BLOOD CIRCUITS

SUNY series in Latin American Cinema
―――――――――――
Ignacio M. Sánchez Prado and Leslie L. Marsh, editors

BLOOD CIRCUITS

Contemporary Argentine Horror Cinema

JONATHAN RISNER

SUNY PRESS

Cover image: *Plaga zombie: Zona mutante – Revolución tóxica*. Pablo Parés, Hernán Sáez, and Paulo Soria, dirs. © Farsa Producciones, 2011.

Published by State University of New York Press, Albany

© 2018 State University of New York

All rights reserved

No part of this book may be used or reproduced in any manner whatsoever without written permission. No part of this book may be stored in a retrieval system or transmitted in any form or by any means including electronic, electrostatic, magnetic tape, mechanical, photocopying, recording, or otherwise without the prior permission in writing of the publisher.

For information, contact State University of New York Press, Albany, NY
www.sunypress.edu

Library of Congress Cataloging-in-Publication Data

Names: Risner, Jonathan, author.
Title: Blood circuits : contemporary Argentine horror cinema / Jonathan Risner.
Description: Albany : State University of New York Press, [2018] | Series: SUNY series in Latin American cinema | Includes filmography, bibliographical references and index.
Identifiers: LCCN 2017041904| ISBN 9781438470757 (hardcover : alk. paper) | ISBN 9781438470764 (pbk. : alk. paper) | ISBN 9781438470771 (e-book)
Subjects: LCSH: Horror films--Argentina--History and criticism.
Classification: LCC PN1995.9.H6 R57 2018 | DDC 791.43/61640982--dc23 LC record available at https://lccn.loc.gov/2017041904

10 9 8 7 6 5 4 3 2 1

For Gretchen, Arno, and Ila

CONTENTS

List of Illustrations   ix
Acknowledgments   xi

Introduction   xiii
Argentine Horror Cinema: A Constellation of Miracles

Chapter One   1
Reaches: The National and Transnational Coordinates of
Argentine Horror Film Culture

Chapter Two   35
Telling Carnage: Spectacles and Spaces of Neoliberalism

Chapter Three   61
Cinematic Body Snatching:
English-Language Argentine Horror Cinema and Systems of Paranoia

Chapter Four   93
Where Punk and Horror Meet:
Argentine Punk/Horror, "Cine under," and Gore as Affect

Chapter Five   125
Is It There? It's Not There. Now It's There.:
Spectral Dynamics of the Last Dictatorship in Argentine Horror Cinema

Conclusion   163
Notes   167
Filmography   209
Bibliography   213
Index   237

ILLUSTRATIONS

Table 1.1   Low-Budget Argentine Horror Films   13

Table 1.2   YouTube Hits for Select Argentine Horror Films   14

Table 1.3   Box-Office Performance by Commercially Released Argentine Horror Films   17

Figure 2.1   Still from *Plaga zombie: Zona mutante*   41

Figure 2.2   Still from *No moriré sola*   52

Figure 3.1   Still from *Death Knows Your Name*   69

Figure 3.2   Still from *Dead Line*   78

Figure 4.1   Still from *Sadomaster 2: Locura general*   93

Figure 4.2   Still from *Goreinvasión*   121

Figure 5.1   Still from *Jennifer's Shadow*   128

Figure 5.2   Still from *The Last Gateway*   132

Figure 5.3   DVD cover of *Crónica de una fuga*   139

Figure 5.4   Still from *Crónica de una fuga*   142

ACKNOWLEDGMENTS

"Me. We." Muhammad Ali's verse, allegedly the shortest poem ever composed, lays bare how *Blood Circuits* was realized with the help of many. Writing about Argentine horror cinema has been a protracted and ongoing labor of love and simply would not have been possible without the generous help of strangers, the poignant criticism and suggestions by colleagues, and the encouragement and laughter of friends. While no one can bear responsibility for the errors herein, I owe a lot.

At the University of North Carolina at Chapel Hill, María DeGuzmán, Joanne Hershfield, Juan Carlos González-Espitia, and Greg Flaxman were instrumental in laying the groundwork for the project. Likewise, Eric Downing, Sam Amago, Alice Kuzniar, and Will Nolan opened up new lines of inquiry and exercised considerable influence in shaping my approach to criticism.

I could not ask for better and more supportive colleagues than those at Indiana University Bloomington. In the Department of Spanish and Portuguese, Anke Birkenmaier, Andrés Guzmán, Olimpia Rosenthal, Patrick Dove, Melissa Dinverno, Luciana Namorato, Deborah Cohn, Estela Vieira, Alejandro Mejías-López, Kathleen Myers, Darlene Sadlier, Ryan Giles, Reyes Vila-Belda, Edgar Illas, and Steve Wagschal have consistently provided guidance and acted as soundboards for this project and various other pursuits. I am especially grateful to Steve for allowing me to develop and teach cinema courses in which graduate and undergraduate students occasionally have encountered Argentine horror cinema and its pleasures and unpleasures. Also at Indiana University Bloomington, Shane Greene, Morten Oxenbøll, and Michael Crandol lent a helpful ear or eye to *Blood Circuits* at various stages of gestation. Elsewhere in the academic universe, Tamara Falicov was a catalyst for this project from its outset and offered encouragement and sound advice. Juana Suárez has long been a valued mentor and friend, and was always helpful with suggestions. I am amazed and humbled by the generosity of the horror, *cine bizarro*, "cine under," and genre cinema communities in Argentina. Their love for cinema is remarkable and downright infectious. Scores of individuals were willing to graciously provide their insights into the status of horror cinema in Argentina, and I am eternally grateful for their help: Pablo Sapere, Carina Rodríguez, Demián Rugna, Hernán Moyano, Hernán Sáez, Paulo Soria, Walter Cornás, Nicanor Loreti, Pablo Parés, Axel Kuschevatsky, Sebastián Tabany, Fabián Forte, Matías Raña, Javier Diment, Carlos de la Fuente, Germán Magariños, Alejo Rébora, Daniela Giménez, Marcelo Leguiza, Lisandro Berenguer, Gonzalo Quintana, and Paula Pollachi. Beyond Argentina, Todd Brown from *Screen Anarchy*, Raymond Murray at Artsploitation, and Ray Perez at Alebrije Entertainment answered questions that allowed a better understanding of how Argentine horror circulates in the United States and elsewhere.

Crucial institutional support came from the Department of English and Comparative Literature and the Institute for the Study of the Americas, both at the University of North Carolina at Chapel Hill. At Indiana University Bloomington, a research travel grant from the College Arts and Humanities Institute also was decisive in the realization of this project, and *Blood Circuits* is partially funded by the Office of the Vice Provost of Research at Indiana University Bloomington through the Grant-in-Aid Program.

I would like to thank Beth Bouloukos, Rafael Chaiken, Kate Seburyamo, Jenn Bennett, and others at SUNY Press for their astute guidance. Many thanks are due to the anonymous readers whose suggestions were instrumental in developing *Blood Circuits*.

My families—immediate and otherwise—have always been a source of unstinting support. My parents have long encouraged me in my various pursuits, and I owe them the world. My siblings, Eric and Amelia, consistently offer encouragement as do my extended family: Scott, Lucy, and Will; John; and Martha and Ray. Arno and Ila provide endless moments of joy, anarchy, and unforeseen comedy while ensuring there is a world beyond toil and Dad's "inappropriate" movies. Last, Gretchen has been a steadfast partner and constant source of love and support in this journey. This book would not exist without her.

Select parts of chapters 1 and 3 originally appeared in an article published in volume 7, issue 1 of *Studies in Spanish and Latin American Cinema*. A version of the first section in chapter 2 appeared in Spanish in a collection of essays titled *Horrofílmico* (2012), published by Isla Negra. A version of the first section in chapter 5 appeared in a collection titled *Filme in Argentinien/Argentine Cinema* (2012), published by LIT Verlag. I am grateful to the journals, publishing houses, and editors for granting me permission to reprint parts of those essays here.

INTRODUCTION

ARGENTINE HORROR CINEMA
A Constellation of Miracles

In June of 2008, I briefly ventured to Buenos Aires to research Argentine horror cinema after reading about several low-budget productions in *Variety*. Shortly before departing from Buenos Aires, I entered *Mondo macabro*, a small store that sat tucked inside an unassuming *galería comercial* on Avenida Corrientes. Now shuttered, *Mondo macabro* was a horror/fantasy movie store that provided me with a confounding firsthand introduction to Argentine horror cinema and how its cultural and economic links stretch out to parts known and unknown. Entering the store, DVD and VHS cases lined the shelves with fantasy, exploitation, science-fiction, and horror films from all over the world. Amid the cases, Argentine horror titles that I had read about online caught my eye: *La casa de las siete tumbas*/ "The House of the Seven Tombs" (Pedro Stocki, 1982), *Chronicle of a Raven* (aka, *Jennifer's Shadow*; Daniel de la Vega and Pablo Parés, 2004), *The Last Gateway* (Demián Rugna, 2007), *Habitaciones para turistas*/*Rooms for Tourists* (Adrián García Bogliano, 2004), and *Plaga zombie* (Pablo Parés and Hernán Sáez, 1997), among others.[1] I asked the clerk if it would be possible to purchase copies of the films, and he explained I could give him some pesos to receive a bootlegged version by the week's end. Since I was leaving Buenos Aires the next day, I refrained. The clerk asked where I was from, and I answered, "Los Estados Unidos." He explained that the more recent Argentine horror movies in the store were distributed in the United States and just as easily could be purchased there. Dumbfounded, I thanked him for pointing this out, and continued to peruse the shelves before exiting the store. That evening an online search indeed corroborated what the clerk had said. I found Argentine horror DVDs on amazon.com, and I purchased the DVDs while still in Argentina. My first brush with Argentine horror cinema was a range of flows and exchanges. Argentine horror films circulated "legally" in the

United States and "illegally" as bootlegged copies in Argentina proper. Capital, the Internet, scales of distribution—all components of a well-oiled machine of media and commerce—enabled me to purchase films made in Argentina, and the DVDs would be arriving at my doorstep in the United States within days.

Contemporary Argentine horror cinema (roughly 1997 through the present, a periodization that I explain below) is a tale of two economies— a formal and informal one—which overlap and must be taken together to ascertain any comprehensive understanding of Argentine horror and its consumption and circulation. As Ramon Lobato and Julian Thomas have written, "While television studies, media policy studies, and the political economy of communications tradition have tended to focus on large-scale, nationally regulated industries, this does not always help us to understand what lies outside this space—pirate DVD and VCD [Video Compact Disc] economies, off-the-books cable TV systems, video-hosting sites, BitTorrent, user-created virtual worlds, and so on" (379–380). Argentine horror cinema resides both within and outside nationally regulated industries. If a coupling and blurring of informal and economies are a prerequisite for a discussion of Argentine horror cinema, then so is a blurring of ostensibly distinct horror film cultures that potentially disperse according to any number of factors, such as differing and uneven modes of distribution (DVD, YouTube, informal markets), exhibition (commercial cinemas, film festivals, museums, rock concerts), and/or marketing (professional marketing, social media).

Argentine horror cinema fragments according to its relationship with INCAA (Instituto Nacional de Cine y Artes Audiovisuales; National Institute of Film and Audiovisual Arts), the national government's production agency. INCAA is charged with myriad tasks, such as supporting productions and coproductions through contests, grants, and scholarships; regulating exhibition, or at least attempting to do so; and promoting Argentine cinema abroad. INCAA operates as one, if not the primary, filmic gatekeeper for national cinema production. As Perelman and Seivach write, "La particularidad de promoción argentino es que las decisiones sobre qué tipo de cine fomentar está totalmente concentrada en manos del Estado, a través del INCAA" ("The unique nature of promoting film production in Argentina is that the question of which films will be made rests exclusively in the hands of the state through INCAA") (30). Given INCAA's central role, it possesses the capacity to determine which films reach domestic and transnational audiences, how, and when. As Sean Cubitt argues, "Nations' role in distribution is shaped by the same priorities as corporations: promoting some flows and delaying or denying others"

(203). Prior to the 2008 theatrical release of *Visitante de invierno/Winter's Visitor* (Sergio Esquenazi), twenty years passed without a single nationally produced horror film appearing in commercial cinemas in Argentina.[2] During the 1990s and early 2000s, INCAA's support for domestic horror cinema production was null; Argentine horror cinema was largely off the grid and unfolded beyond the confines of commercial cinema. Argentine horror cinema was nevertheless sustained and flourished by a confluence of factors that initiate and enable an outpouring of horror cinema: inexpensive camcorders and digital cameras; home computer editing software; the Internet as an exhibition circuit, publicity mechanism, and forum for critique and creation of a virtual fan culture; the formation of alternative exhibition venues for horror in Argentina and beyond.[3] During the late 1990s and early 2000s, such facets would make visible a heretofore obscured production of horror cinema within Argentina that would play out largely within national and transnational cultural zones of horror consumption. In other words, with its emergence, Argentine horror in its low-budget form would register in online forums, websites, and film festivals in Argentina, with various seismic cues being recorded elsewhere, such as *Fangoria* magazine in the United States, Sitges Film Festival in Spain, horror fan websites in Japan,[4] DVD distributors in Germany, and the ubiquitous gray zone of the Internet.[5]

While INCAA largely refrained from supporting domestic horror film production for two decades, its relationship to horror cinema has drastically changed.[6] To allude to one indication, as of September 2016 INCAA has sponsored the production or coproduction of fifteen horror films since 2008. INCAA, abetted with a range of production and distribution companies in Argentina and beyond, must be credited for exponentially increasing the level of visibility for Argentine horror cinema and positioning it within a commercial juncture that facilitates its domestic and transnational reach. INCAA ostensibly stabilizes a flow of horror. Yet, not all horror cinema comes under the productive auspices of INCAA. Underground punk cinema that possesses salient moments of horror—such as the films of Gorevisión, Sarna, and Mutazion—remains beyond its INCAA reach, though, as I describe below, select films nevertheless benefit from INCAA's small-screen exhibition initiatives such as CINE.AR PLAY and INCAA TV.[7]

Among other phenomena, Argentine horror augurs and embodies larger dynamics of contemporary cinema in general. In March of 2011, the film journal *Kilómetro 111* published a two-part essay by Silvia Schwarzböck that scrutinizes the relationship between cinema and the state. In the second essay, titled "La posibilidad de un arte sin Estado: El cine después de Internet," Schwarzböck ponders the question of the Internet's consequences for cinema, one of which being the possible obsolescence of a government film agency, such as Argentina's own INCAA. The Internet as a distributive and viewing platform could obviate INCAA as a body regulating exhibition, among other facets of the country's film industry. While many of Schwarzböck's observations are valid, low-budget Argentine horror cinema—films made for less than $20,000—anticipates the author's observations by more than a decade.[8]

The critical blind spot that elides low-budget horror from studies of contemporary Argentine cinema begs the question of whether a genre film cycle exists if films rely on marginal exhibition venues and alternative forms of distribution which occlude those films from particular echelons of film criticism that would endow a genre with a certain visibility and cultural cachet. The short answer is a resounding yes. As I describe in chapter 1, Argentine horror cinema culture has long possessed its own critical mechanisms and articulations within that film culture which, among other tasks, create canons, chart the genre's history, and recover classical Argentine horror films.

Over the past fifteen or twenty years Argentina has emerged as a producer of genre films that diverge from more established national film genres, such as melodrama, detective cinema, auteur cinema, and documentary. Screwball comedies, animation, martial arts, horror, trash cinema, and science fiction all compose a loosely conceived "wave" of contemporary filmmaking that is periodically dubbed "Cine Independiente Fantástico Argentino" ("Argentine Independent and Fantastic Cinema") and "Nueva Ola de Cine de Género Argentino" ("New Wave of Argentine Genre Cinema"), among other monikers. At first glance, such a wave appears to exist parallel to that of commercial cinema. Scores of genre films are produced on microbudgets and rely on exhibition and distribution that is largely independent of INCAA. Other higher-budgeted commercial films made with the support of INCAA—such as the superhero spoof *Kryptonita* (Nicanor Loreti, 2015) and the giallo *Necrofobia 3D* (Daniel de la Vega, 2014)—nevertheless are couched as part of a larger surge of genre cinema that unabashedly traffics in and reworks transnationally established genres with a stated objective of filmmakers almost invariably being to "entertain" the audience. In an article describing the creation of La Liga de Cine de Género ("The League of Genre Cinema"), a collective of directors, script writers, and various professionals devoted to the promotion of the fantasy genre (horror, fantasy, thriller, science fiction) in Argentina, director

Gustavo Cova stated, "Queremos que el público se divierta, reencontrándose con un cine que le habla directamente, sin intermediarios, que se realiza de manera consistente en nuestro país" ("We want the public to have fun, reconnect with a cinema that speaks to them directly without intermediaries and a cinema that is produced consistently in our country") ("Se presentó La Liga").

The goal to make cinema to "entertain" flies in the face of a domestic critical apparatus that elevated a neorealist auteur cinema over genre cinema produced in Argentina, a point to which I will return in chapter 1. And while I hesitate to assign Argentine genre cinema, or even Argentine horror cinema, a high level of coherency based on filmic style, the current wave of genre cinema assumes the form of a "movement" through the rhetoric of filmmakers, programmers, and fans. In a recent article appearing in *Haciendo Cine* about the trajectory of Argentine genre cinema (science-fiction, horror, and action films), the headline reads "El próximo movimiento" ("The Next Movement") (Oliveros). Likewise, in the prologue to Matías Raña's *Guerreros del cine: Argentino, fantástico e independiente*, director Pablo Parés repeatedly alludes to a low-budget genre cinema made without the support of INCAA as "un movimiento" ("a movement") (13) and "nuestro movimiento" ("our movement") (15) that has come to include those genre films made with INCAA's support. Genre cinema, irrespective of budget, becomes the calling card that makes for a national film culture centered around genre cinema.

Owing to the volume of films belonging to the genre, the breadth of audience reception registered on fan websites in Argentina and in other countries, alternative and commercial exhibition, the circulation of films in Argentina and beyond, horror cinema is the most salient of genres that compose the aforementioned genre film wave in Argentina. It is crucial to note that the emergence of horror is a resurgence of sorts that achieves a sustained rhythm. Argentine horror does not emerge from a vacuum. As Carina Rodríguez, Darío Lavia, Pablo Sapere, and Fernando Pagnoni, among others, have demonstrated, horror and horror/detective and horror/science-fiction hybrids dating back to the 1930s precede the current crop of productions, even anticipating some of contemporary Argentine horror's dynamics. Though León Klimovsky worked in genres other than horror, his transatlantic movements as a director precede Adrián García Bogliano's more recent transnational trajectory and productions in Argentina, Mexico, the United States, and Sweden. Moreover, the dubbing into English of Emilio Vieyra's horror and exploitation productions (e.g., *La venganza del sexo*/ *The Curious Dr. Humpp* [1969]) to appeal to US English-speaking audiences during the late 1960s and early 1970s, anticipate the crop of contemporary Argentine English-language horror films (Dapena 95–98). What distinguishes the contemporary Argentine horror cinema from the past is the sustained rhythm of production resulting in a score of horror productions. At present, Argentine horror is not defined by a single great film or an iconic ghoul that internationally defines the country's horror output. Instead, Argentina asserts its presence in a transnational chain of global horror and other genre cinema through consistent production, as evident in a November 2016 headline about Blood Window that appeared in *Variety*: "Latin America genre powerhouses Argentina and Mexico dominate section" (Mayorga).

Production and consumption provide a guiding axis of the study of Argentine horror cinema here. Argentine horror films and their multitude of circulatory paths set into motion the potential of poaching on a transnational scale. Albeit most associated with Henry Jenkins's seminal *Textual Poachers*, de Certeau coins the notion of poaching to describe those activities that readers or viewers perform with the consumption of a text or television program. In lieu of reading conceived as a passive and inert exercise, "readers are travellers; they move across lands belonging to someone else, like nomads poaching their way across fields they did not write, despoiling the wealth of Egypt to enjoy it themselves" (de Certeau 174). Reading can entail the "advances and retreats, tactics and games played with the texts" as well as affective resonances: "subconscious gestures, grumblings, tics, stretchings, rustlings, unexpected noises, in short a wild orchestration of the body" (de Certeau 175). I depart from de Certeau (and Jenkins) by conceiving poaching as a scalar concept that entails not only the activities of individual fans, but also those activities enacted by entities. INCAA, private production and distribution companies, exhibition venues, presses, film publications, retail stores, cable companies, and "media pirates" *do things* with Argentine horror films and arguably exercise a stronger degree of poaching that push the relay of a film across space and time. Taken concurrently, entities and fans fashion a transnational Argentine horror film culture whose coordinates stretch across geographies.

The notion of production and consumption illuminates the emergence of Argentine horror cinema as an instance in which a sufficient number of consumers of horror become producers of horror to such a degree that horror registers nationally and transnationally as a critical mass. While Argentina lacks a sustained horror cinema tradition of production, horror cinema has long been consumed among a range of other genres. *Sábados de Súper Acción* was a television program broadcasted from 1961 to 1993 on Teleonce (which became Telefé in 1990), and consisted of marathons featuring a vast range of film genres (Westerns, horror, science-fiction, dramas, action films, comedies, giallos, B cinema) from all over the world.[9] While numerous Argentine channels imitated Teleonce's program, several Argentine horror directors and programmers have alluded to *Sábados de Súper Acción* as an inspiration (Rugna 2009; Sapere 2009; Raña 2014).[10] The advent of cable television, VHS, DVD rental stores, Video-on-Demand, and the Internet likewise enabled an expanding catalog of viewing platforms in Argentina that exposed consumers to horror cinema from elsewhere as well as permitting the recovery of national horror films, such as *Una luz en la ventana*/"A Light in the Window" (Manuel Romero, 1942) or *Si muero antes de despertar*/"If I Die Before I Wake" (Carlos Hugo Christensen, 1952). Factors such as the advent of digital cameras and home editing software, combined with a remarkable tenacity on the part of filmmakers to make films, enable Argentina to become a node of horror production.

Argentine horror films evince a keen understanding of transnational horror cinema subgenres (zombie films, vampire films, slashers, trash horror, rape-revenge, body horror, Gothic horror, etc.) that have become transnational owing to a transnational mediatic circuit. The reach of that circuit at the level of film content perhaps is most evident in the end credits of several films directed by Adrián García Bogliano's, in which he acknowledges the "Ayuda espiritual" ("Spiritual guidance") of different films of various genres, directors, and other media (e.g., comics), such as Lucio Fulci, Frank Miller, Kaneto Shindô, and Nicolas Roeg, to name a few. Such a convergence of influences can be witnessed in other Argentine horror films, and complicates any notion that Argentine horror is a composite copy of US horror. Indeed, US audiovisual media (films and television) dominate Argentine commercial cinemas and various private viewing platforms, such as cable television (Getino 240; 332). Argentine horror, however, is a product of the multiple flows of transnational cinema which, in turn, "[...] mov[es] beyond any tendency to reduce the centers and peripheries of present-day capitalism to the past familiar binary of cultural imperialism" (Newman 9). The Argentine horror films hardly constitute an imitation of cinema arriving from elsewhere. Instead, the films rework transnational horror codes and bend the syntax of various horror subgenres to conjoin with a larger global flow of horror cinema.

A second axis of my examination of Argentine horror cinema is the question of the pleasures of horror. Numerous critics of horror cinema have attempted to understand what Julian Hanich describes as "the paradox of fear" (3), or how a fear-inducing genre such as horror could even be deemed pleasurable. Isabel Cristina Pinedo, for instance, posits that horror affords its spectator, especially its female spectators, "a simulation of danger that produces a bounded experience of fear not unlike a rollercoaster ride" (5). In *The Philosophy of Horror*, Noël Carroll locates a pleasure of horror in narrative: "For what is attractive—what holds our interest and yields pleasure—in the horror genre [is] situated as a functional element in an overall narrative structure" perhaps best exemplified through the gradual revelation of a monster over the course of a narrative (179). Special effects and intertextuality among horror films, likewise, provide other sources of pleasure. Most significantly for my purposes, however, Hanich and Matt Hills contend that horror affords a multitude of pleasures, and enumerating those pleasures runs the risk of essentializing particular spectatorial dynamics of horror (Hanich 8; Hills 51–52). Akin to Hills and Hanich, I refrain from stating that Argentine horror cinema affords its audiences a finitude of pleasures. Yet, while refraining from preemptively closing the possibility of other pleasures, Argentine horror cinema and its various subgenres afford new kinds of pleasures that range from hermeneutical pleasures, such as allegory and paranoia, or affective ones, in which low-budget punk/horror gore potentially undermines any settled pleasure. Finally, I conceive of such a catalog of pleasures not as a "construction of pleasure hierarchies" (Frost 22) in which affective or somatic pleasures are conceived as lesser than intellectual, but rather as a cluster with the chance that the affective can feed into the hermeneutical and vice versa.

As a circulating media object, Argentine horror cinema offers unprecedented kinds of pleasures to distinct audiences. For Argentine viewers, the films may appeal to a pleasure of seeing *argentinidad* coded within a horror film made in Argentina by Argentine filmmakers and actors. Director and actor Pablo Parés has described his youthful admiration for films such as the *Star Wars* trilogy and *The Neverending Story* (14). Behind such admiration, however, Parés expresses a desire "ver el cine que más me gusta, pero hecho en mi país" ("to see the cinema I like the most but made in my country") (14), which inspired him to actually make films. Argentine horror films not only provide the pleasure of seeing a horror film that adheres to genre conventions, but also achieve a level of national or local specificity through language, cinematic landscape, and/or humor. For audiences elsewhere, pleasure may come with the drop of an ax and the ensuing spectacle of blood, witnessing the motifs of a horror subgenre twisted and reworked, seeing a film realized on a shoestring budget, and/or taking delight in panning or praising an Argentine horror film in an online comments section.

This question of pleasure departs from and is entangled with already existing scholarship on Argentine and Latin American horror cinema. Carina Rodríguez's seminal *Cine de terror en Argentina: producción, distribución y mercado, 2000–2010/ Horror Cinema in Argentina: Production, Distribution, and the Market, 2000–2010* (2014) provides a crucial foundation for a discussion of contemporary Argentine horror's political economy. The anthologies *Horrofílmico: Aproximaciones al cine de terror en Latinoamérica y el Caribe* (eds. Rosana Díaz-Zambrana and Patricia Tomé, 2012) and *Latsploitation, Exploitation Cinemas, and Latin America* (eds. Victoria Ruétalo and Dolores Tierney, 2009) provide additional cornerstones, namely for their positioning of Argentine and Latin American horror cinema or particular films among national, regional, and transnational film cultures and endowing the films with the capacity of horror to allegorize national sociocultural crises.

An analysis of cinematic pleasure does not omit an engagement with the political economy of Argentine horror or the question of allegory. Pleasure sustains the production, distribution, and exhibition of cinema. Commenting on film history's capacity to make "visible" the films and industries "that produce the renewable and repeatable side of the cinema experience" (50), Thomas Elaesser observes, "These [histories] point not towards a finite object, but, if anywhere, towards a finite subject, namely the spectator, whose desire sets into motion the other machines of the institution [of] cinema" (50).[11] I, too, read allegorically and rely heavily on Walter Benjamin's theories of the "antimonies of allegory" (*Origin* 174) in which "the false appearance of totality is extinguished" (*Origin* 176). Totalities of meaning and pleasure buckle under weight of the films' transnational circulation. However, at the same time I circumscribe my own tendency to view Argentine horror cinema purely as allegories of national crises in a mode of reception that I concisely designate as "crisis eyes." Argentine horror cinema initially can be received as a doubling down of crises—first, as an Argentine film, and, second, as a horror film.[12]

While select critics have associated Argentine cinematic history with crisis,[13] recent studies on contemporary Argentine cinema, particularly *New Argentine Cinema*, only tighten a formula in which the national cinema is denoted in shorthand as Argentine cinema equals crisis. Noting the low-budget filmmaking characteristic of New Argentine Cinema, Joanna Page writes, "The 'new' filmmaking techniques of New Argentine Cinema have, then, as much to do with a crisis in film as they do with a crisis in society" (36). Jens Andermann comments how on "production process, subject matter and film form have collapsed into one" (New Argentine Cinema 10) in New Argentine Cinema, and how "political crisis is encountered not at the level of film content but, rather, any sort of content becomes actively and self-consciously political in the way it is taken through a production process and its formal resolution, in which cinema inscribes [...] its contemporariness and reasserts its autonomy" (10). In other words, political crisis inscribes itself in the very process of producing the film and in the film's formal elements. Similarly, in *Desintegración y justicia en el cine argentino contemporáneo*, Gabriela Copertari privileges select Argentine films—both those associated with New Argentine Cinema and commercial productions such as *Nueve reinas/Nine Queens* (Fabián Bielinsky, 2000) during the late 1990s and early 2000s—for their capacity to register "transformaciones políticas, sociales, económicas y culturales que marcan distinctivamente la década de los noventa [...] y que habrían de culminar dramáticamente en la crisis del 2001" ("political, social, economic, and cultural transformations that mark as distinct the 90s and which would culminate dramatically with the crisis of 2001") (1).

Likewise, numerous critics, including myself, endow horror cinema with a capacity to allegorize societal dilemmas or crises. Carol Clover famously deemed slasher films from the 1970s and 1980s to be "a transparent source for (sub)cultural attitudes toward sex and gender in general" (22). Adam Lowenstein locates national traumas through allegorical moments in horror films and contends that "the modern horror film may well be the genre of our time that registers most brutally the legacies of historical trauma" (*Shocking Representation* 10).[14] While asserting that most contemporary horror productions have lost their critical edge, Christopher Sharrett Holder observes, "[T]he horror film is the most honest and forthright art form in discussing the relationship of the Other to the heteronormative, the bourgeois family, 'normal' community life, and/or 'functional' society under capital" (56).[15]

Given its geography and generic tagging, Argentine horror tenders a horizon of expectation that potentially overdetermines a critical tendency to receive a film as making visible or allegorizing economic and/or cultural crises: the carnage reaped from the imposition of neoliberal policies, the economic and political collapse of 2001, and the legacies of the last dictatorship. Again, crisis eyes. And a critic's charge, in turn, is to tease out which crisis, or crises, manifests themselves on-screen. To be sure, instances of Argentina's political and economic crises are present at times in Argentine horror. In *Mala carne/Carnal* (Fabián Forte, 2003), one briefly sees *cartoneros* making their rounds at night as the two male protagonists return from a restaurant. Yet, at the very least, the question of Argentine horror cinema's relationship to a single or multiple crises varies with each film. To receive Argentine horror cinema exclusively as allegories of crises brings to mind Page's notion that Argentine cinema is expected to "supply a First World demand for images of poverty and social unrest in the Third World" (56). Particular Argentine horror films can satiate such a demand, although horror also provides a possible out from such an exclusive reception. Reading Argentine horror allegorically is not wrong per se. However, I position reading allegorically and reading crises in Argentine horror film as part of a larger horizontal mass of pleasures.

Argentine low-budget horror cinema offers a corpus of films that further diversifies the precarious modes of Argentine filmmaking noted by Andermann and others and, which, at times, predate many films associated with New Argentine Cinema. A crop of Argentine horror films were made without INCAA's support starting in the late 1990s and required filmmakers and their crews to be incredibly innovative with little money. While economic strictures understandably prompted select New Argentine Cinema filmmakers to emulate the likes of Italian neorealism, John Cassavetes, and US independent cinema from the 1980s (Wolf, "Las estéticas" 37–38), among others, as models for filmmaking, directors of low-budget horror productions have longed imbibed lessons from low-budget genre productions by the likes of Peter Jackson, Lloyd Kaufman, John Carpenter, and Sam Raimi. Making horror, or even genre cinema, on a shoestring budget in Argentina has become a collective identity among particular directors and producers. The sentiment is perhaps best captured by a kind of slogan once emblazoned on Paura Flics's website and, for filmmaker and producer Hernán Moyano, boils down the ethos of genre filmmaking in Argentina: "Nosotros los desconocidos, trabajamos para los ingratos. Estamos tan acostumbrados a hacer tanto con tan poco, que ahora somos capaces de hacer todo con nada" ("We, the unknown, work for the thankless. We are so accustomed to working with so little that now we are capable of doing everything with nothing").[16]

With the possible exception of the trash-gore-underground cinema of Germán Magariños, Argentine horror filmmakers making low-budget productions do not aim for an aesthetic of "strategic carelessness" (Aguilar 15), or play up a precariousness characteristic of New Argentine Cinema. And while one can only do so much to mask budgetary strictures, genre filmmakers do their utmost to make a quality film. Many of the low-budget horror films gain DVD distribution in Argentina, the United States, several European and Asian countries, as well as circulate through YouTube and digital piracy networks, an achievement that constitutes a miracle of sorts; hence, the introduction's title.

In chapter 1, I map the reaches of contemporary Argentine horror cinema culture across physical and virtual sites of production and reception on national and transnational scales. Irrespective of its origin, the horror genre yields a multiplicity of pleasures for global audiences. Abetted by an ever increasing range of distribution and viewing platforms (theaters, festivals, pirated and "legal" DVDs, cable, streaming, downloads), flows of horror accord Argentine horror cinema a timely and auspicious instance in which it, too, can circulate and be consumed nationally and transnationally. The construction of an Argentine horror cinema culture hinges on how the films are consumed in multiple geographies. The flow of Argentine horror films through physical and virtual sites of consumption enables the films to potentially incite "secondary forms of production" (de Certeau 31) around a film or corpus of films; the film, in turn, constructs a culture. The "paper trails" and virtual traces of exhibitions, distribution deals, and range of critiques illuminate the films' movements within Argentina and beyond and, if taken as a map, connect different publics (i.e., audiences at public film screenings) and otherwise atomized consumers (i.e., those who watch the films via the Internet).

Chapter 2 begins with the notion that violent film spectacles operate as a source of pleasure, with horror possessing its own spectacular facets (i.e., gore, music, choppy editing, active camera movement) that are distinct from other genres such as action films or musicals. In Argentine horror cinema, spectacle operates as a means of forging new kinds of filmic spaces, and I analyze how spectacle and spatial dynamics in select horror films allegorize socioeconomic transformations and crises that have unfolded under neoliberalism. Argentine cultural production, including its cinema, has often been viewed through Domingo Faustino Sarmiento's foundational text *Facundo*, and hinges on the dyad of city as civilization versus country as barbarism. Argentine horror conforms to and departs from Sarmiento's city/country binary in significant ways, and the chapter's three sections consider how screen violence upends ostensible spatial divisions. Spectacular violence in the *Plaga zombie* trilogy (1997, 2001, 2012), reconfigures the on-screen urban spaces and engages with national (e.g., neoliberalization and the 2001 economic crisis) and transnational events (e.g., the War on Terror). The chapter's second section takes up the rural imaginary in the rape revenge film, *No moriré sola/I'll Never Die Alone* (Adrián García Bogliano, 2008). Highlighting the films' adherence to the rape-revenge subgenre, female characters wield forms of violence that are traditionally conceived as masculine to survive, and reflect the changing status of women and gendered spaces in Argentina. In the final section, I examine the suburban environs of *La memoria del muerto* and how the film queers the haunted house genre and forms of masculinity.

To date, there are twelve English-language Argentine horror films, and in chapter 3 I perform close readings of three: *Dead Line* (Sergio Esquenazi, 2005), *Death Knows Your Name* (Daniel de la Vega, 2007), and *The Last Gateway*. Though filmed in Buenos Aires or Buenos Aires province, the on-screen narratives are set in anonymous US cities, and Argentina generally is obscured. A generic United States is constructed through props, cultural allusions, brand placement, English, and, most crucially, paranoia, which in the past decade has become a source of global visual pleasure as signaled by the popularity of television programs and films that fit under the broad rubric of the "thriller."[17] The imagining of the United States and US characters from Latin America happens to a degree never seen in any non-US cinema. If the rest of the world and its stories have long figured into mainstream US cinema, then Argentine English-language horror turns the table, so to speak, and projects the United States from the Global South. The films embody a form of what I call "body snatching" that attempts to mimic US culture amid the War on Terror. All three films were made on incredibly low-budgets and feature occasional flaws. Yet, flaws are not problems per se, but rather an opportunity to alert a viewer that something is off.

My examination of Argentine punk/horror cinema in chapter 4 contends that punk film production is pleasurable for directors and spectators, given that the films operate largely beyond a market logic by eschewing mainstream distribution, narratives, and aesthetics that would appeal to large audiences. In short, punk cinema is made for a love of cinema in lieu of a profit. Over the past five years, Argentine punk/horror filmmakers and collectives, such as Germán Magariños of Gorevisión, Mutazion, and Sarna have attracted attention from publications such as *Rolling Stone* in Argentina and various national newspapers for their unconventional films. In addition to marking out what is punk about Argentine punk/horror, I consider how punk and horror meld through modes of gore that are distinct from Argentine films that fit more squarely into the horror genre. The gore in punk/horror films is crude and makeshift and drastically differs from the spectacles of gore in films with higher budgets. Focusing on a particular scene of gore from Magariños's *Goreinvasión* (2004), I treat punk/horror gore as a potential cinematic form of affect by invoking a fundamental definition of affect as arising "in the midst of in-between-ness" (Seigworth and Gregg 1), that is, between emotions.

Chapter 5 addresses the complicated relationship between film violence in Argentine horror cinema and the Dirty War, which lasted from 1976 to 1983 and during which nearly thirty thousand people were kidnapped, tortured, and killed by a brutal dictatorship. Argentine horror cinema's relationship to the Dirty War varies, and, over three sections, I position select films and the question of pleasure vis-à-vis the tragedy. In the first section, I consider how Argentine horror filmmakers contend with a cultural saturation of filmic memories of the Dirty War, and how horror operates as a pleasurable and resistant genre in order to move away from the theme of the Dirty War. For directors, horror potentially allows for an escape from the dominance of Dirty War films. In the second section, I focus on Adrián Caetano's *Crónica de una fuga*/*Chronicle of an Escape* (2006), a film that draws on motifs of escape films, Westerns, thrillers, and horror to loosely adapt to film a testimonial account written by Claudio Tamburini, one of the only prisoners to ever escape from a detention center during the Dirty War. A mainstream film that was made with the help of INCAA, *Crónica de una fuga*, established the possibility of using horror in a pleasurable, compelling, and ethical mode to represent the Dirty War in a filmic genre other than documentary, melodrama, or political thriller, all of which have repeatedly narrativized the Dirty War. In the final section, I analyze four specific films that are unprecedented in their mode of representation of the last dictatorship. *Nunca asistas a este tipo de fiesta* / "Never Go to This Kind of Party" (Pablo Parés, Paulo Soria, and Hernán Sáez, 2000), *Nunca más asistas a este tipo de fiesta* / "Never Again Go to This Kind of Party" (Pablo Parés, Paulo Soria, and Hernán Sáez, 2010), *Sudor frío*/ *Cold Sweat* (Adrián García Bogliano, 2010), and *Malditos sean!*/ *Cursed Bastards* (Fabián Forte and Demián Rugna, 2011) rely on humor with slapstick gore while caricaturing police and torturers of the dictatorship by frequently portraying them as buffoons. The four films evidence different modes of filmmaking and film receptions among younger audiences in Argentina who reside at a temporal remove from the atrocities of the last dictatorship. The dictatorship becomes less a source of fear and more a source of comedy in these four films.

In diagnosing the consequences of the critical narrative surrounding New Argentine Cinema, Jens Andermann locates a lacuna.

> [...] what this critical narrative missed was the wider, more contradictory and multilayered landscape of film-making in Argentina, including for example the recent resurgence of a middlebrow entertainment cinema or the boom of political documentary and of activist film and

video, not to speak of ongoing work by film-makers established well before the 1990s such as Hector Olivera, Fernando Solanas or Leonardo Favio. (*New Argentine Cinema* xii–xiii)

Argentine horror cinema supplements such a landscape of emerging filmic strains that compose a national cinema and add to the filmmaking practices and cultures that escape critics who inevitably cannot perform the Panopticon-like charge of surveilling all that is cinematic within Argentina. With low-budget productions and a catalog of genres, Argentine horror cinema is a shape-shifting entity that continues to morph with time and has effectively emerged into the cultural fields of national and transnational cinema.

1 REACHES

THE NATIONAL AND TRANSNATIONAL COORDINATES OF ARGENTINE HORROR FILM CULTURE

In *La globalización imaginada*, Néstor García Canclini prescribes how to make feasible a study of cultural globalization: "El vértigo e incertidumbre que produce tener que pensar a escala global lleva a atrincherarse en alianzas regionales entre países y a delimitar—en los mercados, en las sociedades y en sus imaginarios—territorios y circuitos que para cada uno serían la globalización digerible, con la que pueden tratar" ("The vertigo and uncertainty that comes with thinking on a global scale leads one to entrench oneself in regional alliances between countries and to delimit—in markets, societies, and their imaginaries—territories and circuits that make for a a digestible globalization, with which one can deal") (13). In a similar move, I conceive Argentine horror cinema as an instance of cinematic globalization that becomes imaginable and comprehensible by focusing on a single film genre—horror—emerging from a single national node. In lieu of the totalities implied by global or world (e.g., the catchall category of "World Cinema"),[1] here transnational functions as an approach that demands a certain degree of precision in order to isolate and take stock of cultural flows with and around Argentine horror films. While YouTube and file sharing—again, the so-called gray zone of film distribution—endows select films with a remarkable geographic reach, Argentine horror does not spread out over the planet like an amorphous mediatized blob availing itself of each and every viewing platform. Instead, more akin to a phantom that leaves clues for detection, the films and how they are consumed leave material and virtual traces in their wakes. Riffing on yet another horror motif, the study of Argentine horror cinema necessitates a sewing together of a monstrous body composed of disparate parts from different times and places. Part detective work and part surgery, assembling a narrative of Argentine horror cinema requires collecting and piecing together a range of appendages and agents.

As will become evident below, Argentine horror cinema moves through a plurality of geographical registers: local, national, regional, hemispherical, and transnational. In his study of Italian cinema between 1896 and 1996, Pierre Sorlin defines a national film culture as "not a set of films which help to distinguish a nation from other nations, [but rather] the chain of relations and exchanges which develop in connection with films, in a territory delineated by its economic and juridical policy" (10). If Sorlin focused on a national cinema with Italy as a node at which flows of various national cinemas converged, then I modify and complicate those directional flows. With their national and transnational circulation, Argentine horror films and the film culture that emerges around those films in Argentina only spill over its borders to arrive at geographically dispersed zones of consumption. Such an approach echoes that of Andrew Higson in his seminal article, "The Concept of National Cinema," in which he proposes, "[T]he parameters of a national cinema should be drawn at the site of consumption as much as the site of production of films" (36). Similarly, Yingjin Zhang performs what he calls a site-oriented investigation in his study of contemporary Chinese cinema, in which he examines a national cinema beyond a single geographic entity. For Zhang, a site-oriented mode of examination allows one "to map out the changing networks and locations of film production and distribution [and film consumption] in or between mainland China, Hong Kong, and Taiwan as well as their complex relationships with other regions in Asia (especially Japan) and around the world" (40).

Needless to say, contemporary Chinese cinema differs from Argentine horror. However, the site-oriented impulse to account for the transnational cultural flows of Argentine horror cinema in and beyond Argentina resonates and is replicated here almost by necessity. There is seemingly always an elsewhere with Argentine horror cinema. Distribution companies in Argentina and elsewhere, exhibition spaces in Argentina and elsewhere, websites and blogs that cover Argentine horror in Argentina and elsewhere, a film's content that beckons to viewers in Argentina and elsewhere. However, while I trace the cultural flows of Argentine horror, it should not be presumed that those flows achieve a kind of globalized fantasy with the unchecked and seamless movement of a cultural product (a film) within Argentina and across national borders. As Ďurovičová suggests, "the prefix 'trans-' implies relations of unevenness and mobility" (x), and, for Argentine horror cinema, plenty of obstacles arise both within and outside Argentina and vary with each film.

In lieu of distribution, I conceive a film's physical or virtual movement as circulation, with "circulation" encompassing the myriad forms in which Argentine horror cinema becomes an object of consumption for viewers in different geographies. That is, a film's transformation into a media object that passes through different locales is not exclusively owing to the auspices of national or multinational companies producing and distributing a horror film for screening in a multiplex. As Ramon Lobato's writes in *Shadow Economies of Cinema*, "Today, film distribution is everywhere, in every city—and not just within the infrastructure of multiplexes, arthouses, retail chains and broadcasters that make up the formal film economy. Parallel to this official circuit is another world of grey-market and counterfeit media, of cheap straight-to-video films that never register in DVD sales data, a digital ecology of file-sharing and online video" (vii). Taking stock of the transnational dimensions of Argentine horror film culture, in turn, is a question of gauging varying scales of cinematic production from microbudget horror cinema to commercial films. As I will detail below, Argentine horror films have an amorphous existence circulating via any number of channels and venues, including movie theaters, film festivals, universities, planetariums, bars, cultural centers, parties, and rock concerts. Many films, and especially low-budget films, possess a high degree of "spreadability," that is "the potential—both technical and cultural—for audiences [and filmmakers] to share content for their own purposes" (Jenkins, Ford, and Green 3). YouTube is perhaps the most common forum in which most low-budget Argentine horror filmmakers share their work, and the site provides a film with incredible geographic reach. Film circulation, thus, encompasses the diverse ways a film arrives on a screen (distribution companies, film festivals, DVD distributors, on-demand cable, the Internet, informal street markets, etc.), and becomes viewable in Argentina, Mexico, Peru, Brazil, the United States, England, Germany, Sweden, Japan, Australia, and all points in between.

Taking stock of Argentine horror film culture also requires an attention to extratextual materials. As Acland observes, "[. . .] the mere existence of film texts tells us little if we do not also consider their circulation and availability. The way films move about in the world, where they are presented, for how long they might be seen, and the information obtainable about films and film events establish parameters that mark out who has access to them" (x). The extratextual materials around Argentine horror cinema illuminate the films' breadth of circulation, access, and availability. Moreover, to return to Sorlin's aforementioned definition of an Italian national film culture and its "exchanges which develop in connection with films" (10), Argentine horror cinema is composed of more than just films. The notion of a national Argentine horror film culture rests with the proliferation of virtual spaces in which a viewer can articulate his or her opinion of a film. While scholars of film studies continue to map film cultures with a transnational dimension in mind,[2] Thomas Ryall's definition of "film culture" in his study on Alfred Hitchcock's British films offers an ideal point of departure for considering the national and transnational coordinates of Argentine horror cinema culture.[3] For Ryall, "film culture" encompasses all "the ensemble of practices," including "the immediate contexts in which films are made and circulated such as studios, cinemas, and film journals, and those contexts which have to be constructed from the material network of the culture, the philosophies and ideologies of film" (2).

Modes of production and consumption are intricately linked with the idea of a film culture. For his part, Ryall considers select fan responses alongside the work of studios in his assessment of Hitchcock's British films.[4] Michel de Certeau's articulation of production and secondary production helps to couch the practices that make Argentine horror cinema culture, and the cardinal mechanisms that disperse Argentine horror film culture transnationally is how the films are produced and consumed transnationally. In *The Practice of Everyday Life*, de Certeau deems consumption as "another production," or "secondary production" that encompasses the ways in which consumers use a product (xii–xiii). While he refrains from entering into a detailed discussion, de Certeau's allusion to television and the need to study "what the cultural consumer 'makes' or 'does' with the images" (31) offers a framework to think about what Argentine consumers and those in other countries do with Argentine horror cinema. That act may be posting a montage lauding Argentine horror on YouTube,[5] posting a comment or review on a website about an Argentine horror film, making fan art inspired by the dystopic science-fiction/horror film *Daemonium: soldado del inframundo/ Daemonium: Underground Soldier* (Pablo Parés, 2015),[6] publicizing the screening of a film on Twitter, or attending a screening of an Argentine horror film at a festival in Argentina, Holland, the United States, or South Korea; or even writing an academic monograph about Argentine horror cinema. I, too, am embedded in Argentine horror film culture, and what you have before you is what I do with Argentine horror cinema.

De Certeau's calculus effectively blurs the line of demarcation between production and consumption as well as the boundaries between producers and consumers to generate an Argentine horror film culture. The film directors and production companies are not the sole producers of an Argentine horror cinema culture. Moreover, consumption is not only a means of participating in a culture (a film culture, in this instance), but it also composes and defines that culture: "Culture is not something already made which we consume; culture is what we make in the varied practices of everyday life, including consumption. Consumption involves the making of culture" (Storey 132). Yet, to extend the range of consuming agents, consumption as secondary production can be performed by larger entities, both governmental and nongovernmental (e.g., *concurso* [contest] committees at INCAA, film festivals, distributors, production companies, film magazines), as well as individual consumers.[7] As Harbord observes, "production strategies, marketing, film festivals, reviewing, distribution channels and sites of exhibition" as "practices [that] engender [...] particular film cultures, embedding film within practices of everyday life [...] filling the contours of the existing socio-cultural formations" (5).

Argentine horror film culture is an instance of cultural circulation in which films are wedded to and enable modes of production and consumption to emanate around those films. Yet, albeit intertwined, the textual (the film) *and* the extratextual (what individuals and entities do with a film) do not circulate in a homogeneous fashion. To again refer to Harbord, "practices [...] *shape* the flow of film" (5), and select extratextual forms of consumption impact a film's reach more than others. A DVD distribution deal or posting a film online does more for a film's circulation than commenting on the movie in an online forum. To further underscore the point of practices shaping a film's flow, a horror film's marketing campaign on the streets of Buenos Aires along with a film's presence at an esteemed horror film festival such as Sitges in Spain can grease the wheels, so to speak, and facilitate a film's national or transnational circulation through DVD distribution deals in multiple countries. In contrast, another Argentine horror film may rely on physical and virtual word-of-mouth and exhibition purely on YouTube. Acland's comments on the capacities of capital and media corporations to fragment and atomize cinema into subgroups further flush out this point about a film's flow:

> The industrial will to orchestrate commodities and markets leaves us with a multi-tiered environment as [capital] unevenly circulates forms and establishes zones of consumption. This unevenness extends to the velocity of culture, such that audiences confront varying speeds for the arrival and departure of cultural forms. Consequently, these dynamics fix in place a core of popular texts, while other works find themselves as part of a "minor" cinema, eking out parallel, noncommercial and alternative venues. (244)

Argentine horror films circulate at different speeds, in different forms, and through different spaces. However, for those interested in hierarchies of national horror cinemas, Argentine horror most certainly is "minor" compared to canonical horror films from the United States, Italy, and Japan. Yet, as I will describe below, the splaying of Argentine horror films into its own internal hierarchy of canonical and minor productions does not necessarily happen.

If pleasure figures into the transnational circulation of Argentine horror cinema culture, then extratextual materials, such as concise reviews written by fans on sites such as YouTube, ostensibly afford the clearest instance of the pleasures, and unpleasures, of Argentine horror. Though I occasionally allude to viewers' receptions of a film to illustrate or flush out the nuances of an argument vis-à-vis a particular film, my attention to how Argentine horror cinema films are consumed does not reside chiefly with the receptions of a "real audience" insofar as that audience is conceived through the comments section of an Internet message board. In fact, I would argue that the majority of comments posted on sites such as YouTube, as well as Facebook or CINE.AR PLAY, are not exceptionally revealing about how a film is received beyond a laudable remark or outright vulgar flaming.[8] Instead, I am interested more in mapping a social imaginary composed of material and virtual sites that make visible an Argentine horror cinema culture. Albeit distinct in scope, my approach to Argentine horror cinema emulates that of Jeff Himpele's analysis of cinematic and television cultures in La Paz, Bolivia, in his book *Circuits of Culture*. In the introduction, Himpele describes the study of film distribution and ethnographies of consumption that enable him to "delineate the pulsing circuits of film traffic and that connect the city's imagined urban publics" (24). Film screenings in La Paz, for Himpele, constitute occasions in which "movie going publics [that] are suspended come into being in events along the circulatory systems of cinematic media" (23). With a film screening, a public materializes and, in turn, makes visible paths of circulation.

Whereas Himpele takes a keen interest in the ethnography of how films and television are consumed by *paceños*, I am concerned more with enumerating the sites of production and consumption of Argentine horror cinema as evidence of the films' circulation and a film culture. Both material and virtual sites of production and consumption constitute an organic transnational Argentine horror cinema culture. And though I attempt to isolate national and transnational paths of Argentine horror cinema culture à la Canclini, it is nearly an impossible exercise and a snapshot at best. Argentine horror cinema culture folds and unfolds on other cinematic genre cultures in Argentina and abroad (cult cinema, psychotronic, trash, thrillers, etc.), and, as described in the introduction, Argentine horror takes its place among a wave of independently produced genre cinema in Argentina. With a mere splattering of fake blood and a quick edit, Argentine horror can hide amid the weeds of other genres.

Along with action cinema, romantic comedies, detective films, and pornography, horror is among the most transnational of film genres, and pleasure cannot be overlooked as an engine for horror's reach. In reference to the films and videogames that various authors analyze in *Transnational Horror across Visual Media*, Dana Och and Kirsten Strayer note, "These texts are not significantly constrained by traditional cultural or cinematic binaries. They are regional and national; they traverse generic and media forms; and they emphasize the horror genre's ability to circumvent borders and delimit territories" (2). While money can never be omitted from any discussion of film's circulation, pleasure, as with any popular film genre, swells a demand for horror, a transnational dynamic in which Argentine horror partakes. Recalling Hills's remarks about the plurality of cinematic pleasures offered by horror, it is near impossible to catalog a finitude of pleasures that are shared among transnational audiences. For the time being, we nevertheless should see the unceasing transnational supply and demand for horror and its distribution as maintained by an assembly of pleasures in which the market, technologies, and various viewing platforms temporarily satiate those pleasures.[9] Conceived in terms of its national origin, Argentine horror cinema is a single flow of horror that contributes to a larger transnational stream of horror.

In *The Imaginary Signifier*, Metz articulates a connection between "a libidinal economy (filmic pleasure in its historically constituted form) [which] reveals its 'correspondence' with the political economy (the current cinema as a commercial enterprise)" (8). For Metz, the cinema industry's capacity to cultivate a desire to see a film [i.e., marketing] enables its perpetuation and "inaugurates the circuit of return which brings the money back eventually, if possible with a profit, from the pockets of the individual spectators to those of the production companies or the banks supporting them, thus giving the go-ahead for new films to be made" (8). Yet, the minimal amount of profit returned to horror filmmakers—especially those who produce low-budget horror films that are screened at small film festivals and released solely on YouTube—complicates Metz's "circuit of return." However valid, Metz's conjecture applies to a film industry abetted by financial institutions, and Argentine horror cinema, or even Argentine cinema in general, does not necessarily attain a centralized form à la a studio system (Perelmann and Seivach 75).[10] Instead, the production of Argentine horror cinema can take the form of a fragmented and precarious affair of often making do with scarce resources. Moreover, with Argentine horror cinema culture it is not all about the pleasures of actually seeing the film. Pleasures come with secondary production (i.e., a blog, a Tweet, a Facebook post) and those pleasures stretch across geographies.

ARGENTINE HORROR FILM CULTURE IN ARGENTINA

A loose historical periodization for contemporary Argentine horror cinema commences at the end of the 1990s, owing to the confluence of different factors, one being the premiere of a key horror-comedy film: *Plaga zombie*. *Plaga zombie*'s significance for the development of Argentine horror cinema cannot be overstated. Director Javier Diment's laudatory comments about the film are typical and instructive: *Plaga zombie*'s formal elements, specifically its cinematography and special effects, surpass scores of national commercial films that receive support from INCAA and/or from the country's largest film production companies, such as a Pol-ka or Patagonik (*Rojo sangre*). Farsa Producciones, the collective that made the film, qualifies as one of the most esteemed producers of horror and genre cinema in Argentina.[11] Made by a group of teenage friends in Haedo for six hundred pesos, shortly after its premiere, *Plaga zombie* became a cult hit within Argentina and gained DVD distribution in the United States, Spain, and Germany. *Plaga zombie*'s success and Farsa's capacity to make films using a home video camera and performing multiple tasks themselves and/or with the help of friends (special effects, script writing, cinematography, editing, set design, acting) are crucial to the development of Argentine horror cinema. The subsequent influence of *Plaga zombie* on other genre filmmakers constitutes one instance of secondary production as production of additional films; critics frequently credit the movie with inspiring other horror filmmakers to make their own films on shoestring budgets.[12] As Matías Raña's writes, "No es exageración decir que *Plaga zombie* fue el punto de partida de una generación nueva y libre de cineastas, que rompieron los esquemas y se animaron a hacer lo que querían" ("It is not an exaggeration to say that Plaga zombie was the starting point for a new generation of filmmakers who broke with the typical schemes of making movies and were encouraged to do what they wanted") (*Guerreros del cine* 27). Raña's sentiments are echoed by others, and Carina Rodríguez describes *Plaga zombie* as the film that "encendió la mecha de la producción de terror" ("lit the fuse of horror production") (75).

Following the premiere of *Plaga zombie*, other producers of low-budget horror working outside the auspices of INCAA emerged at the end of the 1990s and 2000s, many of which would become primary figures associated with contemporary Argentine horror: Daniel de la Vega; Demián Rugna; Sergio Esquenazi; Adrián García Bogliano, Ramiro García Bogliano, and Hernán Moyano of Paura Flics; Hernán Findling; Mad Crampi; Sergio Mazurek; Paula Pollachi; Fabián Forte; Nicanor Loreti; Javier Diment; and Germán Magariños and Gorevisión. The profusion of low-budget horror films produced in Argentina at the end of the 1990s and the lack of places to screen those productions led to the creation of Buenos Aires Rojo Sangre (BARS), a cine bizarro and fantasy film festival specializing in independent and low-budget productions, in 1999.[13] Given its sustained presence and significance to the horror film culture in Buenos Aires, the festival's start in 1999 and *Plaga zombie*'s release in 1997 makes for a kind of bifurcated foundational moment for Argentine horror cinema culture that boasts its own national horror productions. As noted in the introduction, Argentine directors and viewers in Argentina have long been consumers of horror cinema from elsewhere. The emergence of horror made in Argentina changes the game, so to speak, with a more pronounced presence of horror made within the country.[14]

Cinema clubs in Buenos Aires such as Cine Club Nocturna and Cine Club La Cripta have been instrumental in cultivating and maintaining a horror cinema culture in Buenos Aires (Scherer), and BARS builds on a culture of exhibition that includes horror. Commenting on the importance of studying film festivals to understand the history of cinema, Brendan Kredell characterizes film festivals as "the public squares in which its hidden audiences gather" (16). However, festival audiences can only be so hidden. BARS provides the context in which a community of cinemagoers that includes fans, directors, journalists, programmers, publishers, and distributors materialize to assert the popularity of horror as well as other kindred genres such as science-fiction and exploitation cinema in the *porteño* and, thus, Argentine contexts.[15]

Exhibition constitutes a secondary production: it is what a group of programmers, directors, and distributors do with Argentine cinema and initiate a potential relay for what other viewers (blogger, journalist, distributor, etc.) might do with a film. In other words, exhibition enacts a moment of consumption that holds open the possibility for other modes of material secondary production. Lázaro-Reboll has described how the San Sebastián Horror and Film Festival in Spain "enabled the creation of spaces and networks of communication [...] where fanzines have regularly presented their work to the horror fandom community and competed for financial reward" ("Peversa" 38). Likewise, many directors and horror film aficionados in Argentina credit BARS for providing them an exhibition space as well as space for other facets of a horror film culture to emerge: book presentations, film production workshops, and meeting spaces for filmmakers to coordinate projects. The comments of Paula Pollachi, director of *Baño de sangre*/"Blood Bath" and *Inzomnia* (2007), illustrate BARS's venerated status among filmmakers. Pollachi describes BARS as "la columna vertebral" ("the back bone") of the horror community in Buenos Aires (Pollachi).[16] While recent scholarship stresses the transnational nature of film festivals—to which BARS conforms given the diverse national origins of the films screened—the festival's significance for directors and fans as a copresent community within Argentina should not be discounted.[17]

In a brief ethnographic study of the 1997 Sundance Film Festival, Daniel Dayan characterized the festival's various facets as separate narrative threads that dissociate and converge: "There is a story of young directors; a story of sales; a story of films shown; a (mostly unsung) story of the audience; a story of journalists; and, first of all, of the festival itself. Each of the stories proposes a temporal continuity, a plot, and a specific form of suspense. Each is often condensed in striking images" (45). In short, festivals are more than just massive amounts of films being shown, and BARS is similar. Supplementing Dayan's enumeration of narratives and akin to other film festivals that have expanded beyond exhibition,[18] BARS itself serves as a node around which additional features of an Argentine horror film culture materialize. Throughout the year via Facebook and Twitter, BARS holds contests for posters and tickets for new national and international horror releases and publicizes horror film cycles in Buenos Aires and beyond. It has also organized film production workshops during the festival as well as in other contexts such as a filmmaking workshop for kids.[19] In 2015, in collaboration with the production company Findling Films, BARS announced a competition for best Spanish-language horror script, which came with an initial cash prize and an additional one upon the film's completion.

In *Screen Traffic*, Acland examines a plurality of sites for "ideas about cinematic life" (media sources, advertising, editorials, industry reports, etc.) as evidence of the dispersed global film industry (21). Argentine horror film culture is likewise dispersed geographically beyond Buenos Aires. Within Argentina, exhibition unfolds amid different circuits and subcircuits, including commercial cinemas and festivals. The International Festival of Independent Cinema in Mar del Plata (MARFICI) has shown several national horror films, and Pantalla Pinamar, an international film festival taking place in the coastal town of Pinamar, has screened several Argentine horror films. Since 2010 in Mendoza, Mendoza Rojo Sangre has screened national horror films, as well as other genres. Since 2014 in La Plata, the series *Gritos en el planetario* (Screams in the Planetarium) has showcased contemporary Latin American genre cinema (horror, disaster films, comedies, and action films) and has screened national horror productions such as *Necrofobia 3D* and *2/11: Día de los muertos*/"2/11: Day of the Dead" (Ezio Massa, 2012). Festival exhibition venues in Argentina are appearing to proliferate. The year 2015 marked the first Muestra Internacional de Cine Terror Córdoba, which primarily screened short films from various Latin American countries, Spain, and Portugal, and in 2016 Mar del Plata hosted the first Festival Internacional del Cine Fantástico. Exhibition amplifies a mapping of Argentine horror cinema culture within Argentina based on production. A survey of the short films and feature-length shown at the festival in Córdoba as well as BARS signals that horror cinema production in some form happens in a number of Argentine cities in addition to Buenos Aires: La Plata, Jujuy, Salta, Santa Fe, Neuquén, Córdoba, Mendoza, Río Negro, Catamarca, Santiago del Estero, Chubut, and Tucumán, among other cities.[20]

Geography nevertheless matters in Argentine horror cinema culture, and Buenos Aires is the indisputable hub of Argentine horror.[21] Saskia Sassen's notion of a global city captures the role that specific cities perform in contemporary globalization via the centralization of financial operations with links to a network of other global cities with Buenos Aires counted among them. While Sassen refrains from delving into the cross border cultural exchanges that can happen among cities (31), the presence of a vibrant horror film culture and its transnational dynamics that I describe below suggest that Buenos Aires functions as a productive and consuming node within a global circuit of horror cinema culture. The quantity of films produced in Buenos Aires is not accidental; numerous cultural entities, specifically the national government's production agency, INCAA, are located there. Multiple film production companies exist or have existed in Buenos Aires, including Furia Films, Cruda Films, Buenos Aires Rojo Shocking, Findling Films, Gorevisión, Argentina Druida Film, El Desquicio Producciones, C y K Films, Mutazion, and Sarna, among others. Buenos Aires boasts a high number of public and private film schools, and many, though not all, horror film directors who are from Buenos Aires have attended these schools, such as Universidad del Cine, Escuela Nacional de Experimentación y Realización Cinematográfica (ENERC), and Centro de Investigación Cinematográfica (CIC). The opening of schools specializing in special effects and special effects agencies such as Metamorfosis EFX and Rabbid EFX also help establish Buenos Aires as the epicenter of Argentine horror. While some producers and critics point to a lack of professionalization among horror directors,[22] the training that directors and other personnel receive at film schools and universities is a crucial factor in the recent development of Argentine horror cinema.

In her study of the political economy of contemporary Argentine horror cinema, Rodríguez distinguishes and groups contemporary Argentine horror in three groups according to different criteria: (1) higher-budget films mainstream films made with INCAA's support; (2) horror films primarily oriented to external markets and with English-language dialogue; (3) and "producción subterránea" ("underground production"), or low-budget films that lack production support from INCAA (109–10). I maintain these same categories while underscoring their mutability and capacity to coexist in the same exhibition and critical spaces, which appears to be a distinct characteristic of Argentine horror cinema culture. For example, BARS has screened low-budget films, films with English-language dialogue, and higher-budgeted productions. With the exception of *Jennifer's Shadow*, Argentine English-language horror films also can be grouped under the rubric of low-budget films, since the English-language films generally are produced with a minimal budget. Irrespective of budget or language, such conditions do not preclude a film from being esteemed by horror aficionados in Argentina and elsewhere. As I will describe in subsequent chapters, low-budget films offer their own distinct pleasures that move beyond a reductive "so bad it's good" spectatorship (Mathijs and Sexton 18–19). While Argentine horror cinema lacks a definitive canon of films, low-budget films such as *Plaga zombie*, *Habitaciones para turistas*, and *Death Knows Your Name* are often considered among the referential films on Argentine websites (e.g., *QuintaDimensión*, *Cinefania*) and print publications (e.g., *Cine fantástico y bizarro*, *La Cosa*) that regularly cover national horror cinema production.[23] The truncated list of films in table 1.1 provides some understanding of the costs of some lower-budget productions.

The impact of low-budget Argentine horror cinema within a larger national horror film culture is hard to measure empirically with box office numbers, and thus escapes the circuit of profitable returns that Metz conceived. Simply put, the films' paltry budgets and collaborative approach prevent the films from entering a circuit of national cinemas. INCAA functions much like a gatekeeper, given its centrality to the country's filmic output. As Perelman and Seivach write, "La particularidad del sistema de promoción argentino es que las decisiones sobre qué tipo de cine fomentar está totalmente concentrada en manos del Estado" ("The unique nature of the Argentine system of film production rests on the fact that decisions about what type of cinema to promote is entirely concentrated in the hands of the State") (30). The government agency provides crucial funding and an imprimatur so that a film can be made and screened in a national circuit of cinema. For instance, INCAA's support allows for a project to comply with the rules and regulations as set by the Sindicato de la Industria Cinematográfica Argentina (SICA; "The Union of the Cinematic Industry of Argentina"), the national cinematographic film union. SICA regulates working conditions in the film industry, and its rules run the gambit from establishing pay scales, setting the minimal number of technicians working on particular types of films (feature length, animation, documentary, etc.), and specifying holidays. Films that do not comply with the union's statutes will not be "classified," or approved, by INCAA (Sindicato 33). Such films, in turn, are not released in any national cinemas, thus restricting their presence from mainstream movie houses.

By necessity, low-budget Argentine horror films rely on alternative exhibition venues, both physical and virtual, in Argentina and elsewhere. The Internet, for instance, has provided a crucial platform through which Argentine horror filmmakers can showcase their work. Consumers can access the films with relative ease, and the Internet enables a virtual chain of secondary production through comments on the films. Many production companies such as Paura Flics, Sarna, Mutazion, Altaris Video, Farsa Producciones, Gorevisión, and Furia Films and distribution companies such as Videoflims have YouTube channels on which they post films, trailers, music videos, and/or demo reels. Lobato has observed that "the ability to

TABLE 1.1 Low-Budget Argentine Horror Films[24]

TITLE	BUDGET
Plaga zombie	$150
Sadomaster	$50
Habitaciones para turistas	$3,000
Death Knows Your Name	$15,000
Mala carne	$125

monitor media consumption drops off sharply as we approach the informal end of the distributive spectrum" (44), and that "[t]he further we move away from the consolidated, rationalised accounting models of formal Euro-American film industries, the greater degree of invisibility and variation" (44) increases. While sites such as Ultracine and Taquilla Nacional maintain excellent databases on contemporary commercial releases,[25] Lobato's point holds true with those films distributed through YouTube or other online sites. Despite its imprecisions, a survey of the hits of particular low-budget films (see table 1.2) underscore their popularity and how important YouTube is to production companies and distributors for both exhibition and income.

The Internet aside, Buenos Aires offers a range of screening venues, which

TABLE 1.2   YouTube Hits for Select Argentine Horror Films[26]

TITLE	YOUTUBE CHANNEL	QUANTITY OF HITS
Plaga zombie 2	Farsa	2,549,953
Death Knows Your Name	Maverick	90,840
Sonríe	Mutazion	683,526
No moriré sola	Hernan Moyano-Paura Flics	533,665
Sadomaster 2: Locura general	Gorevisión	27,758

includes universities, cultural centers, bars, concerts, and museums and collectively constitute an alternative circuit for low-budget horror films.[27] Though such a circuit does not allow for a regular rhythm of exhibition that approaches a weeks-long run at a multiplex, film screenings nevertheless give low-budget Argentine horror some level of visibility that compliments the films' availability on YouTube or Vimeo or through DVD distribution in Argentina and elsewhere. Festival de Cine Inusual in Buenos Aires has provided vital exhibition spaces for select Argentine horror films since its start, and Fantabaires, a Buenos Aires comic convention that began in 1996 and lasted until 2001, screened a number of Argentine horror films (Rugna, Sáez, and Soria). In 2009, Club Cultural Pachamama screened *Run, Bunny, Run!*, a punk horror film along with *Jennifer's Shadow* as part of its ongoing film series, "No todo el cine argentino es aburrido" ("Not all Argentine cinema is boring"). Also in 2009, the Museo de Arte Latinoamericano de Buenos Aires (MALBA) screened *Jennifer's Shadow* along with a *Filmatrón* and Esteban Sapir's *La antena*. Espacios INCAA, cinemas run by the national government and which primarily show national films, has also screened some low-budget horror films.[28]

INCAA's support for horror cinema has changed markedly over the past five years with the support and release of some thirteen horror films in national cinemas. While Rodríguez has demonstrated in very concrete terms through interviews with directors the long and circuitous routes that Argentine horror films have taken through INCAA's system of production support,[29] INCAA's backing represents a watershed moment in the contemporary development of Argentine horror. And though INCAA enables a horror film to enter a commercial circuit of theaters potentially splitting Argentine horror cinema into subgroups, exhibition nevertheless remains a primary way in which low-budget and higher-budgeted Argentine horror films remain in contact. No sólo en cines ("Not only in cinemas") is a mobile cinema that follows a circuit largely composed of cultural centers and theaters in Buenos Aires, Greater Buenos Aires, La Plata, Mar del Plata, and the Argentine interior. With ticket sales that contribute to INCAA box office data for national productions, the screenings often are preceded by music and poetry readings and then followed by question and answer sessions with the director. While *No sólo en cines* does not exclusively show horror films, a number of horror films have been included among its offerings, such as *La memoria del muerto*, *Mujer lobo*/*She Wolf* (Tamae Garateguy, 2013), *Sonno profondo* (Luciano Onetti, 2013), and *Sangre negra: Aldo Knodell debe morir*/"Black Blood: Aldo Knodell Must Die" (Elián Aguilar, 2013).[30]

The exhibition of Argentine horror cinema of various budgets also can be a private experience at times enabled, or not, by INCAA's support. INCAA TV and CINE.AR PLAY, "el Netflix criollo" (Lerer, "Odeón"), provide additional platforms to consume Argentine horror cinema privately with low-budget and commercial releases appearing alongside each other.[31] While commercially successful horror films, such as *Sudor frío*, achieve DVD distribution, lower-budget films do as well. Videoflims is located in Buenos Aires and distributes a number of national horror films (e.g., *Habitaciones para turistas*, *Recortadas*, Sadomaster, Nocturnos, and *Inzomnia*) from its catalog that is composed mainly of genre films as well documentaries and series. SRN Distribution also distributes a number of low-budget Argentine horror films with a catalog of films produced by Sarna, Mutazion, Gorevisión, Cosamostra, and Mondolila Producciones. In addition to DVD distributors, retail stores that specialize in horror cinema DVDs have been integral to the maintenance of horror cinema culture in Buenos Aires. Splatter

House, Dark Room, and the now defunct Mondo Macabre are retail stores in the capital city featuring horror cinema from Argentina and elsewhere. Finally, while there is no precise data available that indicates the extent of the practices, file sharing and informal markets that sell pirated DVDs constitute additional modes of circulation of Argentine horror cinema that enable a film to be consumed privately.

The myriad ways in which one can view an Argentine horror film (festivals, online streaming sites, pirated DVDs from informal markets, a commercial cinema, a mobile cinema such as *No sólo en cines*) make for varied and fragmented circuits of exhibition in Argentina. As intimated above, those circuits in and of themselves shape what people or entities like producers or distribution companies do with an Argentine horror film and, in turn, create points of departure for other forms of production and consumption within mainstream and peripheral film cultures. Print, television, and virtual media are significant modes of consumption that grow around Argentine horror cinema. Argentine horror cinema has acquired a greater presence in national newspapers such as *Clarín*, *Página 12*, and *La Nación*, especially given INCAA's support for particular horror films. Mainstream online and print versions of publications specializing in cinema, such as *La Cosa*, *EscribiendoCine*, *24 cuadros* and *Haciendo cine* also increasingly cover Argentine horror. And though operating on a lesser budget than the aforementioned publications, additional print and online sites provide extensive coverage of Argentine horror, such as *Cine fantástico y bizarro*, the short-lived *Cinefania Macabra*, *QuintaDimensión*, *Zona Freak*, *Cinefania*, *Terror Universal*, *Terrorífilo*, and *Horas de Horror*. Finally, the small publishing company Fan Ediciones has published a number of books devoted to horror and genre cinema that often focus on or include information on contemporary Argentine horror films.[32]

The growth of BARS and the emergence of other festival venues, the release of INCAA-supported films in commercial cinemas, and increasing coverage of horror cinema by national news outlets suggest a mainstreaming of Argentine horror cinema. Yet, such a claim of Argentine horror's arrival to the mainstream requires several caveats. First, the arrival of Argentine horror within a mainstream domestic film culture is, at best, partial. Argentine horror cinema, especially low-budget films, continues to reside within cultural margins and rely on alternative exhibition circuits and the Internet to be seen. Moreover, as indicated by table 1.3, with the exception of *Sudor frío*, horror films supported by INCAA generally attract low numbers of spectators, which broaches the unpleasures of Argentine horror as evidenced by the absence of the audience.

The low box office numbers have been received by directors and critics as indicative of any number of possibilities, such as the lack of support from INCAA for marketing campaigns to compete with mainstream Hollywood films (Raña 2014) and the continued need for professionalization and specialization of production. Argentine films must contend with the dynamic that national audiences, especially spectators under twenty-five years of age, often prefer to watch films from elsewhere in lieu of domestic fare ("Un cine en busca de jóvenes"). A particular intriguing hypothesis that is related to transnational horror cinema circuits is the issue of language and Argentine spectatorship. Journalists Matías Raña and Alexis Puig, and filmmaker Fernando Spiner have alluded to the peculiarity of watching a horror or genre film with Spanish-language dialogue as opposed to watching and reading subtitles simultaneously.[33] In turn, Argentine horror runs counter to an Argentine spectator's horizon of expectation for how a horror film should appear; that is, with English-language dialogue.

TABLE 1.3   Box-Office Performance by Commercially Released Argentine Horror Films[34]

TITLE	RELEASE DATE	NUMBER OF SPECTATORS
Los inocentes	9/29/2016	3,340
Eslabón podrido	6/16/2016	3,421
Resurrección	1/7/2016	60,888
El desierto	4/9/2015	3,278
Still life: Naturaleza muerta	3/5/2015	10,076
Necrofobia 3D	10/2/2014	14,389
La segunda muerte	3/13/2014	9,384
El día trajo la oscuridad	5/1/2014	7,638
2/11: El día de los muertos	11/20/2014	3,207
La memoria del muerto	3/28/2013	15,580
Hermanos de sangre	6/6/2013	3,320
Penumbra	2/9/2012	16,094
Sudor frío	2/3/2011	80,516
Fase 7	3/3/2011	36,249
Lo siniestro	11/24/2011	7,132
Visitante de invierno	4/3/2008	10,818

COHERENCE IN THE MARGIN

The sheer range and fragmented status of Argentine horror cinema culture in Argentina ostensibly suggest multiple horror film cultures. In *Film Cultures*, Harbord asserts that particular sites of exhibition (the nickelodeon, the art gallery, and film club) "cultivate a culture of film that distinguishes it from other sites" (10). In short, an exhibition space intimates the boundaries between film cultures. Given that Argentine horror cinema relies on a range of commercial and alternative circuits of exhibition, one would expect some degree of atomization within Argentine horror culture with exhibition affecting a horror film's visibility on other fronts, such as criticism. Irrespective of the number of cinema screens a film appears on or the number of weeks a film remains in cinemas, a horror film's release in commercial cinemas requires it to be reviewed by national newspapers and film publications. Such horror films would expectedly enjoy a higher and qualitatively different level of visibility than those that do not.

While a line of demarcation can be drawn between commercial and low-budget releases that are consigned solely to alternative circuits of exhibition, cracks in Argentine horror cinema culture do not necessarily take hold across different sites of consumption. Akin to select exhibition spaces (i.e., *No sólo en cines* and CINE.AR PLAY), commercial and low-budget Argentine horror films frequently occupy similar critical spaces. In film reviews appearing in mainstream newspapers and film magazines, low-budget horror frequently is alluded to alongside other higher-budget productions as a critic demonstrates an awareness of Argentine horror's trajectory or a director's developing oeuvre during the preceding years. In his review of *Naturaleza muerta* (Gabriel Grieco, 2014) on the website Alta Peli, Lisandro Liberatto begins his piece by stating that the film "es el primer largometraje de Gabriel Grieco, de quien ya vimos una gran cantidad de cortos a lo largo de los años en el Buenos Aires Rojo Sangre" ("is the first feature-length movie from Gabriel Grieco, from whom we have seen a number of short films over the years in Buenos Aires Rojo Sangre").

A possible fragmentation of Argentine horror film culture is also curtailed by the movement of directors among genre projects that would ostensibly be distinct from a higher-budget horror or genre film. In a footnote explaining the three categories of Argentine horror (mainstream productions, productions oriented to the international markets, and underground production), Rodríguez writes, "Esta segmentación no se puede aplicar a las productoras, ya que algunos directores participan tanto de producciones independiente o underground como de proyectos internacionales" ("This segmentation does not apply to producers, since some directors participate in both independent or underground productions as well as international commercial productions") (109). The separate work of Nicanor Loreti and Javier Diment substantiate Rodríguez's point. Loreti directed the action/comedy *Diablo* (2011) and, with Fabián Forte, codirected *Socios por accidente*/"Partners by Chance" (2014), a comedy, and *Kryptonita*, a skewering of the superhero genre. These productions enjoyed wide domestic theatrical releases. Nevertheless, Loreti has collaborated with Sarna, a punk collective, in the making of *Trash 2: Las tetas de Ana L.*/"Trash 2: The Tits of Ana L." (Alejo Rébora, 2012), and Sarna and Loreti have worked together to make several music videos (Rébora and Giménez). Similarly, Diment directed *La memoria del muerto*, wrote the scripts for numerous films including *Aballay, el hombre sin miedo/Six Shooters* (Fernando Spiner, 2010), a Western that was Argentina's nomination for the Academy Awards Best Foreign Language Film in 2011. Yet, Diment has collaborated in the making of films with Gorevisión, a production company that makes underground/metal/trash/gore cinema. Diment was executive producer for Gorevisión's *Los super bonarenses*/"The Super Bonarenses" (Germán Magariños, 2014), acted in *Goretech: Bienvenidos al planeta hijo de puta* / "Welcome to the Planet Son of a Bitch" (Germán Magariños, 2012), and, with support from INCAA, made a documentary about Gorevisión titled *El sistema Gorevisión: Cine z, micropolítica y rocanroll*/"The Gorevisión System: Z Cinema, Micropolitics, and Rock 'n' Roll" (2015).

Support from INCAA for their respective projects hardly accords Loreti and Diment the sort of celebrity/auteur director status that comes with, say, a Latin American director's arrival at the echelons of Hollywood or global commercial cinema à la Fede Álvarez or Alejandro González Iñárritu. Nevertheless, INCAA's assistance does count for something and bestows a certain notoriety on Loreti and Diment, which underscores something exceptional about Argentine horror directors: a fluidity among horror genres that might otherwise be hierarchized in another context. Jeffrey Sconce analyzes the critical reception in the United States of *Nightmare on Elm Street* and *Henry: Portrait of a Serial Killer* as evidence of a critical disparagement of slasher films and an elevation of art-house horror of the likes of *Henry* ("Spectacles" 103–04). Diment's and Loreti's fluid movements between horror and other genres embody the absence of a generic hierarchy that would elevate or relegate one horror subgenre over another within the Argentine context.

THE PLEASURE OF A MARGIN: ARGENTINE HORROR AS PARACINEMATIC

The grouping of low-budget, commercial, and English-language Argentine horror films together are further consolidated through the notion that horror cinema operates as a paracinematic pleasure for viewers and directors that pits Argentine horror cinema (or even, genre cinema) against New Argentine Cinema. Sconce famously conceived paracinema as "less a distinct group of films than a particular reading protocol, a counteraesthetic turned subcultural sensibility devoted to all manner of cultural detritus. In short, the explicit manifesto of paracinematic culture is to valorize all forms of cinematic 'trash,' whether such films have been either explicitly rejected or simply ignored by legitimate film culture" ("Trashing" 372). Given its traditionally disreputable status among domestic critics, Argentine horror may be conceived as a "lesser" genre than films directed by the likes of Lucrecia Martel and Lisandro Alonso, two figures often associated with New Argentine Cinema. Besides considering an instance in which the paracinematic plays out in the Argentine context, examining the relationship between Argentine horror and New Argentine Cinema also explains, in part, horror cinema's marginalization and reception during much of the 1990s and the 2000s, in which criticism and exhibition inadvertently elevate one domestic film culture over another.[35]

Though almost invariably and self-reflexively admitting the risk of pigeonholing, select critics make coherent New Argentine Cinema and distinguish it from other cinemas through a criteria of budgets, exhibition, and aesthetics. In the introduction to *Nuevo cine argentino*, Horacio Bernades, Diego Lerer, and Sergio Wolf assert that films associated with New Argentine Cinema are generally made on shoestring budgets and, though often produced with assistance from INCAA and/or a film production fund outside Argentina such as the Hubert Bals Fund or Fonds Sud, attain a kind of independent financing structure (10). Gonzalo Aguilar likewise describes the low-budget and precarious conditions of production (8–10), the sundry modes of distribution in national and international film festivals (10–11), and an aesthetic of "strategic carelessness" (15).[36]

Positioning Argentina horror cinema and New Argentine Cinema as marginal cinematic "movements" or "waves" can be a difficult task given the frequency with which such terms are bandied about these days. David Oubiña's prologue to *Cines al margen* provides an index to consider ways in which marginal films are conceived in Argentina. Oubiña traces common characteristics in the essays that apply to select filmmakers associated with New Argentine Cinema (Martín Rejtman,

Lisandro Alonso, Albertina Carri), video collectives in Patagonia, film genres (documentaries, science fiction, art house), and theoretical topics (metacritical forms of documentary, postnational identities, representations of global capitalism in Argentine film, realism). For Oubiña, marginal films are defined by their crucial reliance on "formas de financiamiento no convencionales, circuitos alternativos de exhibición y aproximaciones críticas desprejuiciadas" ("unconventional forms of financing, alternative circuits of exhibition, and impartial critical interpretations of films") (Prólogo 15).[37] Oubiña further defines marginal films by how they are made, a characteristic through which he creates a binary between mainstream and marginal cinemas: "por un lado, [cine del mainstream tiene] la forma de un espectáculo omnipresente gobernado por reglas muy precisas y, por otro, [cine marginal tiene] diversas formas cuya característica principal consiste en seguir apostando por la experimentación y el riesgo" ("On one hand, [mainstream cinema has] the form of a ubiquitous spectacle governed by strict norms and, on the other hand, [marginal cinema] has diverse formas whose main characteristic consists of relying on experimentation and risk") (Prólogo 15). Oubiña thus assigns a level of spontaneity and adventure to marginal cinema. In contrast, mainstream cinema is characterized by an adherence to established rules and, as Oubiña notes later in the same paragraph, a fixation with new technology (Prólogo 15).[38]

Argentine horror cinema, particularly low-budget Argentine horror cinema, largely conforms to Oubiña's criteria of a marginal cinema. The horror films are almost invariably produced on a small or miniscule budget with different sources of funding (crowdfunding or even self-financed by the director and/or crew), a dependence on alternative forms of exhibition, and a reliance on film critics for visibility, although critics of Argentine horror rarely, if ever, command the same cultural cachet as Oubiña and others who have championed New Argentine Cinema. Still, the parallels between New Argentine Cinema and Argentine horror have limits. Albeit grossly simplifying the differences among Argentine horror films, the horror films' awareness and manipulation of generic horror cinema codes set the films apart from the most iconic films associated with New Argentine cinema that instead opt for a slow-paced and loose narrative structure (i.e., *Pizza, birra, faso/Pizza, Beer, and Cigarettes* [Israel Adrián Caetano and Bruno Stagnaro, 1998], *Mundo grúa/Crane World* [Pablo Trapero, 1999], and *Silvia Prieto* [Martín Rejtman, 1999]).

Juxtaposing Argentine horror films and its domestic film culture against New Argentine Cinema and its film culture signals different registries of marginality and independence within a larger Argentine film culture and the need to account for the relationality that terms such as marginal and independent denote (marginal and independent to what?). New Argentine Cinema was and continues to be abetted by a critical apparatus and exhibition circuit both in Argentina and beyond. There is no shortage of book-length studies and academic articles in Spanish and English that examine the films that compose New Argentine Cinema. Page (3) and Andermann (*New Argentine Cinema* 8) have noted the crucial role of journals such as *El amante de cine* and *Kilómetro 111* played in the emergence of New Argentine Cinema, and such journals appear to have overlooked national horror cinema in its entirety. The August 2009 issue of *El amante de cine* represents a curious but instructive omission. The first quarter of the issue is devoted to horror cinema, and a still from *Drag Me to Hell* (Sam Raimi, 2009) braces one side of the cover that announces "Especial sustos y terrores" ("Special [issue] with scares and terrors").[39] Inside, any mention of a contemporary and classical Argentine horror film is conspicuously absent.

Exhibition similarly provided a crucial vehicle for the emergence of New Argentine Cinema both nationally and transnationally. Carlos Gutiérrez and Monika Wagenberg have alluded to the "symbiotic" relationship between New Argentine Cinema and BAFICI (Buenos Aires Festival Internacional de Cine Independiente / "Buenos Aires International Independent Film Festival") at the end of the 1990s: "they have grown hand in hand, travelling similar paths as they have exerted regional influence, and won international recognition" (299) and developing a film culture with transnational ramifications. Gutiérrez and Wagenberg describe how "programmers from Cannes, Venice, Rotterdam, Toronto, Tribeca, and many other festivals began to flock to BAFICI to find new talent in as early as it third edition" (300), thus making concrete the notion that film festivals possess the capacity to upend facile notions of center and periphery in which the primary nodes of film production (e.g., select European and North American cities) merely distribute films to cultural peripheries in a dynamic of one-way film traffic (Loist 51–52). An exhibition venue of BAFICI's stature and a national/transnational critical apparatus that feted New Argentine Cinema posed ramifications in other facets of Argentine film culture, such as film schools in Buenos Aires with horror and genre film directors occasionally grousing about how auteur cinema was generally esteemed while genre cinema was disparaged (De la Vega interview 2007; Rodríguez 97). In turn, audiences at BARS operate as a counterpublic of sorts whose cinematic tastes are largely at variance with those of BAFICI (Wong 90). While BAFICI regularly screens horror and fantasy films from outside Argentina and has screened national horror productions in 2012 and 2014, the festival's offerings in general are vastly different from those of BARS.

Argentine film culture presents an instance in which an auteur cinema (New Argentine Cinema) acquires a degree of dominance that renders marginal other cinematic genres, such as horror, that retain a commercial viability elsewhere. In an interview, Pablo Sapere, a critic and programmer for BARS, remarked that critics championing New Argentine cinema in the early 1990s had the effects of relegating genre cinema, such as horror, to near invisibility, thus necessitating the creation of BARS and other exhibition venues for genres, such as horror, science fiction, and exploitation. While the aforementioned collection of essays titled *Cines al margen* describes auteur cinema among other categories, it is telling that Argentine horror cinema is nowhere to be found among its pages. While Oubiña is correct to characterize the films discussed by essayists as examples of marginal cinema, the absence of horror cinema produced in Argentina suggests a plurality of margins within Argentine cinema in which a cinematic category attains its marginal status in which marginal is relational to more than one center. Again, both New Argentine Cinema and Argentine horror are marginal to Hollywood's films. Yet, pitted against each other, New Argentine Cinema and Argentine horror have traditionally not occupied an equal footing. Numerous horror directors have remarked about what appeared to be a bias against genre cinema on the part of INCAA during the 1990s and early 2000s that prevented any national horror film being released for twenty years between the releases of *Alguien te está mirando* (1988) and *Visitante de invierno* (2008). While it is difficult to ascertain the precise reasons why, horror's absence is glaring during those two decades. A lack of support from INCAA, the absence of a domestic and transnational critical apparatus and exhibition circuit are all factors that prevented Argentine horror filmmakers during the late 1990s and 2000s from plying and developing their trade under the auspices of INCAA. INCAA's newfound support for horror cinema signals how crucial a national cinematic infrastructure is to nurturing the emergence of film movements in Argentina.

Irrespective of the budget of an Argentine horror film, the traditionally marginalized position of Argentine horror vis-à-vis New Argentine Cinema can make for a paracinematic pleasure. For Sconce, the pleasures of paracinema are based on an audience's ironic readings ("Trashing" 383–84) or " 'seeing through' the diegesis" ("Trashing" 389).[40] While Argentine horror certainly affords a viewer such pleasures, the paracinematic pleasures of Argentine horror also can take a more generalized form with horror being consumed in oppositional taste to some other body of films. That opposition is laid bare when consumers, filmmakers, and critics sometimes couch the wave of Argentine genre cinema, which includes horror, as contestatory vis-à-vis other Argentine films that likewise coagulate around similar discourses of independence, such as New Argentine Cinema.

The issue of labeling Argentine horror cinema as "independent" in a deluge of independent films, at times, has generated a range of rubrics among Argentine horror film critics, fans, and directors. Some critics and fans have designated Argentine horror films as belonging to a larger wave of genre cinema by using designators, such as "*ultraindependiente*" ("super-independent"), as do the organizers of BARS ("Historia del festival"), or positioning horror cinema within a "movement" christened "Cine Independiente Fantástico Argentino," with the designator "fantástico" encompassing the genres of horror and science fiction. Javier Diment has perhaps best articulated and boiled down the relationship between an independent auteur cinema (New Argentine Cinema) and independent genre cinema, such as horror in Argentina. On various occasions Diment has described how conditions of genre cinema in Argentina as being distinct from those conditions elsewhere, such as the United States (*Rojo sangre*; Diment). If genre cinema is dominant in the United States with auteur cinema as an expression of independence, in Argentina the formula gets reversed: genre cinema operates as a countercinema contrary to what has been esteemed by "serious" film critics.[41]

If differentiating Argentine horror cinema from New Argentine Cinema underscores the existence of distinct film cultures in Argentina, then the two "movements" nevertheless blur. Directors often associated with New Argentine Cinema have made genre films that are clearly indebted to horror. With Adrián Caetano's *Crónica de una fuga* (2006), a movie that I will examine more closely in chapter 5, the horror elements are unmistakable. Lucía Puenzo's *El médico alemán: Wakolda/The German Doctor* (2013), a drama based on her novel about Josef Mengele's sojourn in Patagonia, depicts Mengele as a mad scientist–like figure ogling bodies and maintaining copious notes while prescribing unconventional remedies for ailments. Additional films that could conceivably fit within the aforementioned template of New Argentine Cinema—low budgets, an ad hoc style, and/or an aesthetic that differs from mainstream Hollywood or Argentine cinema—possess moments of horror or a muted and lingering sense of dread. Several critics have pointed to the dynamics of Gothic horror cinema in Lucrecia

Martel's films,[42] and, when asked about the horror elements in films such as *La ciénaga*, Martel herself acknowledged, "Ésa es mi gran debilidad: el cine de terror. Todo mi vida va hacia eso" ("That is my big weakness: horror cinema. My entire life revolves around it") (Oubiña, *La ciénaga* 66). In the climax of *La araña vampiro/The Vampire Spider* (Gabriel Medina, 2012), Jerónimo (Martín Piroyansky) places a large poisonous spider on his eye so that he will be bitten and be cured by the same spider bite. The scenario and the multiple images of the spider would not be out of place in a film like Lucio Fulci's *The Beyond*, or spider horror films from the United States during 1950s and 1970s, such as *World without End* (1956) or *Tarantulas: The Deadly Cargo* (1977) (Salmose). Finally, despite a provocative title that betrays its excruciating slow pace, *Historia del miedo/History of Fear* (Benjamín Naishat, 2014) draws on ambient horror to suggest an ominous fear that seeps into different characters' lives. Horror, in turn, can make Argentine horror and New Argentine Cinema estranged siblings.

ARGENTINE HORROR FILM CULTURE ELSEWHERE

Miriam Ross has written about the difficulties of Latin American countries creating a historical legacy through the preservation of national cinema: "[...] cinematic products have a certain kind of spatiality which is intensified by their transference through global locations from one cinema screen to the next, with a trail of reviews and discussions tracing their mark on different locales" (35). While contemporary Argentine horror films presently are exempt from preservation in any official archive, Ross's characterization of a residual "trail of reviews and discussions" is helpful to understand the transnational breadth of Argentine horror cinema. What precedes and what follows in the wakes of Argentine horror films illuminates the paths of Argentine horror film culture.

Conditions in horror film cultures outside Argentina appear ideal for Argentine horror cinema to circulate transnationally. The production of horror cinema in various countries signals the existence, however modest, of vibrant horror cinema cultures in those very countries. Akin to the conditions in Argentina in which consumption of horror translates into its production, the contemporary emergence of horror from numerous national sites intimates the same sites in which an Argentine horror film may garner interest among consumers. In the anthology *Horror International* (2005), various authors examine horror films from countries with a tradition of horror cinema production—Spain, Britain,

Germany, Australia, New Zealand, and Japan—as well as countries that do not, such as Belgium, Romania, and Thailand.

Transnational horror spectatorship enacts a demand for horror cinema irrespective of the origin, or origins, of its production qualities, a dynamic of which enables Argentine horror avails itself. The paracinematic consumption within Argentina described above can extend beyond its borders, with an Argentine horror film participating in a local flipping of hierarchical tastes in which horror and other marginal genres are valued over those genres esteemed by domestic critics. Lobato, among others, has written about the transnational dimensions of the straight-to-video market that usually have low-budgets and how producers specialize in particular genres, such as horror, and produce films that clearly adhere to genre tenets so as to be recognizable by consumers and to facilitate categorization in DVD rental stores or websites (25). "The STV market bases its continued existence on the voracious appetites of genre buffs for whom the number of films released theatrically each year is never quite enough" (Lobato 25), whose appetite, in distinction from higher-budget films, is sustained by its "own logics and pleasures" (Lobato 25). Lobato himself alludes to "the pleasures of mediocrity" with STV productions, and Argentine horror cinema potentially affords such pleasures (34).[43]

Yet, Argentine horror also offers its viewers another pleasure: innovation on a limited budget. Spectators, both in Argentina and beyond, profess an admiration for a film's or director's ingenuity for crafting a film on a budget that pales in comparison to more commercial films. Remarks posted on message boards about Argentine horror films illustrate such a dynamic of pleasure. In the comments section for *Grité una noche*/"I Screamed One Night" (Adrián García Bogliano, 2005) on YouTube, the poster "corpusvile" writes, "36 Pasos was a work of micro budgeted genius," and "Animaciones Pro" writes of *Plaga zombie* on Farsa Producciones YouTube page: "analisemos [sic] esto[:] en toda la pelicula [sic] estuvieron en su casa o el patio! O sea armaron un guion [sic] de 1:09:56 solo con esos dos escenarios! es increivble [sic]! la trama de la pelicula [sic] esta [sic] muy bien echa [sic] [. . .] ("Let's analyze this[:] in the entire film they were in their house or the patio! In other words, they wrote a script based on those two settings! it's incredible! the film's plot is really well done"). In lieu of mediocrity, the posters articulate a deep appreciation for making do with little resources. In an interview, critic Matías Raña referred to Sam Raimi's original *Evil Dead* (1981) as a kind of proverbial Bible for low-budget horror filmmakers in Argentina given the film's innovations and restrictive budget. Argentine filmmakers emulate Raimi's *Evil Dead* out of necessity.

If horror film cultures in different geographies signal where an Argentine horror film may find success, then those same geographies also constitute a site that potentially sets off additional chains of secondary production around that film. The commodity circuit of *La memoria del muerto* that led to its distribution in the United States is instructive for understanding the mechanisms that enabled the film to circulate with various links between exhibition, distribution, critics, and moviegoers with the movie being consumed at each stop. In 2012, *La memoria del muerto* was screened at several horror and fantasy film festivals, such as Fantastic Fest in Austin, Fantaspoa in Porto Alegre, Brazil, Fantasia Festival in Montreal, and Feratum Film Fest in Tlalpujahua, Michoacán, Mexico. At each festival, the film was described in print and online programs and subsequently reviewed by writers for various websites that specialize in exploitation and horror cinema, such as *Bloody Disgusting* and *Horror Not Dead* in the United States and *Cinefagia* in Mexico. In March of 2013, *La memoria del muerto* premiered in Argentine cinemas with modest success. The movie was reviewed widely in national newspapers, magazines, and blogs in Argentina. In December of 2013, the movie was shown at Blood Window in Buenos Aires, which is the horror-thriller-fantasy-science fiction sector of Ventana Sur.[44] During the first Blood Window in December of 2013, Artsploitation, a U.S. distributor of exploitation/horror/art cinema, acquired US and Canadian distribution rights for *La memoria del muerto* after its founder, Raymond Murray, viewed the movie (Murray). As is customary for distributors, Artsploitation sent acquisition and release announcements to its vast number of media contacts in the United States and Canada (Murray). The distribution deal was covered by sites in the United States such as *Screen Anarchy* and *Daily Dead* with scores of additional sites covering Artsploitation's actual release of *La memoria del muerto* in February of 2014. With the film's DVD release, select consumers of Diment's film posted their reviews of the film on sites, such as amazon.com and imdb.com.

Other Argentine horror films replicate to varying degrees *La memoria del muerto*'s circuit of consumption with distribution being the crucial mechanism that makes for transnational blocks of consumers and sites of secondary production. As Cubitt states, distribution "can be considered as the management of space-time flows of product and money" (202), with distributors possessing the power "to direct and delay the flow of mediation" between producers and consumers (196). Yet, not all films circulate homogenously with some relying exclusively on alternative exhibition circuits outside actual cinemas, in festivals, and/or via YouTube.

Festivals can be especially important for Argentine horror films by constituting its own circuit of hemispherical and transnational exhibition in which a film's exhibition at a festival is invoked in a film's marketing as a kind of imprimatur. While a prevailing definition of a "festival film" denotes an "art house" film,[45] the circuit of horror film festivals in Latin America and elsewhere reiterates the possibility of a genre-specific festival film (Falicov, "The 'Festival Film'" 213–15). In her introduction to *Horrofílmico*, Díaz-Zambrana provides an overview of Latin American horror cinema and, among other aspects, enumerates a list of horror and fantasy film festivals that include BARS, Otrocine (Bogotá), Fantaspoa (Porto Alegre, Brazil), Macabro (Mexico City), Mórbido (various cities in Mexico), Montevideo Fantástico (Uruguay), and the Puerto Rican Horror Film Festival (Guaynabo and San Juan) (29).[46] Collectively, the festivals offer an alternative subcircuit for horror films produced in Argentina, Latin America, and elsewhere. Though festivals only provide an ephemeral moment of exhibition with finite distribution (i.e., the film is distributed to a single location at a time), the festivals nevertheless serve as a potentially significant stop in the life of an Argentine horror film given that a festival event can enable a more substantial form of distribution and secondary production around a film's presence at a festival. Dayan describes "a Niagara of printed paper" (52) that preceded and followed film screenings at the Sundance Film Festival. The deluge of paper at Sundance constituted "the written festival" (Dayan 51), a festival running parallel to the actual film screenings. Similarly, Argentine horror cinema enters into the print and/or virtual arms of a festival in which films are being consumed and undergo secondary productions outside Argentina through festival guides, reviews of festivals by journalists covering the event, and fan reviews of films on Facebook and Twitter. Festivals beyond Latin America likewise provide a venue of crucial visibility and a subsequent circuit of consumption for Argentine horror. Argentine horror has figured into the programming for modest-sized festivals such as Tabloid Witch Festival in Santa Monica, California, as well as more esteemed ones, such as Sitges, the Brussels International Fantastic Film Festival in Belgium, Bucheon International Fantastic Film Festival in South Korea, and the aforementioned Fantastic Fest and Mórbido Film Fest.

Given the secondary production that can emerge around DVD releases (à la *Memoria del muerto*), DVD distribution appears the most effective way to attract secondary consumption around a film. The DVD distribution of Argentine horror cinema constitutes a crucial mode of circulation for Argentine horror cinema and highlights the existence of horror film cultures outside Argentina. Argentine horror is largely distributed by small and midsize companies, such as Maverick (*Death Knows Your Name*), SRS (*Sadomaster*), and Maya Entertainment (*36 Pasos*) in the United States; Star Films in Peru (*Penumbra*); Oh My Gore! in France (*No moriré sola*); and Lighthouse Entertainment (*La segunda muerte*) in Germany with London-based One Eyed Films having worldwide distribution for a handful of Argentine horror films such as *2/11: Day of the Dead*.[47]

Nevertheless, the DVD distribution of Argentine horror films within select countries hardly limits the geographic scope of the films' circulation. A film's circulation on the Internet constitutes a channel of circulation of almost immeasurable reach. Typing the title of virtually any Argentine horror film into a search engine along with the words *DVD rip* illustrates the multitude of sites in which the number of viewers and locales of those viewers consuming a particular film escape any empirical determination. For example, using a search engine to find a site from which to download *Resurrección* (e.g., typing "DVD rip Resurrección Gonzalo Calzada") yields more than twenty different sites from which one can download the films, while, of course, running the risk of acquiring a virus.

The traces of fan and journalist criticism of Argentine horror cinema in different forums beyond Argentina further illuminate the films' transnational reach and provide instances in which the pleasure and unpleasures of Argentine horror are most discernible. Argentine horror is written about and reviewed on horror and fantasy cinema websites in Uruguay (*Terrorífilo*), England (*Horror Cult Films*), Spain (*Scifiworld*), Sweden (*FromBeyond*), Germany (*AngstRated*), Japan (*Killer Demons, Aliens, and Rabbits*), and Australia (*Horror Society*). The presence of Argentine horror on particular sites reiterates the existence of nodes of consumption for Argentine horror and possibly supports Steffen Hantke's observation that horror fans have turned to local and foreign horror cinema as a way to solidify subcultural capital (Introduction xxii).[48]

Argentine horror film culture achieves a transnational reach and makes for what Rick Altman calls a constellated genre community whose glue, in this instance, is the mere consumption of Argentine horror (161). Occasional instances of "lateral communication" ("exchanges between viewers") often transpire via the websites with such communication conducted in Spanish between those viewers dispersed through Latin America and/or Spain (Altman 162). Otherwise, specific bilingual journalists facilitate the linkages among horror film cultures in which Argentine horror cinema is the common topic. Nicanor Loreti used to write English-language articles about Argentine horror films, in addition to films from other countries, for *Fangoria*. According to Todd Brown, a film critic and founder of *Twitch* and *Screen Anarchy*, Loreti's English-language articles have helped to bring attention to Argentine horror cinema through *Fangoria* (Brown). Loreti's own crossing over into English-language journalism has helped Argentine horror cinema cross over into other markets. Brown's own work about Argentine horror cinema on *Twitch* and *Screen Anarchy* has brought the films to the attention of English-language readers. Finally, John Hopewell, a correspondent with *Variety*, has written extensively about the growth of genre cinema in Argentina.

THE LOOP OF HORROR

Argentine horror cinema culture can be fractured and conceived through physical geographies: production and consumption within Argentina and production and consumption outside Argentina. Nevertheless, the splices that tie sites together constitute the circulation of the actual films. As noted above, consumption as secondary production emerges around the films in a multitude of physical and virtual locations. The linkages among geographies do not make for a one-way traffic for Argentine horror cinema culture. The circulation of Argentine horror film culture unfolds as a loop that moves beyond Argentina and then feeds back only to move out again, creating a cycle of national and transnational relays. Such a dynamic for contemporary Argentine horror cinema has always been the case. At the end of the 1990s and the early 2000s, Argentine horror cinema was made without the support of INCAA. Select Argentine directors and producers of both English-language and Spanish-language films actively sought audiences within Argentina and outside it to gain visibility for their films and, at times, reasoned that the visibility gained outside Argentina through exhibition and criticism could translate into visibility within Argentina, as if the vindication of one's craft comes from elsewhere. Daniel de la Vega poignantly captures such a sentiment in an interview conducted in 2007 several years prior to his first film produced with INCAA's support, the horror-comedy *Hermanos de sangre/Blood Brothers* (2012): "Se nos reivindicado porque afuera nos han reivindicado" ("We have been vindicated because we have been vindicated outside Argentina"; Conde and Mérida 57).

To conceive the circulation of Argentine horror as a loop is underscored on numerous fronts. In addition to De la Vega's films, those directed by García Bogliano, Nicanor Loreti, Farsa Producciones, Javier Diment, Demián Rugna,

Paula Pollachi, Santiago Fernández Calvete, Germán Magariños, Alejo Rébora, Fabián Forte, and Tamae Garateguy, among others, have received international coverage, which appears to have collectively alerted INCAA to horror genre's transnational appeal. INCAA historically has been acutely aware of the various transnational repercussions of the Argentina's cinematic output. Regarding testimonial films and Manuel Antín's policies during his tenure as INCAA's director from 1983 to 1988,[49] Falicov describes how "Antín stressed in [an] interview in 1995 that [a] push to promote Argentine cinema abroad worked as effectively for a nation as any ambassador, and that it would help revitalize Argentina's image as a newly democratic and free country" (*The Cinematic Tango* 48). While at loggerheads with Antín's approach, Mario O'Donnell, Antín's successor, sensed that the transnational reception of Argentine cinema, "was firmly in accordance with the proponents of 'un cine rico' ('a wealthy cinema') and promised to promote national films as an export product" (Falicov, *Cinematic Tango* 93).[50]

INCAA's awareness of the export potential for horror cinema can be discerned with the creation of the Blood Window sector of Ventana Sur and INCAA's initiatives that focus specifically on horror film production. Ventana Sur has taken place in Buenos Aires since 2009 and bills itself as "indisputably [...] the main Latin American film market" (Blood Window). Held in and around Puerto Madero, the event is a collaboration between INCAA, the Marché du Cinema arm of the Cannes Film Festival, and the European Commission. Ventana Sur facilitates meetings between international distributors and producers with Blood Window serving as the fantasy (horror-thriller-dark comedy-science fiction) sector of Ventana Sur since 2012. The transnational dimensions of Blood Window are immediately apparent upon looking at Blood Window's website with genre productions from across Latin America, multiple fantasy film festival representatives in attendance, spaces reserved for pitches to international distributors and distributors, and prizes sponsored by entities located in different countries (Mórbido Film Festival and Labo Digital in Mexico, Full Dimensional Entertainment in Argentina, Roma Lazio Film Commission in Italy, among others) to support particular aspects of a film's production, such as color correction, sound, graphic design for a movie poster, and subtitling (Blood Window). Moreover, Blood Window's collaboration with Cannes and multiple well-known fantasy film festivals (Sitges, Fantastic Fest, Mórbido, Bucheon, among others) enables select Argentine and Latin American horror films to be showcased within different exhibition spaces and increase their likelihood of theatrical and DVD distribution outside Argentina. While the

Argentine dimension of Blood Window is conspicuous, the transnational orientation of the event is all the more so.

INCAA further underscored its understanding of horror's transnational orientation in 2015 when it announced the creation of annual *concursos* specifically earmarked for the production of two fantasy films with separate "vías" ("tracks") (1).[51] In the document issued by INCAA announcing and describing the *concurso*, fantasy cinema is conceived as horror, science fiction, and gore.[52] Under "Capítulo 03: DE LAS VIAS" ("Chapter 03: About the Tracks"), the document specifies that "Ambas [propuestas que ganan] deben contemplar la creación de un proyecto de CINE FANTASTICO, de estándares aptos para el mercado internacional en condiciones de ser ofertado a un Coproductor Internacional para su producción integral" ("Both [winning proposals] should reflect a production belonging to the fantasy genre with standards in line with the international film market so as to be offered to an international co-producer for the film's complete production"). The stipulation that filmmakers collaborate with a producer from outside Argentina greases the rails, so to speak, for a film to enter into markets in addition to the domestic one.

INCAA, however, is not exclusively a mechanism for launching Argentine horror into a global film market. CINE.AR PLAY, the Argentine government's online streaming initiative, features a number of contemporary horror films, such as *Trash*, *La segunda muerte*, *Los super bonarenses*, and *Mujer lobo*, along with horror short films such as *Alexia* (Andrés Borghi, 2013), *Infierno grande* / "Big Hell" (Jonathan Hofman and Paula Venditti, 2004), and *Best-Seller* (Matías Rispau and Boris C.Q.). CINE.AR PLAY is accessible solely to Argentine residents. INCAA TV likewise provides an additional platform for Argentine horror cinema available only to residents of Argentina. INCAA's program *Trasnochados* ("Up All Night") has screened numerous Argentine horror films such as *Necrofobia* and *Plaga zombie*, as well as a series of shorts titled *Cortos para perder el sueño* ("Short Films to Lose Sleep To"), which were originally screened at BARS (Brennan). In addition, INCAA TV produces behind-the-scene segments of Argentine films in a series called *Making of* and posts them on its YouTube channel. Multiple Argentine horror films (*Sangre negra: Aldo Knodell debe morir*, *Goretech*, *Sudor frío*, *Malditos Sean!*) have been the subject of the *Making of* series. INCAA's national and transnational initiatives fragment Argentine horror cinema with distinct circuits of exhibition that determine which audiences have access to what. Nevertheless, all the films partake in a transnational loop of horror cinema that exists on national and supranational scales.

In his tract *The Circulation of the Blood* (1628), William Harvey eloquently describes his suppositions and experiments to arrive at the conclusion of the circular movement of blood through the human body: "In attempting to discover how much blood passes from the veins into the arteries I made dissections of living animals, opened up arteries in them, and carried out various other investigations. [...] I began privately to consider if [blood] had a movement, as it were, in a circle" (57–58). The geographic travels and returns of Argentine horror cinema culture—its films, its critiques, its directors, word-of-mouth—signal that it, too, moves in a loop. Horror is only one of many transnational genres that have long moved over national borders, and, though the films circulate at differing speeds with distinct obstacles, the multiplicity of distribution channels and viewing platforms and forums of secondary production facilitate the movement and construction of an Argentine horror film culture.

In addition to the circular path of blood, Harvey discovered that the heart functioned as an engine that pumped blood through the body. Here, for Argentine horror, or even genre cinema in general, pleasure is what primes the pump of horror with the potential for pleasure to slow or even cease or convert to an unpleasure; horror cinema is not for everyone. Moreover, the production of Argentine horror cinema and the realities of its transnational reach is not necessarily a glib call for celebration. As Mette Hjort writes regarding the different types of transnational cinema she outlines, "There is nothing inherently virtuous about transnationalism and there may even be reason to object to some forms of transnationalism" (15). Daniel de la Vega and Germán Magariños, among others, have shared instances of being fleeced by producers and short changed by distributors (Panessi; Rodríguez 138–42). Still, pleasure sustains Argentine horror cinema at different points in its circulation, and I now turn to select spectatorial pleasures.

2 TELLING CARNAGE

SPECTACLES AND SPACES OF NEOLIBERALISM

Genre film critics often conceive cinematic spectacles in terms of an audience's pleasure. Larry Gross's speculative musings about the violent sequences in action films typify an affective relationship between pleasure and cinematic spectacles: "Seduction by spectacle, providing sensuous and visceral pleasures, is now considered characteristic of many contemporary Hollywood films (though some critics regard it as an infantile characteristic)" (11).

Cinematic spectacles may be conceived as particular to a specific genre with formal elements marking off the moment of a spectacle.[1] If sequences of singing and dancing in musicals characterize the spectacle particular to that genre, then spectacles in horror cinema possess their own facets that revolve around screen violence. Indeed, violence is intrinsic to the very genre of horror. As James Kendrick notes, "[...] Violence of some kind, even if understood as simply the *threat* of violence, is absolutely essential to the horror genre; otherwise, there would be no suspense and no reason to fear the film's threat, whether it be human or supernatural" (J. Kendrick 79–80). In his article "Spectacle Horror and *Hostel*: Why Torture Porn Does Not Exist," Lowenstein coins the category of "'spectacle horror': the staging of spectacularly explicit horror for purposes of audience admiration, provocation, and sensory adventures as much as shock or terror" (42). While simultaneously negating the subgenre,[2] Lowenstein cites so-called torture porn films to flesh out the characteristics of spectacle horror and turns to Tom Gunning's notion of cinema of attractions to ground spectacle horror: direct address of the audience; "inciting visual curiosity," shock, or surprise in the audience; and "theatrical display [that dominates] over theatrical absorption" (Gunning 64–65).

Select critics contend that a spectacle qualifies as a vacuous instance or gap in a narrative that short circuits a critical reception. Dana Pollan exemplifies such a view with his remark that "spectacle works to convert the critical into the merely watched and watchable" (140). As if a spectacle was a moment that snuffs out any cerebral flicker, and a viewer is rendered into a passive receptacle that, at best, can simply follow a sequence. Yet, spectacle and spectacular violence have the capacity to generate meaning within a narrative.[3] In her introduction to *The Violent Woman*, Hilary Neroni outlines different theoretical notions of screen violence and alludes to David Bordwell's lack of discussion of screen violence in *Narration and the Fiction Film* as an example of how screen violence refrains from rupturing the narrative: "[...] Bordwell never mentions filmic violence as such but rather describes violent scenes in terms of their place within the larger narrative structure" (Neroni 3). Spectacle acquires meaning within a narrative chain with violence in a horror film advancing the plot or constituting the climax via a standoff.

What is crucial in my analysis of Argentine horror cinema here is whether a horror spectacle possesses the capacity to generate meanings beyond a narrative and to project sociopolitical allegories to weigh in on the imposition and repercussions of neoliberal policies in Argentina. Such a charge is fraught with pitfalls, especially given that a mediatized violence in amateur documentaries, television news broadcasts, and newspapers have captured moments in which neoliberalism has been contested in spectacular fashion in 2001 with massive protests, roadblocks, and the looting of supermarkets.

Horror spectacle, in turn, runs the risk of merely joining with a larger flow of spectacular images. Yet, horror, as intimated above in the distinction between musical and horror spectacles, sets itself apart and the genre performs its own defamiliarization.[4] As broached above, the horror spectacle is specific to the genre and a film. More importantly, horror scholars have recognized the capacity for viewers to receive a horror spectacle as more than a vacuous narrative gap. In lieu of horror spectatorship being simply characterized by shock and alarm (Baird), several critics writing about horror cinema hold out the possibility of the spectator being able to wade through a spectacle to acquire another meaning.

In a point to which I will return in my discussion of punk/horror, Isabel Cristina Pinedo has alluded to the critical distance fans acquire that enable them to deconstruct the use of special effects in horror (56). Similarly, commenting on the EC-comic-inspired color palette in George Romero's *Dawn of the Dead*, Caetlin Benson-Allott writes that "*Dawn* thereby reminds its spectator that she can learn to be critical of spectacle, too, if she can begin to recognize the limitations of its shallow, gaudy values" (44). Setting aside Benson-Allot's claim of spectacle's values, both academics and nonacademics, can make a horror spectacle signify by explicating that spectacle.

Concomitant with an examination of horror spectacle is the consideration of how the eruption of violence in horror pluralizes Argentine filmic spaces at a moment when neoliberalism restructures space and even mints new kinds of spaces in what Guillermo Tella calls "el marco de un laissez-faire territorial absoluto" ("the frame of an absolute territorial laissez-faire"), with a suburbanization achieved by private initiatives and are perhaps most emblematic with the growth of *countries*, or gated communities (108). And it is with spectacles that Argentine horror multiplies Argentine filmic spaces. A zombie horde running through the streets of Haedo in *Plaga zombie*; misogynists hunting women in the rural countryside in *No moriré sola*; and the queering of suburban space in *La memoria del muerto*: horror tenders new spectacles and, thus, new filmic spaces. Argentine horror cinema is not an inevitable reflection of neoliberalism in Argentina. As stated previously, I consistently hold out the possibility of the films doing something else. However, here, I will consider select films and their horror spectacles as moments that present a cinematic Argentina under the sign of neoliberalism.

SIGNS OF NEOLIBERALISM: ZOMBIE MULTITUDES IN *PLAGA ZOMBIE: ZONA MUTANTE*

In her book *Pretend We're Dead: Capitalist Monsters in American Pop Culture*, Annalee Newitz coins a subgenre of horror cinema and literature which she calls "economic horror." For Newitz, "capitalist monsters" are a fixture of the subgenre and embody the moral and economic ramifications of capitalism, most particularly in the United States. Capitalist monsters, in all their unseemly forms, "are allegorical figures of the modern age, acting out with their broken bodies and minds conflicts that rip our social fabric apart" (Newitz 2).[5]

Newitz's notion of economic horror provides a fitting point of departure for considering the capacity of the zombie genre in Argentina to project allegorically the country's neoliberalization. Marx's use of horror metaphors for various facets of capitalism—specters, vampires, werewolves, dead labor—are well known and wielded by different critics. Upon alluding to Marx's notion that a capitalist's asceticism nevertheless enables capital to operate as a ghost availing itself of pleasures denied, Terry Eagleton locates a zombie in such a characterization: "The more the capitalist forswears his self-delight, devoting his labours instead to the fashioning of this zombie-like *alter ego*, the more second-hand fulfilments he is able to reap. Both capitalist and capital are images of the living dead, the one animate yet anaesthetized, the other inanimate yet active" (200).

If zombie cinema possesses the ability to function as a cultural barometer (Dendle), then the zombie genre in Argentina acquires a capacity to present select tenets of Argentine neoliberalism in a cinematic form. Neoliberalism in Argentina during the 1990s has generally been characterized by "the defense of free trade, privatization, and deregulation of market and workplace" (Grimson and Kessler 70). Given that the Argentine economy was susceptible to external problems such as the Mexican peso crisis of 1995 (Grimson and Kessler 71), unfortunate and tragic repercussions followed, such as soaring foreign debt and increased poverty levels.

A contagious disease; the mass annihilation of bodies; precarious and impromptu human alliances; the incompetence of a government body to defend its citizens and its collusion with an invading entity; and spectacles of crowds and gore: as I will describe below, the zombie subgenre's iconography embodies the *consequences* of neoliberalism that are, at times, comparable yet distinct from other Argentine films that engage with neoliberalism's repercussions. Copertari locates the common theme of disintegration in dramas (*Buenos Aires viceversa/Buenos Aires Vice Versa* [Alejandro Agresti, 1996]), a comedy (*76-89-03* [Cristian Bernard and Flavio Nardini, 2000]), and a heist film (*Nueve reinas*) that allegorize neoliberalism. Moreover, though Gonzalo Aguilar resists using a corpus of films as a means of critiquing or explaining neoliberalism (3), he nevertheless relies on national cinema to "investigate the decade's transformations" during the 1990s. Similarly, the zombie genre in Argentina holds out the possibility of an allegorization of neoliberal forces.

While *Plaga zombie: Zona mutante* is hardly the sole zombie film produced in Argentina,[6] it provides a work in which to examine neoliberalism condensed into a narrative.[7] The second film in a trilogy, *Zona mutante* adheres to and plays on a number of the aforementioned subgenre's characteristics: a communicable disease, legions of undead, buckets of comedic gore, and "ordinary" heroes. Aliens conduct experiments with government approval and infect the populace of Haedo, an Argentine city located in Greater Buenos Aires. Three friends—John West (Berta Muñiz), Bill Russell (Pablo Parés), and Max Giggs (Hernán Sáez) arm themselves with makeshift weaponry of garden tools and cutlery to fight scores of zombies not to save the city, but simply to escape.

Zona mutante and the other two films that compose the trilogy are often heralded as the best Argentine zombie films.[8] Yet, the movie is rarely received as an allegory of neoliberalism. The comments on Farsa's YouTube message board range from insults to laudatory remarks over the film's comedy, its special effects, the use of particular weapons to fight the zombies (e.g., a spoon), or a moment in the film during which John West and Max dance to a John West theme song.[9] Nevertheless, the draw to examine *Zona mutante* as a projection of neoliberalism is buttressed by an instance of marketing by VideoFlims Fanpage on Facebook. Beneath a postcard that originally announced the film's premiere appears the following: "En diciembre del 2001 en pleno colapso nacional los amigos de Farsa estrenaban [*Zona mutante*]" ("In December of 2001 in the midst of a national collapse, friends at Farsa premiered [*Zona mutante*]"). An apocalyptic film, in turn, premieres amid a real apocalypse.

Zona mutante's setting provides a compelling site for examining a cinematic depiction of a neoliberal crisis in Argentina. First, its urban environs provide an expected yet slightly distinct backdrop. Andermann deems Buenos Aires "as the principal location in which crisis is being staged" (*New Argentine Cinema* xvi). Likewise, writing in December of 2002, Adrián Gorelik refers specifically to Buenos Aires and contends, "La ciudad es hoy una de las formas más concretas del colapso del ciclo democrático, su marco material" ("The city today is one of the most concrete embodiments and material framework showing the collapse of the democratic cycle") (245). At a slight remove from Buenos Aires proper, Haedo, in turn, initiates a spatial joke whose punch line is rooted in a dark humor. A zombie apocalypse unfolds not in the financial or political centers of Buenos Aires, but at a slight distance. The residents of Haedo provide a disposable population for lucrative experiments. As a voiceover by a government agent states at the beginning of the film, "Cierren las fronteras. Corten las líneas de comunicación. Ese pueblo jámas existió" ("Close the borders. Cut the lines of communication. That town never existed").

The invasion of Haedo and its fissure from the country's center initiates a cardinal mode by which neoliberalism as an aesthetic figures into the film: fragmentation *writ large*. Absent any approximation of a discontinuous and elliptical narrative style; the film is unabashedly propelled by cause and effect. Fragmentation, instead, transpires in other ways, including spatially. Haedo is first physically fragmented simply by virtue of being on film. As James Donald writes, absent a pilot's view, urban space is inevitably "fragmented" (77), and the city achieves a degree of coherence and integrity as a representation (8). One does not look at *Zona mutante* to ascertain a "realistic" depiction of Haedo; there is no truth revealed here. Henri Lefebvre professed an acute skepticism of the capacity of cinema and other visual media to "embody and 'show' the truth" about space

(96), while still empowering it with the ability to present "a truth and a reality answering to criteria quite different from those of exactitude, clarity, readability and plasticity" (97). Lefebvre leaves open such criteria, which I fill by contending that a particular image in *Zona mutante* underscores an experience of neoliberal space, one of absolute spatial discontinuity. "As free market capital accumulation plays across a variegated geographical terrain of resource endowments, cultural histories, communications possibilities, labor quantities, and qualities [...] so it produces an intensification of uneven geographical development in standards of living and life prospects. Rich regions grew richer leaving poor regions poorer" (Grimson and Kessler 178). While neoliberalism operates distinctly in different geographical contexts, its capacity to render discontinuous the space in Argentina can be seen, for example, in the increasing numbers of private neighborhoods, or "homogeneous, highly segregated and protected areas" in which the middle and upper classes are separated from the lower classes, who may have formerly occupied the same space (Janoschka and Borsdorf 96).

Zona mutante begins in media res. After a conversation between a government minion ("Agente") and a faceless "Señor," Bill, John, Max, and another individual, who remains in a body bag for nearly half the movie, are dropped off separately in different vehicles bearing FBI vanity plates. Shortly thereafter, Bill is captured by a horde of zombies, manages to escape, and is subsequently separated from John West and Max. As John and Max look for Bill, they arrive at the city's limit, which is marked with a sign: "Límite de la Ciudad." The camera frames the pair in a medium close-up from a low angle as they stand on the edge of a steep cliff. Any bridge that was formerly there has now been destroyed.[10] The humans are confined to the same space as the alien/zombie threat; there is no exit. With buildings looming in the background in the long distance shot of Max and John at the precipice, Buenos Aires appears out of reach and its government—metonymically contained in the city—is aloof (see fig. 2.1). Such an image recalls a conception of the Argentine government that was seen to be in retreat during and following the events of December of 2001. Rafael Olarra Jiménez and Luis García Martínez observed, "La vida social está desarticulada cercana al caos y la disintegración. El Estado se muestra incapaz de cumplir de manera aceptable sus funciones [...]" ("Social life is broken up and close to chaos and disintegration. The state shows itself to be incapable of acceptably fulfilling its functions [...]") (7).

The conspicuously missing state—itself a fragmentation between government and its citizens—is immediately evident and constant in *Zona mutante*. The Argentine government is not only absent but colludes with aliens and the FBI. At the start of the film, a government operative speaks to "Señor," a liaison to the president, about the alien experiments that the government has allowed on its citizens. The president is occupied with more important mat-

FIGURE 2.1 Still from *Plaga zombie: Zona mutante*. John and Max stand at the edge of a cliff at the city limits. Buenos Aires sits in the background. Directed by Pablo Parés and Hernán Sáez. 2001, Farsa Producciones.

ters. Andrew Tudor has traced various aspects of "paranoid" (post-1968) horror cinema, one of which is the absence of and/or ineffectiveness of government agencies, such as the military or police. Such an element acquires a particular resonance in the case of an Argentine zombie film made at a historical moment in which neoliberalism was at foot and helped to precipitate the mass chaos in December of 2001—"una suerte de apocalipsis" ("a kind of apocalypse") (Copertari 1)—that appeared in global media. Just as the government shrank through neoliberal policies under Menem, its on-screen presence in *Zona mutante* is largely missing and, when present, is guilty of colluding with foreign powers (aliens and the FBI) against its own citizens. Aliens can double as foreign capital that "invaded" and then abruptly exited the country ushering in chaos in Argentina. While an incomplete and impossible endeavor, *Zona mutante* then operates as a way of intimating a global totality with nefarious outside forces working with domestic entities and acting on unassuming citizens. If Jameson deemed the conspiracy film an exercise in cognitive mapping of global proportions—"an unconscious effort, collective effort at trying to figure out where we are and what landscapes and forces confront us in a late twentieth-century whose abominations are heightened by their concealment and their bureaucratic impersonality" (*Geopolitical* 3)—then the global zombie film may be employed in a similar fashion.[11] *Zona mutante*'s allegorical accuracy is unimportant; "it is the intent and the gesture that counts" (Jameson, *Geopolitical* 3).

Neoliberalism's spatial fragmentation extends to a social fragmentation. Numerous Argentine scholars and cultural critics have characterized an Argentine citizenry under neoliberalism during the 1990s as woefully atomized. Maristella Svampa and Damián Corral point to the "loss of social ties" (119), and Reati observes a "loss of the earlier sense of collectivity" ("Fractures" 187). Beatriz Sarlo's characterization of conditions would not be out of place in a postapocalyptic novel: "En este marco, proliferan las violentas armadas para la autodefensa o las iniciativas barriales para que se les reconozca a los vecinos el derecho de organizarse en defensa propia, lo cual implicaría inducir a un estado de guerra de ciudadanos contra ciudadanos" ("In this atmosphere, violent bands who practice self-defense or neighborhood initiatives proliferate so that neighbors recognize the right to organize in their own defense. Such actions imply a state of war with citizens against citizens") (*La ciudad* 56).

The social fragmentation in *Zona mutante* is ubiquitous and unmistakable. Humans aggregate only in small groups. The vacuum left by any government necessitates new human alliances and points to an additional mode in which neoliberalism's consequences appear. *Zona mutante* resembles other contemporary horror films, especially those of the zombie subgenre, in which groups form in an ad hoc fashion often with "average" heroes (i.e., not police or military officers) and are inevitably precarious.[12] Bill, John, and Max compose such an alliance, and their ordinary stature comes through in numerous ways. In lieu of superhero strength, the friends arm themselves with makeshift weaponry such as a hedge trimmer, forks and spoons, and a body contained in a bag. The coalition, however, is remarkably fragile. Max allows zombies to capture Bill, John allows Max to be captured, the three argue, and, toward the end of the film, they knock each other unconscious. If three characters constantly mend their differences, the resolutions are only temporary.

Such alliances in *Zona mutante* bring to mind the newly formed organizations that emerged during the 1990s and after the December collapse in 2001. The *piquetero* movement began during the mid-1990s and, while there is no single *piquetero* group, unemployed workers, their family members, and/or sympathizers participate (Epstein 95).[13] According to Edward Epstein, the *piqueteros* emerged with the undermining of conventional labor unions and "traditional neighborhood-based clientelist [networks]" (96).[14] With a ubiquitous distrust of conventional forms of governance, numerous self-organized groups emerged after the government collapse: "neighborhood assemblies, barter clubs, workers' self-managed factories, and counter-cultural collectives" (Svampa and Corral 118).

Human alliances, however, are not the only ones in *Zona mutante*. Zombies constitute a collective force that ostensibly appears homogeneous and unified, which is distinct from that of the quarreling humans. Although the zombies differ in dress and appearance, they are all undead. They amble about and pursue humans with a stubborn resolve. The desire to conceive the zombie multitude here as allegorizing politics emerges given Argentine's literature occasional fixation with crowds in depictions that hew close to zombie-like. Sarmiento in *Facundo* locates "the savage horde" (56) on the pampas and famously places the group in opposition to those civilized individuals residing in the cities. In Esteban Echeverría's *El matadero/The Slaughter Yard*, a political allegory of the country under then governor of Buenos Aires province, Juan Manuel de Rosas, the masses participate in the slaughter of animals in a kind of open-air abattoir. Descriptions of children playing with cattle tripe and adults covered in blood evoke filmic images of zombies feeding on and toying with intestines. Jorge Luis Borges and Adolfo Bioy Casares's "La fiesta del monstruo"/"The Monster's Party" is a first-person narrative told from the perspective of a lower-class Peronist militant. Often seen as a rewriting of *El Matadero*, the narrator uses obtuse lower-class slang to describe to a friend his experience with other militants in which they kill a young Jewish boy. The mob violence and muddled and abstruse language in "La fiesta del monstruo" suggests a zombie element at work. While the aforementioned three works portray crowds in a negative fashion, they also acknowledge the multitudes' role as a political force in national politics. The multitudes are brutal yet crucial in power relations, as are the zombies in *Zona mutante* for global domination.

Perhaps no work offers a more germane tool to assess *Zona mutante*'s zombies as a national multitude than José María Ramos Mejía's *Las multitudes argentinas/*"The Argentine Multitudes." Published in 1898, Ramos Mejía traces the evolution of the Argentine crowd in three stages, which mirrors that of the country. Ramos Mejía distinguishes his portrayal of the masses from the works mentioned above by considering the multitude as a potentially positive entity. Still, his descriptions of crowds, which are steeped in positivism and indicative of his medical training, simulate zombies.[15] Ramos Mejías speaks of "la abdicación de la personalidad consciente" ("the abdication of the conscious personality" (16) in which an individual becomes part of a multitude. A multitude is "firme y homogénea dentro de su misma heterogeneidad" ("firm and homogeneous in its own heterogeneity") (90) and "falta la inteligencia directiva" ("lacks a directive intelligence") (73). While the zombies in *Zona mutante* are different in appearance, they are similar in their ontologically undead condition. Where Ramos Mejías considers how a multitude "imprime a todas las cosas un sello violento por una especie de contagio o de sugestión profunda" ("imprints everything with a violent stamp through a kind contagion or profound suggestion") (89), the zombies in *Zona mutante* do much of the same, laying waste to the interiors of houses. Ramos Mejías's use of the word *contagio (contagion)*, which he borrows from his French contemporary Gustave Le Bon, describes an individual's provisional state of mind and is, of course, significant for a zombie film to be classified as such.[16] The contagion essentially creates the sickened multitude in *Zona mutante*.

Beyond classifying the zombies in *Zona mutante* as a multitude, the zombies are by no means a continuation of Ramos Mejías's taxonomy of Argentine multitudes; placing the zombies on some kind of artificially historical continuum is, literally and figuratively, a dead end. Instead, the film's zombie multitude is a multitude unto itself that politically and culturally allegorizes other multitudes in contemporary events in Argentina, such as the aforementioned *piqueteros* and massive *cacerolazos* that formed in protest against government officials in 2001. The zombies are not precise depictions of *piqueteros* or any specific group protesting. In this sense, the zombies operate much like the way Jameson sees the shark in *Jaws*, as he boasts a "capacity to absorb and organize [. . .] quite distinct anxieties together" (*Signatures of the Visible* 26). Yet, the zombies attain the status of a political force in many respects insofar as they have aims. A marked departure from zombies in other films, who appear to have no scheme or design, *Zona mutante*'s undead are organized. They have trucks that go around picking up humans and possess a headquarters to which they transport Bill and John West following Max's capture, during which he loses his arm (it is replaced with a zombie appendage). When Max addresses the zombies as a kind of demagogic leader drunk with power, the populist dimension of the zombies is unmistakable; even if they are being manipulated by aliens, the zombies are a structured and militant force.

In turn, the zombies in *Zona mutante* offer a sustained collective presence that is distinct from that of other contemporary Argentine films. Aguilar points to depictions of the masses in recent Argentine cinema as being distinct from "the people" portrayed in political cinema of earlier decades. Alluding to films such as *El bonarense* (Pablo Trapero, 2002), *Pizza, birra, faso*, and *Silvia Prieto*, the "underclass constitutes not the promise of liberation (as the people could be) but fits of disorganized and rash violence" (Aguilar 126, 127) with the images of the masses being relegated off-screen. The zombies in *Zona mutante* embody Aguilar's characterization of the masses as prone to violence and take that characterization to an extreme. Although organized, the zombies attack humans and trash houses with reckless abandon. Then again, if the zombies are the perpetrators of violence, they are also primary and mass recipients of violence. Zombies suffer at the hands of humans in spectacular episodes of screen violence; they have their spines and intestines ripped out, their scalps and various appendages torn off, and they suffer decapitations with copious amounts of blood gushing.

Such spectacles of violence allegorize neoliberalism and graphically highlight the consequences of political and economic policies. Steven Shaviro's commentary on David Cronenberg's body horror films is instructive here: "Power does not work merely on the level of images and ideologies; it directly invests the flesh" (Shaviro 143). The violence committed against zombies shows neoliberalism's capacity to mark the flesh in no uncertain terms. Neoliberalism does not sever limbs, cut people in half, or decapitate them. The over-the-top violence of *Zona mutante* is characteristic of the zombie subgenre, and, in questioning what triggers the violence, one arrives at how allegorization of neoliberalism appears off-screen. An invasion of foreign forces in collusion with domestic entities precipitates an apocalypse much like Argentina's transformation into a market economy transpires through the actions of multiple parties: governments, foreign investment, the International Monetary Fund. *Zona mutante* does not show the imposition of neoliberalism but rather its consequences on a massive and gory scale.

Spectacles of gore and violence in *Zona mutante* transforms an urban Argentine space that is itself already a spectacle in some respects. Podalsky writes of Buenos Aires being transformed into a "spectacle and a protagonist of films" decades ago in films such as *El Jefe* (1958) (*Specular City* 85–86), and Andermann describes the capital as a spectacle in his analysis of contemporary "gay-lesbian cinema" (*New Argentine Cinema* 46, 47). Yet, the space in *Zona mutante* is recast via horror spectacles. And there are pleasures here in this recasting. As mentioned previously, spectacles of violence afford audiences a pleasure. To return to Gross, "It is the cumulative effect of such spectacles—the sustained provision of visual and kinetic motion—which makes good gunfire sequences so enjoyable" (13). *Zona mutante* possesses several protracted fight scenes with hyperactive camerawork and special effects that showcase the different ways in which zombies can be annihilated. This is the pleasure that Gross describes. Yet, another pleasure lurks: the creation of new Argentine film spaces via horror spectacles. Writing about his own selection of travel literature, paintings, novels, poems, and films in order to write about Buenos Aires, Gorelik writes, "[L]as diferentes representaciones culturales de la ciudad no habilitan la composición de una imagen unívoca, ni en la narración de una historia, ni en la articulación de una fórmula para las relaciones ciudad-sociedad" ("The distinct cultural representations of the city do not enable the creation of an absolute image of the city, not in its historical narrative and not in its articulation of a formula for a relationship between city and society") (11). *Zona mutante* adds to the plurality of visions of Buenos Aires.

The film shoots the city's environs through a prism of horror spectacle and comedy to refashion that space and, in some sense, renew that space. In an essay titled "La posibilidad de un territorio" ("The Possibility of a Territory"), Marcos Adrián Pérez Llahí opens with a broad and bold diagnosis of Argentine cinema: "El cine argentino está enfermo del realismo" ("Argentine cinema is sick with realism") (69). For Pérez Llahí, throughout the history of Argentine cinema—from *cine tanguero* ("tango cinema") to *Nuevo cine argentino*—directors have largely subscribed to cinematic realism, as evidenced by recognizable spaces on-screen. In other words, the audience's recognition of a space as Argentine qualifies the greater part of Argentine cinema as realist. But all is not lost for Pérez Llahí. Anomalies do exist, and Pérez Llahí alludes to films such as Hugo Santiago's *Invasión/Invasion* (1969), Esteban Sapir's *Picado fino/Fine Powder* (1998), and Aldo Paparella's *Hoteles/Hotels* (2004) as movies that depart from realism by undermining the stability of familiar spaces. With a premiere in December 2001, *Zona mutante* defamiliarizes Argentine film space and renders it into an apocalypse precisely when an apocalypse was unfolding off-screen.

MALE/FEMALE, CITY/COUNTRY

In his assessment of the low-budget action/comedy *Operación Cannabis/* "Operation Cannabis" (Eduardo Peduto, Juan Oyharcabal, Marcelo Estévez and Belisario Amador, 2009); Matías Raña locates a peculiarity in Argentine genre cinema: "Sigue una línea que parece haber florecido en el cine de género argentino: la figura de la mujer fuerte, que se sobrepone a cualquier situación y abandona el rol de víctima" ("It follows a trend that seems to have flourished in Argentine genre cinema: the figure of the strong women, who overcomes any situation and abandons the role of the victim") (164). While scores of other genre films (slashers, action films, exploitation films) uphold Raña's observation, the figure of the "strong woman" in Argentine genre cinema is perhaps most saliently, if not problematically, on display in the rape-revenge subgenre in films such as *No moriré sola*, *Recortadas*, and *Cuando tu carne grite ¡Basta!/ When Your Flesh Screams!* (Guillermo Martínez, 2015).[17]

    Jacinda Read rightly points out that rape-revenge may be conceived not as genre but instead as a "narrative structure" that plays out across multiple genres (e.g., melodramas, comedies, action films, detective films, and horror films) (25). Nevertheless, a strain of rape-revenge films (e.g., *Teeth*, *I Spit on Your Grave*, *The Last House on the Left*, etc.) achieve the status of a horror subgenre given a consensus among critics and consumers. One is not hard-pressed to find articles and message board discussions centering on rape-revenge films on sites that cover Argentine horror such as *Cine fantástico y bizarro* and *Terrorífilo*. Moreover, the tendency to conceive of select rape-revenge films as a horror subgenre is bolstered by the films' gore and capacity to horrify (Davis and Natale, 38, 40–41), two hallmarks that can define a film as horror. The subgenre's primary tenets are explicit in its name and operate as the narrative's fulcrum (Lehman 105). A film's first-half relates events leading up to the rape of a single character (usually, a woman) by another individual or group (usually, a man or group of men). Subsequently, the exacting of revenge ensues by the victim and/or her or his family or friends killing the perpetrator(s) in an assortment of vicious ways. Claire Henry has pointed to a "loose iconography," "stock characters," and "key themes" and conflicts of rape-revenge films (4).[18] And while not entirely consistent in the subgenre, Carol Clover's analysis of the tense "city/country axis" and "the politics of gender and the politics of urban/rural social class" (160) that play out in a film such as *I Spit on Your Grave* and *Last House on the Left* proves particularly germane to an analysis of *No moriré sola*.

    No moriré sola, recounts the story of four young women—Carol (Gimena Blesa), Leonor (Marisol Tur), Yasmín (Magdalena De Santo), and Moira (Andrea Duarte)—making their way home from Buenos Aires to an unnamed interior town. While the atmosphere inside the car is carefree, matters quickly take an ominous turn when the group discovers the body of a woman on the side of a highway who has been shot. Gun shots ring out as the young women stop to help and carry the young woman's body to the car. The camera provides a blurry subjective shot from the car and indistinctly captures a gaggle of three male hunters in some dense woods beside the highway. The wounded woman succumbs to death, and the four women seek help at a police station in a nearby town, Trinidad. The hunters, one of which is a police lieutenant in charge of the station, arrive at the station. As the four women pull away from the police station, the hunters pursue their car eventually forcing them to stop. Using a chain, the hunters pull the women's car into the woods and shoot Yazmín as the women try to escape on foot. The three men then proceed to rape the women in an excruciating prolonged and cruel scene. The hunters kidnap Yazmín and eventually kill her, and Carol, Leonor, and Moira walk through the woods to arrive at a cabin. Extending the horrific episode, the hunters arrive at the cabin and immediately shoot Carol dead. One of the hunters is left behind at the cabin, and Moira and Leonor begin to enact revenge bludgeoning to death one hunter with a hammer, choking another with barbed wire, and shooting and chasing the last rapist into a nature reserve where he is dismembered off-screen by wild animals.

No moriré sola largely conforms to the tenets of the genre and provide an instance to consider how spectacles of gendered violence project select facets of neoliberal transformations in Argentine culture. Critics have empowered the rape-revenge films, especially low-budget horror films, with a capacity to map a politics of gender that is particular to a historical moment with the United States as the de facto geography of the analysis. Read receives the proliferation of US rape-revenge films during the 1970s and 1980s as "part of an ongoing historically [...] specific cycle" that reflects "the confluence between the rape-revenge structure and the discourses of second-wave feminism" that emerged at that time (23, 25). Henry makes a similar contention about the genre's penchant for being a "flexible genre that can allegorically explore various sociopolitical issues" that can operate in different contexts (55). While Argentina lacks a quantity of rape-revenge films comparable to that to the United States, *No moriré sola*, as well as the other aforementioned Argentine rape-revenge films, nevertheless provide a window into gender relations during neoliberalism that is deeply imbricated with space and, thus, giving those relations a spatial dynamic.

The two rape-revenge films buttress Lucía De Leone's claim that the Argentine *campo* ("countryside") is "un espacio polisémico" ("polysemic space") with contemporary literature, theater, and cinema revealing "las inestabilidades de su estatuto, la copresencia de realidades o elementos heterogéneos [y] las relaciones heterodoxas con el tiempo" ("the instabilities of its rule, the coexistence of heterogeneous realities and elements [and] heterodoxical relations with time" (199, 200). The Argentine countryside proves to be as malleable as its cityscapes and recalls Sarlo's observation regarding the "valores" ("values") that cast rural and urban spaces as "dos grandes espacios más simbólicos que reales" ("two spaces that are more symbolic than real") (*La ciudad* 33).

In "Cinematic Landscapes," Chris Lukinbeal delineates a taxonomy for film geographies and uses the term *landscape* to "emphasize landscape and cinema as a cultural production, a space that is mediated by power relations" (4). Cinematic landscape can operate as place, space, spectacle, or metaphor, and in *No moriré sola* landscape operates as a metaphor only to be disrupted by the performance of violence, as I will describe below. For Lukinbeal, "Through the use of metaphor, meaning and ideology are appropriated into landscape" and "naturalized" (13). *No moriré sola* wastes little time recycling an ideology of gender often inherent in the rape-revenge genre that pairs masculinity and the rural in opposition to femininity and an urban modernity. The film's opening shot is a long take from a low height that moves over a stretch of asphalt and simulates the movement of a car as the film's opening credits roll. The camera eventually catches up to the car of young women who embody a modernity instantly by virtue of their movement through space, or what Guillermo Giucci calls a "kinetic modernity" (xi). Yet, unlike the train's capacity to provide a "panoramic perception" (Kirby 44), the sequence largely lacks any open landscape shots from the car. Again, the camera remains at the level of the road and, save a series of telephone poles, the open landscape is obscured. In turn, the rural environs remain under wraps as the camera sits inside the women's car giddily capturing the young women with tight framing as they paint their nails, send text messages on their phones, and joke around about studying at a university and living in Buenos Aires. The film soon expresses a profound misogyny spatially while solidifying the close relationship between movement and femininity. Carol, Moira, Yazmín, and Leonor happen up a mortally injured woman bleeding profusely who has been shot by the male hunters on the side of the road. Tellingly, the anonymous woman has fallen off her bicycle, immobile and stationary. On two occasions during the film, the camera captures two signs that each warn "Animales salvajes" ("Savage animals"), perhaps a clumsy and dire warning for the four women at the start of film. The woman's bloody body, however, serves as a more blatant signpost in a vein similar to how Susana Rotker described the bodies of captive women in nineteenth-century Argentine narratives, such as Echeverría's *La cautiva*: "bodies are used to trace clear frontiers, to demarcate spaces, and to leave well differentiated who is who" (97).

The four young women have entered into a space in which violence governs. García Bogliano's film inevitably taps into Sarmiento's *civilización y barbarie* dichotomy which juxtaposed an enlightened Buenos Aires with its surrounding rural areas and which is oftentimes retained in Argentine cultural production.[19] For Sarmiento, both the land itself and its inhabitants constitute a savagery beyond the confines of the city: "To the south and the north, savages lurk, waiting for moonlit nights to descend, like a pack of hyenas, on the herds that graze the countryside, and on defenseless settlements. [...] If it is not the proximity of savages that worries the man of the countryside, it is the fear of a tiger stalking him, of a viper he might step on" (46). Here, however, the rural confines in *No moriré sola* are hostile exclusively to women and those attempt to help them, such as a feckless police officer.

Argentine rape-revenge films engage with the contemporary period through an allegorization of symbolic gains for women in Argentine politics and losses for men under neoliberalism. The first decade of the twenty-first century witnessed an increasing role for women in Argentine politics that culminated with Cristina Fernández de Kirchner's assumption of the Argentine presidency and Felisa Miceli's and Nilda Garré's appointments as economic and defense ministers, respectively, prior to Kirchner's election.[20] Such gains can be contrasted with an emasculation of men, especially those of the middle class, which has been laid at the feet of neoliberalism. In her study of masculinity in contemporary Argentine commercial cinema, Carolina Rocha finds that "the cinematic representation of middle-class masculinities in crisis is related to the inception of neoliberalism in Argentina" (2). For Rocha, a middle-class Argentine masculinity is pegged to the State and, as precarious conditions ensued with the imposition of neoliberal policies and the shrinking role of the State, "unemployment, lack of prestige, and the inability to achieve glory made Argentine men feel emasculated" (12).

The rape-revenge genre and its rural environs enables the distillation of tensions that undergird gendered relationships and effectively narrativizes those relationships. In short, the subgenre's rape and revenge are brutal crystallizations of gendered rage. According to Massey, "[p]laces are not so much bounded areas as open and porous networks of social relations" (121) with the identities of places "constructed through the specificity of their interaction with other places rather than their counterposition to them" (121). Rape-revenge *is* the social relation. The countryside becomes the site in which city women meet country men, with the women in *No moriré sola* as mobile metonyms of urbanism. The cinematic landscapes in García Bogliano's film is not so much about images of *pampas* and trees. The Argentine countryside is menacing, lurking, and ominous precisely because the narrative is focalized through young women in a rape-revenge film, a genre that dictates a cinematic landscape precisely be a menace to its focalizers. Moreover, the violence between genders impinges on the landscapes stifling the picturesque.

Any idyllic dimension of the rural in *No moriré sola* is absolutely annihilated in the rape scene that is unsettling in its brutality. Henry describes the rape scene in *Last House on the Left* as an "escalation from humiliation to rape, stabbing, dismemberment, mutilation, more rape, and a final shooting" (33). Such a parsing only begins to capture the spectacle of rape in *No moriré sola*. The scene commences with Yazmín tied to a tree, stripped, and beaten with a stick. The other three women are forced to lie down facing the ground and close-ups of their faces create a series of terrifying eye line matches. As two of the women's clothes are ripped off, one of hunters penetrates Yazmín who now lies unconscious on the ground and then extinguishes a cigarette on her breast. Carol, the youngest of the four women, attempts to flee but is stopped. After she is ordered to strip, she is anally raped until she vomits. The other two women cry and attempt to fight back but are overpowered. Shots reminiscent of pornography figure into the sequence when Carol has a rifle placed into her mouth as she is raped, and one of the hunters masturbates on Moira's breasts. The scene's soundtrack begins with distorted and caricatured screams and eventually grows quiet with only the buzz of insects and the occasional grunts of the hunters and cries of the four women.

The spectacle here both resembles and departs from the horror spectacle characterized by Lowenstein in his assessment of torture porn films. Provocation and shock, indeed, are intact. However, in lieu of a rapid montage with sleek images and special effects that one finds in films such as *Hostel* (Eli Roth, 2005), realism abounds in the rape scene from *No moriré sola*. The sequence boasts several takes that linger on the acts of the hunters and the horror of the women's faces. As intimated above, the sound reflects the film's low budget and does nothing to detract from the gruesome nature of the scene. Extradiegetic music is absent.

Stephen Prince conceives of a graph consisting of two axes to describe the "stylistic encoding" of a particular violent act in a film. "The referential component of violence—the behavior that is depicted—is the x-axis, while its cinematic treatment—the stylistic design—is the y-axis" (Prince, *Classical Film Violence* 35). Prince coins another term to describe the *y*-axis—"stylistic amplitude" (*Classical Film Violence* 35)—which measures the graphicness and duration of a violent screen act. Lasting nearly fifteen minutes, the rape scene in *No moriré sola* possesses a stylistic amplitude that is off the charts and equals, if not surpasses, other films' notorious scenes of rape, such as *I Spit on Your Grave* and *Last on the Left*, all of which appear in the opening credits of García Bogliano's film and are cited as "Ayuda espiritual" ("Spiritual guidance"). While plainly distasteful, the scene registers the horror of rape as exactly that and does nothing to make it appear palatable. Devin McKinney's notion of strong screen violence is instructive here to understand the likely receptions of the rape scene: "Strong violence, while it often has the physical effect of acting on the body genres, also acts on the mind by refusing it glib comfort and immediate resolutions. [...] And it amounts to carnage that is haunting in the truest sense" (McKinney 17).

A facile reception of the rape scene is further complicated by the insertion of images that temporarily disturb a narrative logic of cause and effect and render the setting an "autonomous landscape" that can be contemplated (M. Lefebvre 65–66). The sequence in *No moriré sola* is preceded by an image of treetops swaying in the wind (see fig. 2.2), which reappears toward the end of the rape. A shot of the sky also appears toward the end of the rape that derails any advancement in a plot. Rancière describes a pensive image as that which "arrives to suspend narrative logic in favor of an indeterminate expressive logic" (122). The pensive image as part of a novel or film (e.g., a moment of abstraction) perturbs the primary "narrative chain" and creates multiple regimes of expression (Rancière 124). That is, a novel's or film's main narrative sequence in which "intrigue and dénouement" persists, yet the pensive image ruptures that chain and introduces

FIGURE 2.2 Still from *No moriré sola*. A pensive image wanders into the midst of the rape scene. Directed by Adrián García Bogliano. 2008, Paura Flics.

a "chain [or chains] of micro-events" (Rancière 124) that defies the narrative logic typical of classical Hollywood cinema. If *No moriré sola* takes some of its cues from US rape-revenge films, then it also carves out its own space with pensive images and suggest the women's desubjectification owing to the rape.

The rape infuses the Argentine country side with a violent masculinity injecting the landscape with what Jean Franco calls an "extreme masculinity":

"a meltdown of the fundamental core that makes humans recognize their own vulnerability and hence acknowledge that of the other" (*Cruel Modernity* 15). Violence is the social relation that defines the space. For Neroni, "[s]erving as a fundamental signifier of masculinity, we not only consider violence more the province of men than women, but it is also an activity that inevitably enhances a man's masculinity as much as it would conversely detract from a woman's femininity" (42). Yet, the women's own vengeance in *No moriré sola*, and not a proxy vengeance, produces its own violence that unhinges an exclusive gendering of violence and, in turn, the gendering of the film's rural space. Jeffrey Brown turns to Judith Butler's theory of gender performativity to consider how a heroine in an action film "confounds essentialism through her performance of traditionally masculine roles" (56). In *No moriré sola*, as in many other rape-revenge films, the performance of extreme physical violence puts into relief masculine modes of violence and those tools that are employed to carry out that violence, such as a gun. If masculine violence is construed as shooting, raping, and/or stabbing, a feminine violence would be poisoning.

Moira and Leonor undergo a sort of masculinization through performance of violent acts that could be deemed masculine. A hammer is wielded repeatedly against one of the rapists as blood splatters on Moira's face. Leonora uses a piece of barbed wire to choke another rapist. Finally, Moira grabs a rifle and fires repeatedly at the last remaining rapist. In each instance, Moira and Leonora breathe heavily as if unable to contain the trauma and rage of the predicament, bringing to mind Neroni's observation about horror films from the seventies and eighties: "[T]hese films can only imagine a woman as capable of violence if she is entirely enraged, and this anger can only occur when she is tortured, violated, and pushed into a state of total fright" (32). If the hunters commit violence as if for pleasure, feminine violence remains defensive. Furthermore, if violence destabilizes the female characters' gender, it only reinforces the violence that dominates the space. Initially, the four women were excluded from the space by violence. Only after they themselves have exacted a bloody carnage and emptied the space of threats are the women permitted to remain in that space without being assaulted or pursued.

Critics of rape-revenge films generally have centered a discussion of the subgenre's pleasure by pointing to a hypothetical spectator's gratification at seeing graphic acts of revenge committed by a victim (Henry 6; Read 40). Besides the pleasure of seeing an Argentine entry into the genre for an Argentine spectator,[21] another pleasure of *No moriré sola* is precisely its unpleasure. Frost contends that a "fundamental goal of modernism is the redefinition of pleasure: specifically, exposing easily achieved and primarily somatic pleasures as facile, hollow, and false, and cultivating those that require more ambitious analytical work" (3). *No moriré sola* is resoundingly not a modernist film. Yet, its incredibly brutal rape scene, its revenge, and pensive images prevent the film from being easily imbibed. Its violence and derailment of narrative flow reverberates and obstructs an easy pleasure.

Violence, whether within a film or elsewhere, is rarely allowed to not be indexical. Lest they be deemed gratuitous, interpretations of violent acts are often received as pointing to some cultural symptom. In the case of *No moriré sola*, a rape-revenge film operates as an allegory of gender relations wrought by neoliberalism in Argentina, specifically symbolic gains of female politicians and an emasculation of men. Clover conceives the rape-revenge genre as possessing a "double-axis revenge plot so popular in modern horror: the revenge of the woman on her rapist, and the revenge of the city on the country" (115). The young women in *No moriré sola* complicate such a formulation: they are in transit from Buenos Aires to their hometown in the interior. Moreover, the film's cycle of violence elides the distinction between city and country. With discourses of "*inseguridad*" ("insecurity") figuring saliently in news media in Buenos Aires and other metropolitan cities, *No moriré sola* suggests an economy of violence that binds the city and the country. In other words, violence circulates.

QUEERING THE SUBURBS

Guillermo Tella, among others, has described "una etapa de *desurbanización*" ("stage of desuburbanization") (45) of Buenos Aires that has accompanied neoliberalism's imposition in Argentina over the past twenty years. Abetted by highways, such an "etapa" has entailed an expansion of fragmented spatial developments away from the city's center with the emergence of acutely contrasting spaces, perhaps best emblematized by juxtaposing the private gated communities of the middle and upper classes against rising poverty in Gran Buenos Aires (Tella 45–48; Stang). As with other large cities in Latin America, such as São Paulo, Lima, and Managua (Scorer 20–21), and elsewhere in the world, fragmentation captures the spatial dynamics of Buenos Aires under neoliberalism in which scores of people have voluntarily moved away from the capital or have been involuntarily pushed away. While *La memoria del muerto* is not set in a gated community, the film nevertheless provides an instance to briefly consider how horror manages to subvert, and even queer, a space that ostensibly appears as an escape from the city.

La memoria del muerto is a horror film that flirts with melodrama and dark comedy. Jorge (Jorge Gabriel Goity) and Alicia (Lola Berthet) are a childless and fashionable middle-aged couple who reside in a large country house that is enclosed by a tall iron fence in a neighborhood with similar houses. In Alicia's ominous nightmare that initiates the film, Jorge and Alicia walk about their neighborhood and converse about Jorge going on a weeklong retreat to meditate, two random children approach Alicia and vomit, and Jorge smashes his skull by jumping headfirst twice into an empty cement pool. Alicia awakens to find Jorge bleeding from his nose and convulsing. Jorge dies, and, forty-nine days later, Alicia invites her husband's closest friends to the couple's house to spend the night and ostensibly to celebrate Jorge's life. However, when the clock strikes midnight Alicia, with the help of Hugo (Luis Ziembrowski) and Nicanor (Matías Marmorato), exacts an elaborate occult ritual using the blood of various animals along with that of Jorge's closest friends to revive Jorge. The guests suffer "real" hallucinations as they are forced to confront past traumas that gradually kill each guest. For example, in one of the house's bedrooms Mauro (Rafael Ferro) encounters an apparition of an ex-girlfriend, who committed suicide, and his mother, who disapproved of her. Another one of Jorge's friends, Ivana (Flora Gró), is dragged to a room by an unseen force where she confronts holograms of her sexually abusive father and her mother, who ignored the abuse. The plan to reanimate Jorge goes awry at the film's end when Hugo reveals Nicanor's false obsession for Alicia and supposed lack of love for Jorge.[22] With the hope of completing the ritual, Hugo commits suicide, and Alicia forces Nicanor to kill her. In turn, Nicanor is the only survivor, and Jorge is revived. At the film's end, Jorge and Nicanor meet in front of Jorge and Alicia's former home and passionately hug and kiss. Their conversation reveals that Nicanor manipulated Alicia during the ritual so that he would be the sole survivor and be able to live openly with Jorge.

The entire film unfolds in what appears to be an unlikely place for a story steeped in the macabre. At the start of the film and in Alicia's dream, Alicia and Jorge walk down the road that runs in front of their home. Tall light poles and spacious houses with brick walls grown over with vegetation line each side of the road. A large steel gate serves as the entrance to Alicia and Jorge's house and property, which sits on a large parcel of land. The house ostensibly is a bourgeois domestic space that gets drastically subverted. If the couple's house and marriage serve as a refuge of sorts, it is a poignant instance of cruel optimism, "a relation of attachment to compromised conditions of possibility [. . .] the condition of maintaining an attachment to a problematic object in advance of its loss" (Berlant 21).

Haunted house tropes abound in *La memoria del muerto*. The camera renders the space disorienting with exterior and interior shots of the house framed with canted angles (Curtis 39). On numerous occasions, the camera jumps outside the house and tilts the structure as a storm rages. Moreover, as it typical of the haunted house subgenre, the house acquires a degree of agency (Curtis 49). Characters' dead family members and past lovers appear and, in one instance, clocks and decorative figurines jump about and howl with laughter. The home in *La memoria del muerto*, indeed, is destabilized and possessed. More significantly, the film plays with and departs from the haunted house trope of an architectural structure harboring a dark secret that is eventually revealed. A haunted house film's gradual explication of space is almost invariably accompanied by the revelations of a past crime or injustice. The peeling away of memories pregnant in the space often comes with the peeling back of the house's actual physical structure or discovering a hidden quarter (i.e., *The Conjuring, Insidious*). However, the house's structure in *La memoria del muerto* remains largely intact and does not contain a dated memory of some crime or injustice within its interior. Instead, the house becomes the site in which repressed traumas that reside within characters are teased out and return with fatal consequences. The house, in turn, becomes the crucial site that elicits those traumas. In addition to the aforementioned predicaments of Mauro and Ivana, Nicanor confronts his sister who died before his own birth, and Fabiana (Jimena Anganuzzi) contends with the fear of losing her newborn baby and the profound grief of losing her grandmother.

Barry Curtis captures the cardinal importance of haunting in haunted house films and the haunting's capacity to "seek to restore to attention something—such as injustice, neglect, murder or slavery—that is absent from the record" (24). While traumas, guilt, and fears are brought to light in *La memoria del muerto* and which constitute the film's narrative chain, the true haunting film is the homosexual relationship between Jorge and Nicanor. The film does little to disclose the characters' relationship or even anticipate their kiss once Jorge is reanimated. Yet, the kiss retroactively queers the domestic space. Make no mistake, *La memoria del muerto* is not a queer film and does not conform to Vinodh Venkatesh's notion of a New Maricón cinema that he locates and develops among several contemporary Latin American films, including the Argentine films *XXY* (Lucía Puenzo, 2007), *Plan B* (Marco Berger, 2009), or *El último verano de la Boyita/The Last Summer of Boyita* (Julia Solomonoff, 2009). While Diment's film is set away from an urban milieu, a typical facet of New Maricón cinema, *La memoria del muerto* refrains from playing on "aural and visual affective intensities" to cultivate positive empathy for queer characters (Venkatesh 60). Nevertheless, as a horror film, *La memoria del muerto* holds out something distinct for its insertion of a queer kiss tacked on at the end.

In his investigation of the parallels between homosexuality and monsters in US horror cinema, Harry Benshoff offers varied definitions of queer, and his conception of queer as a narrative mechanism is helpful here: "Queer can be a narrative moment, or a performance or stance which negates the oppressive binarisms of the dominant hegemony [...] both within culture at large, and within texts of horror and fantasy. [...] queerness disrupts narrative equilibrium and sets in motion a questioning of the status quo, and in many cases within fantastic literature, the nature of reality itself" (5). The "narrative equilibrium" or reality in *La memoria del muerto* is offset, first, by the film's haunted house tropes. Characters suffer traumatic blowbacks that pervade the house's interior and thicken the story with narrative threads that eventually merge around a deadly ritual. The queer kiss between Jorge and Nicanor further disrupts an equilibrium by undermining any expectations that the film will return to the "normative" heterosexual relationships that preceded the kiss. Alicia and Jorge and Mauro and Ivana are two couples whose relationships initially mark the house as a heteronormative space. Yet, the queer kiss that follows a *Hamlet*-like accumulation of corpses effectively nixes the return to such a heteronormativity.

Horror cinema frequently has dissected and undermined gender paradigms. While its cinematic codes have changed over the course of time (Benshoff 4), US horror cinema has long critiqued dominant systems of gender and sexual norms. More specific to the haunted house subgenre, *The Old Dark House* (James Whale, 1932) and *The Haunting* (Robert Wise, 1963) are two well-known films in which queer relationships unfold within the space of a haunted house. Patricia White's following remarks about the unconsummated lesbian relationship in *The Haunting* broaches how the strange happenings characteristic of a haunted space can project a queer element: "The film, resisting the visualization of desire between women, displaces that desire onto the level of the supernatural, Theo's seduction of Eleanor onto the 'haunting' " (150). In other words, the queer desire that cannot be openly aired in *The Haunting* is transformed and allegorized through the abnormal events that unfold in the possessed space of a house. Similarly, in *La memoria del muerto*, the strange happenings both conceal and allegorize the queer desire between Jorge and Nicanor that can only come to light at the film's end. Zombies lumber about outside the house; the figure meant to resemble Nicanor's dead sister pries open

Nicanor's mouth to extract his teeth and insert them into a vertical slit in her face; Mauro locks tongues with his own mother. However, *La memoria del muerto* is not a pure repetition of the sexual repression in *The Haunting*. The strange happenings in Diment's are necessary to eventually air the occluded homosexual relationship between Jorge and Nicanor.

In *Gender and Sexuality in Latin American Horror Cinema*, Gustavo Subero privileges horror cinema produced in Latin America as a site for witnessing the reworking of gender and sexuality. In moving away from an analysis of spectatorial identification or rejection with a monster, Subero states his preference to consider "[. . .] the way in which horror cinema in Latin America provides new avenues to map out the changes in the politics of gender and sexuality as experienced in popular culture" (viii–ix). In this vein, the haunted house of *La memoria del muerto* offers an instance in which the filmic spaces in an Argentine film are queered and shift an understanding of how masculinity is portrayed in Argentine cinema.

Aaron Betsky offers varied definitions and examples of what constitutes a queer space. A queer space "[. . .] is a useless, amoral, and sensual space that lives only in and for experience. It is a space of spectacle, consumption, dance, and obscenity. It is a misuse or deformation of a place, an appropriation of the buildings and codes of the city for perverse purposes. It is a space in between the body and technology, a space of pure artifice" (Betsky 5). Moreover, "[b]ecause [a queer space] separates itself off from reproduction, it does not have a part in the establishment of the most basic territory of all, that which perpetuates the self through offspring" (Betsky 19). Regarding the latter point, Alicia and Jorge's home constitutes a queer space, first, by virtue of not having any children given the couple's age. The home is an unproductive and barren space. Otherwise, the house in *La memoria del muerto* only partially adheres to Betsky's notion of a queer space. The film's spectacles, albeit spectacles characterized by horror violence, indeed deform the domestic space of a home. Shortly after leaving the confines of the home to speak to an apparition of her dead daughter who sits on a swing, veins emerge under Ivana's skin and her body explodes before her fellow guests who stand dumbfounded within the home. Mauro panics after using a pair of scissors to separate his tongue from that of his mother's. Yet, while the space of the home is warped by spectacles of violence, it remains remarkably useful and departs from Betsky's notion of a queer space. As broached above, the home is wedded to a singular goal: to revive Jorge.

While the film risks repeating the trope of violence committed by homosexual characters, the queer element in *La memoria del muerto* is arguably contestatory and subversive. Lisa Duggan has commented on the New Homonormativity in the United States, in which the legalization of gay marriage can serve as "a strategy of privatizing gay politics and culture for the new neoliberal order" (188). Traditions of collective and public queer politics in the United States, in turn, are replaced and constricted to private life. Argentina legalized gay marriage in 2010, and a discourse of "homonormatividad" occasionally appears in discussions about discrimination against transgender individuals in Argentina (Trerotola) with gay marriage enabling that discrimination. In turn, a sexual orientation once deemed subversive—homosexuality—becomes hegemonic vis-à-vis other queer sexualities.

In *La memoria del muerto*, queer defies all normativity, first, by subverting dominant models of Argentine masculinity. Eduardo Archetti's studies of soccer, polo, and tango—"Argentinian male masks and mirrors" (19)—elevates that triad as sites in which national masculinities can be studied and scrutinized. However, *La memoria del muerto* and its take on homosexual desire suggests that horror cinema can function to refashion a national masculinity or even a complicate an association between a national queer identity and a particular space, that is, beyond typical queer urban spaces. Regarding the latter, while acknowledging that a handful of works of literature dealing with queer topics have been set outside Buenos Aires, David William Foster observes, "[T]he totality of Argentine cultural production dealing with lesbian and gay issues is centered in Buenos Aires" (12). Akin to *Tan de repente*/*Suddenly* (Diego Lerer, 2002), Lucrecia Martel's feature-length films, and the aforementioned films belonging to New Maricón cinema, *La memoria del muerto* expands the filmic spaces in Argentine cinema that are queered.

Diment's film, however, should not be received as a glib celebration of a queer male identity in Argentina. Jorge and Nicanor's relationship appears largely closeted and can only be revealed once Jorge's closest friends and wife are dead with many of them killed in brutal ways. In lieu of the Jorge and Nicanor coming out of the closet, the exterior of the closet is utterly annihilated. Betsky refers to the palace in the Marquis de Sade's *120 Days of Sodom* as a "queer space [that] became negative" (55). "What was frightening about this space is how desire turned into violence. [...] Queer space here was desperate, a place that killed all those that entered it" (Betsky 54). The queer space of *La memoria del muerto* hardly begins to approach the extremes of the palace in *120 Days of Sodom*. Though the characters do not perpetuate the stereotype of a murderous queer character, Jorge and Nicanor are patently complicit in the realization of an intricate plan to murder friends, harbor their blood, and enable a queer relationship to proceed beyond the eyes of friends.

3 CINEMATIC BODY SNATCHING

ENGLISH-LANGUAGE ARGENTINE HORROR CINEMA AND SYSTEMS OF PARANOIA

In their article "Uruguay Disappears," David Martin-Jones and María Soledad Montañez coin the concept of auto-erasure to describe how a corpus of Uruguayan films "since the mid-2000s have reframed to the background, obscured, or erased recognizable features of the nation in order to appeal to international markets" (26), such as film festival circuits. Auto-erasure underscores the realities of film production and "local-level negotiations of global markets" that change among different Latin American countries (45).

English-language Argentine horror films perform auto-erasure in ways similar to those described by Martin-Jones and Soledad Montañez, especially when the authors refer to different ways in which Uruguay almost fully disappears from the diegesis either as a stand-in for a story's location or an anonymous backdrop as in *Blindness* (Fernando Meirelles, 2008).[1] As I will describe below, the Argentine English-language horror films make Argentina largely invisible with camera placement and mise-en-scène and nearly inaudible through language. Despite similarities with *Blindness* and other films shot in Uruguay,[2] the Argentine English-language horror films suggest ways in which the practice of auto-erasure can differ not only across Latin American countries but within different transnational genre films, such as low-budget horror, that must negotiate conditions specific to local production.[3] While INCAA did not support a horror production between 1988 and 2008, Argentine English-language horror films are symptomatic of INCAA's protracted disinterest and lay bare a tactic by filmmakers to work beyond the auspices of the state to register some presence in a larger market of horror—the United States—where demand for horror appears insatiable (Lobato and Ryan 9).

To date, there are twelve Argentine English-language horror films, some of which have DVD distribution in various countries and/or can be streamed through different legal and "gray" Internet sites. Those films are: *Left for Dead* (Albert Pyun, 2007), *Bone Breaker* (Sergio Esquenazi, 2005), *The Last Gateway, Death Knows Your Name, Chronicle of the Raven, Dead Line, Dying God* (Fabrice Lambot, 2008), *Ultra-Toxic* (Jimmy Crispin, 2005), *Breaking Nikki, They Want My Eyes* (Sergio Esquenazi, 2009), *Mondo Psycho* (Mad Crampi, 2006), and *Run, Bunny, Run!* (Mad Crampi, 2003).[4] What bounds the films together, first, is the Argentine nationality of the directors and production team, and, second, the films' deliberate omission of Argentine filming locations. Though not precluding other national markets, the horror films orient themselves to the US market, as if they were films made in the United States. In turn, each film's respective portrayal of the United States must attain a loose standard of realism, which includes language. Hiding the setting's actual location is not a question of making some part of Argentina appear to be New York, Miami, or some other major US city, but rather to make an Argentine space appear to be Anytown, USA, or, better, Anycity, since the films generally are set in urban locales with the exception of *Left for Dead* and *The Last Gateway*. The Argentine English-language films attain a certain level of modernity and traffic in urban technologies—communication towers, stoplights, high-rise apartments, sidewalks, subway trains—that could appear in any major global city.[5] The films lack an iconography that anchors them to a particular US metropolis (e.g., The Sears Tower = Chicago, Golden Gate Bridge = San Francisco), and we never see superimposed captions or diegetic street signs that indicate an on-screen city that actually exists. In *Left for Dead* and *The Last Gateway*, a filmic United States hinges not on urban codes rather than on generic tenets that are traditionally salient in US cinema: the Western in *Left for Dead* and what can be loosely referred to as "hick flicks" in *The Last Gateway*.[6] In all of the English-language Argentine horror films, actors speak in English, sometimes with an accent or with their voices dubbed over in English. Some films, such as *The Bone Breaker* and *Dead Line*, also use US actors residing in Argentina (Rodríguez 144). No regional US accent prevails in any of the films' dialogues that would tether the diegesis to a single US geography or region (i.e., a Boston accent or a southeast US accent) (Kozloff 35). Camera placement and movement, lenses, sound, global product placement, set design, and English-language dialogue collaborate to forge anonymous US spaces on-screen. Those same elements simultaneously efface Argentina. However, as I will discuss below, Argentina is not hermetically sealed off; rather, its presence seeps through in various ways, such as the aforementioned accented-English or a fleeting image of Buenos Aires.

HERE, HAVE SOME PARANOIA

In an interview in 2009, Daniel de la Vega referred to his English-language films as "caballos de Troya" ("Trojan horses"). Keenly aware of the cinematic dominance of US cinema in Argentina, De la Vega considers his films as exercises in "sending something back in a losing battle." Given the historical and continuing dominance of Hollywood cinema in Argentina and the number of Hollywood productions made in the country,[7] to conceive of *Death Knows Your Name* and other English-language Argentine horror films as "caballos de Troya" is apt. The films largely obscure their Argentine origins and instead project a United States, in order to enter into the US low-budget DVD market. English-language dialogue is crucial to a film's distribution in the United States. Alebrije Home Entertainment is the US distributor of *The Last Gateway*. When asked about the reasons for distributing the film, Al Perez, who was vice president of Sales and Acquisitions for the company, responded, "A horror film in English can do better in the US [than one in Spanish]."

To enter the US market, the Argentine English-language horror films essentially send back to the US that which Hollywood has been exporting to Argentina and elsewhere for decades: English, English-language films, urban and rural filmic spaces, as well as televisual and filmic narratives besieged with paranoia that straddle the multiple genres of the thriller, and, most germane for my analysis, horror. If claiming that Hollywood exports paranoia appears to be a stretch, Ray Pratt's *Projecting Paranoia* charts paranoia's centrality in Hollywood films over decades and across different genres. Pratt's most provocative claim, however, seems unintentional. In the opening chapter titled "Our Greatest Export Is Paranoia," Pratt refrains from attributing the quote to a specific person, fleshing out the title's significance, or alluding to the sheer number of films the US exports around the globe. Yet, the title's implication for what US cinema has given and continues to give to Argentine and other audiences is incredibly suggestive for understanding what the Argentine English-language horror films as "caballos de Troya" do: in lieu of a one-way flow in which the United States sends paranoid film narratives to Argentina, the Argentine English-language films create a circulating loop of paranoid cinematic expressions between the two countries (and beyond) by sending back paranoid narratives that ostensibly appear to be US horror films. If Argentine horror cinema folds itself into a transnational flow of horror cinema, then it also fuses with an even larger transnational deluge of paranoid narratives that revolve around characters confronting localized and global threats. While not ignoring the gross asymmetry that flows between US and Argentine cultural production, for a fleeting instance Argentine English-language horror films illustrate the possibility of how a transnational cinema can "overcome all the uneven relations of power of other scales such as the national, regional, continental, or international scales" (Newman 10).

Along with the English-language dialogue and anonymous settings, paranoia is crucial for the Argentine English-language films to "pass" as US films. In *Monsters and Mad Scientists*, Andrew Tudor provides a cultural history of horror films distributed in Britain between 1931 and 1984, most of which are US films. Tudor posits "the [horror] genre's major developmental pattern: the passage from secure to paranoid horror" (213). While not precluding a film's mixture of the two categories, Tudor dates the emergence of paranoid horror to the 1970s, which contains several common narrative elements: (1) the ineffectiveness of human intervention and experts (e.g., government, scientists, military forces) to subdue a threat; (2) the proximity of a threat to characters such as a neighbor or a person within one's family; (3) the "diffuse" nature of a threat; and the play of oppositions between "conscious/unconscious, normal/abnormal sexuality; social order/disorder; health/disease"; (4) and the lack of narrative closure (211–24).[8] Tudor's category of paranoid horror also rests on a threat's spatialization and invasiveness which ramps up the paranoid dimensions inherent in the horror genre. For Tudor, "[...] the horror movie itself is a paranoid form: it is founded on the supposition that we are constantly under threat from many directions" (66). What proves exceptional about paranoid horror from the 1980s that extends to the transformations initiated in the seventies are "[t]he typical threats of [the 1970s] invade our houses, our communities, our institutions and our bodies" with the defeat over the threat often failing (77).[9] The Argentine English-language horror films exhibit their awareness of transnational horror codes by conforming to Tudor's generalizations about paranoid horror cinema.

The Argentine English-language horror films squarely fit into the category of Straight-to-Video (STV) productions; none of the films was released in a cinema in any country. However, the films' STV credentials transcend that of mere exhibition. Regarding STV productions, Lobato observes, "The STV labour force extends far beyond North America: films are commonly shot in the Philippines, Thailand, Romania, Mexico, and Canada. STV movies are usually more likely to be made in these interstices of the global film economy, or to feature one locations masquerading (often unsuccessfully) as another or to feature an incoherent polyphony of accents and costumes" (Lobato 24). While reiterating Latin America's and Argentina's position in global film production where "[film-making] is cheap!,"[10] the masquerade of a subgroup of Argentine horror films is composed of English, anonymous US cities and towns, and paranoia. These elements abet the Argentine horror films to achieve what I deem to be an unprecedented instance of cinematic body snatching happening *from* Argentina, and, perhaps, *from* Latin America. The extraterrestrials in Don Siegel's *Invasion of the Body Snatchers* (1956) replicate actual people in the town of Santa Mira with one exception: they lack emotion. In a similar vein, the Argentine films simulate the United States in a form that US and other national audiences will recognize as the United States. The Argentine horror films appear to succeed in their venture. In the YouTube comments sections for *Death Knows Your Name* and trailers for it and *The Last Gateway*, numerous viewers writing in English praise the films or disparage the acting, but no comments note that the film was made in Argentina by an Argentine director with an Argentine cast. What makes the Argentine English-language horror films body snatchers are their supposed flaws (e.g., accented dialogue, transitory images of Argentina) that potentially alert a viewer that something is amiss or off and, in turn, possibly lead to the discovery that the United States has been studied, constructed, and projected *from* Argentina and *from* Latin America, a feat that I deem unparalleled.[11]

Here, I will examine three Argentine English-language horror films—*Death Knows Your Name*, *Dead Line*, and *The Last Gateway*—as instances of cinematic body snatching that unfold within different horror subgenres conceived according to the primary space in which the movie takes place: medical/hospital horror (*Death Knows Your Name*), apartment horror (*Dead Line*), and rural horror (*The Last Gateway*). My examination of the films will center on the cinematic constructions of a United States that project it through narrative systems and aesthetics steeped in paranoia. My analysis of paranoia as a mechanism that organizes a narrative begins with Freud's suggestive analogy between a subject's narcissism and "the characteristic tendency of paranoics [sic] to construct speculative systems" (*Three Case* 26). Or, to take cinematic paranoia a step further, as Eve Sedgwick has written, "paranoid knowing [. . .] is inescapably narrative" in which a willing listener holds out the promise for a paranoid subject that his or her story will finally be "truly known" (138). In turn, Argentine English-language horror films perform a double paranoiac ruse: while communicating a narrative of paranoia for US audiences, the films also reveal to the willing listener that Argentine horror cinema indeed exists at a time when INCAA and other facets of Argentine film culture preferred to do otherwise.

DEATH KNOWS YOUR NAME: SYSTEMS WITHIN SYSTEMS

In *Death Knows Your Name*, a young psychiatrist, Bruce Taylor (Ricardo Aragón) works at a mental hospital. The hospital is connected to an older and abandoned mental institution, a structure with which Dr. Taylor is acutely obsessed. Dr. Taylor locates a skull beneath the older hospital and, following its reconstruction, the face is identical to that of Dr. Taylor.[12] With the help of a patient and a colleague, Dr. Taylor learns that one hundred years ago, he was William Vanhess and was buried alive by his twin brother, Gregor Vanhess (also played by Ricardo Aragón), where the abandoned hospital now stands. Gregor remains living despite being 130 years old due to a Faustian-like pact with a diabolical mirror, and he resides in a local nursing home. In a convoluted and carefully executed scheme, Gregor harnesses the space of the hospital and the energy of its inhabitants to be reborn in the form of Bruce Taylor/William Vanhess, through the womb of Dr. Taylor's wife, Melissa (Veronica Mari). Gregor returns with the aim to rebury Bruce Taylor/William Vanhess alive. By the film's end, Gregor assumes the identity of Bruce Taylor and exits the grounds of the hospital.

If a nondescript villa/mansion provides the backdrop for many STV films that seek to stand-in for another location (Lobato 24), *Death Knows Your Name* strikes a more daring pose in its range of spaces that construct a diegetic United States. An anonymous Buenos Aires provides the filming locations for *Death Knows Your Name*, and an apartment, nursing home, university lecture hall, hospital, and streets and thoroughfares are strung together to fashion a coherent on-screen urbanism. All of the film's interiors and exteriors lack any signage in Spanish, and Buenos Aires is recognizable only to familiar eyes in extreme long shots. All of the actors and actresses speak English stitching together a panoply of accents.

The hospital, or more specifically, the mental institution, is crucial for projecting paranoia and intimating various systems of logic at play and which consume each other in *Death Knows Your Name*. The institution's corridors, exteriors, and rooftop constitute spaces with multiple modes of organization, including architecture, medicine, and, of course, bodies. The film wastes no time foregrounding the hospital's order. Toward the start of the film, the camera jumps among various levels in the hospital and glacially tracks forward and rotates.[13] One sees a winding staircase from above, a narrow corridor beset with white tiles and shadows, a room divided with shelves of medical files, and the cellar beneath the hospital where Bruce Taylor discovers his own skull. Other sequences from the film's first half cement the central place of order through an iconography of medicine. Soon after he finds the skull beneath the hospital early, Dr. Taylor dutifully subjects it to microscopes. Hospital personnel in surgical scrubs and white coats mill about and X-rays blanket the background of some shots.

Akin to the powers of observation and the physical sciences constituting a "model of rationality" (Foucault 125), the hospital and its multiple systems of medicine, archives, architecture, and human biology make for a vast interlocking system. Gregor inserts himself into such a system. He cuts the figure of a sort of Dr. Mabuse with omniscient and omnipotent abilities, and his plan to rebury Bruce Taylor/William Vanhess unfolds through his manipulation of events and human bodies within the mental hospital. Gregor holds the reins to a vast network through which he pursues his brother and precipitates in him an unmitigated blitz of paranoia.

Gregor is an invisible and amorphous force at the film's start and asserts his presence, at first, as a diffuse being. Shortly after Bruce finds his own skull, patients and hospital workers begin to suffer what seems a vigorous form of yellow fever, the first instance in which Buenos Aires figures obliquely into the narrative.[14] Characters in *Death Knows Your Name* begin to appear jaundiced, and corpses soon pile up while still maintaining its status as a "body count film" (Sconce, "Spectacles" 105). The physical absence of a monster figure for the first half of *Death Knows Your Name* undergirds a shared paranoia whose contagiousness at first appears owing to an invisible disease. The film lacks what Noël Carroll calls "a geography of horror [that] situates the origin of a monster" (34): a sewer, a graveyard, the sea, outer space. In *Death Knows Your Name*, Gregor's origin is unexplained and, even worse (or better?), Gregor is conspicuously missing for more than half the movie. There is no material villain for Dr. Taylor or the audience to locate and anchor a fear. Paranoia here is bolstered by an ambience fraught with anxiety, "an objectless affect" in lieu of an object-directed emotion (Hills 26).[15]

In *Cinematic Prophylaxis*, Kirsten Ostherr unpacks the relationship between cinema's indexicality and disease and its various capacities to make visible the spread of a contagion. Ostherr alludes to the growing number of Hollywood productions that narrativize the spread of disease and contribute to a "heightened perception of the omnipresence of contagion" (177). And so it is with Gregor. He is a ubiquitous disease, and the visible manifestations of yellow fever on people's bodies give Gregor an amorphous spatialization. We see no sign of Gregor, but only the evidence of his work postinfection, and the yellow fever gives the character a horrifying shape precisely because he lacks a shape that blankets the diegesis. Such a dynamic recalls Foucault's observation that "... the solid, visible body is only one way [...] in which one spatializes disease" (3). Invoking another Foucaultian trope, if medicine is to operate as a panopticon to surveil disease, Gregor goes undetected. Only jaundiced bodies can register Gregor's presence, and there is no refuge in the institutional space of the hospital that is supposed to be just that.

Gregor stokes the embers of paranoia most forcefully in his brother, Bruce Taylor. Dr. Taylor cannot know how his brother will manifest himself; Gregor is an all-pervasive system. If Gregor communicates his presence by infecting physical bodies with yellow fever, then he privileges the bodies of the insane to carry out the most extreme and elaborate parts of his plan for rebirth. Susan Sontag describes insanity as "... the repellent, harrowing disease that is made the index of a superior sensitivity, the vehicle of 'spiritual' feelings and 'critical' discontent" (*Illness* 35). The bodies of the insane in *Death Knows Your Name* are privileged insofar as they alone are attuned to Gregor's machinations. The patients in *Death Knows Your Name* hear the voices of restless spirits buried beneath the institution and, in multiple shots, patients dawdle on the hospital lawn seemingly aloof, but move their heads acknowledging screams audible only to them. The mental hospital's patients alone possess an ability to perceive the impending force of Gregor and, at the film's end, the burying alive of Bruce Taylor.

Gregor uses patients' bodies as conduits, vehicles, and mouthpieces to realize his plan. Perhaps allegorizing Hollywood's commandeering of smaller national markets for its own gains, Gregor appropriates smaller systems for his own ends. Gregor harnesses Richard Ian Patterson (Kevin Schiele), who is Dr. Bruce Taylor's patient and has been at the hospital for several years. Gregor employs Richard as a go-between to communicate with Dr. Taylor rendering Richard a paranoid subject who mediates between a reality since "only he can see the way our world is shaped by their influence" (Paradis 17).[16]

A scene on the hospital's roof in which Dr. Taylor confronts Richard lays bare the nature of Richard's possession by Gregor and illustrates a specific instance of how Buenos Aires is concealed while the United States is projected. Hospital personnel inform Dr. Taylor that Richard is on the hospital's roof cutting himself. With Bruce's arrival on the roof, the camera slowly tracks to the right with close-ups

CINEMATIC BODY SNATCHING   69

of the mortified faces of a nurse and three orderlies. The camera eventually frames Dr. Taylor and Richard in an establishing shot (see fig. 3.1). The shot is the sole instance in the film in which Buenos Aires is in focus and is remotely recognizable to those viewers familiar with the city. A large telecommunications tower cuts the image in half separating the two characters. The characters' positions in relation to the tower give symmetry to the shot: on one side, Richard is possessed and fully comprehends Gregor's plans, while, on the other side, Dr. Taylor remains ignorant of the situation at hand. If the tower distinguishes the two characters' conditions, it also fuses them together. All three vertical figures in the image—tower, Richard, and Dr. Taylor—are vehicles, vessels, and instruments for receiving and communicating some kind of message or plan. Just as the tower receives and transmits signals, Richard does the same for Gregor. Dr. Taylor, for his part, is only a receiver of messages at this point in the film.

The shot of Buenos Aires, coupled with the English-language dialogue, exemplifies the construction of an on-screen United States, which obscures Argentina. Whereas Jameson underscored the importance of writing technologies in

FIGURE 3.1 Still from *Death Knows Your Name*. Dr. Bruce Taylor confronts Richard as an anonymous Buenos Aires looms in the background. Directed by Daniel de la Vega. 2007, Maverick Entertainment Group.

All the President's Men that a "hermeneutics of detection [...] transforms into traces and signs" (*Geopolitical* 76), *Death Knows Your Name* possesses its own technology that eschews detection. The telecommunications tower looming over buildings and a single smoke stack is an unequivocal symbol of an undisclosed global metropolitan city as a mediatized node. The tower composes a no-place, and Buenos Aires's disguise is ensured by the scene's physical elevation. One does not see the city's sidewalks where one could encounter advertising in Spanish or some other cultural element that might give away the film's location. Instead, we see a copse of vertical facades and telecommunication towers with the larger tower slicing and bisecting the image.[17]

The interaction between Richard and Dr. Taylor on the hospital roof merits attention for underscoring Gregor's capacity to subsume systems—here, a body—and marks a point in the film in which Bruce Taylor's paranoia becomes full-blown. Richard declares himself possessed, and he tells Dr. Taylor, "Doctor, what you just found [the skull], won't leave either of us alone. It's horrible. It's all your fault, and I got to get it out of my body." His admission of knowing about Dr. Taylor's discovery of the skull reveals Gregor's omniscience through Richard; Dr. Taylor discovered the skull alone and only has revealed his discovery to his father and a handful of colleagues. Gregor speaks through Richard. The patient's voice changes slightly, and he addresses Dr. Taylor by his full name rather than by "Dr. Taylor," as Richard did in previous scenes: "You can't help anyone Bruce Taylor. You are making the same mistakes as before. It's inevitable." We then see a close-up of Richard cutting himself, after which the camera moves to his face and Richard says, "It's making nests in my head. I can feel it. It's making me say and do things I don't want to do." Richard then slowly lifts the sharp end of the mirror shard and trembles as if fighting his own arm. Richard then bites the shard. Orderlies wrestle the patient to the ground, pull the bits of mirror from his mouth, and take him away.

Richard alludes to "it" repeatedly and how "it" operates on him. "It" invades his brain and makes him speak and acts in ways against his will, an element epitomized by Richard's self-mutilation. The entrance of "its" voice (presumably Gregor's) into the scene, the lack of "it" having its own physical shape, and the power of "it" gives the voice the status of what Michel Chion calls an *acousmêtre*. In *The Voice of Cinema*, Chion defines the *acousmêtre* as "a voice, and especially when this voice has not yet been visualized—that is, when we cannot yet connect it to a face—we get a special being, a kind of talking and acting shadow" (21).

One can think of any number of films, especially horror films, that contain *acousmêtres* and whose narrative concerns the revelation of the *acousmêtre*'s body: *Scream* (Wes Craven, 1996), *Black Christmas* (Bob Clark, 1974), and *Halloween* (John Carpenter, 1978). Chion ascribes four powers to the *acousmêtre*: "ubiquity, panopticism, omniscience, and omnipotence" (24). Gregor possesses these very powers that enable him to inspire in Dr. Taylor a paranoia over threats coming from multiple directions. Gregor's spatialization in the form of yellow fever and his abilities to spread the disease and to know of Dr. Taylor's discovery of the skull renders Gregor a consummate *acousmêtre*.

After being restrained, Gregor through Richard tells Dr. Taylor, "You are making the same mistakes," as if Dr. Taylor is unwittingly hurling himself to an end he has already suffered. Gregor's creation of a repeating system—within the genre of horror that is prone to repetition—infuses Bruce Taylor's paranoia with the uncanny. Toward the beginning of his essay, "The 'Uncanny,'" Freud lays out two possible methodologies to investigate the uncanny only to spell out a shared conclusion and a concise definition: "the uncanny is that class of the frightening which leads back to what is known of old and long familiar" (*Das Unheimliche* 220). While repetition is implicit in Freud's definition, he explores repetition as a source of the uncanny and, in one part, underscores how helplessness can accompany the uncanny. Freud describes his own experience of being lost in a skein of streets in Italy. His attempts at finding his way back to a particular site invoke the uncanny and helplessness when he returns to the same place three times (*Das Unheimliche* 237). Dr. Taylor/William's fate is essentially an inevitable and horrified return to the familiar: the rediscovery of his death at the hands of his brother. Such a return is filled with the collateral damage of dead colleagues and his spouse, Melissa. Dr. Taylor/William is without recourse as he tries to understand the origin of the skull and the plans of Gregor.[18] By the film's end, like Freud's return to the same place from which he tries to escape, Dr. Taylor/William returns to the exact spot where his brother buried him alive a century ago, the same spot where Dr. Taylor discovered the skull at the beginning of the film.[19] Eager to connect the dots, Dr. Taylor's paranoia nevertheless fails him. Paranoia can be conceived as a subjectivity of emboldened agency seeking to synthesize and master disparate phenomena and bits of information. A paranoiac may stand resistant or even victorious in the face of a perceived threat: "[...] God strikes me above all [...] as being ridiculous and childish," declares Dr. Schreber after God's rays have lost their power (*Three Case* 103). Albeit paranoid, Dr. Taylor achieves the opposite:

"a paranoid subject disempowered by virtue of all-encompassing plots and systems that surround [him]" (O'Donnell 190).

DEAD LINE: MY OWN PRIVATE PARANOIA

Dead Line's aesthetics of paranoia emerge, first, from the clash of two conflicting systems of perception and, second, in a passing engagement with Freud's reading of the memoirs of Dr. Daniel Schreber, paranoia's patient zero, even broaching the red herring of paranoia as an outburst of homosexual panic (Freud, *Three Case* 118–23).[20] One system is shot through with paranoid delusions and is focalized with and through the film's protagonist, Martin (Andrés Bagg). Martin suffers from an acute fear over being pursued from multiple directions by threats residing at different proximities. His paranoia is most pronounced within the claustrophobic space of his apartment whose narrow dimensions are exacerbated by tight framing, camera movement, and sound. The apartment's interior, in turn, becomes a space that projects Martin's paranoia, which is fraught with aural and visual hallucinations. Martin's system of delusions is at loggerheads with a second system, a "reality" shared among characters, including Martin at times. The boundary between the two systems of perception at first appears a question of playing interior and exterior spaces against each other. If Martin's apartment operates as a kind of pressurized interior in which his decline hastens, then the images of sidewalks, streets, and urban skylines temporarily relieve a spatial tension. Yet, *Dead Line* reiterates paranoia's contagious dimension, and Martin's system of delusions spills out from the apartment and infects exterior spaces as the character descends into a murderous insanity.

Dead Line is set entirely in an unnamed city. Martin is a twenty-something professional who loses his job at an advertising agency.[21] His wife Ann (Alejandra Lapola), a former prostitute that we learn Martin used to visit, has left him for her personal trainer, Alex Vinelli (Martin Capuccio). Despite help from two friends and former colleagues, Laura (Virginia Lustig) and Aaron (Oliver Kolker), Martin has fallen into a depression that morphs into murderous paranoia. He suffers from the delusions of persecution and hallucinations that originate from his apartment telephone. Martin believes he is able to eavesdrop on the conversations of a male neighbor who hires prostitutes only to murder them. Martin tries to intervene to find out the murderer's identity until he believes the murderer has begun to pursue him. By the film's end, we learn the extent of Martin's delusions. Martin himself is the murderer. He killed his wife and her lover and stores their heads in his apartment's refrigerator. Martin's eavesdropping and seeking out the prostitutes' murderer was simply not possible; his telephone service had been cut off and no murders were reported. The phone conversations are entirely imagined by Martin. Soon after Laura asks Martin to seek professional help, he fatally stabs her and a neighbor. In the film's final sequence, Martin, who has become a nearly unrecognizable bum rummaging through trash cans at a metro stop, presumably stabs Aaron upon encountering him on a train.[22]

The on-screen urban space in *Dead Line* approximates the United States in various ways, and surpasses that of *Death Knows Your Name* with more specific allusions to US culture. The characters' English-language dialogue helps transform the filmic space into a United States seemingly free of regional specificities though particular enough to "pass" as a diegetic United States. Albeit accented at times, the actors speak a US form of English complete with US slang. The film partakes in a product placement that will be recognizable to US viewers and viewers elsewhere. The mise-en-scène features global brands such as Jim Beam, Asics, and Adidas, infusing the diegesis with "[a] paradox of no-place: a foreigner lost in a country he does not know (a 'passing stranger') can feel at home there only in the anonymity of motorways, service stations, big stores or hotel chains. [...] among the supermarket shelves he falls with relief on sanitary, household or food products validated by multinational brand names" (Augé 106). If the mélange of accents makes a US spectator uneasy and suggests a film as impostor, product placement sets him or her at ease.

Dead Line also traffics in clichés of US culture. Martin reads a newspaper titled the *Daily Tribune*. Toward the beginning of the film, he and his friends, Laura and Aaron, meet in Roxie, one of Buenos Aires's US-style diners.[23] A prostitute tells the telephone *acousmêtre* to meet her at "1422 Main St." and to park on "Freedom," a buzzword indicating that the frenzied bouts of patriotism in the United States in the years following the 9/11 attacks reverberated to other end of the hemisphere. Elsewhere, Martin is stopped by a police officer for speeding as he imagines that he must bury a prostitute's corpse that the murderer left in his apartment. Martin convinces the police officer he was speeding to meet his wife, who is in labor, at "Bellevue Hospital," the name of the mental institute in Ken Kesey's *One Flew Over the Cuckoo's Nest*. Film locations, English-language dialogue, product placement, and allusions to the United States collude to present a US urban space sufficiently legible to be of the United States but illegible enough to be nowhere (Lynch 2–3).

If the film's selective fragmentation of Buenos Aires enables the construction of a United States, traces of the Argentine capital still seep through, an instance in which a STV film telegraphs its conditions of production; here, its actual film location (Lobato 24). *El subte*, the city's subway system, figures prominently at times as a backdrop for Martin's wandering through the city and, in the closing scene, one sees a sign for the Florida stop. Martin drives through the on-screen city, and one can occasionally see shop signs in Spanish. In one shot, Palacio Barolo on Avenida de Mayo fills the entire frame before cutting to a shot of Martin's friends knocking at his door; the order of the two shots suggests Martin's apartment is in Palacio Barolo. One also occasionally sees graffiti written in Spanish and numerous images of apartment buildings characteristic of Buenos Aires or shots from rooftops looming in the background.

Dead Line can be categorized under a subgenre of horror cinema and psychological thriller often referred to as apartment horror. Roman Polanski's apartment trilogy—*Repulsion* (1965), *Rosemary's Baby* (1968), and *The Tenant* (1976)—is largely responsible for establishing the subgenre and rendering the apartment as an architectural space ideal for helping to forge an aesthetics of fear and anxiety.[24] If Polanski's *Repulsion* and *Rosemary's Baby* achieve a specificity by analogizing a paranoia over architectural penetration with sexual penetration (Shonfield 55), then *Dead Line* upholds other general tenets of apartment horror. In short, the apartment projects a mental demise, and perhaps most famously evident in the accumulation of garbage and Catherine Deneuve's character's hallucinations of hands springing from the walls in *Repulsion*. The apartment in *Dead Line* embodies its own character's unraveling; garbage piles up in Martin's apartment mirroring his declining condition. As with other Argentine films that feature apartments (*Apartment Zero* [Martin Donovan, 1988], *Fase 7*/*Phase 7* [Nicolás Goldbart], *El hombre de al lado*/*The Man Next Door* [Mariano Cohn and Gastón Duprat, 2009]), *Dead Line* understands apartment horror and mimics it for a US market.

The apartment as a horror film space presents a variation on the motif of the precarious refuge. The security of home in horror constantly is undermined by a threat entering one's domicile, or already existing within if the murderer is a family member (e.g., *The Stepfather*, Joseph Ruben, 1987). The apartment in *Dead Line* operates similarly in that it offers little protection from an imminent threat with the exception of a crucial difference: the location of the threat itself. As is the case of *Dead Line* and the other select aforementioned apartment horror films, the threat is not that of an intruder entering the space, but rather the paranoia over the perceived threat emanates from *within* the architectural space. In other words, the problem is not Michael Myers or Jason Vorhees, or some other boogeyman getting in. The fear is already inside in the apartment, which offers Martin a very finite space to flee or to hide from himself. Akin to the siblings in Julio Cortázar's "Casa tomada," Martin can only retreat to smaller sections of his apartment.

Martin's apartment is a space charged with tension and temporal instability. The on-screen apartment has no windows, thus creating a kind of pressure cooker. The interior appears hermetically sealed, keeping Buenos Aires under wraps, but also depriving the viewer of any escape valve for the on-screen anxiety. Close shots of the apartment and camera movement add to the tension and the notion that Martin is pursued. Images of apartment generally lack a deep focus with the exception of showing a corridor that leads to the front door.[25] The camera is confined to single rooms and never projects a room in its entirety from above or from a single corner. Not unlike the camera that tracks on Mendizábal (Federico Luppi) in Adolfo Aristarain's *Últimos días de la victima* / "The Victim's Last Days" (1982)—the paranoid Argentine film par excellence—*Dead Line* features more than a few sequences that hew to Martin as he paces through his apartment. The camera projects Martin's claustrophobia as if the camera were a pursuer following and hovering with eyes piercing the character's neck.

Various critics of contemporary paranoia and conspiracy theories have credited, or better said, blamed technology for the uptick in individual and collective paranoia. If television expanded a geographic range of threats that could strike at any moment (Freeman and Freeman 25), then the Internet enabled a DIY-ification and "democratization of epistemology" in which individuals and groups fashion a paranoid narrative to make sense of a world that is increasingly difficult to grasp (Jane and Fleming 8, 86). In *Dead Line*, the telephone is a prosthesis that renders ubiquitous an illusory threat. Indeed, as reflected by the film's title, the telephone is a central actant in the narrative and establishes its role in one of the film's opening scenes. Martin sits in a bath and relaxes. A cordless telephone sits next to the bath, and through the static Martin hears the conversation between a man and a woman. Martin learns that the woman is a prostitute, and the man is inquiring about her availability and birthday, a detail that will prove crucial later in revealing the man's identity as Martin.

Dead Line's engagement with Freud's account of Schreber's paranoia begins with Martin's split being, a doubling of sorts expressed via the telephone, not unlike Michael Cane's character, Dr. Robert Elliot, in DePalma's *Dressed to Kill* (1980). Schreber, too, is split by means of an elaborate system of persecutory delusions in which he will be transformed into a woman and, upon being sodomized by God, implanted female nerves will give birth to a "new race of men" (Freud, *Three Cases* 93). Paranoia can acquire a gender dynamic and, more specifically, a feminization when an individual senses he or she is being watched or being rendered into a spectacle to be looked at, to recall Mulvey's characterization in "Visual Pleasure and Narrative Cinema." Schreber feels feminized by God not only on account of the illusion that God wants to penetrate him, but also by God's omniscient scrutiny of Schreber (Melley 115). A telephonic *acousmêtre* plays the role of Schreber's God to Martin. Initially, neither Martin nor we have any clue about the material person attached to the voice. The voice, which is distinct from that of Martin's, quickly acquires omnipotence and near omniscience once it speaks to Martin, or even when Martin hears the voice.[26] The camera's movements when Martin eavesdrops or speaks on the phone often suggest he is being watched. In the aforementioned opening scene, shortly after Martin begins to listen to a conversation between the murderer and a prostitute, the camera cuts to different angles of Martin in the bath and slowly zooms in on the character. The camera cuts to a high angle and slowly zooms down on Martin, suggesting a surveillance camera bearing down on its subject. The camera then cuts to a shot level with Martin's body in the bathtub and, again, slowly tracks forward toward Martin. The camera embodies a gaze that has now shifted and sizes up Martin from a different angle. Martin is unnerved even as a listener. And as typical of horror in which a threat inches closer and closer to its protagonist forcing a confrontation, the *acousmêtre* grows nearer aurally and physically. It speaks directly to Martin divulging Martin's name and phone number and eventually acquires the (hallucinated) ability to enter Martin's apartment at will. Yet, a *deacousmatization*, or "finally showing the person speaking" (Chion 23) never transpires since Martin is the voice.

Frenetic camera movements convey Martin's growing paranoia while also marking Martin's being with a corporeal sensitivity characteristic of a paranoiac. Freud quotes at length the observations of Dr. Weber, who was in charge of the sanitarium where Schreber was interned. As Schreber awaited a natural death after being penetrated by God in order to give birth to "a new race of men" (Freud, *Three Cases* 91), "[i]n the meantime not only the sun, but trees and birds [...] speak to [Schreber] in human accents, and miraculous things happen everywhere around him" (Freud, *Three Cases* 91). In lieu of nature, Martin is keenly attuned to the apartment's doorbell and telephone. And while Walter Benjamin found that the telephone was symptomatic of a modern devices in which "a single abrupt movement of the hand triggers a process of many steps" ("Some Motifs" 174) and a city's traffic "involves an individual in a series of shocks and collisions" ("Some Motifs" 175), the shock resides at home in *Dead Line*. A ring from either the doorbell or telephone sets off the camera's rapid and unsteady tracking. Thirty minutes into the film, Martin has been contacted by the voice through the phone. The doorbell buzzes, and the camera quickly tracks in on Martin's face going from a medium shot to an extreme close-up. On two occasions, the telephone's ring likewise unleashes a frantic camera movement. The phone's ring is accompanied by rapid and unsteady tracking on both Martin and the telephone. The telephone rings and the camera quickly and unsteadily tracks toward Martin ending in an extreme close-up. The camera then cuts to a shot of the telephone and the camera shakes and quickly tracks toward the telephone. The tracking shot on Martin implies an assault on the senses that cancels out the rest of the on-screen space.

The successive and nearly identical tracking on Martin and telephone, as an extension of the voice, brings Martin and the *acousmêtre* face-to-face. The confrontation is created through successive and nearly identical tracking shots that end in close-ups of Martin and then the telephone. In *Cinema 1: the Movement-Image*, Gilles Deleuze articulates how objects resemble faces through close-ups. "The thing has been treated as a face: it has been 'envisaged' or rather 'faceified' and in turn stares at us, it looks at us ... even if it does not resemble a face. Hence the close-up of a clock" (88). The close-up of the telephone, specifically its face plate, provides the telephone, or better, the voice, with a face. The voice's stare, however, is by no means passive. The hectic tracking onto Martin suggests the phone's eyes aggressively bear down on the character. The telephone's ring is given a force that shrinks the on-screen space, as if it had the power of motion through the ring's projection and prosthetic legs to run at Martin. For Martin, the telephone is not just a face, but rather a body that physically and forcefully confronts him and sometimes physically dwarfs him (see fig. 3.2).

Outside Martin's apartment, the city becomes a paradoxical urban space given the exterior shots of Martin's apartment. On several occasions, one sees long-distance shots of an apartment immediately before the camera cuts to the interior of Martin's apartment. The exterior shots create continuity prior to the camera entering Martin's apartment; the viewer assumes she or he is looking at the exterior of the Martin's apartment and then the interior. The exterior shot also plays

FIGURE 3.2 Still from *Dead Line*. The phone's power over Martin is demonstrated by the object's appearance in the frame's foreground. Martin, on the other hand, is dwarfed and out of focus. Directed by Sergio Esquenazi. 2006, C&K Films.

on a common shot in horror or science-fiction horror films in which some particular harrowing scene is about to unfold within the confines of secluded house or ship.[27] A long-distance shot of the house or ship captures the entire structure within woods or a field or, in the case of a space vessel, floating in space. The shot projects the isolation and helplessness that characters must contend with in the face of a human or alien intruder. In the case of the exterior shots of Martin's apartment, he is simultaneously isolated and surrounded. His apartment sits among thousands of other people, yet he remains alone contending with his own paranoid delusions.

TORN AT THE GUT: BODY HORROR AND *THE LAST GATEWAY*

Albeit in different spaces, in *The Last Gateway* a dynamic of paranoia unfolds from directions equally intimate if not more so than those in *Death Knows Your Name* and *Dead Line*. Michael (Ricardo Aragón) and Marianne (Salomé Boustani) are newlyweds and have just moved into a suburban home. Shortly after arriving, Michael becomes violently ill, and his wife seeks help from a next-door neighbor, Victor (Hugo Halbrich), who is a medical doctor and also engages in the occult. Victor eventually confesses to Michael that he attempted to open a gateway to hell and, in a moment of understated comedy between neighbors, erroneously opened the gate on Michael's abdomen. Monsters emerge from Michael's stomach, and Victor instructs Michael to flee and avoid cities at all costs. Michael and Marianne strike out from their home for rural settings, and Michael is pursued by different parties—a cult as well as a good cop–bad cop duo consisting of a priest (Adrián Spinelli) and a practitioner of the occult (Kevin Schiele).[28] By the film's end, Marianne has died in a car accident, those pursuing Michael have been killed, and Michael, who appears homeless and desperately avoiding unknown pursuers, has migrated to an unnamed city.

The pursuit of Michael in *The Last Gateway* transcends an urban space but maintains the typical urban and rural dyad so common to the horror genre as well as other genres, such as the Western and the road movie. Unlike the *acousmètre* in *Death Knows Your Name* and *Dead Line*, in which a ubiquitous and unseen voice alarms a character, the threat is unmoored from a voice. Instead, the threat hinges on the appearance of an unknown individual or group, which unnerves Michael and his spouse and keeps them on edge. After Victor urges Michael to flee near the film's start, he and Marianne depart and remain on the lam and sleep in churches. Michael's paranoia, however, is preeminently multidirectional, not only owing to the ambiguity and possible materialization over who seeks him, but also from what emerges from his innards. The portal to and from hell on Michael's stomach creates a second unknown; he is unaware of what and when some creature will exit his body. Such a dynamic of pursuit and emergence creates a multidirectional and fluctuating paranoia in Michael that intensifies, plateaus, and grows exhausted at moments.

As in *Death Knows Your Name* and *Dead Line*, Argentina is largely absent or obscured in *The Last Gateway* and again effectively transforms the Argentine filmic spaces into a generic United States. In his quest to relocate Michael after he has fled, Victor consults newspaper articles in English. Some characters speak an accented English, and the voices of select characters are noticeably dubbed into English. Globally recognized brands such as Heineken, Peugeot, and Mercedes, and the exchange of US dollar bills among characters offer up a plausible on-screen United States.

As touched on above, what proves unique to the generic United States in *The Last Gateway* is the construction of urban and rural spaces as well as a suburban one. The urban, suburban, and rural are marked as separate through prevailing tropes often present in cinema from the United States or elsewhere. The town to which Michael and Marianne flee is called Plesentville, the deliberate misspelling of a name that recalls the colorless town featured in Gary Ross's *Pleasantville* (1998) and also underscores how rural spaces in US films generally are themselves anonymous, constructed by clichés, and often constitute what Jonathan Lemkin calls archetypal landscapes.[29] In other words, if New York City, San Francisco, and Chicago can rely on their respective monuments to be legible on-screen to viewers who recognize those monuments, the rural United States rarely relies on such specificity and proper names that actually exist; dirt roads, open fields, farmhouses, and some typology of rural denizens (i.e., farmers) suffice. *The Last Gateway*'s Plesentville is simultaneously a US rural everywhere and nowhere. The town is characterized by its isolation, slow pace, and a tinge of religious fanaticism embodied by a town pastor, who in one scene attempts to lay hands on parishioners and drive out evil spirits. The pastor aside, the figure of a single redneck rounds off a general typology of rural characters, recalls any number of hick flicks, and thus further anchors the film to a generic rural US space. The redneck in question, Charlie (Maxime Seugé), chews tobacco, speaks with a US Southern accent, uses coarse language, works on cars, and services the town's septic tanks. Finally, Plesentville solidifies its rural US credentials by offering a space to which one might flee. As seen in scores of US road and/or outlaw movies, a rural space offers an individual or duo an escape either from the law and/or from the stresses of life. Eponymous movies featuring pairs include *Bonnie and Clyde* (Arthur Penn, 1967) and *Thelma and Louise* (Ridley Scott, 1991), as well as Holly (Sissy Spacek) and Kit (Martin Sheen) in *Badlands* (Terrence Malick 1973) and Martha Beck (Shirley Stoler) and Ray Fernandez (Tony Lo Bianco) in *The Honeymoon Killers* (Leonard Kastle and Donald Volkman, 1969); in each film, a rural space offers the possibility of escape. Such a dynamic is at work in countless other movies produced, or coproduced, in different countries, including Argentina. *Caballos salvajes/Wild Horses* (Marcelo Piñeyro, 1995), *Familia rodante/Rolling Family* (Pablo Trapero, 2004), and *El secreto de sus ojos/The Secret in Their Eyes* (Juan José Campanella, 2009) are just a handful of films in which a rural hinterland provides an escape route of some kind to a character or group of characters. And though Michael and Marianne are not evading the police as in some of the aforementioned movies, Plesentville and its rural confines offers the newlyweds in *The Last Gateway* temporary refuge from their unknown and unseen pursuers.

Filmed in Colón in Buenos Aires province, *The Last Gateway* presents a simulacrum of the rural and suburban United States that nevertheless remains somewhat open. Argentina seeps into the diegesis in several ways without fully "outing" itself, so to speak; one notices for instance, the accented dialogue and dubbed voices and the inscription of "La Juanita" on the front facade of Victor's house.[30] Moreover, there are visual references and allusions in the characters' dialogue to being at the end of the world or the other side of the world. The sign marking one's entrance into Plesentville reads: "Welcome to Plesentville ... Welcome to this side of the world." Characters who reside in Plesentville often react to disappointment with a resigned statement of living on "this side of the world." For instance, John (Patricio Schwartz), who runs the rural hotel where Michael and Marianne stay, complains to Michael after dealing with a septic tank problem: "This is a town on this side of the world. You have to depend on shitty people who are used to living in their crap." Such repeated statements of being somewhere antipodal to everything suggests that Plesentville lies elsewhere from anywhere, more specifically elsewhere from its targeted US audience.

The Last Gateway is a body horror film and presents its own dynamics of paranoia distinct from that of *Death Knows Your Name* and *Dead Line*. In Linda Badley's words, body horror depicts "the human anatomy in extremis: the body in disarray or deconstruction, in metamorphoses, invaded or engulfed" (26). Advances in special effects enabled the development of body horror as a subgenre. If films such as *The Blob* (Irvin S. Yeaworth Jr., 1958) and *Invasion of the Body Snatchers* (Don Siegel, 1956) suggested bodily invasion, horror films such as David Cronenberg's *Rabid* (1976) and *The Brood* (1979) took body horror to a new level by graphically showing the body in distress, decayed, and visibly opened (Kuhn and Westwell, 39–40). In the Argentine context, *The Last Gateway* is one of several films that mark the professionalization of special effects in Argentine horror cinema.[31]

Body horror projects paranoia by foregrounding the question of a threat's proximity to an extreme degree. The noxious force—a disease or some creature—threatens to enter one's body and create an "intimate apocalypse" (Badley 26). A rural hinterland, or any other potential refuge from a threat, becomes useless; there is no escape afforded to a victim with the threat both invisible and possibly residing within. The human body, thus, consistently threatens to erupt at random moments and become a spectacle (Williams 11). Michael carries one source of paranoia and transforms his body into an erratic entity unto itself.

Michael's body constantly and potentially runs the risk of becoming a spectacle. The first instance in which he meets Victor and requests medical attention, Michael soon succumbs to a severe pain and, at the end of a sequence that suggests a male giving birth, a large horn cuts through Michael's stomach. The monster's legs emerge, touch the floor, and pull Michael across the room. We never see Michael in such throes of pain again during the film, only his beleaguered state after giving birth again to some creature that kills several residents in a church. Creed underscores the relationship between horror and a woman's womb in horror cinema, and considers films, such as *Videodrome* (David Cronenberg, 1983), *Alien*, and *Total Recall* (Paul Verhoeven, 1990), as expressions of "[m]an's desire to create life[,] to give birth[,] to become woman" (57).[32]

Michael suffers a profound sense of body panic that creates two potential systems of paranoia and thus ramps up feelings of persecution. Not only is he pursued by unseen individuals and groups, but he also becomes an unwitting gate for creatures emerging from hell. While one finds narratives fusing a paranoia and male bodily invasion in accounts of alien abductions,[33] Freud's study of Dr. Schreber offers a point of departure for considering Michael's paranoias. As noted at the chapter's start, Freud surmised that paranoia could serve as a mechanism to organize a narrative, and Freud notes of Schreber, "Patient is full of ideas of pathological origin, which have formed themselves into a complete system" (*Three Cases* 90). Schreber's paranoia over bodily invasion is informed by an illusory mission to be transformed into a woman in order to have sex with God and, thus, "to restore [the world] to its lost state of bliss" (Freud, *Three Cases* 91). Drawing on Schreber's case, Freud theorized that the figure that elicited feelings of persecution in a paranoid subject (God, in this instance) was "either identical with someone who played an important part in the patient's emotional life before his illness, or is easily recognizable as a substitute for him" (*Three Cases* 116). Freud ascribes to that figure a supreme power, "in whose hands all threads of conspiracy converge" (*Three Cases* 116).[34]

Albeit a form of bodily invasion distinct from that conceived by Schreber, from the outset of Victor's exercise in the occult gone wrong, Michael's stomach systematically reformulates his reality as one shot through with paranoia, denying him any anchor of stability. He and his wife abandon their lives, which never return to normalcy. Michael looks upon all others, including himself, with suspicion. At the same time, Michael's predicament is hardly identical to that of Schreber, or, at least Freud's comments on Schreber's case. Michael does not function as a possible redeemer for all humanity, rather an enabling mechanism of its possible downfall. Moreover, Michael's paranoia is not a question of him locating a single figure "in whose hands all threads of conspiracy converge," as Freud described. Instead, Michael, or, more specifically, his stomach, is the supreme power for others, the linchpin in their plots. They need Michael's tummy; he is the missing piece that completes their systems and designs. The duo, the cult, and Victor: all parties pursue Michael for their own ends. When the Catholic priest and occult practitioner finally encounter Michael, he appears in the hotel with his face bloodied after a gigantic creature emerged from his stomach at a local church and slaughtered everyone present. The Man in Black, as he is listed in the credits, demands to know the gate's whereabouts. Michael relents, picks up his shirt, and shows the duo a star-shaped scar that is the gate's physical manifestation on his body. The priest explains the attraction for the gate in one word—"Power!"—and, subsequently, explains to Michael that the gateway from hell on his stomach will endow its keeper with the same power as that of the Vatican, which, according to the priest, has the largest gate.

At first glance, Michael appears to be some literal permutation of a paranoid body without organs (BwO).[35] In *A Thousand Plateaus*, Deleuze and Guattari offer up an abbreviated index of five "sucked-dry, catatonicized, vitrified, sewn-up bodies," whose conditions suggest a lack of caution, which, for the pair of theorists, is of utmost importance to achieving a BwO (150).[36] In the case of the paranoid body, "[. . .] the organs are continually under attack by outside forces, but are also restored by outside energies" (Deleuze and Guattari 150). Freud's analysis of Dr. Schreber serves as the model of the paranoid body, and Deleuze and Guattari poach from Freud's case study to suggest a paranoid and eviscerated human frame.

Michael's paranoia is coupled with a reordering of his innards. His body has been transformed as an entrance to and exit from hell, with an abdominal scar and a wake of destruction to show for it. Anna Powell has considered how Deleuze and Guattari's notion of BwO can operate in body horror films such as *Hellraiser* (Clive Barker, 1987), *Videodrome*, and *Hollow Man* (Paul Verhoeven, 2000). If Powell confesses to taking liberties with the notion of BwO (80), her analysis of "becoming woman" in *Alien Resurrection* (Jean-Pierre Jeunet 1997) proves crucial to understanding the specificity of Michael's paranoia and what it shows about a contemporary human condition. Powell refers to how the scientists' action of splicing together alien and Ripley's human genes in *Alien Resurrection* evokes the mad scientist trope that comes out of Gothic literature and thus taints the notion of an assemblage. While Deleuze and Guattari urge readers to exercise caution with experimentation while forming a circuit to achieve a BwO, Powell uses her comments on *Alien Resurrection* as an occasion to comment, "Assemblages should be consensual" (74). No such consensus exists for Michael. He becomes a paranoid subject precisely because he becomes part of an assemblage to which he does not know how he fits in with the designs and plans of multiple parties and agents closing in on him from various undisclosed directions: Victor, the duo of the priest and the Man in Black, the hooded cult, and, of course, hell.

CRIOLLO BODY SNATCHERS, SHARED PARANOIA, AND ALLEGORIES OF CIRCULATION

In *Looking Awry*, Slavoj Žižek describes the lack of objective shots in the film *Lady in the Lake* (Robert Montgomery, 1947) as producing "a paranoiac effect" (43). With the exception of two brief moments at the film's beginning and end, *Lady in the Lake* is solely focalized on a detective with a framing that captures his point of view. For Žižek, "the field of what is seen is continually menaced by the unseen, and the very proximity of objects to the camera becomes menacing; all objects assume a potentially threatening character, there is danger everywhere" (*Looking* 42). *Death Knows Your Name*, *Dead Line*, and *The Last Gateway* expand a repertoire of aesthetics of projecting cinematic paranoia that Žižek detects in *Lady in the Lake*. Sound, lighting, architecture, camera movement, and narrative all operate to communicate anxiety from the characters on-screen, and possibly to the viewers.[37] Characters suffer from both real and delusional suspicions of pursuit from multiple directions and remain at the mercy of obscured systems of power, sometimes of a character's own making, as in the case of Martin in *Dead Line*. The films' narrative arcs gradually reveal the extent and functioning of those systems at work.

With a general effacement of Argentine culture and the creation of generic United States, which includes the use of English-language dialogue, *Death Knows Your Name*, *Dead Line*, and *The Last Gateway* also share a target audience: an English-speaking US audience. I by no means want to suggest that a single audience of a particular geography precludes other audiences from comprehending the films' intricacies and enjoying the film. Many filmgoers in other countries will recognize the urban and rural codes and global brands as part of creating an on-screen United States. The films' distribution in the United States, along with the projections of generic visions of the United States, nevertheless prioritizes a US audience and complicates a US-Argentine filmic circuit that is largely one-way with US mainstream productions dominating Argentine exhibition. The Argentine English-language films' targeting a US audience hardly translates into a glib pandering or celebration of US culture, but rather a complicated dance of the films' imagining an audience. In addition, the films lay bare the ramifications of Hollywood's historical and continuing dominance of cinematic markets in Argentina and elsewhere, and INCAA's skipping over horror at the start of the twentieth century.

As touched on at the start of this chapter, the foregrounding of paranoia is a primary mode for the film to enter the US market and pass as a US film. Paranoia has long been part of US political culture and cinema. Richard Hofstadter, in his essay "The Paranoid Style in American Politics," published in 1964, detected an alarmist rhetoric about the Free Masons, as well as the existence of anti-Catholic groups, as evidence of the aforementioned "style" whose primary contention was "the existence of a vast, insidious, preternaturally effective international conspiratorial network designed to perpetrate acts of the most fiendish character" (14), namely the undoing of the United States.[38] While Hofstadter focuses on examples contemporaneous with his own historical moment, one of Hofstadter's primary arguments is the recurrence of a paranoid style in US history (7), which is evident in contemporary US cultural production and media. The turn of the last century ushered in a rash of studies about conspiracy theories in US popular culture,[39] and in his article "The Return of the Paranoid Style," Ross Douthat detects a return to a paranoid cinema associated with the 1970s string of conspiracy, slasher, and vigilante films.[40]

Given that the three English-language Argentine films examined here, as well as the other nine films, were released from 2004 onward, the films potentially tap into and allegorize a persistent paranoia afoot in the United States that merely changes shape. Amid the War on Terror and a proliferation of paranoias to fit one's political stripe (fears of homegrown terrorists, government surveillance, gay marriage, immigrants, immigrants' fear of Immigrations and Customs Enforcement, gun control, etc.), the Argentine English-language films mirror and allegorize a paranoid structure of feeling that manifests itself in US culture and cinema. Recalling Benjamin's contention that "the antinomies of the allegorical" (*Origin* 174) enable "any person, any object, any relationship [to] mean absolutely anything else" (*Origin* 175), the Argentine films present a nebulous US paranoia that parallels their presentation of a diffuse and ambiguous United States. The nature of the threats the films present are too vague to allegorize a specific US political and/or cultural event over the past decade.[41] Instead, the films' paranoiac modes and amorphous threats align with Brian Massumi's notion of an "iterative series" of "threat-events" ("Future Birth" 86) that governed the Bush administration's preemptive logic during the Global War on Terror and during which the Argentine English-language films were produced. For Massumi,

> 9–11 belongs to an iterative series of allied events whose boundaries are indefinite. [. . .] The terrorist series includes torpedoing buildings with airplanes, air missile attacks, subway bombs, suicide car attacks, road-side bombs, liquid explosives disguised as toiletries, tennis-shoe bombs, 'dirty' bombs (never actually observed), anthrax in the mail, other unnamed bioterrorist weapons, booby-trapped mailboxes, Coke cans rigged to explode, bottles in public places [. . .] The list is long and ever-extending. [. . .] They blend together in a shared atmosphere of fear. In that atmosphere, the terrorist threat series blends into series featuring other generic identities. There is the generic viral series, including threats, real and nonexistent, as heterogeneous as human-adapted avian flu, SARS, West Nile virus, and the Millennium Bug, just to mention a few from the first years of this century. ("Future Birth" 86–87)[42]

The anonymous filmic spaces likewise enable US paranoia to shift shapes unmoored from a particular geographic center of the likes of New York or Washington, DC, or even a particular town or region. The films' paranoia, in turn, can manifest itself in any US setting and thus embody an ambience of ever present unease.

Death Knows Your Name, *Dead Line*, and *The Last Gateway* do not operate solely as allegories of US culture; the United States hardly holds a monopoly on paranoia. The films allegorize not only a single national culture (the target market for the film: the United States), but also the culture from which the film emerges (Argentina), and possibly beyond. A dynamic of circulation between the two countries leaves open the possibility of the films' allegorizing multiple forms of paranoia within both and elsewhere. Contemporary Argentine cinema reinforces the notion that paranoia figures prominently into its national cultural production. Bosteels detects a proliferation of paranoia and conspiracy theories among Argentine leftist intellectuals that "fill the void in consciousness opened up by the unpredictability of events such as the mass mobilizations of December 19–20" (278–79). And in his study of *el complot* ("conspiracy") in Argentine literature, Pablo Besarón contends that conspiracy theories are littered throughout Argentine literature beginning with Mariano Moreno's *Plan de Operaciones* (1810). A cursory survey of contemporary mainstream Argentine films shows paranoia to be rife among national cinema ranging from films dealing with the last dictatorship between 1976 and 1983 (*Crónica de una fuga*/*Chronicle of an Escape* [Adrián Caetano, 2006]), the predictatorship (*El secreto de sus ojos*) and the country's economic crisis in 2001 (*La mujer sin cabeza*/*The Headless Woman* [Lucrecia Martel, 2008]). Argentine cinema does not mark Argentina as a nation wholly consumed by paranoia, as if all Argentines hide behind windows peeking through blinds. Yet, at the very least, insofar as a national cinema evidences a (and not "the") structure of feeling, a degree of paranoia is indeed present.[43]

Argentine cinema, in turn, reiterates paranoia found in other cultural quarters. Besides Bosteels's and Besarón's arguments, in *El sentimiento de inseguridad*, Gabriel Kessler describes the different connotations that the term *inseguridad* attains in Argentina. Pointing out that *inseguridad* is often misunderstood, Kessler observes, "Al fin de cuentas, hace ya una década que la 'inseguridad' a menudo se usa, en tanto categoría para describir la realidad, sección mediática y problema público, como sinónimo de delincuencia sin que haya una identidad entre delito e inseguridad" ("All told, beginning a decade ago 'insecurity' often has been used to describe reality, the section of a newspaper, and a threat to public safety, as well as functioning as a synonym for delinquency despite the lack of correspondence between crime and insecurity") (11). With specific regards to Kessler's allusion to print media, Argentine national newspapers such as *Clarín* and *La Nación* regularly feature articles under the rubric of "la inseguridad" ("insecurity") relating episodes of violent crime in a sensationalistic manner suggesting a kind of middle- and upper-class paranoia over crime that fuels phenomena such as the country's growth of gated communities over the past two decades. Sociological studies confirm Kessler's suggestions about paranoia during the time in which many of the Argentine English-language horror films began to be made. After conducting scores of interviews with residents of Buenos Aires following the economic crisis that culminated in December of 2001, Alicia Entel enumerates a catalog of common preoccupations that reads like an Argentine version of an "iterative series" of "threat events": "fear of being robbed and of street crime, fear of delinquency in general, fear of losing one's job or not getting a first job, fear of the inhabitants of other neighborhoods or cities, fear of the police, fear of drug dealers, fear of repressions, fear of a lack of future prospects, and fear that people will forget the crimes of the dictatorship" (49–50).[44]

The English-language Argentine horror films thus project a general psychic structure of paranoia present in contemporary US and Argentine cultures. If the notion of allegory allows for the emergence of different meanings, then allegory's range arguably gets redoubled in the horror genre. This expansive facet of allegory gains traction, for example, upon viewing *Going to Pieces*, a documentary about US slasher films from the 1980s, in which interviewees weigh in on the multiplicity of sociocultural meanings expressed by slasher films.[45] *Death Knows Your Name*, *Dead Line*, and *The Last Gateway* project a prevailing paranoia unmoored from a specific geography and, in turn, allegorize multiple systems that are largely beyond the control of both US and Argentine citizens: economics, housing markets, employment, crime, illegal drug networks, corruption, and so on. All such systems are allegorized through the systems projected in the three films.

The films' allegories and paranoia nevertheless acquire a measure of specificity when the films are conceived as cinematic body snatchers that replicate a US film in order to enter the US market. In other words, the English-language films allegorize the dominance of US cinema in Argentina. The characterization of the Argentine English-language films as a body snatcher from Argentina/Latin America analogizes the sometimes paranoid visions of Latin American immigrants entering the United States. Latin American immigration has set off fits of hysteria among some sectors of the US populace, especially since 9/11 and show no signs of abating. Minutemen militias, the controversial Arizona Senate Bill 1070 passed in April of 2010, and alarm over Central American children being placed across the US during the summer of 2014 are only some of the most recent and clear expressions of paranoia over Latin American immigrants.

The accented English dialogue evokes the vision of accented-English spoken by Latinas/os immigrants that sometimes accompanies paranoia in nativists in the United States. In the case of Arizona's aforementioned legislation, police officers were required by the bill to determine a person's immigration status if there was a reasonable suspicion about an individual's status. Accented English instantly becomes something scrutinized by police. Beyond Arizona, the paranoia over accented English is reinforced through the growth of accent reduction courses in the United States—courses that immigrants often enroll in to lessen their own paranoia and the suspicions of others. While Latin American immigrants are hardly the only individuals using the courses, Edgard Jiménez, a Mexican immigrant in Los Angeles, captures what is at stake with accented English: "As soon as you sound foreign, people do give you a different reaction," he said (Gorman). "People do judge you if you have an accent. I've experienced it" (Gorman).

The dynamics of paranoia and accents in English-language Argentine horror films has an oblique precedent in film noir. In *Dark Borders*, Jonathan Auerbach alludes to a catalog of films whose narratives "center on thresholds and border crossing" and, among other conflicts, gesture at "a fear that enemy (Nazi) spies, informers, strangers, and brainwashers have wormed their way into the country and refuse to leave [...]" (17). Among the ways an impostor is discovered in the films Auerbach describes is a German accent in the case of *The Red Menace* (R. G. Springsteen, 1949). According to Auerbach, the US Department of Justice "relies on a foreign and criminal past, if not a strange accent, to purge the state of the unwanted outsider" (22).

The dynamic of accent as indicative of a flaw in film noir and the Argentine English-language horror films recalls Žižek's discussion about the grasp of ideology and anti-Semitism in *The Sublime Object of Ideology*, in which he hypothesizes about how a German in the 1930s would overcome the discrepancies between anti-Semitic propaganda that depicts Jews as monsters and the everyday realities of encountering his kind Jewish neighbor, "Mr. Stern." For Žižek, the lack of correspondence between anti-Semitic propaganda and the everyday would be rationalized by the German as: "You see how dangerous [Jews] really are? It is difficult to recognize their real nature. They hide behind the mask of everyday appearance [...]" (*Sublime Object* 49). And so, with the English-language Argentine horror cinema, the Latinas/os (here, the Argentines!) hide within the well-trod genre of horror complete with US English, the latter of which becomes the flaw to be examined.[46] Diegetic plots of discovery are characteristic of horror cinema and, in the case of the Argentine horror films, potentially spill over to the viewing experience for a US audience who may ask, "What is off here?" and, like a dutiful Blade Runner, may commence to scrutinize the closing credits to solve the ruse.[47]

This is all provocation on my part. The accented English dialogue in an Argentine English-language horror film trying to pass as a US film hardly would inspire a visceral fear in US horror cinema viewers. Such a claim would only add to the unfortunate stereotypes of horror cinema fans as disturbed, bloodthirsty individuals suffering a kind of arrested development that condemns them to continuously live in their parents' basement.

Instead of fear, the accented English-language dialogue and the Latina/o actors potentially tender a pleasurable paranoia for US and other national audiences. Pinedo articulates a pleasure of horror that she calls recreational horror. She argues, "[W]hat makes ... anxiety-inducing elements of fictional horror not only tolerable but pleasurable is the genre's construction of recreational terror, a simulation of danger that produces a bounded experience of fear not unlike a rollercoaster ride" (Pinedo 5). Special effects and a viewer's awareness of special effects as artifice are important in Pinedo's conception of recreational terror. Horror fan magazines such as *Fangoria* are crucial for educating viewers about special effects. For Pinedo, understanding special effects provides the viewer a critical distance from the violence and enables them to recognize "the trick, e.g., the cut from the actor to the prosthetic device" (56). In turn, viewers perform a kind of "deconstructive operation" permitting them "to enjoy the pleasure of seeing (more fully) without taking the effect so seriously that it becomes threatening" (Pinedo 56).

One of "the rollercoaster ride[s]" in the Argentine English-language horror films is the turning of the tables, so to speak, in which the films send back to the United States its English as well as its generic filmic spaces and paranoia in an unprecedented fashion. In *Unthinking Eurocentrism*, Ella Shohat and Robert Stam observe, "Hollywood proposed to tell not only its own stories but also those of other nations, and not only to Americans but also to the other nations themselves, and always in English" (191). English in a film thus becomes a way of denying other countries the capacity of self-representation through one's own language (Shohat and Stam 192), which simultaneously accommodates an English-speaking audience. On countless occasions, US films have been set in a country in which English is not the dominant tongue, yet "native" characters speak a kind of accented English that incorporates and renders a character Other. The "native" is understood linguistically by native-English-speaking characters and an English-speaking audience, but his or her accent still sets them apart. The accented dialogue allows the foreign world on-screen to be both exoticized and accessible to an English-speaking US audience, Chris Hampton's *Imagining Argentina* (2003) and Alan Parker's *Evita* (1996) being two glaring examples set in an Argentine context.

With paranoia, generic versions of the United States, and English-language dialogue, Argentine English-language horror films offer a kind of cinematic blowback for US viewers. The films constitute an instance in which Argentina sends back to the United States salient elements of its cinema. The films target US viewers to an unprecedented degree for a film made outside the United States by non-US directors with non-US actors. Though hardly correcting the gross asymmetry of film distribution that exists between Argentina and the United States, the films chart a way into the US market.

While the Argentine English-language films further diversify the concept and motives of auto-erasure, the films also complicate and make flexible notions of genre marginality based on a production's geographical origins. In their introduction to *Latsploitaiton, Exploitation Cinemas, and Latin America*, Victoria Ruétalo and Dolores Tierney characterize Latin American exploitation cinema as "*doubly* marginalized, firstly as the product of the developing, or 'Third World' [...] and second as disreputable material" (6). The Argentine English-language horror films use English—along with other modes of creating a United States—as a means of overcoming marginality in both Argentina and United States. The creation of a generic United States on-screen *from* Argentina largely obscures the film's origins and arguably allows for the film to enter the US DVD market, as evidenced by the aforementioned remarks of Al Perez from Alebrije Home Entertainment.

A flexible marginality aside, at issue in the Argentine English-language horror films is also the question of what the Argentine films project of US and Argentine cultures. In *Re-takes*, John Mowitt posits the critical theorist's tasks of determining what constitutes US values: "As one often hears: American values are popular abroad because people 'everywhere' can and do identify with American values. [...] [T]he critical theorist is confronted with the task of illuminating how the sheer power to enunciate a properly global spectacle becomes the distinctively American character of the values people everywhere are said to identify with" (xix). In lieu of the usual mores that are associated with the United States (e.g., individualism, an amorphous notion of liberty, etc.), the Argentine English-language horror films suggest that those mores may also include paranoia, which plays out repeatedly not only in US cinema but also in its current cultural and political discourses. The English-language horror films also make visible the paranoia in Argentina and elsewhere over forces that are beyond the average citizen's control and comprehension, such as neoliberalism, drug trafficking, and political corruption. Just as these very forces dwarf the individual in reality, the protagonists of the Argentine films are subjected to systems that far surpass their comprehension.

Lastly, the Argentine English-language horror films take their place among other transnational genres in which paranoia is salient. Horror, as well as thrillers and detective films, circulate in different national markets proving their appeal to audiences on a global scale. Paranoia as a cinematic aesthetic appears a safe and pleasurable attraction for global audiences and can enable a film to circulate in different national markets. Paranoia, in its various forms, seems paradoxical. While paranoia over immigration and disease can elicit calls to close borders and to be extremely vigilant, paranoia as a cinematic aesthetic offers an audience pleasure, structures a film's narrative, appeals to different markets, and, conversely, opens mediatic borders.

4 WHERE PUNK AND HORROR MEET

ARGENTINE PUNK/HORROR, "CINE UNDER," AND GORE AS AFFECT

FIGURE 4.1 Still from *Sadomaster 2: Locura general*. A faux rating box from the opening credits. Directed by Germán Magariños. 2005, Mutazion.¹

THE PUNK IN ARGENTINE CINEMA

In his book *Punk Productions*, Stacy Thompson provides a sustained and rigorous engagement with punk cinema that grows out of his examination of punk production in other forms (music, zines, and fashion) and in different geographical and historical contexts.² Thompson relies on the practices and theories of punk production to formulate criteria for what can constitute punk cinema at the level of aesthetics, production, profits, and distribution. He establishes such criteria by invoking *Blank Generation* (Iván Kral and Amos Poe, 1976) and *The Punk Rock Movie* (Don Letts, 1978), and by juxtaposing *Rude Boy* (Jack Hazan and David Mingay, 1980) with *Fight Club* (David Fincher, 1999), a film that Thompson considers to be masquerading as punk. Among the aforementioned indicators that qualify a film as punk, Thompson includes a filmmaker's lack of formal training and the lack of support from large production studios that result in a film's raw aesthetics.³ Given its rough status, a punk film offers "traces of its production that open itself out to its audience as an open text by pointing up how it came to be rather than reifying its means of production and thereby folding in on itself as a closed text" (Thompson 160). In other words, a punk film must possess some type of visible or audible metafilmic component that demystifies the making of a film and, thus, potentially inspires others to produce, which is a central tenet of punk production irrespective of the medium it assumes.

While somewhat minimalized relative to other tenets, the question of pleasure is equally crucial to punk production and to a corpus of films that I designate as Argentine punk/horror. Thompson alludes to the Marxian dimensions of Jacques Attali's notion of "composition" and links it to the ethos of punk musicians in mid-1970s New York, who sought to blur the line between consumers and producers (Thompson 11–12). Attali privileges music as "the ultimate form of production" and advocates that consumers-listeners compose so as to "create [one's] own relation with the world" and invent "new codes" of communication (Attali 134). Pleasure is intrinsic to Attali's formulation of composition. Such a dynamic of production by the erstwhile consumer creates a new relationship to music: "Playing for one's own pleasure, which alone can create the conditions for new communication. [...] But it reaches far beyond that; it relates to the emergence of the free act, self-transcendence, *pleasure* in being instead of having" (Attali 134; my emphasis).

Thompson's characterization of punk production and punk cinema serves as a starting point to consider how select contemporary Argentine punk films mirror punk cinema from England and the United States from the 1970s and 1980s, only to diverge from those earlier manifestations through the Argentine films' invocation of particular registries of horror, particularly gore. While a canon of Argentine punk/horror films verges on being antipunk, I apply the appellation to the following feature-length films to forge a corpus of Argentine punk/horror and to illustrate the breadth of production that melds punk with horror: *Ultra-Toxic* (Jimmy Crispin, 2005), *Trash* (Alejo Rébora, 2010), *Trash 2: Las tetas de Ana L* / "Trash 2: The Tits of Ana L." (Alejo Rébora, 2013), *Sonríe/Snuff, Inc.* (Marcelo Leguiza, 2012), *KV62* (Marcelo Leguiza, 2013), *Mocosis* (Marcelo Leguiza, 2014), *Run, Bunny, Run!* (Mad Crampi, 2003), *Mondo Psycho* (Mad Crampi, 2006), *Sadomaster* (Germán Magariños, 2005), *Sadomaster 2: Locura general* (Germán Magariños, 2011), *Goretech: Bienvenidos al planeta hijo de puta, Detrás del Horror*/"Behind the Horror" (Diego Adrián de Llano, 2011), *Uritorco: En la cumbre solo te espera el miedo*/"Uritorco: On the Summit Only Fright Waits for You" (Carlos de la Fuente, 2010), *Uritorco II: La casa de la montaña*/"Uritorco II: The Mountain House" (Carlos de la Fuente, 2011), and *Protocolo 48: El experimento final*/"Protocol 48: The Final Experiment" (Carlos de la Fuente, 2012).[4] Akin to how the wave of horror cinema from Argentina has begun to establish the country as a productive node—and not just a node of consumption—in a circuit of transnational horror, the aformentioned catalog of punk/horror films suggests the country possesses its own vibrant punk scenes with cinema as just one manifestation of that scene.[5]

I employ the punk/horror label loosely and account for its limitations and overlapping with other genres below. Nevertheless, the frequent intertwining of punk and horror underscores a dynamic unique to Argentine horror cinema.[6] As in previous chapters, select Argentine punk/horror films may be analyzed for their respective expressions of *argentinidad*. And while I occasionally point out embodiments of the national in select punk/horror films below, the proximity between punk and horror in the Argentine context *is* a facet that proves to be distinct about Argentine horror.

I begin this chapter by describing how punk coheres as its own cinematic category in Argentina through exhibition and criticism, only to have that label to open up to an amalgamation with horror. I will then examine what makes the Argentine punk/horror films punk by tracing the differences and similarities between the Argentine punk/horror films and punk films from elsewhere. Finally, I will analyze how horror manifests itself in the punk/horror films through moments of spectacular punk gore which, in turn, also operate as potential forms of affect for national and transnational audiences.

PUNK UNTO ITSELF: PUNK AS A CINEMATIC GENRE IN ARGENTINA

In an essay in *No Focus: Punk on Film*, Chris Barber writes, "The first rule of punk genre is there is NO punk genre ... Punk sub genre [sic] movies, like punk rock, defy audience expectations" ("Polemics" 11). While I address audience receptions of Argentine punk/horror film below, punk cinema as a genre category in Argentina nevertheless coheres in different ways. In an overview of theoretical approaches to genre cinema, Steve Neale cites Thomas Ryall's and Andrew Tudor's work to highlight the "culturally contingent nature of genres" (18). For Neale, if the parameters of genre rest on "a common cultural consensus," he stresses the need to account for the entities and audiences that participate in that consensus (18).

In the Argentine context, exhibition, criticism, distribution practices, and production all enable punk to cohere as a filmic category unto itself and, subsequently, mesh with horror. Punk's coalescence, first, into a cinematic genre in the Argentine context, underscores the significance of exhibition practices and a domestic critical apparatus so that punk becomes a viable category. Exhibition and criticism also enable punk/horror to meld beyond the film's punk and horror aesthetics. To pay attention purely to the punk and horror on-screen ignores a more substantial approach to punk that evaluates other practices surrounding a film and that render the film to be a punk media object.

Punk cinema as a genre in Argentina gains a degree of specificity through news coverage and film websites that conceive a film as punk. In August of 2012, *NO*, a cultural supplement that accompanies Thursday editions of the national newspaper *Página 12*, focused on "Cine gore" with articles on gore cinema, "cine bizarro," and art house pornography. An article titled "Punk Cine" centers on Mutazion, a punk collective based in Buenos Aires. Though the article alludes to different genres present in Mutazion's films (snuff, zombie, and action films), "cine punk" serves as the primary label by which to classify Mutazion's films and one that Mutazion itself employs (Paz). Similarly, when the web-based periodical *EscribiendoCine* announced the filming of Mutazion's fifth film, *KV62: Tiempo come tiempo*/"KV62: Time Eats Time," the article referred to Mutazion as "la productora indie argentina de cine punk" ("the independent producer of Argentine punk cinema") ("Cine indie").

Despite reiterative gripes over the divide between highly esteemed film criticism and amateurish criticism appearing online, select personal websites and blogs also enable punk to circulate as a valid genre category.[7] The blog *Cine guerrilla* ("Guerrilla Cinema"), for example, covers in its words "Cine under, marginal, trash, independiente y con huevos de Argentina" ("Argentine Underground, Marginal, Trash, Independent Cinema with Balls") and includes interviews with Sarna and Marcelo Leguiza of Mutazion. The interviews appear under various tag words, including *cine punk*.

Criticism aside, exhibition constitutes another way in which punk cinema can operate as a genre unto itself. In *Genre and Hollywood*, Neale alludes to the possibility of "[c]inemas, cinema programming, and cinema specialization" as composing part of an "inter-textual relay" that cues the spectator in as to which genre, or genres, a film belongs (35–36).[8] For example, if a movie house specializes in screening particular film genres (art house, animation, foreign films, pornography), then viewers attend those screenings with expectations for a film's genre. In turn, a movie house's specialization in one, or multiple genres, provides a genre with a degree of public visibility.

While Neale's reference to the role of exhibition and genre cinema implies a repetition of genre films in an established movie house, a single occasion of exhibition (i.e., a festival) nevertheless enables a genre to emerge publicly. In December of 2011, the "Primera semana de Cinepunk de Buenos Aires" ("The First Week of Punk Cinema of Buenos Aires"), a six-day festival featuring punk short and feature-length films, took place. With the support of Festival de Cine Inusual and INCAA, SRN Distribution, a distributor of numerous punk/horror films, including those produced by Sarna, Mutazion, and Carlos de la Fuente, organized "Primera semana de Cinepunk."[9] Films were screened in Espacio INCAA, KM 3 Arte cinema in the capital city. The festival provided a space in which films were exclusively categorized as punk (i.e., "Cinepunk"). Marijke de Valck, among others, has written about how film festivals confer symbolic capital and cultural legitimization on particular films and filmmakers (104–06). Albeit vastly distinct from A-list film festivals such as Cannes and Venice that signal the "arrival" of a filmmaker into a particular critical echelon of filmmaking, the Cinepunk festival nevertheless provides an imprimatur for what constitutes punk cinema.

The program for "Primera semana de Cinepunk de Buenos Aires" intimates the breadth of punk cinema produced in Argentina. Films screened at "Primera semana" included feature-length productions such as *Viajes al sol*/"Trips under the Sun" (Gustavo Sidlin, 2010), a punk opera centering on a young punk, Julieta; the documentary *Yo soy Pocavida*/"I am Pocavida" (Hernán Quintana, 2009), about the legendary Argentine punk rock singer Marcelo Pocavida; and *Mono* (Mariano Goldrob and Mauro Andrizzi, 2009), a documentary shot in observational style, which follows twelve contemporary musical groups on tour in Argentina.[10]

If select film festivals can be conceived as nodes of diverse transnational exchange (Iordanova xiii), the Argentine punk festival traffics in diversity not of a transnational ilk with films from different countries, but rather underscores a diversity of national film styles that fit under the rubric of punk. In addition to the films mentioned immediately above, the festival also intimates the proximity between punk and horror in the Argentine context that is reiterated time and time again. In addition to a session of films titled "Bloque Horror Independiente" ("Independent Horror Block"), many of the festival's punk films draw on horror as implied by titles such as *Un cazador de zombis*/"Zombie Hunter" (Germán

Magariños, 2008), *Mutazombie* (Marcelo Leguiza, 2008), and *Detrás del Horror*. The Festival also screened *Uritorco II* and punk/horror shorts by Vindicta Films and Ballena Negra.[11] In turn, the exhibition of punk cinema in Argentina appears to lack the element of surveillance that often accompanies punk music scenes in which a conception of punk authenticity disqualifies some individuals or bands from being punk.[12] Punk/horror is just as punk as a punk opera or documentary.

THE PUNK IN PUNK/HORROR

Punk/horror filmmakers themselves participate in punk cinema's genre consensus in different ways. However, first, it is crucial to note that the Argentine punk/horror filmmakers differ from the punk filmmakers in Thompson's work on account of their formal film training.[13] Argentine directors of punk/horror films have spent varying amounts of time learning some aspect of filmmaking at the various universities and film schools in Buenos Aires. Germán Magariños studied "Diseño de imagen y sonido" ("Image design and sound") at La Universidad de Buenos Aires (Magariños 2015). Marcelo Leguiza of Mutazion studied one year in ENERC (Escuela Nacional de Experimentación y Realización Cinematográfica) and two years in CIC (Centro de Investigación Cinematográfica), but never completed a degree (Leguiza, Quiroga). According to Leguiza, he preferred to invest his time and money in making his own films and learn experientially (Quiroga), a sentiment that is shared among many horror and punk/horror directors. Alejo Rébora and Daniela Giménez of Sarna studied two years at CIEVYC (Centro de Investigación y Experimentación en Video y Cine, [Rébora 2016]), and Carlos de la Fuente studied cinema at La escuela de cine y realización de Lomas de Zamora in Buenos Aires (De la Fuente 2016). Irrespective of whether they completed a degree, many directors found their cinema schools as crucial for meeting others with shared interests in filmmaking and for collaborating on different projects (Magariños 2015; Leguiza 2016; Rébora & Giménez). Given their schooling, as I will describe below, the raw aesthetics in the Argentine punk/horror films opens up a range of styles with the films' crudeness coming through in ways distinct from the films cited by Thompson.

Various critics have written about subcultures' aim to be autonomous vis-à-vis a cultural mainstream. Ryan Moore, for instance, characterizes punk as a response to postmodernism and hypercommercialism that encompasses a "quest for authenticity and independence from the cultural industry" (307). Argentine punk/horror filmmakers' shared punk approach or attitude to filmmaking embodies a punk freedom to which Moore alludes and solidifies the directors' punk status. In a series of interviews, when asked what makes their films punk, punk/horror filmmakers unanimously identified a punk attitude characterized by an independence from larger entities, a fiercely do-it-yourself (DIY) approach to all aspects of filmmaking, and an aesthetics conceived as antiestablishment in some sense. Magariños, who occasionally uses *punk* interchangeably with metal or *under* (*underground*) refers to "esa actitud under rockera de hacer las cosas por uno mismo, romper las pelotas y no someterse a nadie ni ninguna cosa pre establecida estetica [sic] o formal" [sic] ("that underground rock attitude in which one does things by oneself, to shake things up and to not submit to anyone or any preconceived aesthetic") (2015). Leguiza, likewise, speaks about "la actitud de hacer como sea, sin deberle nada a nadie [y] es joder a lo establecido" ("the attitude to do what one pleases and without owing anything to anyone [and] to fuck with established [modes of filmmaking]") (2015). Rébora considers Sarna as punk since it embodies the notion of "no le debe nada a nadie" ("not owing anything to anyone") and, thus, liberates Sarna to make the films that the collective wants. Finally, when referring to his film *Protocolo 48*, Carlos de la Fuente describes the film as "un dedo erecto en la cara de todos los que nos quieren imponer reglas y manuales" ("a middle finger in the face of all who want to impose rules and guidelines") (2015).

The Argentine filmmakers' rhetoric of independence extends to the punk/horror films' financing that is critical to the object's status as punk. A central axis of Thompson's study of punk production is the tension between a punk object's aesthetics (an album, a zine, fashion, or a film) and its commodification. In Thompson's words, "[t]he entire field of punk can be understood as a set of problems that unfold from a single contradiction between aesthetics and economics, between punk, understood as a set of cultural productions and practices that comprise an aesthetic field, and capitalism and the commodity, an economic field and an economic form in which punks discover that they must operate" (3). In different geographical and historical contexts, Thompson maps the modes in which punk objects have resisted, albeit often temporarily, commodification by capitalism. The commodification of a punk object can happen in concrete ways: punk bands sign to major record labels, or, with a commercial film such as *Fight Club*, appropriate punk discourses of anticommercialism and anticommodification (Thompson 168). In the case of the latter, Fincher's *Fight Club* delivers anti-establishment attitude with a high-budget and star actors, which, for Thompson, cancel out the punk edict of inspiring others to produce (Thompson 174). Punks have relied on both aesthetics and economics to resist commodification, and Thompson rightfully remains adamant about the inextricable relationship between aesthetics and economics for an object (music, clothes, zine, and/or film) to be conceived as punk: "In sum, two vectors run through punk as a whole, aesthetics and economics. [...] Within punk productions, the aesthetics always give voice to the underlying economics and vice versa. Consequently, there is no purely punk aesthetics or economics; neither can stand alone. [...] the punk position is uncompromising on the economic front. Aesthetics simply cannot be separated from economics" (22).[14]

Whether a technical-artistic coproduction,[15] product placement, or the vertical relationship that can unfold between a production company and its financiers, cinema has the capacity to register the influence of money on its content. Regarding the latter point, Tanner Mirrlees writes, "By proposing projects they believe financiers will support, and heeding financiers' content concerns, many production companies find that their creative autonomy is curbed" (67). In the contemporary Argentine context, Joanna Page, among others, has invoked films associated with New Argentine Cinema as examples of how film reflects the influence of money on a film's content (4–5) and alludes to Gilles Deleuze's following statement from *Cinema 2*: "Money is the obverse of all the images that the cinema shows and sets in place, so that films about money are already, if implicitly, films within the film or about the film" (qtd. on p. 5).

Deleuze's statement, however, concerns industrial cinema: "[...] what defines industrial art is not mechanical reproduction but the internalized relation with money. The only rejoinder to the harsh law of cinema—a minute of image which costs a day of collective work—is Fellini's: 'When there is no more money left, the film will be finished'" (Deleuze, *Cinema 2* 77). In light of the availability of select punk/horror films on YouTube and their distribution through companies such as SRN and Videoflims, the films do not entirely exempt themselves from a degree of commodification and the asymmetrical "camera-money exchange" that Deleuze deems "the old curse that undermines the cinema" (*Cinema 2* 77). Yet, the punk/horror films' financing emphatically curtails the ability of capital to impinge on a film's content as in the case of a commercial film. Money is not the obverse of punk/horror images and sets; instead, money is kept in check, and a punk filmic aesthetic can run its course.

The financing of Argentine punk/horror cinema transpires on different scales and constitute a crucial way in which the films conform to Thompson's conception of punk through their respective autonomous economic structures.¹⁶ Again, simply put, the punk/horror films' modes of financing enable the filmmakers to exercise autonomy over the films' distribution and exhibition and their punk content. In the case of Mutazion and its feature-length films, the production costs range from $3,125 in the case of *KV62* ("KV62") to $600 in the case of *Sonríe* ("Sonríe"), and $312.50 with *Mocosis* ("Mocosis").¹⁷ Mutazion's films are completely self-financed with 80 percent of a film's budget coming from members' other vocations along with capital coming from its YouTube channel and music videos that the collective makes for bands (Leguiza 2015).

The costs of making the majority of Gorevisión's films are almost negligible. Germán Magariños, the director of Gorevisión's films, related that when Gorevisión began making films at the end of the 1990s, its films costs "Nada, apenas si era comprar el casette" ("Nothing, only if to buy a cassette tape") (2015). Magariños comments on meeting scores of people over the years who are eager and willing to participate, creating special effects, acting, producing, or taking on another role without asking for compensation (2015). However, such remarks should not be construed as a dogmatic commitment to producing a film with a microbudget. One of Magariños's most recent films *Los super bonarenses* (Germán Magariños, 2014) received some help from director Javier Diment and had an estimated budget of $3,750 ("Los Super bonarenses"). According to Magariños, that level of support was exceptional and allowed for the formulation of a shooting schedule and filming in a single location with real explosions, catering, and better special effects with on-screen appearances by *Playboy* models (2015).

Sarna's films also are made on a miniscule budget, and its feature-length films generally are financed by Sarna in collaboration with other groups or individuals with which it produces a film. As with Mutazion, Sarna generates its own capital by making music videos and providing freelance technical services for other productions. Similar to Gorevisión, Sarna's films cost little, albeit with the exception of *Trash*, which cost approximately $400 ("Trash"), and the budgets for many of Sarna's short films are minimal.¹⁸ However, similar to *Los super bonarenses*, *Trash 2*, to which Rébora refers to as "una super producción para el cine under" ("a super production for underground cinema"), had a budget of $1,000 (Rébora and Giménez 2014).¹⁹

The salient rhetoric of independence and punk modes of financing should not be interpreted purely as Argentine punk/horror filmmakers waging an attack on an "establishment" or "system" with the national government's film production agency, INCAA, being its primary and odious target. In *Performing Punk*, Erik Hannerz notes, "Most often subcultures are defined and explained as a direct reaction to material and sociocultural structures. It is this opposition that is said to provide them with their meaning" (13). An ill-defined and "all-encompassing mainstream" frequently operates as the opposition (Hannerz 15). Argentine punk/horror filmmakers have varying relationships with INCAA,[20] and, thus, underscore a facet of punk/horror that is distinct from punk cinema from elsewhere: a willingness to collaborate with a governmental film production agency. In other contexts in which punk films have been produced (i.e., the United States, England, as well as Pedro Almodóvar's early films in Spain), no such collaboration has transpired between punk filmmakers and any government. Though they may reveal a frustration with dealing with INCAA's bureaucracy in interviews or even in a film, many of the punk/horror filmmakers have sought and received assistance from INCAA. As noted above, SRN Distribution, coorganizers of the Festival de Cinepunk, collaborated with INCAA to secure an exhibition space for the festival, and Mutazion and Gorevisión have both participated in the "Making of" segments of their respective films for INCAA TV.[21]

An exact positioning of Argentine punk/horror cinema against an institution or another film movement or style in some kind of paracinematic duel (punk/horror vs. Hollywood or punk/horror vs. New Argentine Cinema) proves difficult and further sets Argentine punk/horror apart from punk cinema elsewhere.[22] Thompson points out how punk films militate against a Hollywood aesthetic by foregrounding what the film lacks (namely, high production values, and distribution and exhibition under the auspices of a major studio) and, thus, resisting its own commercial success (160, 167). Hollywood, in turn, serves as a bête noire against which a punk cinema can cohere. The relationship between Argentine punk/horror and Hollywood resists a facile characterization. Argentine punk/horror filmmakers acknowledge that select Hollywood films influence their own films, thus showing how a behemoth-like conception of Hollywood simplifies the different modes of filmmaking within Hollywood and overlooks how Hollywood is received and reworked within a punk mode of filmmaking, the latter of which I describe below.[23]

In lieu of casting resistance as the motor or raison d'être of Argentine punk/horror cinema, the production of punk/horror may be conceived as a question of pleasure; that is, a pleasure of punk cinematic production that is shared among Argentine punk/horror filmmakers. Making punk/horror cinema for many Argentine punk/horror directors is not a question of attacking another cinematic and/or cultural movement, but rather a love for making cinema. Magariños has remarked about the general lack of money that comes from making his films and how that eliminates any issue of some being paid for their work while others work for free. Thus, "que todos lo hagamos simplemente por amor a estas películas desquiciadas" ("we do it simply for the love of these deranged films") (Magariños 2015). Similarly, in justifying the use of the label "cine punk" to distinguish his films from others that could be conceived as independent in some sense, Marcelo Leguiza has stated, "No es fácil hacer este tipo de cine, se deja mucho de lado, es pura convicción y amor propio" ("It is not easy to do this type of cinema. One sets aside a lot. It is purely owing to a determined conviction and one's own love") (Quiroga). Similarly, Rébora articulates Sarna's approach to making cinema as irrespective of a film's budget, "lo hace con amor y dedicadamente" ("do it with love and with dedication"). Finally, Carlos de la Fuente justifies his use of the term *punk*, since making cinema provides a source of joy (2015).[24]

Cinematic pleasure has traditionally been construed as the prerogative almost exclusively of the spectator and undergirds the entire field of spectatorship in film studies. In *Cinema and Spectatorship*, for example, Judith Mayne writes, "There would be no such thing as spectatorship if the cinema did not function as a powerful form of pleasure, entertainment, and socialization" (31). Punk cinema production flips the signs, so to speak, making possible a recognition of a filmmaker's pleasure as signaled by the Argentine punk/horror filmmakers' aforementioned comments. To allude back to Jacques Attali's previously mentioned comments on composition, the pleasure of punk is in the doing as a producer and not having as the consumer.

The filmmakers' pleasure of making punk cinema inevitably broaches the question of scale that often accompanies discussions of punk production and punk authenticity. In *Global Punk*, Kevin Dunn initially refrains from offering a definition of punk or punk music. However, eventually he invokes a DIY ethos to forge a binary and differentiate DIY punk from commercial punk by alluding to the band Green Day as an instance in which a band "crossed over from DIY punk to commercial punk" (11). Green Day's scale (the reach of its albums' distribution, its record company's marketing arm, the Broadway version of its album *American Idiot*, etc.) puts its production out of its own hands. A DIY approach to punk/horror filmmaking that departs from a film's financing ensures that a movie will not become a full-scale commercialized media object. A punk film's commercialization via a corporate entity would entail the involvement of multiple parties (marketers, distribution agents, etc.) and, in turn, erode a DIY mode of production, or at least fragment the DIY process; in other words, a film could be produced according to a DIY ethos, yet the exhibition and/or distribution may happen under the auspices of a corporation. As I will demonstrate below, the Argentine punk/horror films punk status extends beyond its production, distribution, and exhibition and manifests itself at the level of content. Argentine punk/horror films do not aspire to enter mainstream cinemas or generate profits comparable to that of films released in mainstream cinemas in Argentina. Instead, with pleasure as a motive for production—a punk pleasure—a punk/horror averts entrance into a mainstream exhibition circuit and diminishes the commodified scale of the film. The punk/horror films remain within a punk scale.

CONVERGENCE: THE MESHING OF PUNK AND HORROR

While much of Argentine punk/horror cinema tends to overlap with trash and exploitation,[25] among other genres, my focus rests with the particular fusion of horror and punk. Punk and horror cinema in Argentina converge in a multitude of ways that create punk and horror hybridities. In addition to the horror subsection of "Primera semana de cine punk de Buenos Aires," other exhibition spaces enable punk and horror to intermingle through malleable cinematic genres. Specializing in the category of *cine bizarro*,[26] Buenos Aires Rojo Sangre allows punk cinema to be paired with horror, among other genres. Punk films directed by the likes of Germán Magariños, Mad Crampi, Marcelo Leguiza, and Alejo Rébora have been screened alongside national and foreign films that fit more squarely in the horror genre.[27] Similarly, Festival de Cine Inusual de Buenos Aires provides another exhibition space in which horror and punk cinema mix with "cine inusual" operating as an expansive category comparable to that of "cine bizarro." Codirector of Festival de Cine Inusual Fabián Sancho has described the festival's offerings: "Muchas de [las películas] adscriben al género de terror, otras al género fantástico y otras al drama" ("Many of the films belong to the horror genre, others to fantasy cinema, and others to the category of drama") ("Empieza en Buenos Aires"). Among other feature-length and short punk/horror films, *Sadomaster 2: Locura general*, *Uritorco*, and a work-in-progress version of *Sonríe* have all been screened at the Festival de Cine Inusual in different years.

The online catalog for the distributor Videoflims offers an additional instance in which punk converges with horror. In *Cutting Edge*, Joan Hawkins demonstrates that home video culture made possible the "desacralization of cultural forms" (34) and, in turn, undermined the demarcations between high-brow and low-brow film genres. For Hawkins, US mail-order video companies' catalogs illustrate this generic slippage in which European art cinema resides within close proximity to exploitation, horror, and pornography. The catalog of Videoflims possesses its own dynamics of generic slippage. In its "Catálogo" section on the Videoflims website, the slippage is confined within a spectrum of low-brow genres (action, science-fiction, comedies, horror), none of which are generally held in high esteem by critics in Argentina or elsewhere. Initially, films are categorized in larger sections, such as "Aventuras, Acción, Ciencia Ficción" ("Adventure, Action, Science-Fiction") and, most importantly for my purposes, "Terror, Gore" ("Horror, Gore"). Though lacking the label "punk," a number of the aforementioned punk/horror films categorized as punk by their directors, festival programmers, and critics in other contexts fall under the genre of "Terror/Gore" on Videoflims' site. *Sadomaster* and *Run, Bunny, Run!* initially are categorized as "Terror/Gore," and *Goretech* appears under "Aventuras, Acción, Ciencia Ficción"/(Adventure, Action, Science-Fiction).[28] One can access specific details about each of these films by clicking on the title; doing so further splinters and intertwines genres and gives credence to Barber's claim above that punk cinema is not a genre but rather an object that defies audience expectations or generic cues. Videoflims' classification system suggests the Argentine punk/horror films' content are an amalgamation of many genres, including horror, albeit with punk tones that I describe below. In *Perverse Spectators*, Janet Staiger wrote "[...] no genre film is pure" (66), and punk/horror is perhaps one of the least pure.

The role of the critic in genre film criticism is undeniable. Altman asserts the importance of critics in their periodic redefinition of a genre vis-à-vis other agents: "In the regentrification process [in which critics modify a genre's iconography], critics regularly take on the cycle-formation function previously associated only with film production" (82). The Argentine context also demonstrates critics' capacity to designate genre mixing like punk/horror by enmeshing punk and horror often within larger and more diffuse cinematic categories such as independent or cult cinemas. In her study of the political economy of contemporary Argentina horror cinema, Carina Rodríguez refers to films directed by Mad Crampi and Mutazion as "punk," while positioning the films within a larger political economy of national horror films (112). Likewise, Matías Raña and Mariano Oliveros describe select punk/horror films under the rubrics of independent and cult cinema in Argentina, respectively. Print publications such as *Cine fantástico y bizarro* and

La cosa regularly feature horror cinema alongside films that are conceived as punk in other contexts, such as criticism and exhibition. Argentine punk films also appear with horror films on numerous websites and blogs that cover Argentine horror and/or genre cinema, such as Cinerd.com. Given the frame of criticism, along with exhibition and distribution, the borders that separate Argentine punk and horror are thus porous at best.

PUNK/HORROR ON SCREEN

Given the possibility that films such as *Amélie* and *Run, Lola, Run* can be conceived as punk, a punk aesthetic appears to have fractured into different registries and transformed into a diffuse and casually applied descriptive term. Thompson's exegesis on punk production thus becomes all the more crucial for delimiting what is punk cinema and how Argentine punk/horror conforms to a punk criterion while slightly departing from that very criterion. In establishing a popular conception of punk cinema that he then disputes, Thompson notes, "'punk cinema' signifies, in loose talk, films that obey a particular aesthetic, that are composed of certain formal properties, that mimic punk's speed, frenetic energy, anger, antiauthoritarian stance, irony, style, anomie, or disillusionment" (159).

With analyses of films such as *Blank Generation*, *The Punk Rock Movie*, and *Rude Boy*, Thompson instead characterizes punk cinema's aesthetics as raw, slow, and largely foregoing narrative. Punk documentaries, such as *Blank Generation*, slip into observational and participatory modes.[29] The film shows footage of bands (Talking Heads, Television, Blondie, the Ramones, New York Dolls, and Marbles, among others) associated with first wave punk in New York City and features short vignettes of the bands without intertitles introducing each group. The sound is asynchronous with the songs being performed on camera, and the songs appear to be dubbed onto the soundtrack in post-production.[30] *Blank Generation*, *The Punk Rock Movie*, and *The Foreigner* (Amos Poe, 1978) consist of long takes with minimal editing. Thompson rationalizes such an aesthetic of slowness as a means for punk cinema to distinguish itself from mainstream fare and to resist commodification by capitalism. Contrary to the popular conception of punk rock music resisting commodification through an acceleration of rhythm and lyrics screamed at a feverish clip (i.e., Minor Threat, Crass, DRI), "punk's shift from music to celluloid demanded an inverse logic: the Hollywood aesthetic—linear, teleological, and fast-paced—had to be diverted, rendered open-ended, and sloweddown" (Thompson 168). Whether a documentary or a fictional film like *The*

Foreigner, Thompson's truncated catalog of exemplary punk films lack a goal-driven and cause-and-effect narrative typically associated with Hollywood productions.

As discussed above, punk production, including cinema, may be conceived according to an object's resistance to its own commodification. Argentine punk/horror films' on-screen meshing of punk and horror and a resistance to commodification begins not with its cinematic predecessors but with a particular strain of punk music. Among the different punk scenes that Thompson examines is crust, a subgenre of Anarcho-Punk that emerged in the 1990s in Great Britain and the United States.[31] The different strategies that crust uses to obstruct commodification include a band's name. According to Thompson, "Crust attempted (and attempts) to surpass, in terms of transgression, these commercial band names and those of all previous punk bands, including early Anarcho-Punk names, in an effort to carve out a cultural sphere upon which commodification could not encroach" (101). Crust band names included Assrash, Carcass Grinder, Bleeding Rectum, and Warcollapse (Thompson 110) and suggest why major record labels would likely refrain from signing bands with such names. The film titles conceived as punk by Thompson and others—*Blank Generation, Repo Man* (Alex Cox, 1984), and *Jubilee* (Derek Jarman, 1978)—are tame relative to select Argentine punk/horror films. *Trash 2: Las tetas de Ana L.*; *Goretech: Bienvenidos al planeta hijo de puta*/"Goretech: Welcome to the Planet, Son of a Bitch"; and *Poltergays: Pesadija en lo profundo del recto*/"Poltergays: Nightmare in the Depths of the Rectum" (Germán Magariños, 2013) approximate the prickly crust band names,[32] and their abrasiveness implies how punk/horror cinema's aesthetics begin to militate against its incorporation within a larger mainstream film culture in Argentina or global commercial cinema culture.

If Thompson favors documentary films in which a linear narrative is suppressed, Argentine punk/horror films are unabashedly narrative. In lieu of a film resisting its own commodification through a suppression of a coherent story, convoluted and farcical storylines from punk/horror films put forth their own mode of resisting absorption into mainstream film culture that pushes the films into comedic registers. *Sadomaster* recounts the adventures of Sadomaster, an unwitting man who is transformed into a vigilante after eating a brain fragment belonging to a victim brutally beaten by a neo-Nazi gang. Sadomaster fights and defeats government-sponsored thugs while wearing S&M bondage gear.[33] *Trash* narrates a day in the life of Ansio Bruselas. Ansio suffers from agoraphobia, and his sister, Ana Ele, is kidnapped. Under the threat that Ana will have her breasts sawed off by the kidnappers unless Ansio delivers a blue box hidden in her house,

Ansio embarks on a hyperpaced adventure in which he must contend with being kidnapped himself by queer evangelicals, high-level drug dealers, and, at the film's end, organ traffickers who remove several of Ansio's interior parts. In Mad Crampi's *Run, Bunny, Run!*, the title character Bunny has gone missing and her various lovers (Illimiora, a masked wrestler named Arcanor, a neo-Nazi named Mr. Fritz, and Satan) all pursue her through Buenos Aires. Simply put, such narratives in punk/horror resist commodification; they are not likely to be picked up for distribution by corporate media conglomerates and screened in mainstream cinemas.[34]

In *The Sense of an Ending*, Kermode conceives the tick-tock of a clock with a tick as "our word for a physical beginning, tock our word for an end" (44–45). Kermode then invokes the tick-tock as indicative of "[...] a model of what we call a plot, an organization that humanizes time by giving it form; and the interval between *tock* and *tick* represents purely successive, disorganized time of the sort we need to humanize" (45). The Argentine punk/horror films, including those directed by Magariños and Carlos de la Fuente, all feature a tight tick-tock narrative organized by some foregrounded telos that organizes and anchors the story. In *Goretech*, Hans Sordo and Salas/Estala must save humanity from Dr. Hell/Heller. The vigilante hero in *Sadomaster* exacts an uncompromising revenge against a ruthless gang of neo-Nazis and a corrupt politician. In *Trash 2*, Ana L. must find her detached breasts and have them reconnected by a clandestine abortionist. In *Protocolo 48*, revolutionary commandos desperately seek to expose the plans of a colluding group of clandestine military officials, scientists, and a priest to conduct zombie mind control experiments. While each of the punk/horror films feature a definitive end and ostensibly follow a conventional narrative structure, the chaos of their respective diegetic worlds nevertheless obviates the possibility of the restoration of normalcy at the end. In a diegesis in which absurdity reigns, an "ordered" world is an illusion.

With speeds that vary from a trudge to bat-out-of-hell fast, often within the same film, a strain of Argentine punk/horror films emulates the plodding speed of the punk films invoked by Thompson. In *Ultra-Toxic* the camera occasionally lingers on Peter Shek as he sits in a hall waiting for a delivery of drugs or digs through a dumpster searching for a jettisoned piece of computer hardware. Gorevisión's films often straddle the genres of horror, action, and comedy, and feature spectacles of violence that are generally not edited at a rapid pace and lack the breakneck cuts characteristic of high-budget films of the same genres. Instead, with the exception of close-ups depicting gore, the fight scenes in Magariños's films often are framed as long shots as in *Goretech*, *Un cazador de zombis*, and *Sadomaster*. Dialogues are framed with plan américains or medium shots in long takes instead of a rapid fragmentation of space and time through shot-reverse shots or various framing. Similarly, *Protocolo 48* does not rely on superfast editing and jump cuts in scenes of violence when zombies attack or when someone is shot.

Other Argentine punk/horror films can be characterized as mimicking the feverish pitch of punk music. Brisk editing and hyperfocused goal-oriented narratives of survival or rescue can feel like runaway trains pausing only long enough to present an outlandish and comical obstacle that a protagonist must overcome. In *The Way Hollywood Tells It*, David Bordwell describes an intensified continuity in post-1960s Hollywood films and considers tightly organized plots, a quickened pace of editing, extreme variation between lens lengths (i.e., wide-angle and telephoto lenses), tighter framing ("singles" framing one actor or actress, medium-shots, close-ups), and a more mobile camera (i.e., tracking shots, moving master shots, creeping zooms, and push-ins) as evidence of such an intensification.[35]

Argentine punk/horror films such as *Ultra-Toxic*, *Mondo Psycho*, *Trash*, *Trash 2*, *Marihuana radioactiva planetaria* / "Interplanetary Radioactive Marijuana," *Mocosis*, *Sonríe*, and *KV62* are an Argentine strain of "intensification of the intensification" that Bordwell identifies and that push the intensity to a higher level.[36] If Argentine punk/horror mimics commercial cinema with narrative structures and a filmic style, then punk/horror cranks up the juice, so to speak. Apart from the torpid moments that project Peter Shek's internal state, *Ultra-Toxic* relies on rapid cuts with deliriously fast sequences of strobe lights, split screens, and extreme close-ups of wires and cables to depict the mind of its junky protagonist. *Trash*, likewise, ramps up the pace considerably and features a camera that is almost invariably unmoored. The camera follows the protagonist, Ansio Bruselas, from point to point in Buenos Aires as he attempts to deliver a package of drugs to a sinister group of drug traffickers who hold his sister captive. A zoom lens often changes focal length opening and closing planes in the image and contributing to frenetic sequences. A similarly intense dynamic is at work in Mutazion's films, which are generally cut at a rapid pace with vastly different angles and, like the other movies, often use a handheld camera. The Argentine punk/horror films surpass Hollywood and mainstream US television vehicles and their "linear, teleological, and fast-paced" aesthetics and narrative, to recall Stacy Thompson's description of Hollywood.

The swift pace of the punk/horror films generally rest on the narrative and mobile trajectory of a single character that revamps the flaneur and flaneuse who often appear in films affiliated with New Argentine Cinema.[37] Contemporary Argentine cinema has its fair share of aimless walkers: the teenage lumpen in *Pizza, birra, faso* (Israel Adrián Caetano and Bruno Stagnaro, 1998), Elsa in *Un día de suerte* (Sandra Gugliotta, 2002), and Mao and Lenin from the start of *Tan de repente* (Diego Lerer, 2002). If Gonzalo Aguilar considers New Argentine Cinema as evidencing a dichotomy between nomadism and sedentarism, then *Trash, Mocosis, Snuff, Inc., Run, Bunny, Run!*, and *Mondo Psycho* compose a particular strain of punk/horror cinema that drives the motif of nomadism to a hyperpace. Aguilar defines nomadism as "the absence of a home, the lack of powerful (restrictive and normative) ties of belonging, and a permanent and unpredictable mobility" (34). While a select number of the punk/horror films feature characters with a home to which he or she could return and, albeit tenuous ties to others, those same characters are extraordinarily mobile. It is not a question of characters pursuing different leads to find a job, something to eat, or money, as in the aforementioned films associated with New Argentine Cinema. Instead, the Argentine punk/horror films offer characters clear and direct goals: find Bunny (*Run, Bunny, Run!*), survive (*Sonríe*), deliver the drugs and save your sister (*Trash*), capture the crooks (*Mocosis*). The characters in punk/horror films are set to different degrees of hyperdrive. Dawdling is not an option.

HORROR IN THE HANDS OF PUNK: HORROR MADE RAW

Raw film aesthetics in Latin American and Argentine cinemas have often been conceived either through New Latin American Cinema and its various manifestos or strains of contemporary neorealist films. For instance, in their well-known essay "Towards a Third Cinema," Octavio Getino and Fernando Solanas juxtapose Third Cinema against "the perfect work of art, the fully rounded film structured according to the metrics imposed by bourgeois culture, its theoreticians" (48). In contrast, "[o]ur time is one of hypothesis rather than of thesis, a time of works in progress—*unfinished, unordered, violent* works made with the camera in one hand and a rock in the other" (Getino and Solanas 49; my emphasis).[38] Similarly, " 'New Argentine Cinema' was heralded by critics at home and abroad as the genuine, 'raw' expression of its own moment: a cinema that, because of the way it experienced crisis as a daily reality of production, became a document and a mode of critique of the present not just through the objects of narrative but also embodied in the very form of cinematographic expression" (Andermann, *New Argentine Cinema* 157).

Punk/horror does not step outside and circumvent the Argentine neoliberal economic crisis described by Andermann. Punk/horror is part of its milieu. Yet, punk/horror production is not "experienced as a crisis." Instead, as described previously, punk/horror production emerges from a love or yearning for cinematic production that pays no mind to a material crisis that would bemoan one's inability to secure funding and make a commercial film. Punk/horror's raw aesthetics, in turn, are not the result of crisis à la New Argentine Cinema, but rather a choice. Moreover, Argentine punk/horror interjects a range of unrefined aesthetics into Argentine cinema as well as Argentine horror. Gorevisión, for example, makes no attempts to hide the low-budget nature of its productions.[39] The films' image and sound quality are generally poor and lack any concern with retakes, realistic special effects, and lighting. Any attention to continuity editing is negligible. *Goreinvasión* thoroughly illustrates this disinterest in high production values and "good" cinema, while often mocking the notion of high-brow tastes, "cine independiente" ("independent cinema"), and Argentine cinema's dependence on INCAA to produce a film. *Goreinvasión* functions as a self-reflexive "making of" a slasher film under the auspices of an on-screen Gorevisión production team directed by the hilariously pompous Roger Franco (Ezequiel Hansen). The film crew is joined by an uninitiated and austere film intern who frequently questions the director's and crew's actions until he commits suicide by shooting himself in the mouth. By the film's end, although Franco admits to a crew member that the entire production is a farce, the slasher film is complete. *Goreinvasión*, like the majority of other films directed by Magariños, foregrounds and even flaunts its unpolished nature. An "Advertencia" ("Warning") appears in the opening credits: "Hemos mantenido la pesima [sic] calidad original de esta cinta infumable, para que la experiencia sea equitativa a su visionado original. Disfrutenla [sic] en familia" (We have maintained the poor quality of this crappy film, so that the viewing may be comparable to that of its original vision. Enjoy with one's family.") The film's image and sound quality are unrefined; the computer-generated imagery (CGI) does not even begin to approach that of Hollywood. As typical of Gorevisión's films, gore consists of ample amounts of fake blood and intestines. When the film intern asks Roger Franco if the crew needs to do a retake of a scene, the director and the rest of the crew howl with laughter and Franco replies: "Acá no hacemos retomas, por eso filmamos rápido. No somos como esa burocracia de estudiantes de cine" ("Here, we don't do retakes. Therefore, we film quickly. We are not like that bureaucracy of film students").

Distinct from Gorevisión's productions, other punk/horror films generally do not revel in their limitations. Loosely inspired by William Burroughs Nova

Express Trilogy (Fernandez Cruz),[40] *Ultra-Toxic* describes the drug/technological addictions that inflict Peter Shek (Juan Manuel Gonzales Araoz) after he escapes from a clandestine laboratory. Scientists have inserted a microchip in his brain that causes Shek to crave a mix of brain matter and technology that he ingests by sticking a needle into his arm. Shek is pursued by operatives of two competing factions who have an interest in Shek's whereabouts and condition. *Ultra-Toxic* is shot mostly in black and white, and incorporates images of trash dumps and jettisoned computer parts such as wires, circuit boards, and skeins of videotape that contribute to a cyberpunk aesthetic.[41] The film's special effects are clearly low-budget and the images are grainy. However, the film is well shot, with select sequences cut at both slow and frenetic paces, and relies on editing and split screens to project the inebriated highs of Shek after he shoots up. Other punk/horror films reflect an attempt to make a technically proficient movie. Alejo Rébora has commented that Sarna aspires to make films that are of high technical quality (Rébora and Giménez 2014). In *Trash*, for example, there are multiple cameras and rapid editing, and attention to lighting and the color and saturation of images. Likewise, Marcelo Leguiza of Mutazion has described *Sonríe* as "bien filmado" ("well-filmed") (2015). It relies on multiple cameras with careful attention to editing. Despite the varying attention to technical aspects among punk/horror films, some degree of rawness nevertheless defines a punk aesthetic in punk/horror when the films are set against higher-budgeted productions.

Hollywood action and horror films are often jilted for their use of spectacles that are received as subordinating and eclipsing narrative. Argentine punk/horror films possess their own ilk of spectacle in what I call a punk spectacle.[42] Despite their formal differences or varied relationship to a narrative, punk spectacle in the Argentine films operates not as excess that detours or halts the narrative. Instead, I concur with Murray Smith's view on spectacle in action films in which "[...] the plot advances through spectacle; the spectacular elements are, generally speaking, as 'narrativized' as are the less ostentatious spaces of other genres" (13). The notion of excess, which is often used interchangeably and/or as a more generalized term for spectacle, presupposes a tight narrative structure that progresses only to cease at the moment, or moments, of spectacle.

Different punk spectacles in Argentine punk/horror have a varied relationship to their respective narratives. Punk spectacles advance the narrative while pushing the envelope of tastes and playing with genre conventions in ways that nonpunk films would refrain from doing. This appears often the case with Gorevisión's films and the tampering with tropes in action and martial arts films and sports films. In *Goretech*, Estala (Vic Cicuta) saves Han Sordo (Leandro de la Torre) from being humiliated by a gang of thugs who orally rape him with what are obviously dildos. Afterward, under the direction of Estala, Sordo embarks on a physical regiment that includes Sordo running with a stick weighed down with bottles of Quilmes beer, doing push-ups standing up, and being verbally abused by Estala who wields a fly swatter. The exercises poke fun at the abusive training sequences in scores of martial arts films. The soundtrack's use of Survivor's "Burning Heart" humorously recalls *Rocky IV* (Sylvester Stallone, 1985), which uses the same song. Sordo completes his training with Estala, and the two sit in front of a rudimentary CGI fire. With flashbacks and two brief clips of pornographic films superimposed, Sordo describes to his trainee/pupil how Earth became a kind of hell and reveals that Estala's lost father is the evil Dr. Hell who rules over Earth. Estala and Sordo's relationship grows closer recalling the homoerotic subtexts of many action films.[43] If the developments in a buddy relationship constitute a typical plotline of a movie such as *Lethal Weapon* (Richard Donner, 1987), then the masculine relationship in *Goretech* takes on a more explicit dynamic that surpasses the homoeroticism typical of Hollywood vehicles. After conversing about Dr. Hell, Estala makes a pass at Sordo. Sordo exposes himself using a dildo in lieu of his actual penis. Estala performs fellatio on Sordo, which is shown in a brief close-up. Afterward, in a postcoital moment, the two are framed in a medium close-up with their shirts open, and Sordo praises Estala's knowledge of both "las artes marciales" ("martial arts") and "las artes de amor" ("the arts of love").

The aforementioned spectacle in *Goretech* exemplifies how a punk spectacle can advance the narrative in a punk film. Estala and Sordo's relationship develops, yet the spectacles acquire a punk sensibility by broaching taboos (homosexual relationships between teacher and student) in a comedic manner, likely offending the sensibilities of a hypothetically highbrow audience. The punk modality of the spectacles and their capacity to advance narrative signal another way in which Argentine punk/horror differs from US and English punk cinema. Thompson writes of a punk film's narrative in films such as *Blank Generation*, "[...] scenes that do not advance a film's narrative signify an unconcern with money and therefore with the commercial market" (168). Argentine punk/horror suggests a distinct relationship between narrative, spectacle, and a commercial market. Spectacle advances the narrative in Argentine punk/horror. However, owing to content that is likely to offend those viewers residing exclusively in mainstream commercial market, the films, along with their narratives, remain uninterested in that market.

The moments of gore in Argentine punk/horror films afford the opportunity to consider encodings of screen violence as punk/horror spectacles. As noted above, instances of gore are crucial to a generic mixing of punk and horror. Gore has served as a way of intermittently defining the horror genre at different points in history and, at times, renewing the genre after consumers' interests have dwindled in the wake of a subgenre cycle.[44] James Kendrick illustrates this dynamic by alluding to Hammer Films' 1950s remakes of classical Universal horror films (e.g., *Frankenstein*, *Dracula*) and a reliance on "Technicolor blood and a newfound willingness to focus directly on ghastliness and gore, rather than discreetly cutting away" (82) as a means of reinvigorating the horror genre following the horror parodies, such as those featuring Abbott and Costello. While critics often conceive of the developments in the aesthetics and stylization of screen violence as the exclusive domain of Hollywood,[45] particular films made both within and outside the Hollywood system serve as mile markers that chart the development of gore in horror. For example, adducing the gory depictions of violence in the films of Herschell Gordon Lewis, Dario Argento's *Deep Red* (1975), and David Cronenberg's body horror films, such as *Shivers* (1975) and *Scanners* (1981), Phillip Brophy summarizes a dynamic in many contemporary horror films: "It is [the] mode of showing as opposed to telling that is strongly connected to the destruction of the body" (8).[46] A sleeker and more graphic gore takes center stage in more contemporary and higher-budget productions associated with the so-called torture porn, such as *Hostel* (Eli Roth, 2005), *Wolf Creek* (Greg McLean, 2005), and *Audition* (Takashi Miike, 1999), and supports Brophy's observation about some horror films being more apt to show violence.[47] For Kendrick, torture porn performed a similar exercise in the first decade of the twenty-first century, following a cycle of "spiritually oriented films" like *The Sixth Sense* (M. Night Shyamalan, 1999) and *The Others* (Alejandro Amenábar, 2000) (Kendrick 82).

Gore in Argentine punk/horror stands in stark contrast to that in high-budget productions and potentially affects how a spectator receives gore. In *Performing Illusions*, Dan North offers a critical and historical overview of cinematic special effects and discusses audience receptions of such effects. After describing special effects in three distinct eras, North observes, "In these spectacular moments, the spectator is challenged to perceive the joins between composited elements: all special effects leave vestigial traces of their means of production, and it is these traces which aid the spectator in their detection. Discrepancies too jarringly pronounced, we dismiss as 'bad' special effects" (4).

While many high-budget horror films these days rely on prosthetics and CGI to minimize "vestigial traces," the traces in the gore in Argentine punk/horror run the gamut from glaringly fake to somewhat realistic. Geysers and buckets of blood and clearly artificial body organs are commonplace in Gorevisión's films and are played up for comedic effect. In *Sonríe*, the tortured bodies of some individuals pass a loose test of verisimilitude, although with a closer look the joins become more noticeable. At the end of *Trash*, Ansio is drugged and has multiple organs removed, which will be sold for money. The haphazard surgery is filmed in black and white. The color, rapid editing, multiple framing, and handheld camera do not allow the effects to be scrutinized, and so the joins are obscured.

The punk/horror films' low-budget special effects contribute to the films' status as punk and recalls Thompson's contention that "[. . .] there is not purely punk aesthetics or economics; neither can stand alone. [. . .] Aesthetics simply cannot be separated from economics" (22). Gore in the Argentine punk/horror films acquires its punk sensibility, first, by foregrounding its limited financial budget. The Argentine punk/horror films reflect their punk condition by reflecting their low-budget in different ways, depending on the film: rough and/or fast editing, image and sound quality, and the absence of stars. The punk/horror film's DIY modes of production generally extend to moments of gore.[48] Gore in Argentine punk/horror reflects the films' punk condition insofar as they intimate or point to a financial structure independent of INCAA and/or a well-heeled production company who could afford professionally created special effects. Punk gore demystifies the cinematic gore that one may encounter in more expensive productions, such as *House on Haunted Hill* (William Malone, 1999) or *The Exorcist: The Beginning* (Renny Harlin, 2004). Insofar as an audience receives it as accessible, punk gore reiterates what Thompson considers a central tenet of punk production: to inspire others to produce. That is, you, too, could throw a bucket of blood, play with fake innards, or film a fake surgery without breaking the bank.

Punk gore relates further to a political economy of cinema when considering the market logic that critics sometimes associate with cinematic spectacles in commercial cinema. In "Spectacle and Narrative in the Contemporary Blockbuster," Geoff King examines two types of spectacle that he detects in contemporary mainstream Hollywood films: large-scale spectacle and spectacles characterized by what King calls an "impact aesthetic" (334–35). For King, such spectacles are imbricated with a market logic: "In the contemporary global-scale moving-picture economy, Hollywood creates a territory on which it, alone, can compete [...]. Spectacle as spectacle is, thus, a matter of strongly market-driven aesthetics" ("Spectacle and Narrative," 339). While King centers the bulk of his analysis on action films and science-fiction films featuring action sequences, market-driven aesthetics can be extended to the horror genre. Stephen Prince comments on film directors' awareness of horror film fans seeking thrills via screen violence, and how the film industry panders to such an audience's need: "These shared and relatively unchanging personality traits [of the audience] are ones that the film industry has significant institutional investment in maintaining due to their revenue-generating potential" ("Violence and Psychophysiology" 255). Gore, in turn, can be subject to a market logic, and the buzz surrounding certain films occasionally foregrounds how gore can be wielded as a marketing tool to attract audiences. For example, the red band trailers for films such as *Evil Dead* (Fede Álvarez, 2013) and *V/H/S: Viral* (Justin Benson et al., 2014) underscore the movies' bloodletting by showing copious amounts of gore. The gore in Argentine punk/horror corresponds with the films' other punk aspects (distribution, exhibition and ethos of production) and further evinces a lack of interest in making a film to be an outright commodified object. Punk gore indeed can imbue a film with a cult aura, which in itself can operate as a marketing ploy. However, gore as spectacle in Argentine punk/horror does not operate as a mass marketing tool unlike in many higher-budgeted productions.

PUNK GORE AND AFFECT

If gore operates as a decisive way in which punk and horror mingle at the level of a film's content, affect presents another channel in which horror and punk mix in Argentine punk/horror. Horror often has been conceived as a genre central to questions of affect. Though his theory of "art-horror" is grounded in cognitive studies, Noël Carroll's *The Philosophy of Horror* departs from a basic definition of the horror genre in which "narratives and/or images [...] are] predicated on raising the affect of horror in audiences" (15). Matt Hills takes up and refines Carroll's contention and puts forth the idea that "horror's texts may be thought of as a "machine" for constructing affect and transforming into its other [emotion]" (28).[49] While the aforementioned theorists consider affect in mainstream horror cinema, to examine affect in punk/horror, a low-budget and lowbrow category is not an unprecedented move. In *Cutting Edge*, Hawkins's examination of paracinematic elements in US mail-order video companies' catalogs demonstrates that

European art cinema resides within close proximity to lowbrow genres, such as exploitation, horror, and pornography. For Hawkins, among the various film categories in the catalogs, "[t]he operative criterion here is affect: the ability of a film to thrill, frighten, gross out, arouse, or otherwise directly engage the spectator's body" (4).

Moments of gore in Argentine punk/horror potentially constitute cinematic forms of affect. Here, I begin with Brian Massumi's often-cited definition of affect, which he positions against emotion:

> An emotion is a subjective content, the socio-linguistic fixing of the quality of an experience which is from that point onward defined as personal. Emotion is qualified intensity, the conventional, consensual point of insertion of intensity into semantically and semiotically formed progressions, into narrativizable action-reaction circuits, into function and meaning. It is intensity owned and recognized. ("Autonomy" 88)

If emotion can be captured by language, "affect is unqualified [. . . ,] not ownable or recognizable, and is thus resistant to critique" (Massumi, "Autonomy" 88).

The notion that affect remains enigmatic and evades examination has been roundly criticized in some instances. In an interview, Lawrence Grossberg responds to a question about how the concept of affect "lets one off the hook" (314): "So, I think there is a lot of theorizing that does not do the harder work of specifying modalities and apparatuses of affect, or distinguishing affect from other non-semantic effects [. . .]" (315). Likewise, in *The Forms of the Affects*, Eugenie Brinkema criticizes work on affect and what she calls "[t]his drive for some magical mysterious intensity X that escapes signification" (xiv). Brinkema offers a methodology that inadvertently responds to Grossberg's call for doing "the harder work" and performs what she calls a "radical formalism" that uses continental philosophy to examine questions of form and how filmic moments give structure to an array of affects, such as disgust, grief, anxiety, and joy.[50] Brinkema thoroughly unpacks historical and contradictory views on particular affects in order to muddle the meaning of a film's moment or scene, which, in turn, gives structure to an affect: a structure of grief in a ten-minute sequence of tableaus in Michael Haneke's *Funny Games* (1997); Laura Dern's vomit in *Wild at Heart* (David Lynch, 1990) presents disgust as "a structure in progress" (Brinkema 132); colors and spaces as a structure of disgust in *The Cook, the Thief, His Wife, and Her Lover* (Peter Greenaway, 1989); anxiety as a "form-in-process" in *Open Water* (Chris Kentis, 2003); and joy as a structure of arbitrary repetition in Hollis Frampton's *Zorns Lemma* (1970).

I follow Brinkema's methodology insofar as I conceive of punk gore as potentially offering moments and structures that function as forms of affect. Here, however, I do not consider a particular affect in punk gore, such as disgust or joy, and so I do not engage any particular critical theories related to an affect. Instead, I consider how punk gore offers cinematic structures that allow not for a specific affect per se, but rather for structures that illuminate how "affect arises in the midst of in-between-ness: in the capacities to act and be acted upon" (Seigworth and Gregg 1). If the examinations of affect center on mapping dynamics of transition and becoming, then punk gore offers—again, potentially—stretched moments of transition in which the turns of becoming can be acutely felt. With punk gore, a viewer's transitions can occur through the unsettling of a stable emotion vis-à-vis a particular instance of gore.

I depart from Brinkema in two additional and crucial ways. First, the question of spectatorship: Brinkema claims to omit the spectator completely (37), but I do not. While I inevitably cannot write out my subjective experiences of a film (who can?), I leave open the possibility that a particular scene does not constitute the same affective experience for another viewer. As Seigworth and Gregg argue, "there are no ultimate or final guarantees [...] that capacities to affect and to be affected will yield an actualized next or new that is somehow better than 'now'" (9). And so with punk gore there are no guarantees of an affective and shared experience among a wide swath of viewers. Second, the question of immediacy: Brinkema argues against the "immediacy or obviousness or corporeality of affects" (4). In contrast, I leave open the possibility that affect (again, here as a question of transition between emotions) can be felt in the immediate and/or transpire in the resonances after an actual viewing of a film. Punk works at a visceral level and also leaves open the possibility of a simmering or even rupturing within a spectator's memory. Serge Daney wrote "[T]he brain functions as a second projector allowing the image to continue flowing, letting the film and the world continue without it. I can't imagine a love for cinema that does not rest firmly on the stolen present of this 'continue on without me" (21). While Daney was writing about the tracking shot in *Kapo* (Gillo Pontecorvo, 1960), punk gore also retains the possibility of reverberating within the brain.

My consideration of Argentine punk gore as a form of cinematic affect allows punk gore to speak to two primary modes of spectatorship that are associated at times with horror or gore cinema: (1) a binary of laughing and screaming and (2) ironic viewing. The laughing-screaming binary is perhaps most forcefully expressed in William Paul's *Laughing and Screaming*, for example, when Paul states that "laughter inevitably follows the most terrifying images in fright movies" (67). Similarly, in his comments on the distinction between conservative horror films, in which violence is projected with an air of seriousness, and gory horror comedies, James Kendrick writes, "Gory horror comedies invite their viewers to laugh out loud at physical dismemberment and other bodily mutilations, and in this sense are perfect distillations of the inherent complexities of defining an act as 'violent' (if it's funny, is it still violent?)" (86). As I will argue, punk gore can protract or lengthen the transition between laughing and screaming or, alternatively, elicit different transitions altogether. The affect of punk gore resides in and among the transitions.

While often discussed in relation to cult cinema, ironic viewing illuminates how some initiated spectators can appreciate punk gore. Mathijs and Sexton chart the overlaps and distinctions among parody, satire, pastiche, and irony in cult cinema, and they contend, "Irony refers to a mode of discourse in which an utterance is double-coded: a conventional sentence may be spoken which actually means something else, but only an initiated audience will understand this other meaning, while the uninitiated may only interpret the overt meaning" (224). The question of the status of "an initiated audience" is crucial for punk gore to operate as a form of affect. The transmission and reception of irony is intertwined with the question of its stability and instability within a particular context. Claire Colebrook differentiates stable and unstable ironies, where stable irony indicates the shared "social norms and assumptions" (16) among a readership. In the case of cinema, a sequence, or a particular element (a song, a lighting scheme, a costume, character, dialogue, framing, etc.) can possess a double meaning for those spectators who recognize it. *Goretech* offers one such nongore example with Sordo's training sequence, which recalls *Rocky IV*. For those viewers who recognize the allusions to *Rocky IV* in *Goretech*, irony is stable. In contrast, for those viewers unaware of intertextual references to Stallone's film, the irony becomes unstable. Again, I cite Colebrook: "Complex, undecidable or insecure ironies, where we are not sure about sense, or where what is meant is not clearly recognisable, would then be regarded as special and marginal cases that deviate from the common ground of human understanding" (16). Though the sequence from *Goretech* does not escape "human understanding" and advances the narrative, irony is destabilized, or even lost altogether, when a viewer does not perceive that irony.

Speaking in very general terms about gore in Argentine punk/horror, when a spectator is "in the know" and possesses a prior sensibility of similar film genres such as trash and exploitation, the irony of punk gore is likely to be stable. Here,

I reserve the possibility that punk gore operates as a possible form of affect more for a spectator uninitiated in trash and exploitation genres. Seeing low-budget special effects with copious amounts of blood played up in a farcical manner does not register as a radically new viewing experience for an audience accustomed to films by the likes of Troma or Todd Sheets, both of which Magariños cites as influences (2015). Yet, Argentine punk/horror films' circulation via platforms such as YouTube and distribution in Argentina and other countries constantly change the films' context. A film can thus find those viewers within Argentina and beyond who are unfamiliar with the styles of gore in the punk/horror films. A sequence or moment of punk gore potentially becomes the juncture in which the transition between a viewer's emotions—an instance of affect—is most keenly felt.

My approach to punk gore as a form of affect conforms with Matt Hills's characterization of the consumption of horror (literature, cinema, and television programs) as alternating between emotion and affect. In *The Pleasures of Horror*, Hills eschews an approach that rejects Deleuzian and poststructuralist approaches to affect. Instead, Hills endeavors to offer correctives to object-directed horror that characterizes cognitive approaches to horror.[51] He posits different instances in horror films in which a spectator's anxiety is not elicited purely owing to the materialization of some boogeyman (i.e., the object). Instead, a spectator's anxiety may rest with an object in one instance and become object-less in another, or create an "objectual indeterminacy" (Hills 26). Hills illustrates this with *The Blair Witch Project*, in which a witch is suggested but never appears. The viewing of a horror film, thus, can be "[. . .] an interplay between 'affect' and 'emotion' as these are defined by cognitivists, with cognitive evaluations transforming affects into emotions, while such evaluations can also be challenged or textually complicated. [. . .] [H]orror's texts [which include films] may be thought of as a 'machine' for constructing affect and emotion and transforming each into its other; a kind of 'dialectical affect-emotion machine' [. . .]" (Hills 28).[52] Moments of punk gore present an affect-emotion dynamic in which gore potentially serves as a momentary stretching of affect that unsettles and delays the fixing of an emotion vis-à-vis a scene.

A specific moment of gore in *Goreinvasión* illustrates a possible stretching of affect. At different moments in *Goreinvasión* multiple storylines unfold and, among other targets, poke fun at the idea of art cinema. One storyline involves the random appearances of a killer (or multiple killers?) wearing a hockey mask. The scene in question takes place around the film's midpoint when an anonymous man has robbed a small wooden box containing poker chips. Shortly after declaring to himself, "Voy a ser millonario" ("I'm going to be a millionaire"), an ominous song of guitar and organ music begins, and the masked killer appears wearing dishwashing gloves and carrying a large pot. The killer approaches the robber from behind. After being stabbed, the man lies on his back on the ground with the assailant standing over him.

With the exception of only a few cuts, the handheld camera moves up and down capturing both the killer and the robber. The killer pulls out a larger knife, and there is a brief shot of what is supposed to be the robber's midsection covered in black clothing. A diegetic knocking sound is audible on the soundtrack. After a similarly brief close-up of the robber's face, the camera cuts back to a close-up of the supposed midsection again. Again, there is a knocking sound. After seemingly breaking the robber's sternum, the killer begins to extract what are supposed to the robber's intestines but appear to be scraps of cloth doused in fake blood. With the exception of a brief shot of the robber's face, the camera remains fixated on the midsection for about forty-five seconds. The guitar and organ dirge continues, and one can hear the sloshing of the cloth intestines. The killer pulls the cloth intestines out and then puts them back in again, as if washing laundry by hand transforms the body's cavity into a wash bucket (see fig. 4.2). After the killer has placed the intestines back in the hole for the final time, the robber and the hockey-masked killer stand up. After a brief pause, the killer finishes off the robber by cutting an internal organ out of him, which happens off-screen. The organ is obviously fake, and, in a close-up, the final image fixates on the organ being squished tightly in the killer's hand, which remains encased in a dish-washing glove.

The forms of gore in Argentine punk/horror are not necessarily uniform and shared among the films discussed here. Agents Johnson and Sedel in *Mocosis* commit acts of fast-edited ultraviolence, biting off ears and ripping out intestines; Ana L. in *Trash 2* frantically removes her own breasts in a sequence of close-ups after a clandestine abortionist incorrectly reattaches them; Peter Shek in *Ultra-Toxic* hooks up pieces of someone else's brain to a machine in

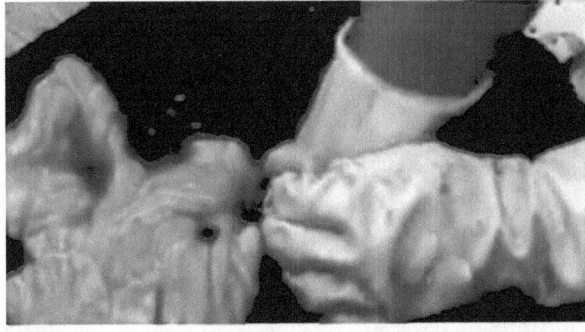

FIGURE 4.2. Still from *Goreinvasión*. In *Goreinvasión*, the killer from the slasher movie-within-a-movie repeatedly removes the victim's intestines and then places them back into a torso. Directed by Germán Magariños. 2004, Gorevisión.

order to get high; *Protocolo 48* relies on basic CGI to simulate blood splattering. The films' gore is inevitably low-budget, which does not disqualify the films from eliciting admiration. The Argentine punk/horror films attract spectators who express their appreciation through reviews on IMDB and/or the YouTube comments section for particular films. Specifically, in the case of *Goreinvasión*, on YouTube, a user named Ernesto lopez (*sic*), posted the comment, "Obra Maestra" ("Masterpiece"). In the case of the comments regarding *Trash* on YouTube, though there is hardly a dearth of hostile reactions, the majority of the comments posted are positive: "Buena fotografía y excelentes efectos!" ("Good photography and excellent effects!") (Alfredo Salvador Musmeci Fernández) and "Me pareció realmente muy buen laburo, los felicito! a ver cuando cuelgan la 2!!! EXITOS!" ("It appears to me as really good work. Congratulations to you all! Let's see when [*Trash*] 2 gets posted!!! What hits!") (Taka Ta-ka).

Some comments by viewers evidence a sensibility and appreciation of punk/gore films. However, again, I prefer to consider the aforementioned scene from *Goreinvasión* as a moment of affect not for the inured viewer, but rather for the uninitiated spectator who is likely to transition between emotions and with states that potentially run the gamut from laughter, bewilderment, revulsion, and/or outright dismissal. The running of the gamut *is* affect, or the transition or the "in-between-ness," to recall Seigworth and Gregg's characterization of affect. The scene from *Goreinvasión* features numerous modes of distanciation that differ from the ostensible aim of Hollywood spectacles in contemporary films "to create the impression of immersion," which can "come down to a question of the absence of flaws [in special effects]" (King, "Spectacle and Narrative," 339). The poor image and sound quality, the editing and camera movement, the low-budget gore and special effects, and the less than stellar acting leaves the supposed flaws and joins in the open. Such formal elements collaborate to break from the stylized violence typical of high-budget productions. In his analysis of moments in *Pulp Fiction* (Quentin Tarantino, 1994), *Natural Born Killers* (Oliver Stone, 1994), and *American Psycho* (Mary Harron, 2000), King refers to the mix of explicit violence with comedic registries. Akin to James Kendrick's comments about the uncertain reception of comical violence, King writes "[a]n uncertain modality can increase the impact of potentially disturbing material such as sudden or graphic outbursts of violence, by leaving viewers in the awkward position of not being able clearly to determine how seriously or otherwise it is meant to be taken" ("Killingly funny," 132). The aesthetics of violence in *Goreinvasión*, as well as other films directed by Magariños, Leguiza, Rébora, De la Fuente, Mad Crampi, and Jimmy Crispin obviously differ vastly from the Hollywood films that King examines. However, the notion of "an uncertainty modality," which leaves the spectator in an "awkward position," is instructive here.

Punk/gore stretches out the uncertainty of reception between emotions for those unfamiliar with such films. Affect is a viewer's passing from one emotion to another. The question of transition between emotions may also be cast as it relates to pleasure. As discussed in a prior chapter, the reception of a horror film, like any film, may be approached according to the multiple pleasures or unpleasures that a spectator derives from consuming that film.[53] The unsettling of emotion that accompanies the viewing of punk gore may be conceived as the unsettling of pleasure by placing the viewer in "an uncertainty modality" as to whether the gore affords pleasure or not.

To be more concrete, the shifts in emotions and/or pleasure may be articulated through a catalog of hypothetical questions running through a viewer's mind, which paraphrase spectators' comments on different YouTube pages featuring punk/horror films: Is this real? Is this "good"? Is this shit? This film cannot be representative of Argentine cinema? Is this comical or gross or both? Is the comedy going too far? Is this a student film? Why would INCAA TV be interested in broadcasting a "making of" segment of such a film? How could *Sonríe* have over 850,000 YouTube hits? Why would INCAA provide support for a documentary to be made about Gorevisión? Such queries do not illustrate a single affect (à la Brinkema), but rather suggest how the transition between emotions—affect—can be presented as an index of unsettled emotions, swirling queries, and/or fidgety pleasures.

5   IS IT THERE? IT'S NOT THERE. NOW IT'S THERE.

SPECTRAL DYNAMICS OF THE LAST DICTATORSHIP IN ARGENTINE HORROR CINEMA

Argentine horror cinema's capacity to allegorize multiple national crises eventually scrapes up against the legacies of the country's last dictatorship (1976–83), and potentially disrupts the polysemous nature of allegory. While Argentina was besieged by a climate of violence committed by both left- and right-wing factions leading up to that moment, an ultraconservative military junta seized power on March 24, 1976, and instituted what the junta itself referred to as *El Proceso de Reorganización Nacional* ("The National Reorganization Process"), or *El Proceso*, for short. The military employed brutal policies of kidnapping, clandestine detentions, systematic torture, and murder against so-called subversive elements or those suspicious of undermining the junta's objectives. The dictatorship's tactics resulted in incredible carnage with some thirty thousand deaths, and the Dirty War understandably reverberates today on numerous fronts.[1]

As is the nature of spectatorship, a legion of factors can influence and shape viewers' horizons of expectation for Argentine horror cinema, including the anticipation that a country's literal and collective horrors, such as *El Proceso*, will figure into its national horror cinema. Though he comments explicitly on literature, Hans Robert Jauss's original formulation of a "horizon of expectation" partially illuminates why a viewer may approach Argentine horror cinema with such a presumption that effectively circumscribes a film's allegorical reach by hemming in its reception to a single event: "A literary work, even when it appears to be new, does not present itself as something absolutely new in an informational vacuum, but predisposes its audience to a very specific kind of reception by announcements, overt and covert signals, familiar characteristics, or implicit allusions" (23). However, a horizon of expectation that inevitably tethers Argentine horror cinema to the Dirty War is untenable. Argentine horror lacks a tradition of engaging with the last dictatorship. Moreover, domestic critics, 'serious' or otherwise, generally refrain from receiving Argentine horror films as allegories of the Dirty War. Nevertheless, *El Proceso* presents a tenacious, preconceived orientation for spectators, especially those outside Argentina, that is shaped by a patchwork of phenomena: a particular strain of academic horror cinema criticism (i.e., national horror cinema = national crises); legacies and memory practices surrounding the Dirty War; and the Argentine government's use of national cinema as a memory practice.

As discussed previously, Argentine horror has long possessed a transnational orientation, and the Dirty War's thematic dominance becomes particularly germane given horror's transnational circulation. However unintended, films such as *La historia oficial* (Luis Puenzo, 1985), *Camila* (María Luisa Bemberg, 1984), *Kamchatka* (Marcelo Piñeyro, 2002), *Garaje Olimpo* (Marco Bechis, 1999), among others, can operate as a de facto primer for transnational audiences in which the Dirty War invariably lingers over any Argentine film irrespective of genre. Given that the Dirty War has been deterritorialized and has acquired a prosthetic dimension in cultural production even outside Argentina, the thematic power of the Dirty War and its capacity to shape generalized expectations for Argentine cinema increases.[2]

A. O. Scott's review of Lucrecia Martel's *La mujer sin cabeza/The Headless Woman* (2008) in the *New York Times* evidences a transnational perception that hems Argentine cinema into a particular reception that prioritizes the Dirty War. Though Scott cites Martel's comment that her own film is "about Argentina's refusal to acknowledge a widening economic disparity between the middle and lower class," Scott himself proposes that the movie is "a meditation on Argentina's historical memory of the Dirty War." His interpretation is not wrong, per se. Svampa, among scores of other researchers, have noted that the last dictatorship's opening of the economy to foreign investors and the deregulation of particular industries marked the first implementations of neoliberal policies in Argentina (Svampa 22–23). For Scott, it appears that the legacies of a dictatorship offer a more concrete villain on which to pin his interpretation: a " 'subjective' violence, violence performed by a clearly identifiable agent" in lieu of a neoliberal economic doctrine, which operates as an inconspicuous, "objective," and "systemic" violence that accompanies "the smooth functioning of [an] economic and political [system] (Žižek, *Violence* 1, 2).

Here, I deliberately insert an examination of the Dirty War's varied relationship with Argentine horror cinema at the end of this study, lest a literal and extraordinary violence hover over all receptions of the films. Such a reading of Argentine horror cinema that haphazardly links content with a particular national tragedy can be exclusionary and, simply put, one-dimensional. Instead, contemporary Argentine horror cinema adds to the already complex relationships between the Dirty War and Argentine cinema with horror films revealing distinct memory practices among filmmakers and memory receptions among different publics.

SOMETIMES A KIDNAPPING IS JUST A KIDNAPPING

In a 1994 essay titled "El cine del Proceso: Estética de la muerte" ("The Cinema of the Process: Aesthetic of Death"), Sergio Wolf analyzes various ways in which the Dirty War manifested itself in movies produced during the last dictatorship. Wolf alludes to "códigos de significación" ("codes of signification") (268)—mise-en-scène, themes, theme songs, and characters—through which the Dirty War figures into films made during the dictatorship. For Wolf, the recurrent themes of confinement, silence, nostalgia for the past, films with didactic lessons, and the images of factions (as in Emilio Vieyra's *Comandos azules*/"Blue Commandos" [1980]), among other elements, allegorize what was happening at the very time of the Dirty War.

Wolf's detection of particular tropes suggests contemporary Argentine horror films ostensibly allegorize the Dirty War through resemblances of what actually transpired some thirty-five years ago, namely torture, kidnappings, and confinement. In Daniel de la Vega and Pablo Parés's *Jennifer's Shadow* (2004), Jennifer Cassi (Gina Phillips) comes to Buenos Aires to claim her inheritance, an old mansion, following the death of her twin sister, Johanna. Mary Ellen Cassi (Faye Dunaway), Jennifer's grandmother, originally came to Buenos Aires to find a cure for an undisclosed disease and discovers that cure in a kind of ritualistic witchcraft called Malam. With the help of other characters, Jennifer learns her grandmother has cast a dark spell on her own family. Various family members (Jennifer's parents, sister, and aunt) are suspended in a liminal state between life and death, which allows the grandmother to feed off their energy and remain alive. The mansion operates as part of Mary Ellen's plot to survive, and her struggle with Jennifer over the mansion is a central conflict in the film's plot. For Mary Ellen, "the mansion is everything," while Jennifer wants to sell off the property quickly and return to the United States. At Mary Ellen's bidding, a raven torments Jennifer in her dreams. By the end of the film, Jennifer burns her grandmother alive in a coffin, only for the grandmother to return to life seemingly unharmed. In the final shot following Jennifer's death, Mary Ellen stands over her granddaughter's coffin, the victor.

Jennifer's Shadow features a scene in which the title character, Jennifer (Gina Phillips) is strapped to a bed and her innards are eaten by a raven. Prior to the raven's attack, Jennifer reads passages aloud from Edgar Allan Poe's "The Raven" one evening before falling asleep.³ She shuts her eyes and an unseen force is put into motion. Ominous music sets in, Jennifer's bedroom door opens, and the lighting takes on more defined contrasts. Upon "awakening" into a dream, the wooden headboard has been replaced by a metal one, and Jennifer's arms and legs are bound to four metal bed posts with leather straps. The camera rests above Jennifer in a full body shot accentuating her powerlessness and cuts to close-ups of Jennifer's tethered hands. A raven flies into the frame and lands on Jennifer's stomach and pecks at her belly (see fig. 5.1). In a rapid sequence of images, we see close-ups of Jennifer screaming and the raven holding pieces of Jennifer's entrails in its beak. The camera's rapid cutting between Jennifer and the raven quickens and is interrupted by an image of Jennifer's grandmother, Mary Ellen, standing over a casket with a point-of-view shot from a corpse in the casket, a framing that foreshadows Jennifer's demise.⁴

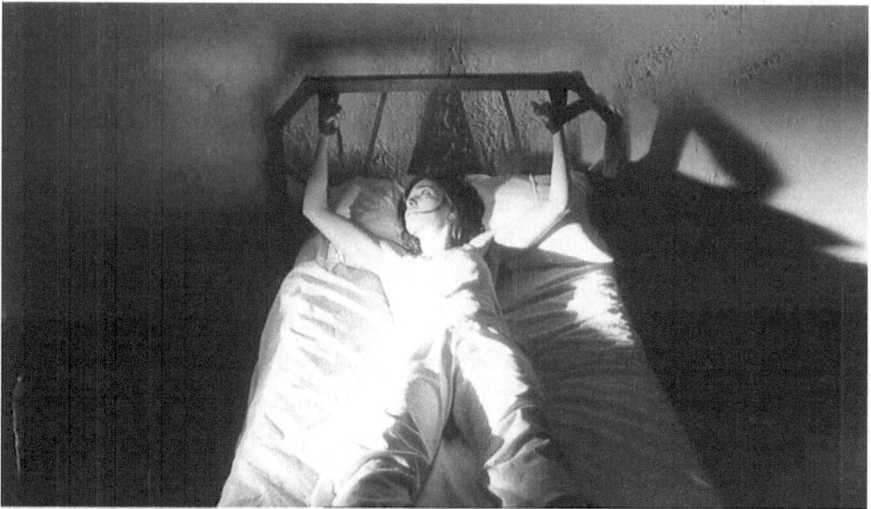

FIGURE 5.1 Still from *Jennifer's Shadow*. In a dream sequence, Jennifer finds herself bound to a bed. Directed by Demián Rugna. 2007, DSX Films.

The scene, or, more specifically, parts of the scene, metonymically approximates incidents of torture during *El Proceso*. The resemblance between the scene from *Jennifer's Shadow* and the actual torture of thousands during the dictatorship stem from the presence of the bed, Jennifer's confinement to it, and her extreme distress. The *Nunca más* ("Never Again") report commissioned by President Raúl Alfonsín upon his election in 1983 is filled with vivid testimonies by people who were subjected to sundry forms of torture, including being severely and repeatedly beaten, waterboarded, shocked with a cattle prod and/or electrodes, and raped. While the methods varied, the authors of the *Nunca más* report boil down the process in which victims were detained and treated. The authors cite the experience of C.G.F., a married woman, by noting her abduction at her workplace and then preface the remainder of her testimony with a generalization: "The usual procedure followed—car without markings ... blindfolded ... ending up in an unknown place ... tied to a bed" (45). The characterization of C.G.F as "the usual" renders being bound to a bed as a kind of Dirty War motif. *Jennifer's Shadow* does not thematically take up the Dirty War at any moment. Yet, Jennifer's bound and tortured state in Buenos Aires may seem to evoke the historical precedents.

Argentine horror cinema is littered with other moments in which the sadism visited upon a diegetic victim ostensibly repeats what actually occurred during *El Proceso*, with the use of electric cables in a zombie experiment in *Protocolo 48* (Carlos de la Fuente, 2012) and the theme of captivity in *Breaking Nikki* (Hernán Findling, 2009) being just two instances. *36 Pasos* (Adrián García Bogliano, 2006) also invokes the dictatorship through a rhetoric of discipline. Six young women (Priscila, Violeta, Marilú, Pilar, Flor, and Emilia played by Priscila Rauto, Andrea Duarte, Melisa Fernández, Noelia Balbo, Priscila Caldera, and Ariana Marchioni, respectively) all attended the same school growing up. The women are kidnapped from various places (a parking garage, an apartment, a country road, a parking lot outside a school, and a stadium) and taken to an isolated rural home. There, the women are forced to obey a regiment of rules based on obligatory fun, "armonía" ("harmony"), and "coexistencia," ("coexistence") with other rules elaborated in voice-overs spoken by Pilar, which are recited at the film's conclusion: "Tengo que aprender a callar. Tengo que tolerar. Tengo que escuchar. Tengo que ceder. Toda coexistencia armónica" ("I have to be quiet. I have to tolerate. I have to listen. I have to comply. All a harmonious coexistence"). The perpetrators of the kidnappings are the family of a former classmate, Tamara (Inés Sabarra), who the six young women bullied in grade school. Tamara's family subjects the young women to a twisted game of survival. Besides adhering to the aforementioned rules during their captivity, the women must wear bikinis, prepare a birthday party for Tamara, and maim or "train" one another with poison or other means. Tamara eventually arrives to the country home pretending to be another young woman,

Lucía, and takes her place among the others in order to carry out the final parts of an intricate and vengeful plot. Only one girl survives, Pilar, and, at the film's end, she is forced to remain with the family and partake in a macabre birthday celebration for Tamara.

The rhetoric of "*reglas*" ("rules") and "*armonía*" ("harmony") in *36 Pasos* quickly recalls the military's own discourse of harmony. Although a simplification of its aims, the dictatorship sought the reestablishment of national values while invoking a form of Christianity to justify the seizure of power and policies of state terrorism.[5] On the day of the coup on March 24, 1976, the military junta released a document outlining their objectives. A discourse of harmony or, better, an establishment of order, is readily apparent. Under a section titled "Propósito" ("Purpose"), the junta professed the aim of "[...] restituir los valores escenciales que sirven de fundamento a la conducción integral del Estado" ("[...] restore the essential values that serve as a base for the comprehensive conduct of the State") (A. García 169). Elsewhere in the same document, the military's leadership also declares its aim for a "[...] [r]elación armónica entre el Estado, el capital y el trabajo" ("[...] harmonious relationship between the State, capital, and labor") (A. García 170). In numerous speeches subsequent to the military's seizure of power, the leaders reiterated and underscored a rhetoric of order that reconciled specific components of society. For example, in 1976, Jorge Videla, General Commander of the Army and Argentina's de facto president between 1976 and 1981, spoke of the "[...] reimplantación de la libertad, la moral, el orden, la justicia y el derecho de la República" ("[...] reimplementation of liberty, morality, order, justice, and law") (A. García 175). Even with the return of democracy in 1983, Law 22.294/83, which pardoned the military for their brutal actions, mentions "[...] la voluntad sincera de reconciliación y la búsqueda de común de caminos para una armoniosa convivencia" ("[...] the sincere will of reconciliation and the shared search for paths towards a harmonious coexistence") (A. García 211). *Harmony* consistently was on the dictatorship's tongue and assumed an echo following its demise.[6]

Judith Filc highlights the various conceptions of family that the last dictatorship promoted and suggests how *36 Pasos* appears to subvert them. Under the dictatorship, family became "[...] el único sostén del orden social" ("[...] the unique support of social order") (Filc 45). The family, a unit specifically based on conservative principles (a father, mother, and children adhering to traditional roles), also acquired a physiological dimension as a "celúla de la nación" ("cell of the nation") (Filc 52). Such an idea made the family both protective of and vulnerable to a so-called subversive cancer or infection and allowed for a dichotomy of "good" and "bad" families (Filc 52). A good family protected their child from corrupting ideas, while a bad family did the opposite and neglected to protect the child. The family in *36 Pasos* appears as a parodic mode of exaggeration given the military's conception of family during the dictatorship. Despite lacking a father, Tamara's family employs a murderous and vengeful way of "protecting" Tamara (i.e., murdering the bullies and tormentors from grade school), and thus skewers a conservative notion of a "good" family. The family's love of their daughter is proportional to an accruing body count of young women.

The Last Gateway likewise features a character that seemingly alludes to the Dirty War. A witchlike figure appears various times in a hotel in the town of Plesentville to which Michael and his wife Marianne flee. The witch is pallid and decrepit (see fig. 5.2), as suggested by the slow thudding sounds that accompany her heavy gait. In a play on the fear of female reproduction, the witch leaves blood in her wake, and the camera often frames the witch's legs in medium close-up shots showing the blood trickle down onto the floor from what one assumes to be her womb. She initially appears within the first ten minutes of the film. She lumbers down a flight of stairs in the hotel and moans, "Where is my son?" The witch later appears in Michael and Marianne's room where she levitates and again asks, "Where is my son?" Towards the end of the film the hotel attendant, John, strikes the witch with a bat, and, for good measure, Marianne also pummels her. John and Marianne then drag the witch's body to the basement where she revives herself and threatens Marianne.

The witch in *The Last Gateway*, more specifically her repeated questioning of "Where is my son?" can easily recall Las Madres de la Plaza de Mayo, an indisputable icon of the Dirty War. Las Madres were generally the mothers of children and wives of husbands who were disappeared by the dictatorship, and, in a very public display of defiance and grief, Las Madres marched weekly, often carrying photos and demanding to know the whereabouts of family members. If, as Subero notes, "the notion of motherhood is intrinsically embedded in the Argentinian social, political, and cultural imaginary" (129), the forlorn but politically energized throngs of Las Madres rendered the mother a trope of *El Proceso*. The witch in *The Last Gateway* is marked as a bereaved mother in numerous ways. She moans and lumbers about as if grieving heavily. She bleeds from her womb and repeatedly demands to know her son's whereabouts.

FIGURE 5.2 Still from *The Last Gateway*, and the abject-mother figure. Directed by Demián Rugna. 2007, Farsa Producciones.

The projection of the Dirty War in the aforementioned scenes appears indisputable by virtue of how the events on-screen match the actual events that occurred during the last dictatorship. The figures of a distraught mother, acts of kidnapping, captivity, depictions of the family, and the rhetoric of "harmony" seem to allegorize the Dirty War through approximate analogies. Yet, the correspondences between the actual acts of violence and scenes of horror film violence ostensibly pierces the "veil" of allegory, that which "indicates that the text is split between surface or literal meanings and an allegorical meaning" (Tambling 30).[7] In other words, the on-screen violence in the horror films evokes real violence through correspondences and facile equal signs—torture in an Argentine horror film = torture under the dictatorship; kidnapping in an Argentine horror film = kidnapping under the dictatorship; and so on.

Yet, a reading that foregrounds the Dirty War is fraught with limitations and pitfalls. First, the specific scenes and narrative elements to which I allude are all staples of global contemporary horror cinema, of which Argentine horror cinema directors are astutely aware. The torture by raven in *Jennifer's Shadow* is a somewhat restrained variation of the gore and torture that is afoot in contemporary horror, especially in so-called torture porn films, such as *Hostel* (Eli Roth, 2005) and *Wolf Creek* (Greg McLean, 2005).[8] Captivity and kidnapping are remarkably common to recent horror film narratives.[9] Likewise, the rhetoric of "*armonía*" and "*reglas*," and the subversion of the family in *36 Pasos* have long appeared in horror cinema irrespective of a film's national origins. The theme of rules echoes the often warped didactic element of horror cinema narratives with lessons most commonly doled out to wayward teenagers in slasher films or feckless adults as in the aforementioned *Saw* series. As for the subversion of family in *36 Pasos*, Tony Williams's *Hearths of Darkness* evidences the ways in which conceptions of family figure into classical and contemporary horror cinema. Finally, the mother-witch in *The Last Gateway* recalls Barbara Creed's notion of the monstrous-feminine, which is indebted to Julia Kristeva's idea of the abject, which plays itself out in scores of horror films.[10] *Jennifer's Shadow* and *36 Pasos*, along with numerous other Argentine horror films, evince a keen understanding of horror genre motifs and manipulate those motifs.

Cultural dynamics of prohibition, saturation, and generational differences in Argentina further complicate the inclination to interpret select moments in Argentine horror as analogies of the Dirty War. In *La imagen justa*, Ana Amado addresses the delicate question of how to represent the violence of the Dirty War in film. Buttressed by debates surrounding the unrepresentability of horror while sharply conscious of the frequency and ubiquity with which stylized violence appears in contemporary media, Amado advocates an ethics of the image that consigns on-screen representations of the Dirty War off-screen: "Las tensiones entre vida y muerte, entre presente y pasado, entre rastro y memoria, solo pueden conjugarse en el marco de una estética limite o, más bien, de una ética de la imagen que [...] opta por desplazarla fuera de la escena, a los bordes del relato, por lo tanto, sometiéndola al régimen de la supresión" ("The tensions between life and death, between present and past, between trace and memory, only can be combined within the frame of an aesthetic limit or, better, within the frame of ethical image that [...] opts to displace that image off-screen, at the borders of the tale, thus submitting the image to a system of repression") (108).

To read the Dirty War into Argentine horror cinema, especially in instances of graphic violence like the torture-by-raven scene in *Jennifer's Shadow*, would obviously contravene Amado's notion of the ethical cinematic depiction of the Dirty War. Considering the horror films as allegories of the Dirty War presumes that a director is willing to project the Dirty War in the most graphic terms and ignore cultural prohibitions that would prevent such representations. While discussions of ethics and film production often center on realism and documentary,[11] Argentine horror directors and critics are sharply aware of such prohibitions. Though his remarks predated the release of horror films that deal explicitly with the Dirty War,

Nicanor Loreti stated in a 2007 interview that Argentine horror cinema simply could not broach the Dirty War. According to Loreti, the Dirty War is off-limits, lest one risk severe criticism, presumably from various sectors, such as survivors of the dictatorship and/or their families, film critics, and moviegoers. For a viewer to automatically and inevitably see the Dirty War in all Argentine horror cinema effectively ignores the prohibitions with which all Argentine filmmakers, horror included, have to contend.

Argentine horror cinema can be enlisted to forcefully refute a stereotype that Latin American cinema ultimately and exclusively adheres to tenets of cinematic realism and constantly confronts the legacies of brutal military dictatorships and political carnage.[12] In his article about Argentine horror cinema's distribution outside Argentina, Fernando Milsztjan alludes to films by Paura Flics and the ways in which the films "demostraron que el terror argentino no sólo tiene que ver con la dictadura militar" ("demonstrated that Argentine horror does not only have to do with the military dictatorship") (28). Argentine horror cinema, or at least a strain of it, delinks national cinema from the dictatorship's legacy. In the same paragraph, Milsztjan cites remarks by Hernán Moyano, a producer of Paura Flics, that intimate how Argentine horror cinema must confront global expectations about which countries or regions make particular genres: "Parece que los americanos pueden hacer cine de acción, horror y suspenso, los europeos el cine dramático y que a los latinoamericanos sólo nos queda la realidad social" ("It seems that the Americans can make action, horror, and suspense movies, the Europeans make dramas, and only films about social reality remain for Latin Americans") (28). Argentine horror cinema thus becomes a foil to the prevailing expectation beyond Argentina that its cinema is fixated on "reality" and that realism is the sole mode that dominates the country or the entire region's cinematic output.

While Argentine horror cinema must contend with foreign expectations as it circulates transnationally, films appear to have escaped a domestic interpretive reflex to view all horror films as allegories of the Dirty War. Speaking specifically to a period that predates the aforementioned Argentine horror films that explicitly treat the Dirty War, reports on Argentine horror cinema in newspapers and online film journals and message boards largely lack any reference to the conflict. Instead, reviews and discussions of Argentine horror films typically revolve around issues of narrative, cinematography, acting, script, and special effects.[13] Diana Taylor famously used the term *percepticide* to describe "the blinding of the population that the military promoted by making what was so obviously visible [...] seemingly invisible" (10), namely the atrocities that were occurring. The absence of discussions about the Dirty War in Argentina is not a form of percepticide or a failure by Argentine horror fans and critics to see the resemblances between on-screen violence and state terrorism under the last dictatorship. Instead, as I have articulated previously, the on-screen violence potentially becomes indexically dispersed, geographically pointing to other national crises (paranoia, neoliberalism, fear of urban violence) and even crises outside Argentina (the War on Terror). The films also can be received in other ways that do not foreground national or transnational socioeconomic dilemmas and can instead center on gore and special effects, affective resonances, a soundtrack, and/or dialogue.

Argentine horror films' circulation abroad enables multiple dynamics of reception contingent on a viewer's familiarity with Argentine horror and to what degree she or he allows the Dirty War to govern an allegorical interpretation. A viewer who is completely ignorant of the Dirty War and Argentine history presumably will not consider the films as allegories of the last dictatorship. On the other hand, for those viewers who are exclusively aware of the Dirty War—either through Argentine films or some other medium—might be inclined to interpret Argentine horror films solely as allegories of the Dirty War. Alternatively, viewers cognizant of the Dirty War and other national crises must consider whether the Dirty War ultimately anchors an interpretation to the exclusion of other events or whether the Dirty War coexists with other possible allegories of crises in Argentina as well as elsewhere.

These three ways of reading Argentine horror cinema embodies Judith Mayne's ideas about spectatorship as a negotiation between the film and the viewer: how the viewer uses, interprets, and appropriates a film, and how the film acts on a viewer. Mayne's idea of negotiation undermines any argument for a viewer's pure agency vis-à-vis a movie or, going to the opposite extreme, a film's working on a passive audience. For all her skepticism of different conceptions of negotiation and spectatorship studies in general, Mayne validates those local studies of spectatorship "insofar as they problematize the ideal reader" (94) and foster a kind of tension that complicates theoretical and one-dimensional abstractions of audiences.[14] Likewise, Mayne asserts the continuing importance of spectatorship identity (race, class, gender, sexual identity, and age) (101). Besides conceiving the readings of Argentine horror films as a question of negotiation, here I simply assert that a viewer's knowledge of Argentine cultural and historical events is yet another facet to consider in terms of spectatorial identity. This knowledge can affect the spectator's negotiations with an Argentine horror film, or group of films. In other words, a spectator's awareness or ignorance of Argentina may or may not result in allegorical readings of a single national crisis (i.e., Argentina's Dirty War), multiple crises (e.g., the Dirty War, neoliberalism, and/or the War on Terror), or no crises. Cultural and historical knowledge of Argentina, how that knowledge interacts with other facets of identity, and the way in which a film works on a viewer are all factors that problematize the notion of an ideal viewer. In turn, there are possibly multiple viewers constructing none or multiple allegories when viewing Argentine horror cinema; as stated previously, allegorical readings are only one mode of pleasurable reception for a horror film, or any film for that matter.

The temptation to consider Argentine horror cinema to be solely about the Dirty War eclipses all other possible allegorical readings and effectively short-circuits the very concept of allegory and its polysemous dimension to enable multiple meanings. If the Dirty War dominates interpretation, then a particular national allegory looms over all readings of all Argentine horror films, reducing the horror films to mere metonyms of the Dirty War. Yet, for all my efforts to undermine a single and particular interpretation of Argentine horror cinema as an allegorization of the Dirty War, that interpretation hovers over the analysis. In *Specters of Marx*, Derrida describes how Marxism continued to haunt Europe despite the supposed triumph of capitalism and liberal democracy accompanying the fall of the Berlin Wall and the collapse of the Soviet Union. According to Derrida, "The European alliance is haunted by what it excludes, combats, or represses" (77).

Derrida's claim gave rise to a philosophy of history—hauntology—in which, despite the claims for an end to a particular ideology, the same ideology remains as "traces of traces" (Derrida xx).[15] In *Ghostly Matters*, Avery Gordon provides a framework for bringing such spectral ideas to bear on fictional narratives. For Gordon, a ghost does not refer to some spooky wraith: "[t]he ghost or the apparition is one form by which something lost, or barely visible, or seemingly not there to our supposedly well-trained eyes, makes itself known or apparent to us, in its own way, of course" (8). Gordon outlines ways to consider knowledge that escapes purely rational systems, and fiction proffers crucial sites to discern the aforementioned ghost: "[...] fictions are what stand on the other side of the facts in our lingering Manichaean scheme, and so they have helped to highlight the problems with 'logical and chronological frameworks' and 'the simplicity of casual chains'" (Gordon 25).

Returning to Derrida's notion about the impossibility of shutting out Marxism, any attempt to exclude the Dirty War from interpretations of Argentine horror cinema likewise allows the conflict to loom precisely due to an attempt at exclusion. A spectator's possible indecisiveness of not knowing whether the Dirty War appears as a trace in Argentine horror forces a move past a glib reception that makes screen violence invoke a national tragedy. Whether aforementioned codes of horror cinema—torture, abductions, captivity, rules—are guises that merely allow Argentine horror films to be categorized as horror, or whether such codes double as allegories of the Dirty War is a complicated dance that resists reductive models of spectatorship. Argentine horror film directors, critics, and fans appear to have largely omitted the Dirty War from discussions of most Argentine horror cinema. Yet, the films' circulation beyond national borders subjects them to various modes of reception and expectation elsewhere by viewers, myself included. Again, referring to Derrida, "[t]he specter is also, among other things, what one imagines what one thinks one sees and which one projects" (125).

FITTING GENRES: MOMENTS OF HORROR IN *CRÓNICA DE UNA FUGA*

In *State Repression and the Labors of Memory*, Elizabeth Jelin refers to an article by Patricia Rojas about youth and memory practices in Argentina. For Jelin and Rojas, graffiti, murals, and street singing illustrate how, in comparison to their elders, younger generations engage with different media to express their perspective of the last dictatorship (111). A similar dynamic of generational differences plays out in select Argentine horror films, of which Adrián Caetano's *Crónica de una fuga* may be included.[16] The film represents *El Proceso* in ways that are distinct from that of preceding films that explicitly narrativize the Dirty War. Horacio Bernades's review of *Crónica* in *Página 12* underscores how the film breaks with cinematic convention, and Bernades places Caetano's film in opposition to national cinema from the 1980s, even going so far as to observe that it "parece enteramente pensada como reacción frente a aquel viejo cine" ("seems entirely conceived as a reaction against that old cinema").[17]

Crónica is based on a testimonial account written by Claudio Tamburini titled *Pase libre: La fuga de la Mansión Seré*, along with the input of Guillermo Fernández.[18] The film commences by recounting the disappearance of Tamburini, a college student in Buenos Aires, in 1977. Falsely tipped off by another prisoner, military operatives invade Tamburini's parents' home, terrorize his sister and mother, and demand to know Tamburini's whereabouts. The operatives eventually locate and capture Tamburini at his own apartment and transport him to Mansión Seré in Morón, a city located outside Buenos Aires. Tamburini is held with other male prisoners close to his age. Told ellipitically over 120 days, their military captors subject the detainees to physical and psychological torture of various kinds. Sensing their impending execution, a group of five prisoners, which include Tamburini and Fernández, successfully escape from Mansión Seré.

Crónica is infused with various genres, including suspense, Western, escape films, and most importantly here, horror.[19] Horror's salient place in the film was immediately apparent to critics following the film's theatrical release. In *Clarín*, Diego Lerer likens the first hour of *Crónica* to a horror film, and, at the moment that five prisoners decide to escape, "termina la [película] de terror [y] arranca la de suspenso" ("the horror film ends and the suspense film begins") ("Un escape"). Writing in *Leer cine*, Santiago García associates particular formal elements with precise forms of horror, even going so far as to link those elements with a particular director: "Los colores, las texturas, el sonido y los encuadres se asocian muchas veces con el cine de terror, pero no con cualquiera, sino con esa estilización clásica y funcional propia del cineasta John Carpenter" ("The colors, textures, sound, and framing often are associated with not just any horror cinema, but rather with a classical and functional stylization typical of director John Carpenter"). Bernades, for his part, identifies "el terror gótico" ("Gothic horror") in the film.

With the possible exception of *Garaje Olimpo*'s use of claustrophobic spaces and scenes of torture, *Crónica* was unprecedented as a commercial film that draws on horror codes to cinematically depict the Dirty War. Unlike the Argentine horror films discussed in the previous section, *Crónica* possesses explicit textual and extratextual markers that invoke a historical moment; the film wears its context and sources on its sleeve. *Crónica* debuted at the Cannes Film Festival in 2005 under its original title *Buenos Aires, 1977*. Intimating its escape film dimensions, the cover of the DVD distributed in Argentina reads, "Basada en una historia real. 120 DÍAS. 4 JÓVENES. UNA OPORTUNIDAD" ("Based on a true story. 120 days. 4 young men. One opportunity"). A circular seal also appears on the cover that reads "Versión libre de la novela Pase Libre: La fuga de la Mansión Seré. Claudio Tamburini" ("Loose adaptation of the novel Pase libre: La fuga de la Mansión Seré. Claudio Tamburini"). As for the film itself, *Crónica* opens with a lengthy epigraph underscoring the film's historical and geographical coordinates and reiterating its testimonial sources. In addition to dating the military coup, the epigraph alludes to the trials of military officials in 1985 for human rights violations. The text's last two lines read: "Esta historia está basada en el testimonio de dos víctimas de dicha dictadura" ("This story is based on the testimony of two victims of the aforementioned dictatorship"). Finally, the film's testimonial sources are repeated some ten minutes into the film during the opening credits. An imposed text reads: "Versión libre de la novela *Pase libre—La fuga de la Mansión Seré* de Claudio Tamburini con colaboración de Guillermo Fernández" ("Loose adaptation of the novel *Pase libre—La fuga de la Mansión Seré* by Claudio Tamburini with the collaboration of Guillermo Fernández").

Crónica's testimonial aspects—on both the film's aforementioned DVD cover and in the film itself—preemptively and immediately situate the film in tension with its horror dimensions while undermining any feasible notion that it will be a typical instance of *cine testimonio*, which prioritizes particular modes of documentary and realism.[20] On the DVD cover (see fig. 5.3), an image of the film's version of Mansión Seré sits in the center between two characters—Tamburini (Rodrigo de la Serna) and Huguito (Pablo Echarri)—and close to the aforementioned testimonial seal.[21] Mansión Seré is presented as a kind of haunted house or Gothic mansion. The structure is faded black and white and sits on a tilted plane anticipating some of the Dutch angles that frame the house in the movie.[22]

Prima facie, the film's adaptation of testimonial interviews and literature and use of horror cinema codes may appear incongruent. Testimonial literature, like its cinematic counterpart, enjoys a vaunted status as evidenced by the popularity of testimonials and the reams of academic criticism on the testimonial genre. Among other factors, testimonial literature's esteemed position among critics is partially built on authenticity and a kind of realism that purportedly yields truth. George Yúdice's definition of the genre conveys such a dynamic: "testimonial writing may be defined as an authentic narrative, told by a witness who is moved to narrate by the urgency of a situation

FIGURE 5.3 DVD cover of *Crónica de una fuga*, distributed in Argentina. The circular seal advertising the film's testimonial source appears in red font in the bottom-left corner. Directed Israel Adrián Caetano. 2006, IFC First Take.

(e.g., war, oppression, revolution, etc.). [...] Truth is summoned in the cause of denouncing a present situation of exploitation and oppression or in exorcising and setting aright official history" (17). Although *Pase libre* was written and published some twenty-five years after the actual escape and was not dictated orally to an intermediary, the film's testimonial credentials appear intact.[23] As stated in the film's opening credits, the film is based on a written text and interviews with another escapee from Mansión Seré. Moreover, the inclusion of the words "*Versión libre*" ("loose adaptation") in the credits allows a certain degree of latitude for the film's adaptation of its testimonial sources.

Horror cinema, in contrast to testimony's position as a respected genre (at least within US leftist academic circles), is generally regarded as disreputable. Brigid Cherry's comments are instructive: "[...] the whole [horror cinema] genre is potentially tainted. It has therefore been denigrated or ignored, never quite wholly acceptable, and relegated to areas of low budget, independent production" (12). One is thus left to ask if *Crónica*, which is based on a work belonging to the venerated genre of testimonial literature, is somehow contaminated by horror?

Crónica's amalgam of testimony and horror is not necessarily unprecedented or at loggerheads. Zeroing in on a single facet of testimonial literature, its basis in reality, the film is hardly the first horror film based on or claimed to be based on real events.[24] Cynthia Freeland's notion of "reality horror" and the subgenre of found-footage horror are just two ways in which registries of reality infuse the horror genre and can be located in Caetano's film.[25] Nevertheless, *Crónica*'s reliance on testimony in concert with horror is absolutely distinct. Moreover, horror's cinematic codes here do not necessarily undermine testimonial sources by somehow rendering the narrative "less real." Rather, in a point I will explore further, such codes operate primarily to imbue scenes with a psychological dimension enabling a cinematic rendering or adaptation of written and oral testimonies. *Pase libre* itself, as well as Alicia Partnoy's written testimony, *La escuelita*, makes use of horror motifs, especially in its textual depiction of Mansión Seré. The use of horror in *Crónica* is apt.[26]

If horror does not undermine testimony, then the testimony likewise does not undermine the horror. The film's basic story adheres to broad definitions of horror. In her study of female spectatorship and classical horror, Rhona Berenstein offers a definition of classical horror: a fantastic monster that defies logic (19). The logic-defying monster in *Crónica* is the military regime. Metaphoric analogies aside, horror manifests itself in *Crónica* not so much in the presence of illogical entities. Formal cinematic elements associated with particular registries of horror are invoked and refined to forge cinematic spaces that project characters' mental state over being kidnapped and detained.

The aforementioned comments by Santiago García and Horacio Bernades have let the cat out of the bag; classical and Gothic horror motifs generally dominate *Crónica*. In the introduction to *Screening the Gothic*, Lisa Hopkins identifies decaying castles and mansions as one of the primary markers of Gothic literature that appear in its cinematic form.[27] For her part, Misha Kavka characterizes Gothic horror cinema according to specific *"visual codes"* (211), which include long shots of a castle on a hill (215), "the close-ups of mad, staring eyes" (210), and, most significantly for my analysis of Caetano's film, the "plasticity of space" in which an on-screen space expands and contracts through camera placement, editing, and lighting (214, 215). Hopkins's and Kavka's concise formulations of a cinematic Gothic both center on the depiction of space, and the Gothic in *Crónica* is no more readily evident than in the on-screen depiction of Mansión Seré, the clandestine detention center where Claudio Tamburini and others are held captive.

Mansión Seré does not appear until some ten minutes into the film following Tamburini's capture by military operatives. The two cars holding the military personnel who capture Tamburini are shown driving through a rural countryside and over railroad tracks. A black wrought-iron gate attached to two large cement columns foreshadows the mansion's dilapidated condition. The operatives' cars stop at the locked gate overgrown with vegetation. A gonglike sound is heard on the soundtrack, and the film's opening credits begin to appear. The mansion, or rather fragmented portions of it, takes center stage for approximately a minute; no actors appear. The first shot of the mansion shows the structure's front door and steps framed from a low angle. The camera is tilted, and eerie violin and single piano notes play. Similar to the gate, vegetation covers the steps. The next shot is of the same door and steps, although the camera now tilts in a different direction. Such shots characterize the sequence of the mansion: the house is repeatedly framed from low angles by an oblique camera. We see Mansión Seré from different sides, but, again, only in fragments—a shuttered window, a portion of the patio, a terrace, a column. The house's dilapidated state is readily apparent from its gray streaks, peeling paint, broken shutter, missing rungs on terrace banisters, partially collapsed ceiling above a porch, and the overgrown plants and vines. The soundtrack is typical of a horror film: a melangé of violin, piano, and an intermittent high-pitched doppler-like sound. The music sometimes gives away to whispering as if the house is haunted. After a nearly a minute, the caravan carrying the military personnel and Tamburini approach the mansion, and the camera is positioned inside the house from a lower-level window. The off-screen absence of the caravan further intimates the mansion's geographically marginal position, as if the caravan had been driving for a minute after passing through the gate in order to the reach the actual house. Only when Tamburini is taken inside the house do we finally see an establishing shot of the entire front facade of the house. The house is framed from a low angle endowing it with an imposing presence.

The sequence equates Mansión Seré with other cinematic depictions of haunted houses. Akin to the hushed voices heard at the beginning of *Death Knows Your Name*, the whispers on *Crónica*'s soundtrack suggest a ghostly presence. The low angles, tilted camera, and fragmented images of the mansion create a kind of visual confusion reminiscent of other horror films that feature haunted structures, such as *The Haunting* (Robert Wise, 1963), *Poltergeist* (Tobe Hooper, 1982), *Evil Dead 2* (Sam Raimi, 1987), and *Insidious* (James Wan, 2010). Mansión Seré maintains its disorienting stature. A quarter of the way through the film, an Air Force jeep pulls up to the mansion with two soldiers. The camera frames the two soldiers from above. The soldiers descend from each side of the jeep and grab a large soup pot. The framing recalls a shot from Carl Theodore Dreyer's *The Passion of Jean of Arc* (1928) in which soldiers and civilians are framed upside down before

FIGURE 5.4 Still from *Crónica de una fuga*. A shot of Mansión Seré as soldiers carry a pot from a Jeep to the front door. Directed Israel Adrián Caetano. 2006, IFC First Take.

Jean of Arc's execution. In *Crónica* the camera captures the Air Force soldiers from behind and above by panning to the left, which frames the soldiers against the tilted backdrop of the mansion (see fig. 5.4).[28]

The mansion's unsettling aspect in *Crónica* extends to the house's interior. Referring to the exploration of a house by new tenants that often initiates the plot of a haunted house film, Barry Curtis considers "the journey through the house [to be] characterized by visual incoherence and disorientation" (35). Shortly after the arrival and torture of Tamburini's character, we see a shot of a dimly lit corridor in which a man appears holding a maté gourd and a tea kettle. The camera does not induce a visual disturbance per se; instead, the set design elicits the disturbance. A kaleidoscope of green wallpaper and nearly indistinguishable floor tiles envelope the man with the maté gourd. He never appears again in the film, giving him a kind of wraithlike quality. Shots of corridors appear in any number of horror films set in part within a house: *Poltergeist*, *Inferno* (Dario Argento, 1980), *The Amityville Horror* (Stuart Rosenberg, 1979), *The Shining* (Stanley Kubrick, 1980), *The People under the Stairs* (Wes Craven, 1991), and *House of the Devil* (Ti West, 2009). Albeit distinct, the corridor shot in *Crónica* further tethers the film to the horror genre.

Other moments that present Mansión Seré's interior conform to a presentation of space common to horror cinema. In her analysis of *Crónica*, Maribel Cedeño briefly focuses on the low-height and neutral-angle shots of a door and a window that appear nearly an hour into the film. For Cedeño, the shots evidence *Crónica*'s depiction of Mansión Seré as a haunted house (57–58). These shots also signal the film's spatial construction as inspired by John Carpenter's films, as Santiago García rightfully pointed out in his review of Caetano's film.[29] Caetano has openly gushed about his admiration for Carpenter's films, and even penned an introduction to a book published in Argentina about Carpenter's oeuvre, titled *Encerrados toda la noche: el cine de John Carpenter*/"Closed in All Night: The Cinema of John Carpenter," by Matías Orta. In an interview with Silvia Schwarzböck, Caetano alludes to the influences of directors or particular films such as Bresson's *Un condamné à mort s'est echappé ou Le vent souffle où il veut*/*A Man Escaped* (1956). In addition to George Romero, Caetano remarks that "[. . .] tenía en mente mucho de Carpenter, con el tema de cómo manejar los espacios, y la música, muy minimalista, muy de clima" ("I definitely had Carpenter in mind regarding the aspect of constructing space, the minimalist and ambient music") (Schwarzböck, *Estudio crítico* 79).

Crónica's presentation of the mansion's interior occasionally departs from Carpenter's influence. Soon after a session of being "submarined," the prisoners are ordered to kneel in the hallway and pray loudly. Suddenly, there is a cut and the camera appears two or three floors below. The camera spins and captures a winding staircase in an extreme high angle before it eventually stops and tracks backward, showing a gaggle of refrigerators, presumably looted from victims who were kidnapped by military operatives, is visible.[30] The prisoners' praying remains on the soundtrack and creates an aural tethering to what we no longer see. By briefly wandering about divorced from any character's perspective, the camera achieves a measure of autonomy and acquires a "unique" presence (Johnson 51–52). If such shots are reminiscent of Antonioni's *The Passenger*, or, more recently, Cuarón's *Children of Men* when the camera leaves Theo's side to briefly linger over the detainment of immigrants, here the camera's wandering suggests something else. In lieu of a ghost presence lingering about the premises, the camera projects the spatial effects of torture that can consists of a vicious receding or brutal expansion. In *The Body in Pain*, Elaine Scarry argues, "It is the intense pain that destroys a person's self and world, a destruction experienced spatially as either the contraction of the universe down to the immediate vicinity of the body or as the body swelling to fill the entire universe" (35). The sequence from *Crónica* suggests both. Having been beaten and blindfolded, the captives in *Crónica* are in the throes of a shrinking world. Nevertheless, the expansion happens not by way of the body, but through the voice. As Scarry notes elsewhere, "[T]he voice becomes a final source of self-extension; so long as one is speaking, the self extends out beyond the boundaries of the body, occupies a space much larger than the body" (33). Yet, the expansion is compromised; the prisoners' words, their prayer, are not of their volition; they pray under duress and, at times, under orders from their captors.

Gothic horror cinema codes further accentuate bodies in pain. The lighting and use of a bleach bypass renders the prisoners' skins especially pallid. Their wounds—bruises and scrapes suffered from beatings—are set in relief by the skins' hue. The prisoners generally wear only underwear and a blindfold which they often lift in the absence of their captors. As Schwarzböck notes, the lack of clothing, their skin, and their wounds recall paintings of religious martyrs (*Estudio crítico* 55), perhaps more specifically El Greco's paintings of Christ and Saint Sebastian. Such a dimension, however, is potentially problematic, as if the prisoners in *Crónica* were invariably all martyrs of sorts, unwilling to renounce some belief the government deemed subversive. Many prisoners, as exemplified by Tamburini, had no political leanings that remotely approached the leftist ideals that the military supposedly was trying to eliminate. Tamburini, as happened to other detainees, was captured for a most unfortunate reason: another prisoner provided his name under the threat of torture. On the other hand, *Crónica*'s depiction of the prisoners' bodies according to religious aesthetics ironically appropriates the very Christianity the dictatorship invoked in justifying their own doctrine. In other words, given the prisoners' physical depiction in the film, the military metaphorically detains and tortures icons of a religious doctrine they allegedly exalt.

The prisoners' wounds are almost the only visual evidence of the torture that takes place almost entirely off-screen and signals *Crónica*'s ethical grounding. Shortly after arriving at Mansión Seré, his captors torture Claudio Tamburini using a *picana eléctrica*, a metal prod charged with an electrical current similar to instruments used in slaughterhouses to goad animals to move from one pen to another. The initial torture of Tamburini transpires entirely off-screen. The camera assumes the point-of-view of Tamburini and shakes with each application of the *picana* in order to simulate the body's jolt.

Such a depiction of torture adheres to tenets of classical horror cinema that suggest violence.[31] Stephen Prince identifies the use of shadows as one such common formal technique to intimate violence: "Silhouetted depictions of violence are a major and recurring visual code in films of the 1930s, providing an indirect means for depicting acts of brutality" (*Classical Film Violence* 75). Suggestion, while not entirely absent from contemporary horror, is by no means the dominant mode of screen violence in recent horror cinema.[32] Instead, graphic depictions of violence usually centered on mutilating the body tend to dominate the genre.

Crónica's invocation of classical horror to depict torture adheres to Ana Amado's formulation mentioned previously, in which violence that happened during the Dirty War should be displaced off-screen. Caetano has alluded to a sort of catch-22 dilemma in portraying torture in a film about the Dirty War and has stated, "Es imposible hacer una película sobre este tema y no mostrar nada de la tortura. La tortura no se muestra, se cuenta" ("It is impossible to make a film about this topic and not show torture. Torture is not shown, it is told") (Schwarzböck, *Estudio crítico* 82–83). Absent the visible torture, the viewer must perceive the act in other ways: auditorily through the battery buzz supplying current to the *picana* and visually through the camera shaking.[33] And while the viewer does see Tamburini tortured once,[34] the camera does not assume some assaultive or predatory point-of-view gaze characteristic of a slasher film, in which the camera mimics a stalker's movements in pursuit of a victim (Balanzategui 167). The camera in *Crónica* never assumes the point-of-view of the torturer, preempting any remote chance that a viewer would assume a sadistic form of spectatorship by identifying with the torturer.[35]

Crónica's depiction of torture largely adheres to classical horror cinema codes. According to Caetano, "No quería hacer gore" ("I did not want to do gore") (Schwarzböck, *Estudio crítico* 84). If Caetano's subsequent remarks refrain from establishing a hierarchy of horror aesthetics that places classical and Gothic horror over more graphic subgenres, his comments exhibit a sensitivity: "Si yo hago una película de terror, hago que al tipo le corten la cabeza, no tengo problema con eso. Pero no me parecía prudente en este caso" ("If I were to make a horror film, I would have some guy get his head chopped off. I don't have a problem with that. But that does not seem sensible in this case") (Schwarzböck, *Estudio crítico* 85). *Crónica*'s uses of classical horror cinema codes—specifically, suggested screen violence—operate as a "safe" mode for depicting the Dirty War, taking the teeth out, so to speak, of a genre that often forces a confrontation with uncomfortable realities. Commenting on Jörg Buttergeit's *Nekromantik* films, Linnie Blake zeroes in on the films' gore as a means of compelling viewers to deal with undesirable legacies of Germany's role in World War II. For Blake, "[...] viscerality forces the audience to look at that which they would rather avoid" (24). Laura Podalsky and Dierdra Reber have pointed out the presence of affect in contemporary Latin American cinema and, for Podalsky in particular, how films "[encourage] audience members to recognize in visceral ways the affective legacies of the recent past as well as newer sensibilities emerging in the contemporary moment" (*Politics of Affect* 83). *Crónica* forces the recognition of gradations of affect vis-à-vis particular topics in which the form or intensity of an affect can be hemmed in or circumscribed according to prevailing cultural mores. *Crónica*'s use of classical horror opts for a less confrontational and accepted way in which horror cinema could project the Dirty War. It is worth noting that film critics in Argentina did not complain about *Crónica* and its use of horror.

One is thus left to ponder the critical reception of more gory depictions of the Dirty War, which explicitly broach the conflict as the main narrative unfolds. Paco Cabezas's *Aparecidos/The Appeared* (2007), Adrián García Bogliano's *Sudor frío*, and *Malditos sean!* are three such horror films that directly allude to the Dirty War. Temporarily setting aside *Sudor frío* and *Malditos sean!*, *Aparecidos*, an Argentine-Spanish coproduction, relates a scenario in which two siblings, Pablo and Malena, travel from Spain to see their father who is being kept alive artificially, and to decide whether to let him die or not. Pablo and Malena travel south from Buenos Aires and, through visions, learn that their father was a torturer during the Dirty War. *Aparecidos* contains graphic depictions of violence with a specter of the father graphically waterboarding and assaulting his own children.[36]

Diego Lerer's review of the film in *Clarín* briefly focuses on the nationality of the director and main actors and illustrates the problem of representing the military's violence in a horror film:

> ¿Una película de suspenso con los desaparecidos de la última dictadura militar? ¿No será mucho? Eso pensarán muchos argentinos que no se atreverían a tratar un tema así para generar sustos en el público. Es por eso que la película, si bien se centra en un misterio ligado a los desaparecidos locales, es de origen español. Su director y sus protagonistas son de allí, más allá de que la acción que transcurra en la Argentina.

> A suspense film featuring the disappeared from the last military dictatorship? Wouldn't that be too much? That is what many Argentines will think who would not dare contend that such a theme be used to scare an audience. Is it for this reason that the film, as it focuses on a mystery linked to the disappeared, is of Spanish origin. Its director and actors are from there, away from where the action took place in Argentina. ("Rodeados")

While Lerer goes on to praise certain parts of *Aparecidos*, his remarks and allusion to the film as a "película de suspenso" in lieu of a horror movie reinforce Álvaro Fernández's view that Argentine film critics appear reticent and even unwilling to entertain the notion that horror would be an appropriate film genre to narrativize the Dirty War (276). Moreover, one aspect of Lerer's critique loosely embodies the aforementioned opinions of Nicanor Loreti concerning the pitfalls of representing the Dirty War through horror genre codes. Yet, Lerer goes further and delves into the nationality of the director and cast: a Spanish director and actors can make a horror film about Argentina's Dirty War precisely because they are Spanish. They are not from where the actual trauma took place, Argentina, and so could not internalize the same cultural and cinematic prohibitions. Despite its global reach, the prosthetic memories of the Dirty War do not instill the same filmic taboos for non-Argentines.[37] Given Lerer's indictment of

Aparecidos, Caetano's use of classic and Gothic horror appears justified insofar as he anticipates the film's critical reception in Argentina and what is permitted at that historical moment. Classic and Gothic horror make the Dirty War palatable for a domestic audience, including critics.

LAUGHTER AND MEMORY: PARODIES OF DIRTY WAR OPERATIVES IN ARGENTINE HORROR CINEMA

In her study of the Dirty War in Argentine cinema released between 1983 and 1993, Constanza Burrucúa charts the movement and narrativization of the Dirty War across different film genres: political and paramilitary thrillers, women's film and melodramas, and more self-reflexive films, such Lita Stantic's *Un muro de silencio/ A Wall of Silence* (1993). Burrucúa considers the appropriateness of the genres in light of political events, and each genre operates as a signpost in a development of how Argentine society confronted filmically the legacies of the Dirty War. For instance, she, along with Octavio Getino, contend that *La historia oficial* was an acceptable way of presenting the Dirty War at that particular historical moment in Argentina (127). While Álvaro Fernández rightfully comments on the reluctance of some Argentine critics to acknowledge horror's capacity to present the Dirty War, *Crónica* appears to signal a sea change with regard to which cinematic genres could be brought to bear on the national tragedy. Whereas Blake alludes to horror's capacity to "[expose] dominant ideologies' will to deny trauma's centrality to national identity" elsewhere (6), Argentine horror films obviously operate under different conditions. With the passing of time, film genres other than melodrama and documentaries were deemed appropriate to memorialize the Dirty War under state auspices as embodied by INCAA.

Subsequent to *Crónica*'s release in 2006, INCAA provided support for three additional Argentine productions, or coproductions, that explicitly deal with the Dirty War and fit squarely within the horror genre: *Aparecidos* (Spain-Argentina), *Sudor frío* (Argentina), and *Malditos sean!* (Argentina). Akin to *Crónica*, the films can be examined for their stylization of screen violence in narratives that expressly broach the Dirty War, and I prefer to take up stylistics of screen violence alongside a recurring trope: caricatures of operatives (police officers, paramilitaries, and military officers) who work or worked for the dictatorship. Though worthy of closer analysis,[38] I switch out *Aparecidos* for two films by Farsa Producciones along with *Sudor frío* and *Malditos sean!*: *Nunca asistas a este tipo de fiesta* / "Never Go to This

Kind of Party" (Pablo Parés, Paulo Soria, and Hernán Sáez, 2000) and its sequel *Nunca más asistas a este tipo de fiesta* / "Never Again Go to This Kind of Party" (Pablo Parés, Paulo Soria, and Hernán Sáez, 2010).

As discussed in the previous chapter, comedy frequently is paired with horror cinema, and *Sudor frío*, *Malditos sean!*, *Nunca*, and *Nunca más* achieve a degree of humor in part by lampooning a character, or characters, who either has some association with the military dictatorship, or embodies some facet of the junta's discourse. Poking fun at heinous dictators and their minions in cinema is hardly unprecedented. Hitler and his supporters were skewered in films, perhaps most notably in Chaplin's *The Great Dictator* in 1940. Moreover, Luis García Berlanga's *¡Bienvenido, Mr. Marshall!* / *Welcome, Mr. Marshall!* (1953) and *Plácido* (1961) ridiculed Francisco Franco's regime, and *Team America: World Police* (Trey Parker, 2004) mocks North Korea's leader Kim Jong Il while scathingly razzing US politics and the War on Terror.

The four Argentine films in question here may appear distinct among Dirty War films in the use of horror in conjunction with comedy. *Crónica*, as well as any number of other Dirty War films (*La noche de los lápices*/ *The Night of the Pencils* [Héctor Olivera, 1986], *La historia oficial*, *Kamchatka*, *Garaje Olimpo*, *Cautiva*/ *Captive* [Gaston Biraben, 2003], *El secreto de sus ojos*, etc.), are largely bereft of comedy. Yet, if I contend that *Sudor frío*, *Nunca*, *Nunca más*, and *Malditos sean!* use horror and comedy in unique ways, they also represent a resumption of comedy to depict the Dirty War. *No habrás más penas ni olvido*/ *Funny Dirty Little War* (Héctor Olivera, 1983) offered the possibility that comedy tinged with sequences of graphic violence could present the Dirty War, or more specifically, the period preceding it. While Olivera's film satirically allegorizes the bitter split between right- and left-wing Peronists factions prior to the dictatorship, allusions to the Dirty War appear through an acrid rhetoric of eliminating subversion, abductions, home invasions, and even torture. The violence, however, never enters into a comedic register. Distinct from *No habrás*, the modes of screen violence in horror films in question here work in concert with comedy to cast an operative of the dictatorship as a buffoon and interweave memory and humor. While Jean Franco rightfully describes an "official policy of amnesia" with some administrations in Argentina and other Latin American countries (*Decline and Fall* 238–42), the fusion of horror and comedy suggests that select modes of remembering the Dirty War by younger filmmakers resonate not only in practices of *escrache*, graffiti, or demonstrations, but also in horror comedies.

THE THREAT OF YOUTH

Though lacking the same notoriety as Farsa's *Plaga zombie* trilogy and *Filmatron*, *Nunca* and *Nunca más* have been screened at alternative exhibition circuits, have DVD distribution through Videoflims, and can be viewed through Farsa's YouTube channel. Both films take place in the same rural setting and feature many of the same actors. In the first film, Colonel Santoro (Berta Muñiz) has taken his adolescent son, Fito (Juani Conserva), on a fishing trip during which the colonel intends to teach his son supposed military survival skills, such as finding and eating "cachos de bosta" ("chips of dried manure"), should he ever lack sufficient food when in the "wild." Shortly after the start of *Nunca*, the colonel's plans for a tranquil father-son excursion are nixed by a homosexual male couple (played by Nicanor Loreti and Urto Urquiza) frolicking in the water and playing paddle ball. Colonel Santoro initially refers to the queer couple as "putos de mierda" ("fucking fags"). Colonel Santoro also must contend with the presence of six teenagers intent on merrymaking with music, drugs, alcohol, and dancing—El Colo (Paulo Soria), Karina (Paz Cogorno), Vicky (Sandra de Vinzenzi), Quique (Walter Cornás), Rolo (Pablo Parés), and Lucho (Hernán Sáez). The band of partygoers constitute "subversive" elements in the eyes of Colonel Santoro. At night, the Colonel and Fito attempt to sleep outside in sleeping bags, but Fito becomes scared and begs his father to leave. The colonel eventually relents and knocks on the door where the teens are cavorting to ask if he and his son can spend the night. The teens allow Colonel Santoro and his son to stay in a spare bedroom. However, despite forbidding Fito from leaving the room and partying with the teens, the son does so twice and gets drunk on the second occasion. In the morning, Colonel Santoro cannot find Fito, and interrogates the teens as to his whereabouts. As Colonel Santoro searches for his son, a masked murderer kills each teen in incredibily gory ways. At the film's end, the murderer removes his mask in front of Colonel Santoro. The killer is, in fact, Fito, a prodigal son who slaughters the teens in hopes of eliciting love and approval from his authoritative father.

Nunca and *Nunca más* never describe Colonel Santoro explicitly as an officer of the dictatorship. However, numerous elements point to his status as such.[39] The father-son relationship frequently assumes the rigid interactions between an officer and a soldier. Colonel Santoro often addresses his son as "Soldado" ("Soldier") and Fito responds to his dad as "Mi coronel" ("Colonel"). Colonel Santoro's railing against delinquency unequivocally recycles and mocks the junta's conservative conceptions of family described above and the subversive elements that supposedly threaten "good" families and, by extension, the nation's very fabric. Here, father and son are the metonym of a conservative family unit setting out for the open country on a clichéd bonding trip, and *Nunca* quickly establishes the centrality of family through a voice-over/dialogue at the film's start set to the strumming of a guitar:

voz 1   Hola. La historia que le vamos a contar es una historia terrible y espeluznante. Empieza con el Coronel Ernesto Santoro y su hijo, Fito.
voz 2   Fito y su pa, Don Santoro, ¿eh?
voz 1   Sí. ¡Qué hombre de bien!
voz 2   Nunca viste una persona más buena. Un corazón de oro. [...]
voz 1   Esa es la historia de que van a ver ahora: la delincuencia juvenil tratando de destruir la felicidad de familia. Terrible, terrible. Un horror.

voice 1   Hello. The story that we are going to tell is a horrible and frightening story. It begins with Colonel Santoro and his son, Fito.
voice 2   Fito and his Dad, Don Santoro, right?
voice 1   Yes. What a proper and good man!
voice 2   You never saw a better person. A heart of gold. [...]
voice 1   This is the story that you are going to see now: juvenile delinquency seeking to destroy family happiness. Terrible, terrible. A horror.

The force of *Nunca*'s comedy, in part, rests on its incongruities. Laughably, the merry band of six teenagers are deemed a threat by Colonel Santoro.[40] Upon seeing Vicky, Rolo, and Quique close to the lake in which they are fishing, Colonel Santoro is immediately bothered, purses his lips, and shakes his head, and, over a soundtrack of a trumpet, snare drum, and organ's dirge, tells his son, "Estos individuos presentan certeros rasgos de promiscuidad, drogaddición, prostitución y comunismo. Es preciso dar de baja subversión sin límite. ¿Comprendes, soldado?" ("Those individuals exhibit certain traits of promiscuity, drug addiction, prostitution, and communism. It is imperative to ceaselessly eliminate subversion. Do you understand, soldier?"). As Colonel Santoro and his son speak, the camera cuts between close-ups of the two characters from different angles and heights. At the mention of "drogaddición, prostitución y comunismo," the camera successively cuts to medium close-ups of a single "subversive" teenager, as if each individual embodies a particular form of subversion: "drogadición" (Quique), "prostitución" (Vicky), "comunismo" (Rolo). Moreover, while almost the entirety of *Nunca* is in color, the images of the teens in this sequence are in black and white and approximates a dated celluloid with small scratches and blots suggesting that the colonel's directives addressed to his son momentarily serve as a kind of dated educational film adaptation of the notorious *Subversión en el ámbito educativo (conozcamos a nuestro enemigo)* ("Subversion in the Education System [Let's Know Our Enemy]"), a manual distributed by the dictatorship to schools and universities in 1977, which allegedly informed educators about identifying enemies of the state at the time.[41]

After 1983, fear was a vestigial psychic structure held over from the dictatorship: fear of another military coup (Nouzeilles and Montaldo 473) or, most acutely felt by victims of torture, fear of meeting their torturers (Feitlowitz 4). *Nunca* turns the tables by assigning fear to a perpetrator of violence. Fear, in the case of Santoro, is not a defensive or self-preserving mechanism, but rather a combative one. Colonel Santoro's hypermasculine and paranoid subjectivity embodies a fear of a dissolution of a postdictatorial society in which a previous "subversive" threat is laughably switched out for wayward teenagers. Hapless and unsuspecting youths provide the grist for Colonel Santoro's paranoid mill. The substitution of threats—again, perhaps best conceived with Massumi's notion of an iterative series discussed in chapter 3—maintains a panic and a totalizing logic without pause. In short, Colonel Santoro cuts the figure of a paranoid right-wing machine who lacks an off switch, but whose son carries out the dirty work and murderous implications of his father's ideas.

The parody of the dictatorship's vision of subversion is ramped up in *Nunca más*, and the association between Colonel Santoro and the regime is more forceful. After Colonel Santoro perishes in the attacks on the World Trade Center while in New York, an adult-aged Fito (Berta Muñiz) returns to the same rural locale where he and his father were in the first film. Fito's psychoanalyst/lover, Nicolás Estevinsky (Sebastián de Caro), accompanies Fito to help the latter realize what his father relates to Fito in a vision that is heard in a voice-over at the start of the movie: "conocer el secreto de la familia [...] completar la lección que hace tantos años intenté darle [...] y convertirse en el hijo con que siempre soñé. Usted va a ser un hombre derecho y humano" ("learn the family secret [...], complete the lesson that I tried to impart to you years ago [...], and become the man that I always dreamed you would be. You will become an upstanding and humane man"). Colonel Santoro's desire for Fito to be "un hombre derecho y humano" recalls the last dictatorship's marketing campaign in 1979, to combat what it called "una campaña antiargentina" ("anti-Argentine campaign") by survivors of clandestine centers, those Argentines living in exile, and relatives of victims. The dictatorship ordered some 250,000 heart-shaped stickers that read "Los argentinos somos derechos y humanos" on a background that resembled the Argentine flag, and instructed citizens to place the stickers on their cars to help improve the image of Jorge Videla in the face of criticism by international human rights organizations and pressure from the US and various European governments to cease human rights violations (Seoane). Colonel Santoro's wish for his son to be "derecho y humano" is an obvious holdover of the dictator's marketing campaign that doubles as an edict for child-rearing in this instance.

With a repetition of an excursion in the country, Fito and Nicolás's therapeutic excursion coincides with the arrival of a motley group composed of two leftist militants—Silvana Zapata (Victoria Hladilo) and Bruno (Paulo Soria) from Organización Revolucionaria del Pueblo ("The People's Revolutionary Organization" [OPR]) and a television news crew, who are doing a report on the two militants' search for the remains of Miguel Monforte, a fictional leader of OPR who was disappeared during the dictatorship.[42] The entire group stays in the same small house from the first movie in which the teenagers lived and which is guarded by a police officer, Oficial Montoya (Hernán Sáez). After the group finds an empty grave, they set out to find the remains of Colonel Santoro to verify that he has not somehow returned from the dead.[43]

During the course of the film, Fito slips into his father's identity to become "un hombre derecho y humano," and Fito's murderous slaughter underscores the violence lurking behind the dictatorial marketing of bumper stickers. After killing and maiming several of the people staying in the cabin and recovering his Dad's bones, Fito shaves his hair close, dons a pair of sunglasses with mirrored lenses, and draws a thin moustache on his lip with a magic marker to more precisely resemble his father in the first film. Fito, however, surpasses Colonel Santoro's vision of his own place in rooting out subversion with a rhetoric that is more intense with a murderous violence to boot. Fito binds to chairs Mariana (Constanza Boquet) and Darío (Walter Cornás), two members of the crew. Fito also binds to chairs Silvana and his Dad's skeleton. Fito slaps the three captives and screams lines eerily recall those of a torturer seeking to render a victim helpless and utterly dependent: "Soy todo para vos. La justicia soy yo. Soy Dios. ¿Entendiste? Hay que dejar de baja la subversión sin límite. ¿Comprende? ("I am everything for you. I am justice. I am God. Understood? It is imperative to ceaselessly eliminate subversion. Understand?"). Fito's diatribes clearly draw on the dictatorship's rhetoric and underscore a linguistic dynamic of torture. As Marguerite Feitlowitz asks, "How can one torture a person who doesn't exist? Be God in a realm of no ones? How can a living being not exist? Be no one in a realm of gods? Through language" (57). Such inflammatory language appears void of comedy on paper. Yet, humor enters the delivery with an acute degree of hyperbole. An active camera that varies in angles and movements intensifies Berta Muñiz's already exaggerated expressions and gestures that forge caricatures of blustering conservative militants paranoid about subversion in a postdictatorial milieu.

In *Film Parody*, Dan Harries conceives of parody as a discursive mode and relies largely on US comedies such as *Blazing Saddles* (Mel Brooks, 1974), *Spaceballs* (Mel Brooks, 1987), and *Airplane!* (Jim Abrahams and David Zucker, 1980) to map different disruptive and ironic techniques characteristic of cinematic parodies that spectators can recognize to various degrees. A fundamental element of Harries's conception of cinematic parody is "the necessary oscillation between similarity and difference from a target [film] that allows parody to maintain either the lexicon, syntax or style while manipulating the others" (9). A cinematic parody thus performs a kind of transtextual invocation of one or more films and preserves some element of the original (e.g., soundtrack, opening title graphics, events, etc.) while toying with the others through various schemes of "reiteration, inversion, misdirection, literalization, extraneous inclusion, and exaggeration" (Harries 26, 37).

Relation to a target text is essential in parody. Dirty War films—of which one can discuss as an Argentine thematic film subgenre—provide a loosely tethered target for the characters of Colonel Santoro and Fito in *Nunca* and *Nunca más*. Dirty War films, in part, furnish the tropes that Colonel Santoro and Fito exaggerate in gross terms: a rhetoric against subversion (*La noche de los lápices*, *Crónica*), paranoia (*Los ultimos días de la víctima*, *La historia oficial*), mirrored sunglasses (*Crónica*), a moustache (*La noche de los lápices*, *Crónica*), and a hidden propensity for violence (*La historia oficial*). The character parodies in Farsa's films never achieve an antipodal relationship with those agents of the dictatorship in Dirty War films, as if Colonel Santoro or Fito were somehow foils of those agents in other Dirty War films. Instead, again invoking Harries's schemes of film parody, the two characters in *Nunca* and *Nunca más* disrupt via exaggeration the tropes composing a filmic version of an operative who worked for the dictatorship.

Colonel Santoro and Fito are not the cool-headed "villains" who practice violence in secret. Rather, the colonel and his adult son hardly maintain a calm attitude that obscures a tendency for violence. Though Fito hides his identity as he kills the teenagers in *Nunca*, he and his father are set off by the mere site of "subversives." Moreover, the violence in *Nunca* and *Nunca más* is extreme and acquires a slapstick tone with hearts ripped out and groins and heads smashed. And the violence is key for the films' laying bare the absurd reality of the dictatorship's invocation of "family" that *Nunca* and *Nunca más* play with and eventually muddy. Beneath the dictatorship's rhetoric was a widespread and brutal violence that left incredible carnage in its wake. Instead of opting for a suggestive violence à la *Crónica*, *Nunca* and *Nunca más* treat the violence in an indirect and temporal fashion some twenty years after the dictatorship to discredit resolutely any notion of the junta somehow being ethically upstanding.

STRIKING BACK: YOUTH AND MAGIC

Similar to *Nunca* and *Nunca más*, *Sudor frío* plays with historical repetition and resilient subjectivities left over from a dictatorial period shot through with violence. Two former torturers affiliated with the dictatorship, Gordon (Omar Musa) and Baxter (Omar Gioiosa), reside in an unassuming house in present-day Buenos Aires, where they lure women to their home via chatrooms, torture them, and eventually kill some of them with explosive chemicals. At the start of the film, Román drops off his friend, Ali, in front of a typical-looking house in Buenos Aires. Ali has corresponded through chat with an anonymous and young blond man, and he and Ali are supposedly going to have a romantic dinner at his home. Before exiting the car, we learn that Román's girlfriend, Jacqui (Camila Velasco), also has been corresponding with the unnamed blond man and contacts Román through e-mail, supposedly to break off the relationship while he and Ali are still in the car. Ali notices that Jacqui's e-mail comes from the same Internet Protocol (IP) address as that of the young blond man; however, Ali still enters the house. Román sees Gordon trying to cross the street and helps the elderly man. Sensing something is amiss, Román breaks into Gordon and Baxter's home. Román eventually frees Ali, and Ali and Román find Jacqui covered in explosive chemicals in the basement of the house and, eventually, help her escape. In a variation of *The People under the Stairs*, the basement also contains a crowd of female cannibals who were presumably disappeared by Baxter and Gordon and served as subjects for different experiments.[44] By the film's end, Baxter explodes after Román throws a bottle of chemicals on him, Gordon is thrown into the basement where he is eaten by the cannibal women, and Ali and Román begin a romantic relationship.

In the US-distributed DVD version of the film, its director, Adrián García Bogliano, appears in an extra titled "Cold Blood," and describes in English the historical context of the Dirty War and the film's popular cultural references. Among other remarks about the attraction of narrativizing some aspect of the Dirty War as a horror film, García Bogliano characterizes as "creepy" the idea that lower-level operatives who actually committed the atrocities on behalf of the dictatorship remain at large in Argentine society. Or as García Bogliano comments in another interview, "Es inquietante que el viejito que uno se puede cruzar en la verdulería puede ser uno de [los torturadores]" ("It's disturbing that the kind old man that one encounters in the produce section of the grocery store could be one of [the torturers])" (Ferri). *Sudor frío*, in turn, engages with the impossibility, or, at least the difficulty, of identifying those people who carried out brutal acts in the name of *El Proceso*. Here, in contrast to *Nunca* and *Nunca más*, a postdictatorial paranoia is imbibed not by those formerly associated with the dictatorship but with those who could have been its victims.

The elderly characters, Baxter and Gordon, provide an ideal shell for broaching the conundrum of identifying a killer, a kind of minority report with the crimes already committed twenty years prior during the Dirty War with similar ones in progress. At the start of the film, Román sees Gordon trying to cross the street using a walker and wearing a hat, glasses, blue jacket, shorts, white socks pulled up, and white tennis shoes; Gordon is a nondescript elderly everyman. Gordon appears as normal and unsuspicious as the façade of his and Baxter's home, where scores of young women have been tortured and kept captive, presumably for years. Román offers his help, and Gordon accepts and eventually remarks, "Ya no se encuentra a chicos como vos, querido, ¿eh? Está muy embrobado para una persona de mi edad salir a la calle. Nadie respeta nada. Gracias, querido" ("Boys like you are hard to find these days, dear. No? Walking down the street is very difficult for a person my age. No one respects anything. Thanks, dear"). Gordon's comments echo those that one occasionally encounters in Argentina, especially among elderly people, who wistfully remember the past during the dictatorship as being better than the present.

Gordon cuts the same figure of dictatorial agents through disparagement of his victims, constantly belittles them and marks out generational differences while torturing them, almost parodying a rhetoric that combines a torturer's contempt for victims and an elderly man's ire over "kids these days": a lack of respect, an absence of knowledge, an antipathy for playing outside, and, last, a degeneration of language and an inability to express oneself without which, in Gordon's words to Ali, "no tenés ninguna libertad" ("You have no freedom"). In a game that postpones physical pain, Gordon ask Ali about the meanings of words. Gordon's use of a dictionary may appear at first an unlikely tool of torture. Yet, Scarry has written about how a torture victim's use of language ceases to exist (30), and how the act of torture "not only converts but announces the conversion of every conceivable aspect of the event and the environment into an agent of pain" (28). The dictionary, in turn, becomes another means through which Gordon diminishes the agency of his victims.

If Baxter as a caricature of the dictatorship appears grounded in an exaggeration of cruelty and rhetoric, Baxter's persistent sadism over time also plays on another trope in Dirty War films, including *Nunca* and *Nunca más*. Though the contexts change in their respective films, Gómez in *El secreto de sus ojos* and Roberto in *La historia oficial* practice atrocities both during and outside of a dictatorial period: Gómez murdering Liliana Coloto, and Roberto grabbing his wife by the throat and threatening her in their home. Right before being eaten by the cannibals in the basement, Gordon has a sort of double flashback. He recalls Baxter and himself sitting in chairs in the recent past, and they remember that they met while killing frogs at the age of six or seven, tortured and killed victims during the Dirty War, and continue the trend in the present day. As Gordon tells Ali shortly after she is taken captive at the start of the film, "Sabes, antes a la gente como vos teníamos que ir y buscarla. Pero ahora no hace falta porque se entregan solitos. Igual, para nosotros, bien porque a nuestra edad ya no tenemos energía de antes ("You know, we used to have to chase down people like you. But not anymore because you kids come here of your own accord. Likewise, it is good for us because we do not have the same energy as before.")[45] Old habits die hard.

Malditos sean! is a film divided into chapters ("El curandero" ["The Necromancer"], "La caja" ["The Box"], and "Cafeomancia") that interlock through flashbacks and flash-forwards and the appearance of select characters in multiple chapters. The film had a limited release in Argentina proper and received mixed reviews among national film critics. In "El curandero," which is set in 1979, agents of the dictatorship arrive at a dilapidated house with a clustered interior searching for Ulises (Carlos Larrañaga), a curandero. Instead, the agents find an old woman who eventually leads them to a door behind which Ulises is performing some kind of ritual. After struggling and eventually shooting the door open, the agents apprehend Ulises and throw him in a cell with two additional prisoners, one of which is Hugo (Hugo Halbrich), who will figure into "La caja." As the police search Ulises's home, one of the three police officers, Jiménez (Simón Ratziel), ventures outside Ulises's home and encounters a collection of ceramic garden gnomes that Ulises has amassed with the help of a mysterious young girl with a disfigured face. Jiménez disappears and, by the film's end, the police ascertain that the garden gnomes abducted Jiménez and scraps of his body are contained inside the gnomes. "La caja" is set years later, and Hugo is an assassin working for Castro (Víctor Cura), a drug dealer. Hugo kills off a young boy after his partner, Carlos (Pedro Di Salvia), shoots the young boy as Hugo kills the boy's father. The murdered boy's ghost continues to pursue Hugo, and he asks for Ulises's help to obtain the boy's forgiveness. In an oblique homage to *Hellraiser* (Clive Barker, 1987), Ulises gives Hugo a box and cryptic instructions by silently pointing at a dagger. Hugo ascertains that he must fill the box up with hearts as retribution for the boy's death, including Hugo's own heart. The third chapter, "Cafeomancia," is set in the future and a group of clairvoyant women practice cafeomancia in a small town.[46] One of the women, Margarita (Gabriela Mocca), has a boyfriend, Leandro (Demián Salomon), who confesses his love to her. However, the situation grows complicated when a demon materializes and tries to kill the women. Leandro learns that Margarita's uncanny mental power is due in part to her chastity and that the demon pursues her because she is a kind of "witch." As the demon closes in on Margarita, Leandro persuades her to have sex, and the demon is defeated.

The caricaturing of the dictatorial agents in *Malditos sean!* does not happen through the physical depiction or mannerisms of the dictatorship's agents à la *Nunca, Nunca más*, and *Sudor frío*. The operatives conform with many of the aforementioned tropes: sunglasses, moustaches, 1970s fashion, and a propensity for sudden violence. Instead, the caricature is based on what happens to the unnamed chief of the paramilitary unit (played by Julio Luparello). After Ulises is detained, he sits in a cell with an unnamed prisoner who hides a gold watch in his stomach. When the guards take the man for interrogation, Ulises asks that he obtain some object that belongs to the officers, or something that one of them has touched. As the police are in another room, the man with the gold watch licks a table and brings back to his cell a small bundle of the chief's nose hairs. Soon afterward, a deluge of hair emanates from the chief's nostrils spilling over his desk, filling up the office, covering walls, and preventing the chief from speaking clearly. The hair grows with vigor even moving objects. At a loss, the police summon two clairvoyant women for help, but they can do nothing except warn the agents that Ulises "es un hombre peligroso" ("is a dangerous man"). Toward the film's end, Ulises pulls the chief by his nose hairs across the police station floor and to his cell. Ulises seizes the chief's keys, and he and Hugo escape. The unnamed prisoner goes with the police to Ulises's home to search for Jiménez.

In her book *The Technical Imagination*, Beatriz Sarlo describes the emergence of a persisting "mythological domain" (129) that takes hold in the 1920s in Argentina, in which new technologies (radio, X-rays, wireless telegraphy) combined with traditional obsessions (apparitions and *curanderismo*) along with new urban discourses such as theosophy and parapsychology. Ulises (along with the clairvoyant women) in *Malditos sean!* suggests that such a domain persists in Argentine culture, albeit perhaps on a smaller scale. Similar to the victims in *Nunca, Nunca más*, and *Sudor frío*, agents of the dictatorship baselessly conceive of Ulises as a subversive, more particularly a communist, and analogize the dictator's police apparatus to an indiscriminate vortex that sucked up any individual deemed inconsistent with a rigid conservative mode of thought or being. Ulises, of course, resides beyond the dictator's prescriptions for citizens and defies the left-right political spectrum afoot in Argentina circa 1979. If Ulises appears a depoliticized individual in the midst of a historical moment immersed in a horrific political violence, he cuts the figure of a character emerging from the pages of a Buenos Aires conceived by Roberto Arlt steeped in an "alternative" knowledge. Ulises does not fight his way out of prison or make a valiant escape in the middle of the night as happens in *Crónica*. Instead, Ulises conjures his way out transforming the chief, the film's metonym for the dictatorship, into an object of derision. Prior to the spell, the chief was fully capable of atrocities directing a squad of police officers arresting subversives. Yet, in the film's final view of him, he is a buffoon. As with the "villains" in *Nunca, Nunca más*, and *Sudor frío*, fifteen to twenty-five years after the Dirty War, a fusion of comedy and horror is possible.

A CRITICAL LAUGHTER

In the introduction to her book-length study of affect in Latin American cinema, Laura Podalsky sets up a straw man by invoking a critical undercurrent that casts young Latin American directors as apolitical and exhibiting an inadequate grasp of past national traumas (*Politics of Affect* 2–3). Akin to how Podalsky shows how the political in contemporary Latin American cinemas assumes forms distinct from, say, the revered New Latin American Cinema of the 1960s and 1970s, the ways in which contemporary Argentine horror films engage, or disengage, with the Dirty War unfold in a plurality of cinematic forms. While I hesitate to call inevitable the Dirty War's narrativization via codes of the horror genre, the Dirty War's mutation into genres other than melodrama and documentary is, at least, unsurprising. In his article on the comedic portrayal of Hitler and the Nazis in cinema, Reimer writes, "Sensitivities change. Material that was passable and accepted as humorous in the past may seem inappropriate to later generations, aware of ethnic and religious genocide." More specific to the Argentine context, in the aforementioned interview titled "Cold Blood," García Bogliano expresses a similar opinion: young Argentines did not want to see the Dirty War in "intense dramas" or documentary because witnessing the calamity would be too "traumatic." Instead, García Bogliano explains that the film narrativizes the component of the Dirty War that "the murderers are among us" within the horror genre, a genre usually ass García Bogliano ociated with younger audiences, to appeal to those very audiences.[47]

Contemporary Argentine horror cinema's engagement with the Dirty War hardly makes for an orderly generic evolution à la Thomas Schatz in which one film initiates a cycle of "Dirty War horror films" and then passes through stages of "transparent social reaffirmation to [arrive at] opaque self-reflexivity" (40–41).[48] If *Crónica* constituted a change in how horror could project the Dirty War, that change happened within a particular hierarchical circle of Argentine culture and cinema. Though stylistically different, Farsa's *Nunca* preceded *Crónica* by nearly six years but remained largely unnoticed by critics, given its exhibition on alternative circuits. Further complicating and diversifying Argentine horror cinema's relationship to the Dirty War, INCAA's support for *Crónica*, *Aparecidos*, *Sudor frío*, and *Malditos sean!* reiterates Marvin D'Lugo's observation that the Dirty War functions as a cinematic "construction of Argentineness" (D'Lugo 108). Though the horror films, with the possible exception of *Crónica*, occupy a lower rung on a cultural hierarchy than the likes of *La historia oficial*, the horror films circulate in national and international markets. Taken collectively, the four films signal a shift in institutional cinematic memory practices among some sectors of the Argentine population for whom the horror genre can render a horrible tragedy into a narrative. While *Nunca* uses parody in its representation of the Dirty War, INCAA's support for *Sudor frío* and *Malditos sean!* suggests that parody and horror have become modes in which the "Dirty War film" as a topical genre can be renewed. The Dirty War's figuration in a horror film is not a case of simple oblivion. Irrespective of whether a film has a serious air or largely engages in parody, a single film hardly drowns out how the Dirty War figures elsewhere in Argentine culture, as if a viewer walks out of a theater or turns off the television or computer with his or her memory emptied. Comedic films are simply not the sites for forgetfulness of a political tragedy. Steven Marsh's study of Spanish dark comedies produced during *el franquismo*, many of which belong to a larger canon of Spanish cinema (e.g., *¡Bienvenido, Mr. Marshall!* and *El verdugo/ The Executioner* (Luis García Berlanga, 1963), thoroughly shows how humor was interjected into film in an oppressive context. Moreover, the current critical appreciation for the films of the Brazilian actor-director Zé do Caixão intimate how some register of camp or comedic horror does not obviate poignant commentary on a ruthless dictatorship. While Spanish dark comedies and the films of Zé do Caixão operate now as comical prosthetic memories, Argentine horror-comedies interject comedy in retrospect.

The significance of reception of the horror films featuring the Dirty War cannot be overstated. While I have tried to undermine or at least problematize the automatic impulse to interpret all Argentine horror films as allegories of the Dirty War, the question ultimately rests with a spectator to determine if the generic elements typical of horror (kidnapping, torture, and captivity) signal the Dirty War. In the case of those films that deal explicitly with the Dirty War, a spectator may weigh in on whether those same generic elements trivialize a catastrophe. Reviews of *Sudor frío* and *Malditos sean!* by Argentine film critics and comments by moviegoers on message boards occasionally evidence reactions that range from surprise that a horror film would broach the Dirty War to acrid resentment.[49] Despite the developments in genre cinema in Argentina and elsewhere in Latin America, horror remains contained within a hierarchy of tastes among critics and audiences and, simply put, horror is not everyone's cup of tea. At the conclusion of a chapter on war photos in *Regarding the Pain of Others*, Susan Sontag writes about the different reactions to a photo, which can transcend that of the photographer: "The photographer's intentions do not determine the meaning of the photograph, which will have its own career, blown by the whims and loyalties of the diverse communities that have use of it" (39). Given Argentine horror cinema's domestic and transnational circulation that follows in the wake of police thrillers, melodramas, and documentaries, Argentine horror films and their relation to the Dirty War have their own career as well.

CONCLUSION

Argentine horror possesses many registries and shapes: English-language horror films; horror films made with the support of INCAA; low-budget films produced beyond the auspices of the state; punk/horror films; films set in generic or distinct spaces; and, last, films that engage with historical and sociocultural dynamics as well as films that ostensibly do not. My study of Argentine horror cinema here has hardly exhausted its object of study; there is, of course, more horror cinema to come. With support from INCAA on numerous fronts (e.g., *concursos*, CINE.AR PLAY streaming service, patronage for Blood Window, among other measures), national horror film production maintains a steady pace. In May of 2014, Ricardo Darín stoked a moment of enthusiasm among horror aficionados in Argentina when he disclosed his wish to make a zombie film. Perhaps Darín's star power—not to mention, his talent—would make Argentine horror even more salient on national and transnational circuits.

Yet, with or without Darín, the production of horror cinema in Argentina will persist. The Internet continues to abet the national and transnational circulation of Argentine horror. A number of titles—*Hipersomnia*/*Hypersomnia* (Gabriel Grieco, 2016); *Ataúd blanco: El juego diabólico*/*White Coffin* (Daniel de la Vega, 2016); *Necrofobia 3D* (Daniel de la Vega, 2014); *Los inocentes*/*The Innocents* (Mauricio Brunetti, 2016); and *Resurrección*/*Resurrection* (Gonzalo Calzada, 2015)—have obtained streaming distribution through Netflix, potentially allowing the films to circulate in the 190 national markets where Netflix is present. However, not all Argentine horror cinema emerges within a mainstream film culture or with institutional support, and horror films produced beyond the state merit critical attention to understand the full breadth of horror in Argentina and its reaches and receptions. With strict regard to film festivals, Buenos Aires Rojo Sangre and Festival de Cine Inusual both continue to exhibit low-budget cinema produced in Argentina. Nevertheless, Sitges, Mórbido in Mexico, and London's FrightFest, among a legion of other festivals, remain destinations for higher-budgeted Argentine horror films.

Irrespective of differences among them, Argentine horror films inevitably search for an audience. Or, better said, the films imagine at least a portion of their audiences. Benjamin Lee and Edward LiPuma have written about cultural circulation in general terms and argue that "circulation always presupposes the existence of their respective interpretative communities, with their own forms of interpretation and evaluation" (192). Argentine horror cinema is keenly aware of "interpretative communities" of horror film viewers, and the films' consumption evinces the existence of audiences—both national and international—who are willing to watch, even if a film is made on a miniscule budget. As stated in the introduction, Argentine horror can be placed within a deluge of genre cinema, and even a larger wave of visual media largely abetted by the Internet. While the Internet has not fully replaced previous forms of distribution, such as theaters and DVDs (Crisp 58), the multitude of channels of circulation that the web affords enables the possibility of Argentine horror films finding new audiences.

Argentine horror cinema embodies many of the facets that often accompany the study of genre cinema, such as the centrality of repetition. Steve Neale, for example, writes, "Most aesthetic theories of genre take as their starting point the issues of repetition and variation, similarity and difference, and the extent to which the elements repeated and varied are simple or complex" (195). Barry Keith Grant has commented on "the repetition and variation of commercially successful formulas" (7) of early Hollywood films, and the "system of signification [...] developed over time and with repetition" (8) associated with particular genres.[1]

If Neale and Grant highlight repetition inherent in the genre cinema production, then film consumption can involve its own repetition with national and transnational genre communities who view and produce film cultures based around a genre. With one foot firmly planted in local and national coordinates, Argentine horror cinema contributes to a larger transnational horror film culture. As stated in the introduction, repetition in horror cinema can be linked to pleasures, or unpleasures, and such pleasures are myriad. In *Spectatorship: The Power of Looking On*, Michele Aaron alludes to Gilles Deleuze's study of masochism and his notion that "pleasure is heightened through anticipation itself" (Aaron 60). For cinema, the anticipation that a film will adhere to genre tenets enriches a viewer's pleasure. The global circulation of horror films irrespective of their geographic origins enables a repetition of anticipation for viewers and, thus, a stream of cinematic pleasure. Yet, a stream of horror cinema does not purely reinforce the same pleasures, but rather leaves open the possibility of the formation of nuanced pleasures.

CONCLUSION

In other words, Argentine horror cinema does not simply deepen and reinforce already established templates of cinematic pleasure but holds out the possibility of new pleasures—and, again, unpleasures—some of which I have attempted to map in this book.

In his comments on repetition in psychoanalysis, Lacan links repetition with the ludic and underscores variation within repetition: "Repetition demands the new. It is turned toward the ludic, which finds its dimension in this new" (61). Argentine horror cinema, along with horror cinema from elsewhere, potentially provides something "new" under the generic rubric of "horror." "Horror" operates as a signifier that proffers variation. Or, as Bruce Fink writes, "It is the signifier, in its polysemy, that allows for a series to be established (allowing, as it does, for substitutions), a metaphorical and metonymic series, along which desire can slide endlessly pursuing difference" (224). Argentine horror takes its place among a larger cinematic circuit of horror—a series—that both maintains a repetition and encompasses, even demands, variations within that repetition.

NOTES

INTRODUCTION

1. When an Argentine horror film is distributed in an English-language market and its title is translated, I provide the English-language title in italics. Otherwise, I translate the original titles into English and enclose them in quotation marks. Unless otherwise noted, all translations are my own.

2. *Alguien te está mirando* / "Someone Is Watching You" (Gustavo Cova and Horacio Maldonado, 1988) was released in Argentine theaters in 1988.

3. It is crucial to note that horror is not the only genre or film movement in Argentina that benefited from cheaper filmmaking technologies. Andermann alludes to similar factors that facilitated the emergence of New Argentine Cinema (*New Argentine Cinema* 9–10).

4. Among the various Japanese fan websites that include reviews of Argentine horror cinema are *Killer Demons, Aliens, and Rabbits*; *Mr. Nama Nick's Killing Time*; and *Horror Treasure Diary*. All of the site's titles have been translated into English from the original Japanese. I am indebted to Japanese horror scholar Michael Crandol for his translations and locating the sites that feature Argentine horror.

5. A film's circulation on the Internet constitutes a *gray zone*, a term that encapsulates online distribution's "grey-zone of semi-legality" with "viewing platforms that integrate legal and black markets" (Lobato 95).

6. It is difficult to ascertain the reasons for INCAA's willingness to fund horror film production. In interviews with directors, journalists, and festival programmers, more than a few interviewees suggested that a generational change and the change in composition of film committees have enabled horror cinema to be made. In other words, the judges who are more open to horror cinema have recently occupied committees within INCAA.

7. CINE.AR PLAY was originally called Odeón, and INCAA renamed the site in early April of 2017. CINE.AR PLAY is the Argentine national government's

free online streaming platform exclusively devoted to national cinema and television series.

8. The figure of $20,000 approximates Rodríguez's categorizations of low-budget and commercial horror productions in Argentina (110–13).

9. For a detailed study of *Sábados de Súper Acción*, see Curubeto and Martín Peña.

10. The centrality of *Sábados de Súper Acción* is reinforced in an article about La Liga de Cine de Género that appeared in *La Nación*. At the bottom of the article, an excerpt from a brief manifesto about La Liga reads, "Crecimos consumiendo Sábado [*sic*] de súper acción" ("We were raised watching Sábado de súper acción") (Montesoro).

11. While Elaesser was writing in the 1980s, Hollywood's trawling of social media data to track spectators' cinematic tastes highlights how spectatorial pleasure remains an engine of the film industry (Barnes).

12. It also bears mentioning that allegory is often conceived as an aesthetic language of crisis. For example, in *Allegories of Underdevelopment*, Ismail Xavier locates a "sense of irony" in Brazilian cinema in reaction to the military dictatorship "hallowing of tradition and nationality" in 1968 (15). For Xavier, "If that was a moment of crisis and transition, then allegory had a chance to show itself as the language of crisis par excellence—and this actually occurred in modern Brazilian cinema" (15). Likewise, in his overview of allegory, Jeremy Tambling observes that "allegory appears to have been produced during periods of emotional and/or religious crises, whether personal or historical or both" and references the works of Dante, William Langland, John Donne, George Herbert, John Bunyan, and Edmund Spenser to support his claim (72–73).

13. For instance, Claudio España describes the conditions of production toward the end of 1986 that preceded an economic decline: "Simultáneamente y ya hacia fines de 1986, una vieja y habitual palabra en la industria de nuestro cine, crisis, sentaba de nuevo sus reales" ("Simultaneously and already towards the end of 1986, crisis, an old word familiar to our cinema industry, again settled in") (14).

14. The relationship between horror and crises can be extended to academic and fan discussions of the genre itself in crises. For example, Hantke examines a number of academic anthologies dealing with the construction of a horror film canon and highlights the discourses of crisis common to each anthology in which the horror genre ostensibly enters a crisis as an exhausted genre ("Academic Film Criticism," 199).

15. I refrain from ascribing a geographic location to an academic tendency to receive horror as allegories of crises. Nevertheless, Mariano Kairuz begins his review of *La memoria del muerto/Memory of the Dead* (Javier Diment, 2013) by pointing out that studies of US horror cinema frequently underscore the relationship between societal crises and horror cinema only to ask, "¿Cómo es que el cine argentino no produjo una verdadera, sólida, profusa antología de espantos nacidos de los infinitos espantos de la realidad nacional del siglo XX?" ("How is that Argentine cinema has not produced a solid, authentic, and vast catalogue of scares inspired by the infinite scares of Argentina's twentieth-century?"). Kairuz's comments, along with Lázaro-Reboll's observations of the allegorical reception of Guillermo del Toro's *Espinazo del diablo/Devil's Backbone* (2001) and *El Laberinto del fauno/Pan's Labyrinth* (2006) by US critics (*Spanish Horror* 260–62), broach the question whether allegorical readings of horror as societal crises may be a general tendency of US-based critics.

16. This same sentiment was expressed by other Argentine horror film directors. For example, in an interview with Nicanor Loreti, when asked what could be considered unique to Argentine horror cinema, he answered that directors are able to make films with much scarcer resources than in other countries.

17. As Martin Rubin writes in *Thrillers*, "The thriller can be conceptualized as a 'metagenre' that gathers several other genres under its umbrella, and as a band in the spectrum that colors each of those particular genres" (4). Those genres include horror, science fiction, detective and crime films, war films, and musicals. Though paranoia has long figured into Hollywood productions beginning in the 1930s, the transnational popularity of superhero films and narcotrafficking series (*Breaking Bad, The Wire, La reina del sur, El patrón del mal*) demonstrate the appeal of narratives in which paranoia, among other characteristics, is a driving force in the narrative.

CHAPTER ONE

1. As demonstrated in Nagib, Dudrah, and Perriam, the term *world cinema* is incredibly fungible. Nevertheless, in the introduction to the collection of essays, the three editors admit "the 'problems' with world cinema begin with the name itself, whose rise as a commercial label in tandem with 'world music' has given origin to a highly questionable, though enduringly popular, opposition between the American mainstream and the rest of the world" (Nagib, Dudrah, and Perriam

xix). This conception of world cinema rests on a simplistic binary and, in contrast to transnationalism, elides the specificity involved with a film's distribution among specific cities, countries, regions, and/or the specificity of the funding that goes into a film.

2. For examples of recent studies of Latin American and US-Latina/o film cultures possessing a transnational dimension, see Jeffrey Middents's *Writing National Cinema* (Dartmouth College P, 2009), Laura Isabel Serna's *Making Cinelandia* (Duke UP, 2014), and Colin Gunckel's *Mexico on Main Street* (Rutgers UP, 2015).

3. Hitchcock's British period, as attested by Ryall's book, is conceived of films the director made with British studios (Islington, Elstree, Sheperd's Bush, etc.) between 1925 and 1938.

4. I am indebted to Barbara Klinger's allusion to Ryall's term in her book on home cinema, *Beyond the Multiplex*. Klinger appropriates and refines Ryall's conception of "film culture" to conceptualize "home film cultures," which Klinger relates to the evolution of home entertainment systems and their attendant viewing practices (11–12).

5. For example, see "Homenaje al cine de género argentino" on YouTube posted by "Victor Von Krueger." While the clip features sequences from different Argentine genre films, horror figures prominently into the montage.

6. For examples of fan art, see *Daemonium*'s Facebook page. The film was originally released in chapters through YouTube over the course of five years and fan art served as one way to publicize the film.

7. For more information about how INCAA's *concursos* operate, see Rodríguez, specifically chapter 3.

8. For an example of the both laudatory and incendiary remarks that often accompany Argentine horror films' presence on websites, see the comments section for *Curas zombis en azul*/ "Zombie Priests in Blue" (Oswaldo Sudak, 2013) on YouTube.

9. For a closer examination of the quantity of horror films produced on a global scale between 1930 and 2006, see Lanzagorta. Albeit a brief article, Lanzagorta describes using IMDb.com to gauge the number of horror films (commercial and straight-to-video releases) produced worldwide during the aforementioned period and the percentage made in the United States during that time. Among other conclusions, Lanzagorta finds that while the United States remains by far the largest producer of horror cinema between 1960 and 2006, the rest of the world dramatically increased its output with the advent of inexpensive movie-making technology and the proliferation of modes to distribute films, such as DVDs.

10. The notion of a fragmented film industry is hardly exclusive to Argentina. In *Global Hollywood 2*, Toby Miller and his co-authors describe what they call "the new international division of cultural labour," in which "creative collaborations" that go into a film production transpire in multiple locations (125). Miller and others allude to animated films to illustrate this idea, with artists located in different countries being contracted for a particular project.

11. Farsa's domestic reception among critics and critical forums beyond genre cinema in Argentina has proved exceptional. The book *Generaciones 60/90: cine argentino independiente* (edited by Fernando Martín Peña, Fundación Eduardo F. Costantini, 2003) accompanied a film series at Museo de Arte Latinoamericano de Buenos Aires (MALBA) that screened select Argentine independent cinema from the 1960s and 1990s. Farsa is the only producer of horror cinema that appears in the collection. Farsa also appears in Fernando Martín Peña's *Cien años de cine argentino* (Editorial Biblos, 2012), and, again, is the only producer of horror cinema mentioned.

12. *Plaga zombie* has also inspired filmmakers outside Argentina. A low-budget production titled *Plaga zombie: American Invasion* is set in New Bedford, Massachusetts, sixteen years following the original story in the *Plaga zombie* trilogy. *Plaga Zombie: American Invasion* is to be released in 2018, and features cameo appearances of several members of Farsa.

13. For more information about BARS's genesis, see its website, specifically the section titled "Acerca del festival" ("About the festival"). The term *bizarra/o* relates specifically to an Argentine context. Here, *bizarra/o* does not translate into *brave* or *courageous*, as generally defined in most English-Spanish dictionaries, but rather, it translates into *strange*. The origins of bizarre/o in Argentine film has been traced back to Fabio Manes, the late critic, programmer, and collector. During the 1980s, Manes first used the term in relation to a film series he and Diego Curubeto organized entitled "Medianoches bizarras. Diego Curubeto's book *Cine bizarro* further cemented the term's meaning (Scherer; Curubeto 15), and the boundaries of *cine bizarro* are incredibly elastic and encompass horror, fantasy, cult, and exploitation cinemas.

14. The emergence of other horror films in Argentina at the end of the 1990s and early 2000s expanded upon and made more visible a small but already existing node of horror cinema production in Buenos Aires. During the 1980s and 1990s, a handful of filmmakers in Buenos Aires were making short horror films, such as Fabio Manes's "Flash sangriento" / "Bloody Flashback" (1986). Such films circulated primarily as VHS cassettes, were available through specialized video stores,

and exhibited in film clubs in Buenos Aires (Curubeto and Peña 99). In addition, *Charly, días de sangre*/"Charly, Days of Blood" (Carlos Galettini, 1990), a low-budget exploitation-slasher film was released direct-to-video and enjoys a cult status in Argentina. The end of the 1990s witnessed a number of low-budget productions belonging to the horror genre, including *El ritual*/"The Ritual" (Paula Pollachi and Pablo del Teso, 1997), and Alexis Puig's *Vendado y frío*/"Blindfolded and Cold" (1998) and *No muertos*/"The Undead" (1999). For a more expansive discussion of the history of Argentine horror production during the twentieth century, see Darío Lavia's work on his site *Cinefania*, chapter 1 of Rodríguez, various articles by Pablo Sapere on QuintaDimension.com, and Pagnoni.

15. *Porteño/a* refers to something or someone from or affiliated with the city of Buenos Aires.

16. Numerous other Argentine horror directors second Pollachi's sentiments in *Rojo sangre: 10 años a puro género*/"BARS: 10 years of pure genre cinema," a documentary film that serves as both an homage to BARS as well as an excellent primer about numerous issues related to Argentine horror cinema, such as distribution, the reception of Argentine horror by national audiences and critics, and the horror genre's evolving relationship with INCAA.

17. Given the screenings of films from Serbia, the United States, Spain, and Mexico, among other countries, BARS also can possess a transnational significance for filmmakers from outside Argentina. For instance, Uruguayan director Fede Álvarez first screened "Ataque de pánico" / "Panic Attack" at BARS in 2009, after which he posted the short to YouTube and was sought after by various US production companies.

18. Dayan's observations of Sundance were based on his experience there in 1997. Albeit speculation, had he observed the festival ten or fifteen years later, a social media aspect would possibly figure more prominently into his ethnography of the event.

19. For example, one film production workshop for children took place during the Feria del Libro Infantil y Juvenil in Buenos Aires in July of 2015.

20. Information about the cities in which particular short films were made and screened at Buenos Aires Rojo Sangre comes from an interview with Pablo Sapere in 2008. The cities in which specific short films were produced and shown at the Muestra Internacional de Cine Terror appears in the festival's program.

21. This is not to imply that other cities, such as Rosario, Mendoza, and, most especially, La Plata, do not merit attention.

22. For example, in the documentary *Rojo sangre: 10 años a puro género*, Fabiana Roth, producer, actress, and president of Druida Films, alludes to the lack of professionalization as an obstacle to horror cinema production in Argentina.

23. Of course, the question of budget can be relative to a particular country, and a horror film deemed to have a low budget in a country such as the United States does not constitute a low-budget production in Argentina. To cite one example, *You're Next* (Adam Wingard, 2011) is one film often referred to as a low-budget horror film in the popular press in the United States (Truitt). However, its budget of one million dollars would make the film anything but a low-budget production in Argentina.

24. The list of films in the table is hardly an exhaustive list of low-budget horror productions in Argentina. For a more complete list, see Rodríguez (110–19). The figures provided in table 1.1 come from various sources. The budgets for *Plaga zombie*, *Habitaciones para turistas* and *Mala carne* come from Rodríguez's study. The budget for *Sadomaster* appears on Gorevisión's website, and the budget for *Death Knows Your Name* appears in an article about Daniel de la Vega (Panessi). The budget for *Breaking Nikki* appears in a personal email from the film's director Hernán Findling. All figures have been converted into US dollars using the rate of peso to dollar conversion at the time of a film's release.

25. In addition to data on spectators, *Taquilla Nacional* has a category of articles titled "Exhibición Alternativa" ("Alternative Exhibition"). While the articles do not offer figures regarding spectators for films circulating outside commercial venues, there is coverage of DVD releases of independently produced films including horror, screenings organized by *No sólo en cines*, and YouTube releases of films such as *Daemonium*.

26. Based on the number of hits a post receives, YouTube will send a check to the individual who posts that material to YouTube. The number of hits for each film appearing in the table is based on findings as of February 8, 2016. The total quantity of hits for *Death Knows Your Name* comes from the movie's posting by Maverick Movies (66,266 hits), the film's US distributor, and another by "komödie deutsch 2015" (24,574 hits).

27. The creation of and need for alternative circuits of exhibition are not exclusive to the horror genre in Argentina. In "El cine argentino: Espacios para una geografía alternativa del cine," Daniela Pereyra alludes to scores of different venues that compose alternative circuits for cinema such as cinema clubs in different cities,

cineambulantes ("mobile cinemas"), and BAZOFI, a festival in the country's capital that shows rare films, which runs parallel to the BAFICI.

28. As Tamara Falicov notes regarding Espacios INCAA, "The idea behind these theatres is not to have to be beholden to the whims of exhibitors, who by and large consider national films to be more risky and less profitable than Hollywood's" (*Cinematic Tango* 138). The exhibition of low-budget horror cinema in Espacios INCAA has seldom occurred. For example, in 2009 the Espacio INCAA KM 2 in the San Telmo neighborhood of Buenos Aires screened Farsa's *Nunca más asistas a este tipo de fiestas*.

29. For information about the process that films go through to be considered by INCAA, see Rodríguez, chapter 3, section 4.

30. For additional information about *No sólo en cines*, see its website: nosoloencines.com.ar.

31. INCAA TV is the television channel belonging to and administered by INCAA, which began operations in January 1, 2011. The channel provides a crucial venue mainly to national film and television productions belonging to different genres as well as Latin American and "presentaciones especiales de films relevantes de la producción mundial" ("special presentations of film relevant to world cinema") ("El equipo"). *Trasnochados* ("Up All Night") is a programming cycle reserved for Argentine genre cinema with series dedicated to specific genres (horror films, short horror films screened at BARS, and fantasy cinema) or stars, such as Isabel Sarli. CINE.AR PLAY exclusively streams national film and television productions with an expanding catalog that includes horror shorts, such as *Alexia* (Andres Borghi, 2013), and feature-length films, such as *Los Super bonarenses* (Germán Magariños, 2014), *Mujer lobo/She-Wolf* (Tamae Garateguy, 2013), and *La segunda muerte* / "The Second Death" (Santiago Fernández Calvete, 2011).

32. For example, see Matías Raña's *Guerreros del cine argentino, fantástico e independiente*, and Mariano Oliveros's *D-culto nacional* (Fan Ediciones, 2014), which deal with national independent genre cinema and cult cinema, respectively.

33. Matías Raña shared this hypothesis in a personal interview, and Alexis Puig and Fernando Spiner proposed similar ideas in separate interviews that appear in the documentary *Rojo sangre: 10 años a puro género*.

34. The figures related to the first four movies listed in the table come from Ultracine's website, and the figures from the other ten movies come from Taquilla Nacional's site.

35. One is hard-pressed to pinpoint the genesis of Argentine horror cinema's marginal status or the overarching reason for its marginalization. Besides the

reasons I cite here, one might also consider horror cinema as an affront to the tastes of potential producers, which, in turn, intimates the position of horror, as well as other genres, within a national hierarchy of tastes. Although such claims would require considerable sociological research among Argentine producers and moviegoers, several years ago in an interview Daniel de la Vega likened the reaction of some producers to financing a genre or horror film to making a pornographic movie: "Conozco a muchísimos productores de la Argentina, y muchos otros me conocen, sin embargo la propuesta de llevar un proyecto de género siempre fue catalogada como pornográfica" ("I know many Argentine producers, and many know me. Still, the proposal to make a genre film always was received as if I wanted to make a pornographic film") (Conde y Mérida 57).

36. Similar characterizations of New Argentine Cinema can be found elsewhere. For example, after alluding to the similarities that other critics have drawn between Italian neorealism and New Argentine Cinema and the latter's capacity to show cultural dynamics, Joanna Page writes, "The grainy, unfinished, 'ad-hoc' nature of these low-budget, independent films expresses with greater eloquence the fissures and imperfections of the present" (34).

37. With regard to Oubiña's last point, he assigns film critics a special task of helping to create a margin in which nonmainstream films can "sobrevivir y puedan hacerse visibles" ("survive and can be visible") (Prólogo 15).

38. Oubiña's differentiation between marginal and mainstream films based on risk and technology can, of course, easily break down. Using new cinematic technology can itself be a form of experimentation and risk-taking even in commercial cinema, as in James Cameron's *Avatar* (2009) or *Hardcore Henry* (Ilya Naishuller, 2016).

39. *El amante de cine* usually has two covers on each side of an issue, as opposed to the back side being reserved exclusively for advertising.

40. Sconce uses the term " 'seeing through' the diegesis" to denote the practice of viewing a film such as Ed Wood's *Glen or Glenda* as one that merges fiction with autobiographical elements, as well as a text that flouts the prevailing cultural norms at the time of its release in the 1950s.

41. It is crucial to note in a discussion about the paracinematic in Argentine horror that the majority of filmmakers are not marginal filmmakers by choice. Diment, Adrián García Bogliano, the collective Farsa, and Daniel de la Vega, among others, aspire to make films that are released in commercial cinemas.

42. See, for example, Deborah Martin's *The Cinema of Lucrecia Martel* (Manchester: U of Manchester P, 2016).

43. While Lobato refrains from an extensive discussion of the "pleasures of mediocrity," he alludes to how STV movies can be "genuinely loved [, while] others are enjoyed in a tongue-in-cheek way, for containing the worst special effects, the silliest dialogue and so on" (34). The notion of mediocrity pertains also to a "mode of production" in which films are made quickly as "something to be bought and sold and watched and forgotten" (34).

44. Since 2009, Ventana Sur has taken place in Buenos Aires and is presently the largest film market in Latin America.

45. Falicov describes a festival film as one "with particular aesthetic and narrative conventions for an educated audience and from a higher economic class stratum," in which the conventions forego a swift pace and spectacles for a more realist and quotidian narrative ("The 'Festival Film'" 214–15).

46. Argentine horror films have been screened at each of the festivals noted as well as festivals that have emerged since the publication of *Horrofílmico* in 2012, such as Zinema Zombie (Bogotá, Colombia) and Fixion SARS (Santiago, Chile).

47. There are exceptions to Argentine horror films being distributed by smaller companies. Lionsgate distributes *Jennifer's Shadow* in the United States, and Cameo distributes *La segunda muerte* in Spain. International DVD distribution of Argentine horror films appear largely part of a straight-to-DVD market, which, as Lobato resoundingly demonstrates "make up the 'invisible' bulk of global [film] production activity" (33). Availing itself of the STV market and its practices, Argentine horror films also run the possibility of distribution impinging upon content, which can be conceived as a form of secondary consumption production, or what distributors do with a film. For example, in an interview Adrián García Bogliano jokingly described how a rape-revenge film he directed, *No moriré sola*, was altered in Japan by omitting the rape scene to become simply a "revenge film" (García Bogliano).

48. Hantke grounds his idea of subcultural capital by using the work of Sarah Thornton, who draws on Pierre Bourdieu's notion of cultural capital. For Bourdieu, cultural capital originally accounted for "the unequal scholastic achievement of children originating from the different social classes" (Thorton 243). In short, cultural capital might refer to the education (in the broadest sense) and societal position that students attained or occupied given their socioeconomic status, factors that influence a student's achievement beyond the confines of a school. For example, a student's membership within a well-connected family may confer on him or her access to particular kinds of social networks that enable his or her

entrance into a prestigious school. In such a case, the student would have higher cultural capital than a student who lacked such a social network. While conceived of three different kinds of cultural capital (the embodied, objectified, and institutionalized states), my, Hantke's, and Thornton's use of *cultural capital* refers to its embodied state, a form of capital that Bourdieu adduces as "culture, cultivation, [and] *Bildung*" (Thorton 244). Thornton writes about certain forms of knowledge that "delineate the boundaries of a subculture" against a "mainstream culture" (11), and, according to Hantke, a horror film fan's knowledge of foreign horror cinema may endow him or her with a particular cachet within a US horror film culture (Introduction 18–20). The websites I list here do not exclusively focus on local and/or foreign horror cinema and do not shun mainstream horror film releases such as *The Shining* (Stanley Kubrick, 1980) or *Halloween* (John Carpenter, 1978). Nevertheless, the inclusion of Argentine horror cinema, as well as other foreign horror film releases, does set the websites apart from other film websites that may limit themselves to horror films that have received theatrical releases.

49. *Cine testimonio* can be defined in various ways. In *Cuban Cinema*, Michael Chanan refers to two forms of *cine testimonio* and several subgenres that are particular to Cuban cinema. Chanan associates one form of *cine testimonio* with the Mexican documentarist Eduardo Maldonado. A film becomes a way for a marginalized social group to "make public their point of view," and the process of making a film enables a kind of *concientización*, the raising of consciousness or awareness, of that social group (Chanan 209). A second form of *cine testimonio* is inspired by testimonial literature, which, loosely defined, depicts the lived experiences of authors. For Chanan, testimonial literature inspires particular modes of documentary: filming "reality without subjecting it to a preplanned mise-en-scène," a focus on social themes, "audacious and intuitive styles of montage," and the use of interviews (Chanan 211). Chanan boils down these four principles of *cine testimonio* in documentaries by relying on a paper presented by director, poet, and journalist Víctor Casaus, "El género testimonio en el cine cubano" ("The Testimonial Genre in Cuban Cinema").

50. Elsewhere in *The Cinematic Tango*, Falicov defines "un cine rico" as having higher budgets, featuring stars, and being "geared toward middle-class audiences and international film festival consumption" (9). In contrast, "cine pobre" denotes an approach to cinematic production in which a country's film production agencies fund "a large quantity of low-budget films for domestic audiences," which conform to New Latin American Cinema's vision for films that depict the "social realities of a Latin America in crisis" (Falicov, *Cinematic Tango* 9).

51. The original announcement for the fantasy film *concurso* by INCAA outlined support for two films and two alternates. However, when the winners were announced, the committee amended the regulations so as to support four films. The winners and their respective directors were *Soy tóxico* / "I am Toxic" (Daniel de la Vega); *La casa acecha* / "The Creeping House" (Mariano de Rosa); *Aterrados*/"Terrified" (Demián Rugna); and *Proyecto Epecuén*/"The Epecuén Project" (Nicolás and Luciano Onetti). The *concurso* for fantasy cinema continued in 2016.

52. The announcement concerning the *concurso* for fantasy films appeared on various websites, such as that of Blood Window.

CHAPTER 2

1. For an overview of spectacle in different film genres, see the collection of essays edited by Geoff King titled *The Spectacle of the Real: From Hollywood to 'Reality' TV and Beyond* (Intellect, 2005). Regarding the formal elements of a spectacle, various critics formally define a cinematic spectacle through the close-up. In "Spectacle and Narrative Theory," an essay that does not appear in the aforementioned collection edited by King, Lea Jacobs and Richard de Cordova characterize spectacle through an array of close-ups and extreme close-ups of Marlene Dietrich in films such as *Scarlet Empress* (Josef von Sternberg, 1937). Likewise, Mulvey adduces close-ups of women's legs and faces as examples of how the camera renders a woman as a spectacle on-screen (11–12). I do not dispute the use of close-ups to create a spectacle. However, the close-up is only one of several formal elements that define violent spectacles in horror cinema. I am primarily interested in screen violence as spectacle, and close-ups alone do not necessarily translate into screen violence.

2. Lowenstein positions "spectacle horror" against another category of horror he refers to as "ambient horror" ("Spectacle Horror" 42), which presumably is a kind of horror that relies on suggestion in lieu of a graphic depiction of violence. As the title of his article suggests, Lowenstein argues against the use of torture porn to describe US films such as *Hostel, Hostel 2* (Eli Roth, 2007), and the *Saw* franchise. He feels such a term sensationalizes a film and obviates any serious critical consideration.

3. For instance, in her discussion on how women in Hollywood cinema often constitute "an indispensable element of spectacle," Laura Mulvey argues that the woman as spectacle "tends to work against the story line, to freeze the flow of action

in moments of erotic contemplation" (11). Such ideas about spectacle rupturing a narrative flow are echoed in academic criticism of horror cinema. In her book, *Body Fantastic*, Linda Badley argues, "Like love scenes in adventure films, the spectacle of effects momentarily [arrests] the plot" (7). Similarly, Annalee Newitz writes of class issues in *Silence of the Lambs* (Jonathan Demme, 1991) as if they are obscured by gore: "The spectacles of murder and mutilated bodies are so heavily foregrounded that the questions about social class and economic mobility which fuel the narrative are safely contained as subtext" (4).

4. My use of the term *defamiliarize* is not accidental and comes from Victor Shklovsky's essay "Art as Technique." Shklovsky, whose essay was published in 1917, observed, "The technique of art is to make objects 'unfamiliar,' to make forms difficult, to increase the difficulty and length of perception because the process of perception is an aesthetic end in itself and must be prolonged" (12). For Shklovsky, "After we see an object several times, we begin to recognize it. [...] Art removes objects from the automatism of perception" (13). Inherent in Shklovsky's notion of defamiliarization is the obstruction and slowing down of perception, specifically in regard to literature. As I will argue, spectacle in many horror films is less endeared to slowing down than the speeding up and constitutes a different mode of defamiliarization.

5. Over the course of her book, Newitz articulates a taxonomy of capitalist monsters that include "serial killers, mad doctors, the undead, robots, and people involved in the media industry" (6).

6. Other Argentine zombie films include *El desierto*/*The Desert* (Christoph Behl, 2013), *Curas zombis en azul*, and *Un cazador de zombis*/"Zombie Hunter" (Germán Magariños, 2008). Argentine zombie cinema may be conceived as part of a larger wave of apocalyptic cultural production that testifies to societal transformations wrought by neoliberalism. See, for example, Fernando Reati's *Postales del porvenir* which examines Argentine science-fiction novels and their capacity to anticipate and show "la manera en que las transformaciones del país en esa década y media de neoliberalismo y globalización impactaron en el inconsciente colectivo y sus productos culturales" ("the way in which a decade and a half of neoliberalism and globalization have transformed the country and impacted its collective unconscious and cultural production") (14).

7. I subsequently refer to *Plaga zombie: Zona mutante* simply as *Zona mutante*. As I explain, *Plaga zombie: Zona mutante* is the second installment in what is supposed to be a zombie movie trilogy. The first movie is titled *Plaga zombie*

and premiered in 1997, and the third part, *Revolución tóxica*/"Toxic Revolution" debuted at the Buenos Aires Rojo Sangre festival in October of 2011.

8. See, for example, Fontana.

9. John West is a wrestler/cowboy who is past his prime.

10. Such a scene is reminiscent of a number of films, such as Sam Raimi's *Evil Dead* and *Evil Dead 2* (1987) and *Cemetery Man* (Michele Soavi, 1994).

11. Among the examples of conspiracy films, Jameson alludes to *Three Days of the Condor* (Sydney Pollock, 1975), *All the President's Men* (Alan Pakula, 1976), and *The Parallax View* (Alan Pakula, 1974).

12. One can think of any number of zombie films in which individuals, who are themselves often metonyms of race, class, gender, and age, are forced into alliances: George Romero and Lucio Fulci's zombie films, *Shock Waves* (Ken Wiederhorn, 1977), *28 Days Later* (Danny Boyle, 2002), and *Zombieland* (Rubin Fleischer, 2009), among others. The alliances, however, are inevitably fragile and often falter for any number of reasons.

13. *Piqueteros* has often been translated into English as "picketers." *Piqueteros* generally refer to associations of unemployed workers who organize various actions such as *cortes de ruta* ("roadway blockades") or blockades of financial buildings to protest government policies and to demand unemployment relief. *Cacerolazos* refer to the massive protests that occurred in Argentina in 1996 and December of 2001. I describe both these terms and their significance later in the chapter.

14. *Piqueteros* conduct a number of actions within communities, but are perhaps most known for *cortes de ruta* in their attempt to solicit government aid.

15. Ramos Mejía considers the multitudes (as opposed to the elites) as largely responsible for helping Argentina to defeat the British in 1806 and 1807, and gain independence from Spain several years later.

16. Despite the similarities to Le Bon's terminology and several of his concepts, Mejías Ramos's text is highly original and constitutes a theoretical lens through which to consider multitudes and crowds at particular historical moments in Argentina and perhaps elsewhere in Latin America.

17. While a word-for-word Spanish-English translation of *Cuando tu carne grite ¡Basta!* would be "When Your Flesh Screams Enough!," the film is invariably translated as *When Your Flesh Screams* in numerous forums, such as imdb.com, YouTube, and various horror film websites.

18. In addition to noting how rape and revenge structure the narrative, Henry's concise summation of the rape-revenge subgenre includes a "loose iconography (mud-covered seminaked rape victims; red lipstick and fetish costumes of the

transformed avenger; castration; women with guns), stock characters (young white, attractive victim turned femme fatale avenger; rapists; rednecks), and key themes and conflicts (transformation; rape trauma; ethics of revenge; vigilantism; torture)" (4).

19. As Ana Laura Lusnich states in her introduction to a collection of essays titled *Civilización y barbarie en el cine argentino y latinoamericano*, "[d]esde 1845, fecha de la publicación del *Facundo* de Domingo Faustino Sarmiento, *civilización y barbarie* se han constituido en conceptos clave no solo en las explicaciones de los procesos históricos y culturales sino también en la producción de textos artísticos" ("[S]ince 1845, the publication date of Domingo Faustino Sarmiento's *Facundo*, *civilization and barbarity* has constituted a key concept not only in historical and cultural explanations, but also in artistic production" 13). With specific attention given to Argentine cinema, the collection of essays edited by Lusnich attests to the persistence of the *civilización y barbarie* dichotomy in national cinema ranging from *Nobleza Gauchal*"Gaucho Nobility" (Humberto Cairo, Ernesto Gunche, Eduardo Martínez de la Pera, 1915) to *El bonarense* (Pablo Trapero, 2002).

20. It is crucial to nevertheless note that symbolic political gains for women in Argentina have not necessarily translated into a wave of women taking additional institutional leadership roles (Di Marco).

21. See, for example, the comments following a review of *No moriré sola*. Though the site is Spanish, a number of commentators on almasoscuras.com are presumably Argentine given their expressions of pride and desire to see the film due to it national origins.

22. It is never clear during the film whether Hugo colludes with Jorge and Nicanor, or if he actually believes that Nicanor is obsessed with Alicia.

CHAPTER 3

1. Martin-Jones and Soledad Montañez refer to *Miami Vice* (Michael Mann, 2006) as an instance in which Montevideo and Atlántida stand in for Havana, Colombia, Miami, and Geneva (49).

2. Among the films that Martin-Jones and Soledad Montañez reference to illustrate ideas of auto-erasure is *La casa muda/The Silent House* (Gustavo Hernández, 2010), a horror film. The film possesses its own dynamics of auto-erasure, namely the minimization of Uruguayan cultures. However, unlike the Argentine

English-language horror films, *La casa muda* uses Spanish-language dialogue spoken with an Uruguayan accent.

3. Latin American Spanish-language genre films frequently have served as stepping stones for select directors—Fede Álvarez, Sebastián Cordero, and Guillermo del Toro—to make higher-budgeted English-language genre productions. Argentine horror adds to the variation of how films with different linguistic dialogues function within the trajectory of a director's oeuvre. While Adrián García Bogliano has progressed from making low-budget horror in Spanish-language dialogue to higher-budgeted productions in various languages (Spanish, English, and Swedish) and countries (Argentina, Mexico, the United States, and Sweden), the case is different for directors such as Daniel de la Vega and Demián Rugna whose first low-budget feature films were made with English-language dialogue. As discussed previously, irrespective of language, Argentine horror films that are well-received abroad often can translate into a laudable domestic reception among fans and critics. However, the English-language films do not necessarily automatically translate into a progression for the filmmakers' careers. INCAA's *concursos* operate on a point system (Panessi), and De la Vega and Rugna's English-language productions did not provide them any points. Nevertheless, both directors have progressed from making low-budget English-language horror films to higher-budget Spanish-language horror productions with INCAA's support.

4. *Death Club* (James Merendino, 2008) potentially could also be counted among the Argentine English-language horror films. However, Merendino is from the United States, the film's dialogue is in Spanish and English, the majority of the films' actors and production crew are Argentine, and *Death Club* makes no attempt to obscure its Argentine locations. This aside, *Mocosis*, *Ultra-Toxic*, *Mondo Psycho*, and *Run, Bunny, Run!* use English-language dialogues not to hide filming locations, but for other motives. Mad Crampi has remarked that English in his films make the cinematic universes more bizarre in lieu of obscuring a film's actual location (2009). In *Ultra-Toxic*, English is part of a dystopia in which the protagonist, Peter Shek (Juan Manuel Gonzales Araoz), loses his command of Spanish and instead speaks English. Shek's loss of Spanish appears to be a consequence of having some kind of microchip implanted in his body by a lab whose operatives all speak accented English. In *Mocosis*, one of the two protagonists, Agent Jhonson, speaks accented English, while the other characters speak Spanish. Marcelo Leguiza, director of *Mocosis*, has commented that Jhonson's accented-English parodies Hollywood films in which a US actor attempts to speak Spanish and mangles the language (2016).

5. The English-language Argentine horror films set in cities are hardly the first films to draw on the accoutrements of urbanism to undermine a film's actual location and to anchor the film's diegesis elsewhere or nowhere. In *Cities and Cinema*, Barbara Mennel alludes to Jackie Chan's kung-fu action-comedy films and how urban visual textuality evacuates the location's specificity, irrespective of the narrative taking place in Hong Kong, Los Angeles, or New York. According to Mennel, "By using generic urban structures, such as parking garages, staircases, and skyscraper walls as the terrain for Chan's acrobatic action style, the cityscape stands in for any city, anywhere" (93). Mennel is obviously focusing strictly on architecture and discounting other filmic elements that can anchor a film to a particular locale such as language (English vs. Cantonese), superimposed words that indicate location, or even the racial makeup of characters. This point aside, the Argentine films are not aspiring to a transnational urban aesthetic or a cinematic anywhere, but rather, as I state above, the specific creation of a generic urban United States.

6. In his book *Hick Flicks: The Rise and Fall of Redneck Cinema*, Scott von Doviak examines films from the 1970s, 1980s, and 1990s and their depictions of rural America. Von Doviak traces redneck cinema across different film genres (horror, comedies, road movies, musicals, among others) with their common thread being a depiction of "the rural American folklore of their time—in this case, the 1970s" (9).

7. See the first chapter for statistics on the imbalance between US cinema distributed in the Argentina and Argentine cinema distributed in the United States. Regarding the production of Hollywood cinema in Argentina and the presence of Argentines in Hollywood, see Diego Curubeto's *Babilonia Gaucha* and *Babilonia Gaucha: Ataca de nuevo*.

8. Tudor's characterization of paranoid horror films partially concurs with other generalizations of postmodern horror cinema, such as the lack of narrative closure and the degradation of authority figures. See, for example, Modelski, Hills, and Pinedo.

9. In *Nightmare Movies*, Kim Newman refers to different subgenres of horror (and nonhorror, such as conspiracy films) in films produced since 1968 within a chapter titled "Paranoia Paradise." Newman does not create as focused and comprehensive a list as does Tudor, rather Newman points out particular motifs and expressions of paranoia among several groups of movies.

10. The allure of Latin America for offering places to produce films that are inexpensive relative to the United States is no secret. My phrasing of "where

'[film-making] is cheap' " is a play on the notorious snuff film *Snuff* (Michael Findlay, Roberta Findlay, and Horacio Fredriksson, 1976) whose provocative tagline was "The film that could only be made in South America ... where Life is CHEAP!"

11. Argentine films with English-language dialogue and oriented to a US market are not without precedence. For example, Gerard Dapena and Diego Curubeto have described how several of Emilio Vieyra's films were oriented toward a US English-language market. Vieyra directed *Extraña invasión/Stay Tuned for Terror* (1965), a US production made in Argentina with almost an entirely Argentine cast with the exception of the film's protagonist, Richard Conte. El Palomar, a section of Greater Buenos Aires where *Extraña invasión* was filmed, was made to look like the US South (Curubeto, *Cine bizarro* 361–62). While the only existing version of the film has Spanish dialogue, Vieyra mentioned a version in which the cast speaks English (Dapena 100). In addition, other films directed by Vieyra such as *Testigo para un crimen/Violated Love* (1964) or *La venganza del sexo/The Curious Dr. Humpp* (1969) were dubbed into English for distribution in the English-language US market in the United States, or produced in English (Curubeto, *Cine bizarro* 361). The dubbed English-language dialogue and racy scenes enabled Vieyra's films to be distributed in the United States.

Tamara Falicov has described a series of US-Argentine coproductions headed by Roger Corman and Héctor Olivera during the 1980s, and those coproductions are similar to Vieyra's films. Falicov divides the films according to genre and the degree of erasure of Argentine culture. On the one hand, the coproductions associated with Corman and Olivera belong to the sword and sorcery genre, and Argentina is entirely absent from the on-screen content, including the ending credits in which Corman insisted that the Argentine film technicians anglicize their names ("US-Argentine" Falicov 33). Otherwise, the films are thrillers and action movies that simplify Argentina and exaggerate unfortunate stereotypes of either the country as being a Nazi refuge or its male population as being extremely *machista*. The English-language dialogue in contemporary Argentine horror films present dynamics that are similar to select films directed by Vieyra and those produced by Corman and Olivera. First, the contemporary horror films are trafficking in a lowbrow genre, and the English dialogue in the Argentine horror films is merely a single aspect that helps to perform the ruse of concealing actual filming locations (Argentina) and anchoring the film within a generic version of another country (in the case of the horror films, the present-day United States). While Argentina is generally muted or omitted from the films of Vieyra, Corman, and Olivera, the projection of a generic United States makes the contemporary Argentine English-language horror films exceptional. As noted above, the mise-en-scène in Vieyra's

Extraña invasión was intended to resemble the United States. However, given the absence of an existing version of the film with English-language dialogue, *Extraña invasión* possesses its own dynamics of projecting the United States from Argentina distinct from those of the contemporary films.

12. Doubles are also crucial for forging an aesthetic that projects paranoia over an approaching death that is cyclical but temporarily and spatially unknown. Besides the presence of Gregor and Dr. Taylor/William, doubles abound in the film. No less than three sets of twins appear at different points, and mirrors appears sometimes at random instances. One may be tempted to draw on Freud's idea that the sets of doubles in the film act as "the uncanny harbinger of death" (235), specifically Dr. Taylor's death. For a detailed reading on doubles in horror cinema, see Steven Jay Schneider's essay, "Manifestations of the Literary Double in Modern Horror Cinema" in *Horror Film and Psychoanalysis* (Cambridge UP, 2004).

13. The opening shot in *Death Knows Your Name* is somewhat reminiscent of the opening shots in *The Cat and the Canary* (Paul Leni, 1927) or *Alien* (Ridley Scott, 1979). However, unlike the sequence in *Alien*, which many consider suggests a womblike space (for example, see Barbara Creed's *The Monstrous-Feminine*), the opening shot of the hospital in *Death Knows Your Name* is hardly maternal.

14. A devastating outbreak of yellow fever that killed thousands of people occurred in 1871 in Buenos Aires.

15. In *The Pleasures of Horror*, Hills takes to task cognitive theories that explain the reception of horror as steeped in emotion and purely "object directed" that do not allow for horror to be conceived as "a mood or ambience" (25). Taking into account music, mise-en-scène, and horror films that never reveal a monster (e.g., *Blair Witch*), Hills contends that horror possesses the capacity to provoke in viewers object-directed emotion and objectless affects.

16. Gregor momentarily invades and possesses Richard's body. Richard's voice does not alter drastically and, with the exception of jaundiced skin, his complexion and physical body do not metamorphose à la Linda Blair's character, Regan, in *The Exorcist* (William Friedkin, 1973). A viewer is sometimes forced to decide whether Richard is speaking as Richard—a patient in a mental hospital, or as Gregor—a malevolent spirit harnessing Richard's body and vocal cords.

17. If the elevation ensures Buenos Aires is kept under wraps, the framing also helps. The DVD extras include a short documentary, "Making of DKYN," with "DKYN" being an abbreviation for the film's title. The short documentary includes some shots of the hospital roof. One sees a large Argentine flag flying to the left of

Dr. Taylor, an obvious symbol of Argentina that had to be excised from the frame if the film's location were to remain anonymous.

18. Dr. Taylor's helplessness as part of the uncanny is visually captured by the circumstances of his death. After Gregor's rebirth, Dr. Taylor goes to a corridor of the abandoned hospital where he eventually encounters Gregor and the end of one corridor opens up onto larger spaces that contain doors. Gregor conjures his monstrous reflection, which resembles a scaly man, and walks with an extremely slow gait. Given the monster's slow pace and the hospital's open spaces and many doors, one might expect Dr. Taylor to escape the monster. However, fate does not allow it.

19. Place is crucial to Dr. Taylor's/William's cyclical fate, and *Death Knows Your Name* appears to draw on a number of ideas from Freud's essay, "The 'Uncanny.'" The manner in which Dr. Taylor/William Vanhess is buried, or reburied, is significant. Freud writes, "To some people the idea of being buried alive is the most uncanny thing of all" ("Das Unheimliche" 244).

20. In *Dead Line*, one of Martin's friends, Aaron, makes a pass at Martin, and kisses him. Martin violently rejects his friend's advances.

21. The character's name is perhaps a tribute to the title character of George Romero's vampire film *Martin* (1977). The Martin from Romero's movie of course suffered from his own kinds of delusions, namely the belief that he is a vampire.

22. The final shot of the film is of a metro train making its way toward a tunnel and one hears Aaron's scream with the violence happening off-screen.

23. Roxie, located in Palermo, exhibits any number of stereotypical characteristics of a US diner: a free-standing structure covered in corrugated metal, a black-and-white checkerboard floor, an OPEN neon sign, a long countertop with cushioned stools that swivel, and of course a menu that includes burgers and fries.

24. Polanski's trilogy aside, one could categorize any number of horror and psychological horror films and dramas as apartment horror: *Pi* (Darren Aronofsky, 1998), *Eraserhead* (David Lynch, 1976), *Rec* (Jaume Balagueró and Paco Plaza, 2007), *Precious* (Lee Daniels, 2009), and *Los inquilinos del infierno* / "The Tenants from Hell" (Damián Leibovich and Juan Cruz Varela, 2004).

25. An apartment as a filming location should by no means preclude deep space or deep focus within a shot or scene. To give one example, in Alfred Hitchcock's *Rope* (1948), the camera usually remains in the sitting room and points toward the kitchen and one can perceive action in the background.

26. The voice's lack of knowing Martin's movements during conversations suggests a level of restriction on the voice that is at variance with other telephone

acousmêtre's in horror cinema. The telephone *acousmêtre*'s in *Scream* (Wes Craven, 1997) and the vignette "The Telephone" from Mario Brava's *Black Sabbath* (1963) possess a level of omniscience in that they know a character's movement and wield that knowledge to generate fear for the on-screen characters and possibly the audience.

27. For examples, see *Scream*, *High Tension* (Alexandre Aja, 2003), *Alien* (Ridley Scott, 1979), or *Event Horizon* (Paul W. S. Anderson, 1997).

28. The repeated presence of the same actors in English-language Argentine horror films could suggest a kind of star system. Ricardo Aragón, Kevin Schiele, and Hugo Halbrich appear in *The Last Gateway* and *Death Knows Your Name*, with Aragón also appearing in *Run Bunny Run!* and Halbrich in *Dying God*. Some English-language Argentine horror productions have relied on Argentine actors who possess a high level of English proficiency of English or US actors who were living in Buenos Aires at the time of a production (Rodríguez 144). A similar dynamic potentially extends to Spanish-language Argentine horror films produced by Paura Flics and Gorevisión, both of which use the same actors in different films. In the case of select short and feature-length films produced by Paura Flics, several of the same actresses appear in different movies such as Andrea Duarte in *36 Pasos* and *No moriré sola* and Victoria Witemburg in *Penumbra*, *Sudor frío*, *No moriré sola*, *36 pasos*, and *Grité una noche*. An anonymous writer on Paura Flics's blog and different bloggers on select horror websites allude to Paura's "star system," and Paura Flics's former website had a section labeled "Star System" ("HorrAR: algo está pasando en Argentina"). Lacking the same financial backing typical of the Hollywood or other star systems affiliated with national film industries, the notion of a star system in the context of Argentine horror cinema adheres more to a cult star system.

29. Lemkin's analysis of archetypal landscapes centers on the cinematic landscapes in Steven Spielberg's *Jaws* (1975) and he observes: "*Jaws* is not a film set in Los Angeles, New York, Washington, D.C., or the plains of the Midwest; it is about America—perhaps an America that does not exist and never did, but one the audience recognizes nonetheless" (321–22). In other words, the filmic spaces in *Jaws* are not an imitation of a single place in the United States, but rather a pastiche of several places that constitute an on-screen United States.

30. La Casa Juanita is a chalet built in a French style and serves as a museum in Colón.

31. Rabbid EFX did the special effects in *The Last Gateway* and *Death Knows Your Name*, along with other horror and nonhorror films produced in Argentina,

such as *Naturaleza muerta*, *Helena* (Milka López, 2014), and *Aballay*. Rabbid EFX also has participated in the production of the science-fiction/horror web series *Daemonium* and in several short films and television programs (Rabbid EFX). Rabbid EFX specializes in special effects and, thus, represent a slight modification in the DIY production of horror films in which individuals with a film crew wear several different hats, including doing the special effects. For an overview of contemporary special effects in Argentina, see Siseles.

32. Michael's stomach serves as a portal from hell; it is a metaphoric womb from which infernal beings emerge. Yet, the narrative device is less an instance of womb envy as in David Cronenberg's films (Robbins 135) and more the showing an abject and masculine body in distress owing to a neighbor's dabbling in the occult. Demián Rugna has acknowledged the influence of US horror cinema from the 1980s (2007), and a transformation of a masculine character into an infernal birthing mechanism brings to mind male characters who endure bodily transformations in several horror films from the 1980s, such as various titles directed by Cronenberg. Male characters in Cronenberg's film served as a supposed "soft" counterweight to cinematic hard bodies that embodied the Reagan-era with the likes of Sylvester Stallone or Arnold Schwarzenegger (Badley 106). In this sense, *The Last Gateway*'s use of body horror traffics in horror subgenre dynamics that may be recognizable to audiences in the United States and elsewhere.

33. See, for example, Brown (2001).

34. In the case of Dr. Schreber, Freud locates this supreme power in Professor Flechsig, who was Dr. Schreber's primary physician and, according to Freud, for whom the patient harbored a sexual attraction.

35. Deleuze first mentions the idea of a Body without Organs (BwO) in *The Logic of Sense* when he refers to Antonin Artaud as "the superior body or body without organs" (88), and the idea is further articulated in Deleuze and Guattari's *Anti-Oedipus* and *A Thousand Plateaus*. While a footnote hardly provides the space to flush out the nuances of the concept, BwO stands in contrast to a psychoanalytic view of the subject in which desire is based on an Oedipal lack (Message 32). Instead, with an individual conceived as a BwO, desire is constantly in flux, and Deleuze and Guattari encourage cautious experimentation to attain alternate modes of experience.

36. The other four bodies to which Deleuze and Guattari allude are the *hypochondriac body*, the *schizo body*, the *drugged body*, and the *masochist body* (150).

37. Numerous contemporary studies of horror film reception have pointed to the variety of responses to screen horror among viewers. In light of these studies, I use the qualifier "possibly" in alluding to the reactions of viewers since

anxiety among viewers is merely one possible response. For studies of audiences' receptions of horror cinema, see, for example, Clover, Pinedo, Berenstein, Cherry, and Hanich.

38. Hofstadter is careful to note that the paranoid style is not exclusive to the United States and is characteristic of groups across the political spectrum.

39. In the recent past, there has been a proliferation of studies of conspiracy theories in US literature and culture, such as Melley, O'Donnell, Fenster, and Uscinski and Parent.

40. According to Douthat, in light of the sheer number of political thrillers, such as the Jason Bourne franchise, and the remakes of scores of 1970s horror films, such as *The Hills Have Eyes* (Alexandre Aja, 2006) and *Halloween* (Rob Zombie, 2007), "another decade entirely seems to have slouched round again: the paranoid, cynical, end-of-empire 1970s" (54).

41. For instance, Dr. Bruce Taylor in *Death Knows Your Name* is pursued by his brother, Gregor, in order to be reborn, a scenario that can be interpreted as a cyclical violence within families. According to Bruce/William Vanhess, Gregor attacked him because "Gregor thought he was unique," which simply does not speak to any larger political rancor that was unfolding in the post-9/11 United States at the time.

42. Massumi counts the following among the "allied events" linked to 9/11: President Richard Nixon's declaration of "war on terror" (perhaps Massumi is referring to the Nixon's declaration of a "war on drugs"), the bombing of the World Trade Center in 1993, and any number of terrorist attacks leading up to 9/11, which, "[i]f the historical and geographical parameters are enlarged, attacks that could be qualified as 'terrorist' stretch indefinitely" ("Future Birth" 86).

43. *Structure of feeling* is a term elaborated on by Raymond Williams in *Marxism and Literature*. The term provides a means for conceptualizing "the undeniable experience of the present" and denotes art's capacity to represent "a social experience which is still in process" (Williams 128, 132). See pages 128–35 in Williams's *Marxism and Literature* for a more detailed discussion of "structure of feeling."

And while the Argentine films arguably prioritize paranoias at work in US and Argentine culture, the narratives make visible paranoia as a psychic condition afoot in the United States, Argentina, and elsewhere, and suggest that a filmic rendering of paranoia is recognizable to transnational spectators. In contrast to other critics, I would argue that paranoia is not a global and totalizing condition that collapses all subjectivity into paranoia (Burgin), or what Emily Apter calls "oneworldness." Instead, the Argentine English-language horror films evidence paranoia as one transnational condition whose aestheticization has become normalized through the circulation of films featuring paranoid narratives.

44. The quote above originally appears on p. 467 of Catherine Leen's article, "City of Fear."

45. In *Going to Pieces*, some interviewees consider the slasher film an allegory of Reaganism and conservative ideologies with a killer brutally disciplining wayward teenagers. Offering a different reading, Robert Oppenheimer, a former assistant editor of the *The Advocate*, a gay and lesbian magazine, observes that the slasher genre alluded to the AIDS epidemic in the 1980s. If in the slasher movie victims and the audience do not know the killer's actual identity, then there is a parallel with AIDS in the 1980s in which one did not why people were falling ill and dying. Finally, for film director Amy Holden Jones, slasher films were about teenage girls' anxiety over having heterosexual sex for the first time.

46. While I am aware of the perils of collapsing Argentina and Mexico within the category of "Latina/o," a commercial for Argentina's national soccer team prior to the start of the Copa América's Centenario in the United States performs just such a collapse. Alternating between a montage of Donald Trump's alarmist campaign rhetoric about scores of people (read: Mexicans) crossing into the United States over the U.S.-Mexico border and images of Argentine soccer players and fans, the connection between Mexico and Argentina is unmistakable.

47. In chapter 3 ("Plotting Horror") of *Philosophy of Horror*, Noël Carroll describes plots typical of the horror genre in which discovery of a threat plays an invariable and crucial role.

CHAPTER 4

1. The faux rating box appears at the start of *Sadomaster 2: Locura general* and can be translated into English as: "The following film has been rated 'Revolting': absolutely prohibited for human consumption."

2. Chris Barber and Jack Sargeant's *No Focus: Punk on Film* (Headpress, 2006), another book whose essays I allude to in this chapter, also engages with punk cinema and conceives punk cinema through different traits, such as a gritty style, a punk attitude, and subversion. Regarding Thompson's analysis of punk in different contexts, he focuses on seven "major" scenes in which "participants in each scene number in the thousands rather than in the hundreds" (9). Those scenes include: (1) the New York Scene (1974–76), (2) the English Scene (1976–78), (3) the California Hardcore Scene (1978–82), (4) the Washington, DC First

Wave Straight Edge Scene (1979–85), (5) the New York Second Wave Straight Edge Scene (1986–89), (6) the Riot Grrrl Scene (1991–95), and (7) the Berkeley/Lookout! Pop-Punk Scene (1990–95).

3. I conceive these raw aesthetics as a lack of editing that would conform to the continuity style, unpolished sound, the absence of a professionally fabricated mise-en-scène—traits that one would expect in a higher-budget production.

4. Such a list is hardly exhaustive and one could include additional punk films by the same directors. Moreover, many of the directors and collectives make short films and music videos, all of which offer other potential visual materials that could be considered as punk/horror. Other Argentine directors and collectives whose work could also be conceived under a rubric of punk/horror include Elvia Serio, Federico James Tarántola, Vindicta Films, and Ballena Negra, among others.

5. Though punk/hardcore zines such as *Maximumrocknroll* have long covered global punk scenes (including Argentina), Argentina has generally not been counted among the primary sites of punk production, like the United States and England. Nevertheless, over the past decade more has been written and filmed about punk production (primarily, music, and zines) in Argentina. The documentary films *Mendoza Territorio Punk* / "Mendoza Punk Territory" (Tomás Makji, 2008) and *Buenos Aires 25 años de Hardcore Punk, El documental* / "Buenos Aires 25 Years of Hardcore Punk, The Documentary" (Miguel Luna y Andrés Lübbert, 2008), and *Una parte* / "A Part" (José Saraiva, 2011) provide an overview of punk music in Argentina and focus on punk music scenes in particular cities (*Una parte* focuses on punk in San Miguel de Tucumán). A plethora of books underscore the presence of punk music and ideologies in Argentina with some more well-known titles being *Punk rock, anarquía y tinta china* / "Punk Rock, Anarchy and Indian Ink" (Maximiliano Vadalá, Tren en movimiento, 2009); *Resistencia: registro impreso de la cultura punk rock subterránea, Bs As 1984–2001* / "Resistance: Printed Record of the Underground Punk Rock Culture, Buenos Aires 1984–2001" (Patricia Pietrafesa, Alcohol y Fotocopias, 2013); and *Derrumbando la Casa Rosada: mitos y leyendas de los primeros punks en la Argentina*/"Razing la Casa Rosada: Myths and Legends of the First Punks in Argentina" (various authors, Piloto de tormenta, 2012). A pair of essays by Pablo Cosso and Ingo Rohrer's *Cohesion and Dissolution* (Springer VS, 2014) appear to be the only academic examinations of Argentine punk.

6. The melding of punk and horror has transpired in a scant number of other films, such as *Return of the Living Dead* (Dan O'Bannon, 1985), a higher-budget

film that Chris Barber categorizes as "punksploitation" for its use of punk rock songs on its soundtrack and punk characters ("Punksploitation" 202–03, 214–06). Nevertheless, the mixing of punk and horror is not particular to cinema. US rock and punk rock bands such as the Misfits and White Zombie, among others, draw on horror iconography through their names, song and album titles, and stage props at their concerts. I credit Shane Greene for bringing this to my attention.

7. The essays in the collection *Film Criticism in the Digital Age* air differing opinions about the status of film criticism and its dispersal and fragmentation wrought by the emergence of personal blogs and websites such as Rotten Tomatoes. In the book's introduction, Mattias Frey provides an overview of the different reactions—negative, positive, and mixed—to the current state of film criticism. Frey alludes to Ronan McDonald's *Death of the Critic* to exemplify a reaction that bemoans critics' loss of aura. Paraphrasing McDonald, Frey writes, "[t]he vacuum of authority has been replaced by a host of nonexpert bloggers and a dispersive field of reviewing that fails to capture the public imagination" (6). While none of the essays in *Film Criticism in the Digital Age* focus on the Argentine context, similar debates have unfolded in Argentina as can be seen in an essay titled "¿El fin de la cinematográfica en la Argentina?" written by Diego Lerer (under the pseudonym "Peacock") and posted on his blog *Micropsia*. Beneath Lerer's essay appears a number of interventions by other critics and film directors and conversations between them as well.

8. *Intertextual relay* is a term coined by Gregory Lukow and Steven Ricci in their article titled "The 'Audience' Goes 'Public': Inter-textuality, Genre, and the Responsibilities of Film Literacy." Lukow and Ricci argue for taking into account the "ensemble of textualities" beyond a film (e.g., marketing campaigns, product synergy, and opening credit sequences) that compose a "network of discourses" and "addressed and recruited an audience, activated its anticipation, pulled it into line, and ushered it into the theater" (29).

9. I discuss SRN Distribution in the first chapter.

10. In *Introduction to Documentary*, Bill Nichols defines the observational mode as "observing lived experience spontaneously" with the filmmaker and/or production crew foregoing control over the "staging, arrangement, or composition of a scene" (110). In addition, the observational mode can be characterized as having "no voice-over commentary, no supplementary music or sound effects, no intertitles, no historical reenactments, no behavior repeated for the camera, and not even any interviews" (Nichols 110).

11. To view the entire program of "Primera semana de Cinepunk de Buenos Aires," as well as other information related to the festival, see semanacinepunk.blogspot.com/. The Cinepunk Festival aside, similar to low-budget horror productions in Argentina, various spaces can become an exhibition space for punk/horror films. A number of directors have commented on the importance and perhaps necessity of showing their films in a multiplicity of spaces. Aside from BARS and Festival de Cine Inusual, Leguiza has mentioned showing Mutazion's films in bars, cultural centers, or at parties (2015). Likewise, Magariños has remarked that Gorevisión's films have been screened in bars or cultural centers and, though less frequently, at metal concerts in which the film initiates the event and the bands perform after the screening (2015). Magariños plays bass guitar in the metal band Velocidad 22.

12. For discussions of authenticity in different punk subcultures, see Hannerz (2015) and Moore (2004). For example, Moore alludes to a "culture of authenticity" that ran through numerous punk rock scenes in the United States and the United Kingdom. Not only was punk couched in opposition to an "artificial" commercial culture; Moore describes how particular scenes (e.g., the hard-core scene in southern California) police "its boundaries" in order to maintain its authenticity that was characterized by an ascetic lifestyle that eschewed drugs, alcohol, and promiscuous sex. Through an ethnography of punk rock subcultures in Sweden and Indonesia, Hannerz likewise documents how notions of authenticity play out among musicians and fans so as to exclude those deemed lacking proper credentials.

13. Thompson counts a filmmaker's lack of formal training as a criteria for punk film production (160). The lack of a director's training anticipates a film's quality raw film aesthetic, since he or she has not mastered the wielding of a camera, editing, mise-en-scène, and/or sound production.

14. Thompson's resolute pairing of economics and aesthetics enables the category of "punk" to maintain some force in light of its ubiquitous application to describe a disparate range of cinematic movements and films. A collection of essays entitled *New Punk Cinema* presents an instance in which critics argue that punk can manifests itself in cinema in different ways. Nicholas Rombes writes in the introduction to the collection that many of the films studied in the anthology do not preclude a film belonging to another genre, and a film's punk dimension is based on "a loose affiliation of stylistic tendencies, narrative choices and production qualities that owe some debt to the punk sensibility" (4). Along with an essay by Thompson in which he reiterates and expounds on the necessity of taking into account a film's punk economics, different critics in *New Punk Cinema* claim that punk applies to movements

or waves, such as Italian neorealism, the French New Wave, and the films of Dogme 95 as well as particular films, like *Memento* (Christopher Nolan, 2000), *Run, Lola, Run* (Tom Tykwer, 1998), and even *Amélie* (Jean-Pierre Jeunet, 2001).

15. Tamara Falicov defines "technical-artistic co-production" in her article about Ibermedia and its relationships to production companies located in one or more member countries in Latin America, Spain, or Portugal. A technical-artistic coproduction "implies that the amount a country invests determines the percentage of actors and/or technicians that will work on a film" ("Programa Ibermedia" 23) as opposed to a "purely financial arrangement" that "has no bearing on the artistic or technical aspects of production" ("Programa Ibermedia" 23).

16. It is crucial to note that Thompson's book is not the last word on punk cinema, and various high-budget films such as *Clockwork Orange* or *Taxi Driver* have been deemed punk in other contexts (Barber, "You Got" 174–78). "Punk," in turn, can operate divorced from the political economy of film production or exhibition construed as punk. In the Argentine context, an appropriation of punk that elides a film's political economy happens occasionally as illustrated with descriptions of Adrián García Bogliano's directorial style. In an interview published in the Mexican newspaper *El Universal* shortly after the premiere of *Ahí va el diablo/Here Comes the Devil*, the journalist and filmmaker Christián Cueva prefaces a transcribed conversation with García Bogliano by alluding to García Bogliano's *36 pasos/36 Steps* (2006) and *No moriré sola/I'll Not Die Alone* (2008) and how "con las que definió su estilo sexy, sangriento y punk" ("with which he defined his style as sexy, bloody, and punk"). As further proof of how punk can be used vis-à-vis García Bogliano's films, García Bogliano himself has referred to *Sudor frío* as "punk" (Rodríguez 136).

17. The budget amounts for *KV62* and *Mocosis* are given in Argentine pesos on their respective IMDB pages. The budgets for the two films in dollars are approximate amounts converted from Argentine pesos to US dollars the year the respective film was released. All subsequent budgets for the Argentine punk/horror films will be given in US dollars, though the amounts are generally provided in Argentine pesos in secondary materials.

18. For example, according to IMDB, Sarna's short film *El día después/The Day After* (2006) costs fifty Argentine pesos ($6.25).

19. Carlos de la Fuente, likewise, describes making his films in a way that accommodates for a low budget. De la Fuente invokes the idiomatic expression

"Hacer vaca," in which all the participants contribute what they can, to explain how his films are made (2015).

20. In most interviews, Argentine punk/horror filmmakers hardly ever criticized INCAA. Instead, the filmmakers almost invariably acknowledged that filmmaking in Argentina would not exist without INCAA. *Goreinvasión* (Germán Magariños, 2004) possesses perhaps the sole moment that openly and jokingly criticizes INCAA. The film's characters frequently mock the notion of auteur art-cinema that INCAA often supports, joke about obtaining support from INCAA, and poke fun at the idea of "good" filmmaking.

21. INCAA TV made and broadcasted "Making of" programs for Mutazion's *KV62* and *Reencarnal*/"Reincarnate" (Marcelo Leguiza, unreleased) and for Gorevisión's *Goretech* and *Los super bonarenses*.

22. See chapter 1 for a discussion of Jeffrey Sconce's notion of paracinema and paracinematic reception.

23. Punk/horror directors cite influences from Hollywood and elsewhere, and their films often appropriate and play on those influences. Magariños alludes to a range of influences such as Albert Pyun's *Cyborg* (1989), films directed by Joe Damato, Lucio Fulci, Umberto Lenzi, Todd Sheets, and Hong Kong martial art films (Magariños 2015). Alejo Rébora refers to the films directed by John Waters, David Lynch, Robert Rodríguez, and the first films of Sam Raimi (*The Evil Dead, Crimewave, Evil Dead II, Darkman*) (Rébora and Giménez 2014). Marcelo Leguiza cites as influences films directed by Robert Rodriguez, Quentin Tarantino, John Carpenter, and Sam Raimi and specific films such as *Back to the Future* (Robert Zemeckis, 1985), *Ghostbusters* (Ivan Reitman, 1984), and *Dick Tracy* (Warren Beatty, 1990) (2015). Leguiza also refers to films and directors that have emerged outside the Hollywood system, such as the Argentine comedy *Esperando la carroza/Waiting for the Hearse* (Alejandro Doria, 1985) and Peter Jackson's *Bad Taste*, as well as specific directors by the likes of Gaspar Noé and Alex de la Iglesia (Leguiza 2015; Quiroga). A similar dynamic of influences emerges for other directors in which select strains of Hollywood cinema or cinema and directors from elsewhere hold sway. Jimmy Crispin has cited Frank Hennenlotter, Jim Jarmusch, and Shin'ya Tsukamoto (Fernandez Cruz). Carlos de la Fuente cites Ed Wood as his primary cinematic influence, with additional ones being literary: Herbert George Wells, Isaac Asimov, and Philip K. Dick (De la Fuente 2015). As regards simplified versions of Hollywood, in *The Way Hollywood Tells It* Bordwell advocates a need to

consider Hollywood's "peaks" (high-budget tent-pole films) and its "valleys" (i.e., indie dramas, children's movies, teen comedies, horror films) (10–11).

24. This element of joy in making punk cinema can be linked to a DIY approach in punk filmmaking. That is, successfully making a movie with the resources at one's disposal affords a joy in itself, as opposed to wishing and waiting for the financial help from a major production company in order to make a film with higher production values.

25. Somewhat unsurprisingly, the fluidity between Argentine horror and punk/horror extends to other disreputable films genres such as exploitation and trash cinema. Jack Stevenson defines trash cinema as a filmic manifestation of "a rebellion against the hypocrisy, fascism and elitism of art and a glorification of all things anti-art, of the transparently cheap [. . .] and [. . .] anti-intellectual movement, if a purposely vague and ill-defined one" (125). For Stevenson, the development of a trash cinema aesthetic in the United States emerged in the 1950s with low-budget B-films and, by the 1970s, "was borrowed by underground film-makers and coupled with a premeditated, ironic, self-aware style of film-making" (126). Critiques of films directed by Germán Magariños, as well as Magariños himself, have designated select films produced by Gorevisión as trash cinema (2011). As for exploitation cinema, according to Eric Schaefer, following World War II, "the designation of exploitation film was gradually expanded to include almost any low-budget movie with a topical bent," with subcategories of exploitation films acquiring specific designations in the 1960s and 1970s according to the taboo theme played up in the film's content, such as blaxploitation, sexploitation, nunsploitation, and nazisploitation (4–8). While Argentine punk/horror is hardly uniform, the films' penchant for presenting taboo subjects is common and readily present in all of the punk/horror films. Joan Hawkins, as well as others, has alluded to the historical exchanges and slippages that have transpired among various high- and lowbrow film cultures and genres that include horror.

26. I discuss the category of "cine bizarro" in chapter 1.

27. For example, in 2012, the punk film *Trash 2: Las tetas de Ana L.* competed for best international feature-length film alongside two Argentine horror films *El día trajo la oscuridad/Darkness by Day* (Martín Desalvo, 2013) and *2/11: Día de los Muertos/2/11: Day of the Dead* (Ezio Massa, 2012).

28. Other movies that have been considered punk which also appear in Videoflims' catalog under the category of "Terror, Gore" are *Sadomaster 2: Locura General* and *Mondo Psycho*.

29. Albeit refraining from a strict prescription of formal elements, the participatory documentary mode "gives [the audience] a sense of what it is like for the filmmaker to be given a situation and how that situation alters as a result" (Nichols 116).

30. Likewise, *The Punk Rock Movie* features concert and behind-the-scenes footage mostly from the Roxy in 1977, during the first wave of punk rock in England. In the case of those punk films featuring a fictional narrative cited by Thompson, *The Foreigner* bears a loose narrative resemblance to a handful of Argentine punk/horror films, such as *Ultra-Toxic* or *Trash*, in which a protagonist is pursued by some obscure entity.

31. Argentina is not without its own crust punk scene, and examples of Argentine crust punk bands include Gerk, Horror Humano, and Acidös Pöpulares.

32. The subtitle of the film *Goretech: Bienvenidos al planeta hijo de puta* is possibly inspired by the White Zombie song "Welcome to Planet Motherfucker." This aside, not all Argentine punk/horror films, including *Run, Bunny, Run!* and *Un cazador de zombis* / "Zombie Hunter" (2008), have abrasive titles. In a comical anecdote about Argentine punk/horror film titles, Germán Magariños's *Alan Smithee's Nosferatu* (2010) was screened at Cine Gaumont (Espacio INCAA KM 0) in Buenos Aires in 2010 as part of the Festival de Cine Inusual de Buenos Aires. Many moviegoers bought a ticket thinking the film to be the actual *Nosferatu* by F. W. Murnau (1922) and quickly left the cinema once they understood their error.

33. According to Magariños (2016), *Sadomaster* is, in part, an exaggerated parody about right-wing politicians and the separation that can exist between a politician's "clean" public image and his or her actual personality. Such a scenario is inspired by films such as *Escape from the Bronx* (Enzo Castellari, 1983). In *Sadomaster*, the character, Mauricio Beccar Varela, who acts as a behind-the-scenes leader of the neo-Nazi gang, is partially based on Mauricio Macri, current president of Argentina. In *Sadomaster 2* (2011), Mauricio Beccar Varela becomes president of the country thus anticipating Macri's own rise to power in 2015.

34. The idea of an Argentine punk film resisting commodification or appropriation by a mainstream becomes more concrete with an anecdote regarding INCAA TV's scheduled broadcast of *Sadomaster* and *Sadomaster 2: Locura general*. *Trasnochados* ("Up All Night") is a programming cycle reserved for Argentine genre cinema and has featured different cycles, such as films featuring Isabel Sarli, horror cinema, and fantasy cinema. Through the distributor Videofilms, INCAA TV obtained the rights to broadcast films from Videofilms catalog, which includes *Sadomaster* and *Sadomaster 2: Locura general*. When the time came for the films

to be shown on the station, the films did not appear. While INCAA TV told the film's director, Germán Magariños, that technical problems prevented the two Sadomaster films from being shown, many viewers were left to wonder if the films' content would have elicited complaints from viewers and, in turn, INCAA TV, decided against broadcasting the movie (Magariños 2015).

35. See, Bordwell, 117–38 (*The Way Hollywood*).

36. Bordwell characterizes John Woo and Tsui Hark's films from the 1980s as an "intensification of intensification" ("Intensified Continuity" 21). Argentine punk/horror films are vastly different from the likes of *A Better Tomorrow II* (John Woo, 1987) and *The Killer* (John Woo, 1989). Yet, in the case of the films by directed by Crispin, Rébora, and Leguiza, an intensification is unmistakable.

37. For analyses on the flaneur in cinema, see, for example, Abel and Gleber.

38. To equate punk with New Latin American Cinema would be a gross oversimplification. Nevertheless, though I cite Getino and Solanas's essay "Towards a Third Cinema" and its emphasis on unrefined aesthetics, it is also worth noting the commonalities between an ethos of punk production and Julio García Espinosa's notion of imperfect cinema in the Cuban context. If a central tenet of punk is to inspire others to produce with a DIY approach, then imperfect cinema echoes those same sentiments: "We should endeavor to see that our future students, and therefore our future filmmakers, will themselves be scientists, sociologists, physicians, economists, agricultural engineers, etc., without of course ceasing to be filmmakers. [. . .] It is only logical that we contribute to the liberation of the private means of artistic production" (García Espinosa 79).

39. Gorevisión also has a "subdivision," Pochito Producciones, whose aim is to make, edit and distribute online a film within a day. Some of the movies made under the auspices of Pochito Producciones include *Alan Smithee's Nosferatu* (Germán Magariños, 2010), *Las orgías inconfesables de Julius Caesar/The Shameful Orgies of Julius Caesar* (Germán Magariños, 2011) and *Poltergays 2: La masacre en la pijamada/Poltergays 2: The Sleepover Massacre* (2011). The movies produced by Pochito Producciones are arguably trashier than those produced by Gorevisión.

40. The influence of Burroughs literary work on *Ultra-Toxic* also comes through in a circuitous way via similarities in its soundtrack and that of David Cronenberg's cinematic adaptation of *Naked Lunch* (1991). *Ultra-Toxic*'s soundtrack features a saxophone played by Tivi Potatoes, a well-known ska-punk musician in Buenos Aires. The prominence of the saxophone recalls Ornette Coleman's work in collaboration with Howard Shore on the soundtrack for *Naked Lunch*.

41. While giving voice to the nuances of the term, Stacy Gillis defines cyberpunk as "engaging with disintegration, fragmentation and discontinuity in *specific* relation to issues surrounding the body, the city and technology [...]" (3). Shek's drug use that couples brain matter and discarded technology and the noir codes that portray Buenos Aires (low-key lighting, dark and menacing streets) in *Ultra-Toxic* help to solidify its cyberpunk aesthetic.

42. I discuss spectacle at length in chapter 2 of the manuscript in which I discuss horror films set in cities. More specifically, my engagement with spectacle in chapter 2 grounds how spectacle can be conceived in a film through formal properties that are momentarily distinct from other parts of the movie.

43. See, for example, Tasker (1993), specifically her comments on *Lethal Weapon* and *Lethal Weapon 2*.

44. The notion of gore renewing the horror genre appears in J. Kendrick and comes from Walter Kendrick (qtd. in James Kendrick 81).

45. Several scholars of screen violence recognize the evolution of stylized and intense violence that accompanies the development of cinema over the years. In his essay "Graphic Violence in the Cinema," Stephen Prince writes, "The history of cinema is, in part, a history of increasingly vivid presentational techniques to stylize violence" (18).

46. Brophy is hardly alone in detecting more explicit depictions of violence in contemporary horror cinema. See, for example, Linda Williams's "Film Bodies: Gender, Genre, and Excess," Stephen Prince's introduction to *The Horror Film*, and Modelski.

47. Gore and explicit violence in horror films should not be considered the sole mode of screen violence in contemporary horror cinema. In addition to recent "spiritually oriented" horror films adduced by James Kendrick, films such as *The Blair Witch Project*, *Paranormal Activity* (Oren Peli, 2007), *Insidious* (James Wan, 2010), *Woman in Black* (James Watkins, 2012), and *The Babadook* (Jennifer Kent, 2014) evidence that suggested violence continues to occupy a place in contemporary horror cinema. In the case of Argentine horror cinema, films such as *Mala carne*, *Tremendo amanecer*, and *El desierto* feature little screen violence relative to other Argentine horror films and gore hardly constitutes the uniform mode of stylized violence.

48. Though the gore in many Argentine punk/horror films is DIY, some films have relied on professional help, particularly from artists associated with Rabbid EFX in films such as *Mondo Psycho* and *Goretech*. Rabbid EFX has done special

effects for higher-budgeted productions relative to punk films such as *Aballay, Fase 7, El desierto,* and *Naturaleza muerta.*

49. A number of other critics underscore affect as a central feature to the horror genre. See, for example, Cherry (39) and Powell.

50. Brinkema positions "radical formalism" against the neo-formalism espoused by the likes of David Bordwell (36–37).

51. Hills juxtaposes and articulates his ideas against a number of different theoretical texts with one of the main ones being Carroll's *Philosophy of Horror.*

52. Hills credits Ed Tan for this characterization of horror as a "dialectical affect-emotion machine" (28). See Ed Tan's *Emotion and the Structure of Narrative Film* (L. Erlbaum Associates, 1996) for an elaboration of this concept.

53. I use the word *consume* in this instance to encompass not just the actual viewing of a film, but also the consumption of paratexts related to the film, such as trailers, movie posters, interviews with directors, and so on.

CHAPTER 5

1. At present, the legacies of the Dirty War can be discerned on multiple fronts, such as the conversion of former torture centers into museums, the trials of a scant number of military officials and the immunity given to others, and news of some young adults discovering that shortly after being born they were taken from their captured parents and given to military families.

2. As for cultural production about *El Proceso* beyond Argentina's borders, Carlos Saura's *Tango* (1998) and Chris Hampton's *Imagining Argentina* (2003), which is based on Lawrence Thorton's novel of the same name, and Nathan Englander's novel *Ministry of Special Cases* (2009) all use Argentina's Dirty War as a substantial backdrop for the narrative.

3. De la Vega has commented that *Jennifer's Shadow* is an "homenaje to Poe" ("homage to Poe").

4. The fleeting shot of the grandmother recalls the abrupt insertion of images of a devil-like figure in William Friedkin's *The Exorcist* (1973) or Lars Van Trier's *Antichrist* (2009).

5. Here, I am omitting the Junta's views on matters of the economy, as well as a discourse that saw Argentina as a potential victim of international Marxism and, thus, a battleground for the Cold War. For a more comprehensive overview of the intellectual foundations for the military's actions, see Donald C. Hodges's *Argentina's "Dirty War": An Intellectual Biography.*

6. Akin to *Jennifer's Shadow*, *36 Pasos* broaches the Dirty War also through both abductions and subversion of traditional concepts of family. The kidnapping of the Tamara's former classmates is a family affair, and Tami's brother, mother, sister, and uncle collectively participate in the abductions. Kidnappings were tragically a common occurrence during the last dictatorship. Victims were not only kidnapped from their homes, but also from other sites such as the street, work, and school (*Nunca más* 11). The different places from which the young women in *36 Pasos* are abducted (home, school, work, a stadium, a roadway) tender another resemblance between a film's profilmic events and the methods employed by the last dictatorship. The government's *Nunca más* report contains different statistical data regarding abductions and the places in which people were detained. Homes were, by far, the most common places where people were captured (62 percent), followed by the street (24.6 percent), work (7 percent), and place of study (6 percent); 0.4 percent of people were disappeared "while legally detained in military, penal or police establishments" (11).

7. My use of the term *veil* comes from Tambling's interpretation of particular moments in Dante's *Inferno* and *Purgatorio* (30–31). Other notions of allegory possessing a veil also appear in the Bible and Boccaccio's "The Genealogy of the Gentile Gods" (Tambling 28–30).

8. Torture porn is characterized by the extremely graphic nature of its screen violence that can feature torture and mutilation against both men and women, and usually is committed by men.

9. Countless horror films throughout history contain instances of kidnapping, such as *Murders in the Rue Morgue* (Robert Florey, 1932), *Last House on the Left* (Wes Craven, 1972), *Silence of the Lambs* (Jonathan Demme, 1991), and *House of 1000 Corpses* (Rob Zombie, 2003), to name only a few.

10. Creed describes various forms of the monstrous-feminine, such as the archaic mother, the monstrous womb, the witch, the vampire, and the possessed woman. Among the various ways in which horror cinema works as "an illustration of the work of abjection" is "the construction of the maternal figure as abject" in films such as *Psycho* (Alfred Hitchcock, 1968), *Carrie* (Brian De Palma, 1976), and *The Birds* (Alfred Hitchcock, 1963) (Creed 10–12). In *The Last Gateway*, the mother's reluctance to allow a child to break away makes her abject because "of her problematic relation to the symbolic realm" (Creed 12). The child attempts to break away and the mother "is reluctant to release it" (Creed 11). The maternal body becomes symbolically unstable because of conflicting desires to keep and to release the child.

11. See, for instance, Nichols for a commentary about ethics and documentary and Lúcia Nagib's *World Cinema and the Ethics of Realism* (New York: Continuum, 2011) for an innovative engagement with ethics and various realist styles.

12. By cinematic realism here, I refer to certain production choices such as using untrained actors and filming on location or themes that foreground a social issue, such as poverty.

13. For examples of such reviews and comments on message boards, see film and horror film websites such as zonafreak.com.ar or quintadimension.com.

14. In chapter 4 of *Cinema and Spectatorship*, Mayne critiques ideas of negotiation in cultural studies and Renaissance Studies.

15. In the case of Derrida in *Specter of Marx*, his notion of haunting was a response to Francis Fukuyama's declaration that the demise of the Soviet Union resulted in the end of history, or better said, the end of the debate between capitalism and liberal democracy versus communism.

16. I will subsequently refer to *Crónica de una fuga* simply as *Crónica*. In addition to the horror genres, other film genres in Argentina evidence different generational relationships to the Dirty War, the documentary *Los rubios* (Albertina Carri, 2003) being the most obvious example.

17. Bernades's point is valid and reiterates a critical perspective that often places Caetano's films as reactions against older national films. *Pizza, birra, faso* (1998), a film Caetano codirected with Bruno Stagnaro, is often considered an important signpost embodying Nuevo cine argentino that emerged in the late 1990s.

18. While Tamburini's book has not been published in English, the title can be translated as "Free Pass—The Escape from Mansión Seré." Regarding Guillermo Fernández's role in the film's production, both Tamburini and Fernández were kidnapped by the dictatorship and held hostage together.

19. While suspense and Western films are more established and critiqued genres, escape films are precisely what the designation indicates: the escape of a character or group of characters is central to the narrative. Examples of escape films include *Stalag 17* (Billy Wilder, 1953), *Escape from Alcatraz* (Don Siegel, 1979), *Crónica de un niño solo/Chronicle of a Boy Alone* (Leonardo Favio, 1965), *Le Trou/The Night Watch* (Jacques Becker, 1960), and *The Shawshank Redemption* (Frank Darabont, 1994). In addition to the suspense, Western, escape, and horror subgenres, Maribel Cedeño points out instances of the thriller in *Crónica* (61–65).

20. See chapter 1 for a definition of *cine testimonio.*

21. Below, I will address the reconstruction and modification of the Mansión Seré in *Crónica*. Shortly following the escape of Claudio Tamburini and three of his fellow prisoners, the Argentine military burned the structure.

22. The cover of the DVD distributed in the United States lacks the same horror cinema motifs or allusions to testimonial literature but still deserves mention. Instead, the US cover engages more with the escape film genre via a single image of an actor that does not even appear in the film. The actor, shirtless and wearing a pair of jeans splattered with white paint, looks backward against a blurred background of buildings and a street suggesting an image still of an escape in progress. The image is a stark contrast to the prisoners in *Crónica* who escape in their underwear and are emaciated after being detained and brutalized for four months. With the exception of a quote from the *New York Times* film critic Stephen Holden, the DVD cover foregoes any allusion to its testimonial sources. Yet, the cover manages to both connect and disconnect the film from actual events with a superlative twist that generalizes the film's historical dimensions while delinking the narrative from Argentina circa 1977: "The true story of the most incredible escape of our time."

23. In her essay on Roque Dalton's *Miguel Mármol*, Barbara Harlow refers to the collaborative nature of not only Dalton's text, but also other *testimonios* by Domitila Barrios de Chungara, Rigoberta Menchú, Leila Khaled, and Elvia Alvarado (11). In each instance, the book is brought to fruition through the collective work of the person who endured an experience and that of the transcriber who writes down the person's experiences.

24. Horror films that are based on, and/or inspired by, real events include *Psycho* (Albert Hitchcock, 1960), *Texas Chainsaw Massacre* (Tobe Hooper, 1974), *The Exorcist* (William Friedkin, 1973), *Open Water* (Chris Kentis, 2003), and *Them* (David Moreau and Xavier Palud, 2006).

25. Freeland defines "reality horror" as a subgenre of horror with a film inspired by real events and "features a possible, realistic monster," such as a serial killer, and "showcases the spectacular nature of monstruous violence" over plot ("Realist Horror" 286, 288).

26. A comprehensive analysis of horror motifs in *Pase libre* is beyond the scope of this chapter. However, the title of the book's second part—"Casa de sombras" ("House of Shadows")—gives a concise and glaring use of Gothic horror in Tamburini's text. *Pase libre*, however, deserves attention especially for its distinctions with other testimonial texts about experiences of being disappeared during the Dirty War, particularly Alicia Partnoy's *La Escuelita/The Little School* and

Jacobo Timerman's *Preso sin nombre, celda sin número/Prisoner without a Name, Cell without a Number*. In contrast to the other two texts, Tamburini's account is much more attuned to space, particularly Tamburini's disorientation, becoming reoriented, and the sensation that he melds with the space as he remains captive. As for the horror motifs in *La escuelita*, at the end of the section titled "Sesión de belleza," Partnoy writes, "La gente está con miedo y parezco un fantasma. Aunque tenga las piernas depiladas" ("People are scared, and I look like a ghost, albeit with shaved legs" (101).

27. Hopkins refers to other Gothic literary motifs that also appear in Gothic cinema: a mansion or castle being haunted by a "real or apparent threat of a supernatural presence, a mysterious and threatening older man and a vulnerable heroine, and a character poised between good and evil" (xi).

28. The mansion receives a similarly eerie and imposing depiction when the prisoners make their escape in the latter third of the film. As the prisoners run in front of the mansion, the mansion dwarves the haggard, almost nude actors. Rain, thunder, and flashes of lightning underscore the structure's looming presence. Regarding the use of Dutch angles, Cedeño notes that Claudio's parents' house is also framed with Dutch angles when the police burst into it looking for Claudio (52).

29. Sheldon Hall characterizes the spatial presentation in Carpenter's *Halloween* by alluding to his trademark use of Panavision anamorphic format with a depth of field to enable a spectator's "systematic exploration of the formal possibilities" of a minimal narrative and the composition of an image (70). Carpenter's filmic style can also be described through meticulously slow tracking shots often in concert with a wide-angle lens. Such a technique abounds in *Halloween*. Gina Wisker relates such shot to the creation of a "sense of doom" in the suburban US, and Carpenter has remarked that "[. . .] if you use the tracking shot, do it very slowly and methodically, be very authoritative about it, then the audience feels there is something strange there" (qtd. in Wisker from Clive Barker 64). The presentation of the door and window shots in *Crónica* recall Carpenter's depiction of space. Of course, with the disappeared prisoners behind the door and the window within the interior of the prisoner's room, the viewer already knows "something is strange." The formal composition of space in *Crónica* merely reinforces that sentiment.

30. Analogous to corridors, staircases are often filmed in such a way as to become a source of disorientation and/or claustrophobia in horror films or similar genres, such as psychological thrillers. Countless horror films include sequences where

stairs feature prominently. However, unlike the sequence in *Crónica*, staircases function as a mechanism of suspense in which any potential fright on the part of the audience comes from not knowing what lies at the bottom of the stairs, which is usually obscured in darkness.

31. In his study of horror film and literature, A.S. Prawer references Fritz Lang's *M* (1931) and various films produced by Val Lewton for RKO studios, such as *Cat People* (Jacques Torneur, 1942), *I Walked with a Zombie* (Jacques Torneur, 1943), and *The Body Snatcher* (Robert Wise, 1945), as examples of films using nongraphic modes to convey murder.

32. For example, in her essay "Horror and Art-Dread," Cynthia Freeland considers *The Others* (Alejandro Aménabar, 2001), *The Sixth Sense* (M. Night Shymalan, 1999), and *The Blair Witch Project* (Daniel Myrick and Eduardo Sánchez, 1999) as examples of contemporary horror films that uphold horror cinema's tradition of suggestive violence.

33. Stephen Prince's analysis of several horror films from 1930s and of the conduct of the Production Code Administration (PCA) in the United States prevents a broad generalization that would contend violence in classical horror films was inevitably suggestive. The PCA did not function as a censorship board; rather it helped production companies anticipate the objections of regional censorship boards in the United States and abroad (Prince, *Classical Film Violence* 51). According to Prince, the PCA gave only a "cursory reading" of the scripts for some of the horror films that came out in 1931, such as *Frankenstein* (James Whale, 1931) and *Dracula* (Tod Browning, 1931). The PCA did not anticipate the controversies that erupted over horror films from the early 1930s, which "unleashed a new wave of imagery depicting cruelty, torture, pain, and murder and disseminated it en masse to the nation's movie screens" (Prince, *Classical Film Violence* 53). Through a comparative analysis of screen violence in *Frankenstein*, *Murders in the Rue Morgue* (Robert Florey, 1932), and *The Black Cat* (Edgar G. Ulmer, 1934), Prince shows the tamping down of graphic violence that relied more on suggestion, following the public outcry of horror films, and a more rigorous participation of the PCA in its recommendations for production companies.

34. Following a brief interrogation shortly after arriving at Mansión Seré, his captors push Tamburini's head underwater in a bathtub. The camera sits beside and outside the tub but never in the water. The torturers are off-screen, and Tamburini's shoulders and face occupy almost the entire frame. The shot is not from the point-of-view of the torturer or torturers, but rather achieves a kind of

omniscience that transcends any character's perspective. The camera sits outside the tub, but we hear Tamburini's voice as if the camera and microphone were in the water. Image and sound do not coincide.

35. In her book-length analysis that focuses on *Crónica*, Schwarzböck simplifies film spectatorship and conceives of a horror-viewing public in near sadistic terms in which a hypothetical horror viewer evades the fear induced by a horror film in order to "identificarse con el verdugo [...] en lugar de la víctima" ("identify with the executioner [...] in lieu of the victim") (69). While Schwarzböck is correct to pick up on the film's play on camera's perspectives in Caetano's film, her depiction of horror film spectators presumes that viewers would not sympathize with the victim.

36. While my comments on *Aparecidos* are brief, Álvaro Fernández offers a compelling analysis of the film, along with *Tras el cristal/In a Glass Cage* (Agustí Villaronga, 1986), Jaume Balagueró's *Los sin nombre/The Nameless* (1999) and *Darkness* (2002), and *Crónica de una fuga*, to comment on the prohibitions and dynamics in Argentina and Spain of using the horror genre to portray the trauma suffered by a population under a dictatorship. For Fernández, "*Aparecidos* es [...] una película de horror que reescribe los miedos de la transición española" ("*Aparecidos* is a horror film that rewrites the fears that have accompanied the Spanish transition [to democracy])" (275).

37. The term *prosthetic memory* comes from Alison Landsberg's book of the same name. For Landsberg, "prosthetic memory" refers to a new kind of memory "that emerges at the interface between a person and a historical narrative about the past, at an experiential site such as a movie theater or museum" (2). An individual's contact with the narrative enables a sort of imbibing of a memory that the individual did not experience firsthand but nevertheless shapes his or her subjectivity.

38. See Fernández (274–76) for intriguing comments about the dynamics of memory in Spain and Argentina and, though *Aparecidos* is explicitly set in Argentina, how the film is more about Spain than Argentina.

39. First, given that the attainment of the rank of colonel in the Argentine army takes an average of twenty years, one can surmise that Colonel Santoro was an officer during the time of the last dictatorship (1976–83).

40. The teenagers hardly constitute a threat of any sort. El Colo is docile compared to his cohorts, wears a neck brace, and must contend with unceasing flatulence; Karina appears as a tough and reserved Goth; Rolo is a parody of a leftist

revolutionary à la Che Guevara; Vicky is bubbly and extroverted and, despite her pursuit of Rolo, oblivious to politics; Quique stereotypes a gregarious and party animal Spaniard; and Lucho is tense and obsessed with keeping the house clean.

41. *Subversión en el ámbito educativo (conozcamos a nuestro enemigo)* can be read online at the website of the Biblioteca Nacional de los Maestros. This aside, Colonel Santoro's vision of the largely depoliticized teens as subversives is reiterated throughout *Nunca* to a comedic effect. After Fito goes missing, his father interrogates the teens, slaps el Colo and Lucho, and, at one moment addresses Lucho as "delincuente" ("delinquent").

42. Miguel Monforte was a programmer for the Festival Internacional de Cine Independiente de Mar del Plata (MARFICI), which has screened several of Farsa's productions (Sabat).

43. In addition to Fito's character in *Nunca más*, the last dictatorship figures into the film in different ways. As Oficial Montoya divides everyone into smaller search parties, he draws a map of the area, which is framed from above the actors. To the right of Montoya's hands, one sees a folder with information on Monforte and, to the left, a copy of the *Nunca más* report.

44. In her analysis of *Sudor frío*, Rosana Díaz-Zambrana describes the zombie-like nature of the women in both physical and metaphorical terms. As regards the latter, for Díaz-Zambrana the women suggest a return of the repressed, or, more specifically, the return of the memory of the disappeared during the Dirty War ("Entre placer" 157–58).

45. My translation of the dialogue is a slight variation of the English subtitles on the US version of *Sudor frío*.

46. Cafeomancia is the practice of telling the future by discerning images in the bottom of a coffee cup.

47. "The murderers are among us" is the English translation of a German drama (*Die Mörder sind unter uns*) released in 1946, and describes a story of a Nazi who committed atrocities during World War II being brought to trial.

48. Schatz's notion is not unique, and Schatz himself alludes to Christian Metz's essay "Textuality and Generality" and Henri Focillon's *The Life of Forms in Art* to buttress his own argument. While self-reflexivity alludes to a genre film's self-awareness, "transparent social reaffirmation" pertains to Schatz's argument that "[. . .] genre films celebrate [a culture's] most fundamental ideological precepts" (31).

49. See, for example, Juan Pablo Cinelli's online review of *Malditos sean!* in *Página 12*, and the message board comments that appear below Diego Batlle's online review of *Sudor frío* in *Otros cines*.

CONCLUSION

1. In his discussion of repetition, Grant illustrates his point by alluding to Colin McArthur's examination of gangster films and the iconography and "visual patterns" typical of the genre (8).

FILMOGRAPHY

Adrián de Llano, Diego, dir. *Detrás del Horror/*"Behind the Horror." 2011.
———, dir. *Rojo Sangre: 10 años de puro género.* 2009; Videoflims.
———, dir. *Sangre negra: Aldo Knodell debe morir/*"Black Blood: Aldo Knodell Must Die." 2013; Farsa Producciones.
Aguilar, Elian, dir. *Rojo Sangre: 10 años de puro género.* 2009; Videoflims.
———, dir. *Sangre negra: Aldo Knodell debe morir/*"Black Blood: Aldo Knodell Must Die." 2013; Videoflims.
Borghi, Andrés, dir. *Alexia.* 2013; Estrella Infernal.
Brunetti, Mauricio, dir. *Los inocentes/The Innocents.* 2016; Aleph Media.
Cabezas, Paco, dir. *Aparecidos/The Appeared.* 2007; IFC Films.
Caetano, Israel Adrián, dir. *Crónica de una fuga/Chronicle of an Escape.* 2006; IFC First Take.
Calvete, Santiago Fernández, dir. *La segunda muerte/*"The Second Death." 2012; Magma Cine.
Calzada, Gonzalo, dir. *Resurrección/Resurrection.* 2015; Buffalo Films.
Crampi, Mad, dir. *Mondo psycho.* 2006; Videoflims.
———, dir. *Run, Bunny, Run!* 2003; Psycho Junkie.
Crispin, Jimmy, dir. *Ultra-Toxic.* 2004; Psycho Junkie.
de la Fuente, Carlos, dir. *Protocolo 48: El experimento final/*"Protocol 48: The Final Experiment." 2012; Altaris Home Video.
de la Vega, Daniel, dir. *Death Knows Your Name.* 2007; Maverick Entertainment Group.
———, dir. *Necrofobia 3D/Necrophobia 3D.* 2014; Del Toro Films.
———, dir. *Ataúd blanco: El juego diabólico/White Coffin.* 2016.
———, and Pablo Parés, dir. *Chronicle of a Raven* (aka *Jennifer's Shadow*). 2004; Lions Gate Home Entertainment.
Diment, Valentín Javier, dir. *La memoria del muerto/Memory of the Dead.* 2011; Artsploitation.
Esquenazi, Sergio, dir. *Dead Line* (aka *Interference*). 2006; C&K Films.

———, dir. *Visitante del invierno/Winter Visitor*. 2008; C&K Films.
Findling, Hernán, dir. *Breaking Nikki*. 2009; 1971 Cine.
Forte, Fabián, dir. *Mala carne/Carnal*. 2003; Timeless Media.
García Bogliano, Adrián, dir. *36 Pasos*. 2006; Paura Flics.
———, dir. *Habitaciones para turistas/Rooms for Tourists*. 2004; Paura Flics.
———, dir. *No moriré sola/I Will Not Die Alone*. 2008; Paura Flics.
———, dir. *Penumbra/Penumbra*. 2011; Paura Flics.
———, dir. *Sudor frío/Cold Sweat*. 2010; Paura Flics.
———, and Demián Rugna, dir. *Malditos sean!/Cursed Bastards*. 2011.
Grieco, Gabriel, dir. *Hipersomnia/Hypersomnia*. 2016; Estudios Crepusculum.
———, dir. *Naturaleza muerta/Still Life*. 2014; Estudios Crepusculum.
Leguiza, Marcelo, dir. *KV62: Tiempo come tiempo/*"KV62: Time Eats Time." 2013.
———, dir. *Marihuana radioactiva interplanetaria/*"Interplanetary Radioactive Marijuana." 2010.
———, dir. *Mocosis*. 2014; Mutazion.
———, dir. *Sonríe/Snuff, Inc*. 2012; Mutazion.
Magariños, Germán, dir. *Goreinvasión/*"Goreinvasion." 2004; Gorevisión.
———, dir. *Goretech: Bienvenidos al planeta hijo de puta* / "Goretech: Welcome to the Planet Son of a Bitch." 2012; Gorevisión.
———, dir. *Los super bonarenses* / "The Super Bonarenses." 2014; Gorevisión.
———, dir. *Sadomaster*. 2005; Gorevisión.
McQueen, Jeff, dir. *Going to Pieces: The Rise and the Fall of the Slasher Film*. 2006; THINKFilm.
Onetti, Luciano, dir. *Sonno profondo*. 2013; Guante Negro Films.
Parés, Pablo, dir. *Daemonium: Soldado del inframundo/Daemonium: Soldier of the Underworld*. 2015.
———, dir. *Filmatrón*. 2007; Farsa Producciones.
———, and Hernán Sáez, dir. *Plaga zombie*. 1997; Farsa Producciones.
———, and Hernán Sáez, dir. *Plaga zombie: Zona mutante/Plaga Zombie: Mutant Zone*. 2001; Farsa Producciones.
———, and Hernán Sáez, dir. *Plaga zombie: Zona mutante: Zona tóxica/*"Plaga Zombie: Mutant Zone: Toxic Zone." 2011; Farsa Producciones.
———, and Paulo Soria, dir. *Nunca asistas a este tipo de fiesta/*"Never Go to This Kind of Party." 2000; Farsa Producciones.
———, and Paulo Soria, dir. *Nunca más asistas a este tipo de fiesta/*"Never Again Go to This Kind of Party." 2010; Farsa Producciones.

Pollachi, Paula, dir. *Baño de sangre*/"Blood Bath." 2003.
———, dir. *Inzomnia*. 1997.
Rébora, Alejo, dir. *Trash 2: Las tetas de Ana L.*/*Trash 2: The Tits of Ana L.* 2013; SRN Distribution.
———, dir. *Trash*. 2010; SRN Distribution.
Rugna, Demián, dir. *The Last Gateway*. 2007; DSX Films.
Sudak, Oswaldo, dir. *Curas zombis en Azul*/"Zombie Priests in Blue." 2013.

BIBLIOGRAPHY

Aaron, Michele. *Spectatorship: The Power of Looking On*. Wallflower, 2007.

Abel, Marco. "Intensifying Life: The Cinema of the 'Berlin School.'" *Cineaste*, vol. 33, no. 4, 2008, isites.harvard.edu/fs/docs/icb.topic432924.files/Cinema%20of%20the%20Berlin%20School.pdf. Accessed 25 May 2015.

Acland, Charles. *Screen Traffic*. Duke UP, 2003.

Aguilar, Gonzalo Moisés. *Other Worlds: New Argentinean Film*. Translated by Sarah Ann Wells, Palgrave Macmillan, 2008.

Altman, Rick. *Film/Genre*. British Film Institute, 1999.

Amado, Ana. *La imagen justa: cine argentino y política, 1980–2007*. Ediciones Colihue, 2009.

Andermann, Jens. "December's Other Scene: New Argentine Cinema and the Politics of 2001." *New Argentine and Brazilian Cinema: Reality Effects*, edited by Jens Andermann and Álvaro Fernández Bravo, Palgrave Macmillan, 2013, pp. 157–72.

———. *New Argentine Cinema*. I. B. Tauris, 2012.

Animaciones Pro. "Re: PLAGA ZOMBIE—Full Movie—Pelicula [sic] Completa." YouTube, 9 Nov. 2010, www.youtube.com/watch?v=09EOSxk-X_M, 9 Apr. 2016. Accessed 21 July 2016.

Apter, Emily. "On Oneworldness: Or Paranoia as a World System." *American Literary History*, vol. 18, no. 2, 2006, pp. 365–89.

Archetti, Eduardo. *Masculinities: Football, Polo and the Tango in Argentina*. Berg, 1999.

Attali, Jacques. *Noise: The Political Economy of Music*. Translated by Brian Massumi, U of Minnesota P, 1985.

Auerbach, Jonathan. *Dark Borders: Film Noir and American Citizenship*. Duke UP, 2011.

Augé, Marc. *Non-Places: An Introduction to Supermodernity*. Verso, 2008.

Bachelard, Gaston. *The Poetics of Space*. Translated by Maria Jolas, Beacon Press, 1994.

Badley, Linda. *Film, Horror, and the Body Fantastic*. Greenwood, 1995.
Baird, Robert. "The Startle Effect: Implications for Spectator Cognition and Media Theory." *Film Quarterly*, vol. 53, no. 3, 2000, pp. 12–24.
Balanzategui, Jessica. "Crises of Identification in the Supernatural Slasher: The Resurrection of the Supernatural Slasher Villain." *Style and Form in the Hollywood Slasher Form*, edited by Wickham Clayton. Palgrave Macmillan, 2015, pp. 161–79.
Barber, Chris. "Polemics: Punk Cinema—Like Punk Rock—Is ANTI-GENRE!" No Focus: Punk on Film, edited by Chris Barber and Jack Sargeant, Headpress, 2006, pp. 9–14.
———. "Punksploitation." No Focus: Punk on Film, edited by Chris Barber and Jack Sargeant, Headpress, 2006, pp. 202–16.
———. "You Got Bad Taste." No Focus: *Punk on Film*, edited by Chris Barber and Jack Sargeant. Headpress, 2006, pp. 168–84.
Barnes, Brooks. "Hollywood Tracks Social Media Chatter to Target Hit Films." *New York Times*, 7 Dec 2014, www.nytimes.com/2014/12/08/business/media/hollywood-tracks-social-media-chatter-to-target-hit-films.html?_r=0. Accessed 9 Sept. 2015.
Benjamin, Walter. "On Some Motifs in Baudelaire." *Illuminations*. Translated by Harry Zohn, Schocken, 1969, pp. 155–200.
———. *The Origin of German Tragic Drama*. Verso, 1998.
Benshoff, Harry. *Monsters in the Closet: Homosexuality and the Horror Film*. Manchester UP, 1997.
Benson-Allott, Caetlin. *Killer Tapes and Shattered Screens: Video Spectatorship from VHS to File Sharing*. U of California P, 2013.
Berenstein, Rhona. *Attack of the Leading Ladies: Gender, Sexuality, and Spectatorship in Classic Horror Cinema*. Columbia UP, 1996.
Berlant, Lauren. "Cruel Optimism." *Differences*, vol. 17, no. 3, 2006, pp. 20–36.
Bernades, Horacio. "Pormenores de una huida increíble." *Página 12*, 27 Apr. 2007, www.pagina12.com.ar/diario/suplementos/espectaculos/5-2401-2006-04-27.html. Accessed 21 July 2011.
———, Diego Lerer, and Diego Wolf. *Introducción: una historia breve. Nuevo cine argentino: temas, autores y estilos de una renovación*, edited by Horacio Bernades, Diego Lerer, and Sergio Wolf, Fipresci, 2002.
Berenstein, Rhona. *Attack of the Leading Ladies: Gender, Sexuality, and Spectatorship in Classic Horror Cinema*. Columbia UP, 1996.

Besarón, Pablo. *La conspiración: ensayos sobre el complot en la literatura argentina.* Ediciones Simurg, 2009.

Betsky, Aaron. *Queer Space: Architecture and Same-Sex Desire.* William Morrow, 1997.

Blake, Linnie. *The Wounds of Nations: Horror Cinema, Historical Trauma and National Identity.* Palgrave Macmillan, 2008.

Blood Window. Bloodwindow.com. Accessed 10 Aug. 2016.

Bordwell, David. *The Way Hollywood Tells It: Story and Style in Modern Movies.* U of California P, 2006.

———. "Intensified Continuity: Visual Style in Contemporary American Film." *Film Quarterly*, vol. 55, no. 3, 2002, pp. 16–28.

———. *Narration in the Fiction Film.* U of Wisconsin P, 1985.

Bosteels, Bruno. *Marx and Freud in Latin America: Politics, Psychoanalysis, and Religion in Times of Terror.* Verso, 2012.

Brennan, Ximena. "TV: Un ciclo de cortos de terror se emite por INCAA TV." *EscribiendoCine*, 6 July 2013, www.escribiendocine.com/entrevista/0006816-tv-un-ciclo-de-cortos-de-terror-se-emite-por-incaa-tv/. Accessed 3 June 2016.

Brinkema, Eugenie. *The Forms of the Affects.* Duke UP, 2014.

Brophy, Phillip. "Horrality: The Textuality of Contemporary Horror Films." *Screen*, vol. 27, no. 1, 1986, pp. 2–13.

Brown, Bridget. "'My Body Is Not My Own': Personalizing Disempowerment in Alien Abduction Narratives." *Conspiracy Nation*, edited by Peter Knight, NYU P, 2002, pp.107–32.

Brown, Jeffrey A. "Gender and the Action Heroine: Hardbodies and the 'Point of No Return.'" *Cinema Journal*, vol. 35, no. 3, 1996, pp. 52–71.

Brown, Todd. "Re: Argentine Horror Cinema." Received by Jonathan Risner, 8 Sept. 2009.

Burgin, Victor. *In/different Spaces: Place and Memory in Visual Culture.* U of California P, 1996, pp. 117–38.

Burucúa, Constanza. *Confronting the 'Dirty War' in Argentine Cinema, 1983–1993: Memory and Gender in Historical Representations.* Tamesis, 2008.

Carroll, Nöel. *The Philosophy of Horror.* Routledge, 1990.

Cedeño, Maribel Rojas. "Estética y estrategias narrativas del cine de terror y el *thriller* en *Crónica de una fuga* de Adrián Caetano. *HeLix*, 2015, pp. 49–70.

Chanan, Michael. *Cuban Cinema.* U of Minnesota P, 2004.

Cherry, Brigid. *Horror.* Routledge, 2009.

Chion, Michel. *The Voice of Cinema.* Translated by Claudia Gorman, Columbia UP, 1999.

"Cine Indie: La productora de 'cine punk' Mutazion filma su nueva película." *EscribiendoCine,* 19 June 2013, www.escribiendocine.com/noticia/0006702-cine-indie-la-productora-de-cine-punk-mutazion-filma-su-nueva-pelicula/. Accessed 15 June 2015.

Cine Inusual. festivaldecineinusual.blogspot.com/. Accessed 5 June 2015.

Clover, Carol J. *Men, Women, and Chainsaws: Gender in the Modern Horror Film.* Princeton UP, 1993.

Colebrook, Claire. *Irony.* Routledge, 2004.

Conde, Pedro, and Pablo Mérida. *Cine bizarro y fantástico hispano-argentino entre dos siglos.* Gráficas Medina, 2008.

Copertari, Gabriela. *Desintegración y justicia en el cine argentino contemporáneo.* Tamesis, 2009.

corpusvile. (2013). "Re: *Grite una Noche.*" *YouTube,* 2013, https://www.youtube.com/watch?v=pcM1RPypDHc. Accessed 9 Apr. 2015.

Crafton, Donald. "Pie and Chase: Gag, Spectacle, and Narrative in Slapstick Comedy." *The Cinema of Attractions Reloaded,* edited by Wanda Strauven, Amsterdam UP, 2006, pp. 355–64.

Creed, Barbara. *The Monstrous-Feminine: Film, Feminism, Psychoanalysis.* Routledge, 1993.

———. *Phallic Panic.* Melbourne UP, 2005.

Crisp, Virginia. *Film Distribution in the Digital Age: Pirates and Professionals.* Palgrave Macmillan, 2015.

Cubitt, Sean. "Distribution and Media Flows." *Cultural Politics,* vol. 1, no. 2, 2005, pp. 193–214.

Cueva, Christián. "Terror mexicano con sangre argentina." *Domingo: El Universal,* 2 Dec. 2012, moviles.eluniversal.com.mx/sites/all/modules/domingo/images/diciembre_2012_02.pdf. Accessed 5 June 2015.

Curtis, Barry. *Dark Places: The Haunted House in Film.* Reaktion Books, 2008.

Curubeto, Diego. *Cine bizarro.* Sudamericana, 1996.

———. *Babilonia Gaucha.* Planeta, 1993.

———. *Babilonia Gaucha: Ataca de nuevo.* Sudamericana, 1998.

———, and Fernando Martín Peña. *Cine de super acción: cine clásico y de culto en la TV argentina 1961–1993.* Norma, 2001.

Daney, Serge. "The Tracking Shot in Kapo." *Postcards from the Cinema*. Translated by Paul Douglas Grant, Berg, pp. 17–35.

Dapena, Gerard. "Emilio Vieyra: Argentina's Transnational Master of Horror." *Latsploitation, Exploitation Cinemas, and Latin America*, edited by Victoria Ruétalo and Dolores Tierney, Routledge, 2009, pp. 87–101.

Davis, Blair, and Kial Natale. " 'The Pound of Flesh Which I Demand': American Horror Cinema, Gore, and the Box Office, 1998–2007." *American Horror Film: The Genre at the Turn of the Millennium*, edited by Steffen Hantke, UP of Mississippi, 2010, pp. 35–57.

Dayan, Daniel. "Looking for Sundance: The Social Construction of a Film Festival." *Moving Images, Culture, and the Mind*, edited by Ib Bondebjerg, IU Press, 2000, pp. 43–52.

De Certeau, Michel. *The Practice of Everyday Life*. Translated by Steven Rendell, U of California P, 1988.

De la Fuente, Carlos. Personal interview. 20 June 2015.

———. Personal interview. 24 Feb. 2016.

De la Vega, Daniel. Personal interview. 9 June 2008.

De Leone, Lucía. "Imaginaciones rurales argentinas: el campo como zona de cruce en expresiones artísticas contemporáneas." *Cuadernos de literatura*, vol. 20, no. 40, 2016, pp. 181–203.

Deleuze, Gilles. *Cinema 1: The Movement-Image*. 1985. Translated by Hugh Tomlinson and Robert Galeta, U of Minnesota P, 1989.

———. *Cinema 2: The Time-Image*. 1985. Translated by Hugh Tomlinson and Robert Galeta, U of Minnesota P, 1989.

———. *The Logic of Sense*. Edited by Constantin V. Boundas. Translated by Mark Lester with Charles Stivale, Columbia UP, 1990.

Deleuze, Gilles, and Félix Guattari. *A Thousand Plateaus: Capitalism and Schizophrenia*. Translated by Brian Massumi, U of Minnesota P, 1987.

Dendle, Peter. "The Zombie as a Barometer of Cultural Anxiety." *The Monsters and the Monstrous: Myths and Metaphors of Enduring Evil*, edited by Niall Scott, Rodopi, 2007, pp. 45–57.

Derrida, Jacques. *Specters of Marx: The State of Debt, the Work of Mourning and the New International*. Translated by Peggy Kamuf, Routledge, 2006.

De Valck, Marijke. "Fostering Art, Adding Value, Cultivating Taste: Film Festivals as Sites of Cultural Legitimization." *Film Festivals: History, Theory, Method, Practice*, edited by Marijke de Valck, Brendan Kredell, and Skadi Loist, Routledge, 2016, pp. 100–16.

Díaz-Zambrana, Rosana. "Entre placer y conciencia. El horror (real)ista en el filme argentino Sudor frío." *Polifonía*, vol. 2, no. 2, 2012, pp. 147–61.

———. Introduction. *Horrofílmico: Aproximaciones al cine de terror en Latinoamérica y el Caribe*, edited by Rosana Díaz-Zambrana and Patricia Tomé, Isla Negra, 2012, pp. 19–43.

Dika, Vera. *Games of Terror: Halloween, Friday the 13th, and the Films of the Stalker Cycle*. Fairleigh Dickinson UP, 1990.

Di Marco, Laura. "Mujeres al poder." *La Nación*, 4 Dec. 2005, www.lanacion.com.ar/761830-mujeres-al-poder. Accessed 11 July 2011.

D'Lugo, Marvin. "Authorship, Globalization, and the New Identity of Latin American Cinema. From the Mexican 'Ranchera' to Argentinean "Exile": *Rethinking Third Cinema*, edited by Anthony Guneratne and Wimal Dissanayake, Routledge, 2003, pp. 103–25.

Donald, James. *Imagining the Modern City*. U of Minnesota P, 1999.

Douthat, Ross. "The Return of the Paranoid Style." *The Atlantic*, Apr. 2008, www.theatlantic.com/magazine/archive/2008/04/the-return-of-the-paranoid-style/306733/. Accessed 9 May 2014.

Duggan, Lisa. "The New Homonormativity: The Sexual Politics of Neoliberalism." *Materializing Democracy: Toward a Revitalized Cultural Politics*, edited by Russ Castronovo and Dana D. Nelson, Duke UP, 2002, pp. 175–94.

Dunn, Kevin C. *Global Punk: Resistance and Rebellion in Everyday Life*. Bloomsbury, 2016.

Ďurovičová, Nataša. Preface. *World Cinemas, Transnational Perspectives*, edited by Nataša Ďurovičová and Kathleen Newman, Routledge, 2010, pp. ix–xv.

Eagleton, Terry. *The Ideology of the Aesthetic*. Basil Blackwell, 1990.

Elaesser, Thomas. "Film History and Visual Pleasure: Weimar Cinema." *Cinema Histories, Cinema Practices*, edited by Patricia Mellencamp and Philip Rosen, University Publications of America, 1984, pp. 47–84.

Elejaiek Rodríguez, Gabriel Andrés. "Transilvania-Cali-Bogotá: 'Tropicalización' en tres películas de horror colombiano." *Horrofílmico: Aproximaciones al cine de terror en Latinoamérica y el Caribe*, edited by Rosana Díaz-Zambrana and Patricia Tomé, Isla Negra, 2012, pp. 163–82.

El equipo de INCAA TV. "Re: INCAA TV." Received by Jonathan Risner. 23 June 2014.

"Empieza en Buenos Aires el IV Festival de Cine Inusual." *Ñ: Revista de cultura*. *Clarín*, 21 May 2008, edant.revistaenie.clarin.com/notas/2008/05/21/01677114.html. Accessed 26 June 2015.

Entel, Alicia. *La ciudad y los medios: La pasión restauradora*. La Crujía Ediciones, 2007.

Epstein, Edward. "The Piquetero Movement in Greater Buenos Aires." *Broken Promises: The Argentine Crisis and Argentine Democracy*, edited by Edward Epstein and David Pion-Berlin, Lexington Books, 2006, pp. 95–115.

España, Claudio. "Diez años de cine de democracia." *Cine argentino en democracia: 1983–1993*, edited by Claudio España, Fondo Nacional de las Artes, 1994, pp. 12–53.

Falicov, Tamara. *The Cinematic Tango: Contemporary Argentine Cinema*. Wallflower, 2007.

———. "The 'Festival Film': Film Festival Funds as Cultural Intermediaries." *Film Festivals: History, Theory, Method, Practice*, edited Marijke de Valck, Brendan Kredell, and Skadi Loist, Routledge, 2016, pp. 209–29.

———. "Programa Ibermedia: Co-Production and the Cultural Politics of Constructing an Ibero American Audiovisual Space." *Spectator*, vol. 27, no. 2, 2007, pp. 21–30.

———. "U.S.-Argentine Co-productions, 1982–1990: Roger Corman, Aries Productions, 'Schlockbuster' Movies, and the International Market." *Film & History: An Interdisciplinary Journal of Film and Television Studies*, vol. 34, no. 1, 2004, pp. 31–38.

Feitlowitz, Marguerite. *A Lexicon of Terror: Argentina and the Legacies of Torture*. Oxford UP, 2011.

Fenster, Mark. *Conspiracy Theories: Secrecy and Power in American Culture*. U of Minnesota P, 2008.

Fernández, Álvaro. "Horror o política. El selectivo anclaje de los fantasmas del pasado a ambos lados del Atlántico." *Horrofílmico: Aproximaciones al cine de terror en América Latina*, edited by Rosana Díaz-Zambrana and Patricia Tomé, Isla Negra, 2011, pp. 261–80.

Fernandez Cruz, Martin. "Entrevista a Jimmy Crispin." *Revista El Bondi*, n.d., www.elbondi.com/cineyteatro/entrevista-a-jimmy-crispin#.WFngkFMrKpo. Accessed 7 Apr. 2015.

Ferri, Leonardo. "El terror de la mano desocupado." *Página 12*, 1 Feb. 2011, www.pagina12.com.ar/diario/suplementos/espectaculos/5-20646-2011-02-01.html. Accessed 4 Nov. 2015.

Filc, Judith. *Entre el parentesco y la política: familia y dictadura, 1976–1983*. Editorial Biblos, 1997.

Fink, Bruce. "The Real Cause of Repetition." *Reading Seminar XI: Lacan's Four Fundamental Concepts of Psychoanalysis*, edited by Richard Feldstein, Bruce Fink, and Maire Jaanus, SUNY, 223–29.

Fontana, Juan Carlos. "El ritual de espantar alienígenas." *Diario La Prensa*, 29 Mar. 2012. http://www.laprensa.com.ar/389481-El-ritual-de-espantar-alienigenas.note.aspx. Accessed 15 Aug. 2016.

Foster, David William. *Queer Issues in Contemporary Latin American Cinema*. U of Texas P, 2003.

Foucault, Michel. *The Birth of the Clinic*. Translated by A. M. Sheridan Smith, Pantheon, 1973.

Franco, Jean. *Cruel Modernity*. Duke UP, 2013.

———. *The Decline and Fall of the Lettered City: Latin America in the Cold War*. Harvard UP, 2002.

Freeland, Cynthia. "Horror and Art-Dread." The Horror Film, edited by Stephen Prince, Rutgers UP, 2004, pp. 189–205.

———. "Realist Horror." *Aesthetics: The Big Questions*, edited by Carolyn Korsmeyer, Blackwell Publishers, 1998, pp. 283–94.

Freeman, Daniel, and Jason Freeman. *Paranoia: The Twenty-First Century Fear*. Oxford UP, 2008.

Freud, Sigmund. "Das Unheimliche." *Sigmund Freud: Collected Papers*. Translated by Alix Strachey, vol. 4, Basic Books, pp. 218–52.

———. *Freud's "On Narcissism: An Introduction,"* edited by Joseph Sandler et al., Karnac, 2012.

———. *Three Case Histories*. Collier Books, 1963.

Frey, Mattias. Introduction. *Film Criticism in the Digital Age*, edited by Mattias Frey and Cecilia Sayad, Rutgers UP, 2015, pp. 1–20.

Frost, Leslie. *The Problem with Pleasure: Modernism and Its Discontents*. Columbia UP, 2013.

García, Alicia S. *La doctrina de la seguridad nacional: (1958–1983)*. Centro Editor de América Latina, 1991.

García, Santiago. "Para la libertad." *Leer cine: Revista de cine y cultura*, n.d., www.leercine.com.ar/nota.asp?id=22. Accessed 12 July 2011.

García Bogliano, Adrián, dir. Interview with Adrián García Bogliano. *Cold Sweat*. 2012. DVD. Dark Sky Films.

García Canclini, Néstor. *La globalización imaginada*. Paidós, 2000.
García Espinosa, Julio. "For an Imperfect Cinema." *New Latin American Cinema*, edited by Michael Martin, vol. 1, Wayne State UP, 1997, pp. 71–82.
Getino, Octavio. *El capital de la cultura: las industrias culturales en la Argentina*. Ediciones CICCUS, 2008.
Gillis, Stacy. Introduction. *The Matrix Trilogy: The Matrix Reloaded*, edited by Stacey Gillis, Wallflower, 2005, pp. 1–8.
Giucci, Guillermo. *The Cultural Life of the Automobile: Roads to Modernity*. Translated by Anne Mayagoitia and Debra Nagao, U of Texas P, 2012.
Gleber, Anke. *The Art of Taking a Walk: Flanerie, Literature, and Film in Weimar Culture*. Princeton UP, 1999.
Gordon, Avery. *Ghostly Matters: Haunting and the Sociological Imagination*. U of Minnesota P, 1997.
Gorelik, Adrián. *Miradas sobre Buenos Aires: historia cultural y crítica urbana*. Siglo Veintiuno Editores Argentina, 2004.
Gorman, Anna. "To Sound More American." *Los Angeles Times*, 2 Nov. 2007, articles.latimes.com/2007/oct/23/local/me-accent23. Accessed 12 July 2011.
Grant, Barry Keith. *Film Genre: From Iconography to Ideology*. Wallflower, 2007.
Grimson, Alejandro, and Gabriel Kessler. *On Argentina and the Southern Cone: Neoliberalism and National Imaginations*. Routledge, 2005.
Gross, Larry. "Big and Loud." *Action/Spectacle Cinema*, edited by José Arroyo British Film Institute, 2000, pp. 3–25.
Grossberg, Lawrence. Interview. "Affect's Future." *The Affect Theory Reader*, edited by Melissa Gregg and Gregory J. Seigworth, Duke UP, pp. 309–38.
Gunning, Tom. "The Cinema of Attraction: Early Film, Its Spectator and the Avant-Garde." *Wide Angle*, vol. 8, no. 3/4, 1986, pp. 63–70.
Gutiérrez, Carlos, and Monika Wagenberg. "Meeting Points: A Survey of Film Festivals in Latin America." *Transnational Cinemas*, vol. 4, no. 2, 2013, pp. 295–305.
Hall, Sheldon. *The Cinema of John Carpenter: The Technique of Terror*. Edited by Ian Conrich and David Woods, Wallflower, pp. 66–77.
Hanich, Julian. *Cinematic Emotion in Horror Films and Thrillers: The Aesthetic Paradox of Pleasurable Fear*. Routledge, 2010.
Hannerz, Erik. *Performing Punk*. Palgrave Macmillan, 2015.
Hantke, Steffen. "Academic Film Criticism, the Rhetoric of Crisis, and the Current State of American Horror Cinema: Thoughts on Canonicity

and Academic Anxiety." *College Literature*, vol. 34, no. 4, 2007, pp. 191–202.

———. Introduction. *American Horror Film: The Genre at the Turn of the Millennium*, edited by Steffen Hantke, UP of Mississippi, 2010, pp. vii–xxxii.

Harbord, Janet. Film Cultures. SAGE, 2002.

Harlow, Barbara. "Testimonio and Survival: Roque Dalton's Miguel Mármol." *Latin American Perspectives*, vol. 18, no. 4, 1991, pp. 9–21.

Harries, Dan. *Film Parody.* BFI, 2002.

Harvey, William. *The Circulation of the Blood and Other Writings*. Tuttle, 1993.

Hawkins, Joan. *Cutting Edge: Art-Horror and the Horrific Avant-Garde*. U of Minnesota P, 2000.

Henry, Claire. *Revisionist Rape-Revenge: Redefining a Film Genre*. Palgrave MacMillan, 2014.

Higson, Andrew. "The Concept of National Cinema." *Screen*, vol. 30, no. 4, 1989, pp. 36–47.

Hills, Matt. *The Pleasures of Horror.* Continuum, 2005.

Himpele, Jeffrey. *Circuits of Culture: Media, Politics, and Indigenous Identity in the Andes*. U of Minnesota P, 2008.

Hjort, Mette. "On the Plurality of Cinematic Transnationalism." *World Cinemas, Transnational Perspectives*, edited by Nataša Ďurovičová and Kathleen Newman, Routledge, 2010, pp. 12–33.

Hofstadter, Richard. "The Paranoid Style in American Politics." *The Paranoid Style in American Politics and Other Essays*, Vintage, 1965, pp. 3–40.

Holder, Christopher Sharett. "The Horror Film as Social Allegory (And How It Comes Undone)." *A Companion to the Horror Film*, edited by Harry M. Benshoff, Wiley Blackwell, 2014, pp. 56–72.

"Homenaje al Cine de Genero [sic] Argentino." *YouTube*, uploaded by Victor von Krueger, 10 July 2014, www.youtube.com/watch?v=mbKZIZUYlsU.

Hopkins, Lisa. *Screening the Gothic*. U of Texas P, 2005.

"HorrAR: algo está pasando en Argentina." *Que no se culpe a nadie*, 19 Apr. 2007, quenoseculpeanadie.blogspot.com/2007/04/horrar-algo-esta-pasando-en-argentina.html. Accessed 20 Feb. 2015.

Iordonova, Dina. Foreword. *Film Festivals: History, Theory, Method, Practice*, edited by Marijke de Valck, Brendan Kredell, and Skadi Loist, Routledge, 2016, pp. xi–xvii.

Jacobs, Lea, and Richard de Cordova. "Spectacle and Narrative Theory." *Quarterly Review of Film Studies*, vol. 7, no. 4, 1982, pp. 293–308.

Jaffe, Ira. *Slow Movies: Countering the Cinema of Action.* Wallflower, 2014.

Jameson, Fredric. *The Geopolitical Aesthetic: Cinema and Space in the World System.* Indiana UP, 1992.

———. *Signatures of the Visible.* Routledge, 1990.

Jane, Emma A., and Chris Fleming. *Modern Conspiracy: The Importance of Being Paranoid.* Bloomsbury, 2014.

Janoschka, Michael, and Axel Borsdorf. "Condominios Fechados and Barrios Privados: The Rise of Private Residential Neighbourhoods in Latin America." *Private Cities: Global and Local Perspectives*, edited by Georg Glasze, Chris Webster, and Klaus Frantz, Routledge, 2006, pp. 92–108.

Jauss, Hans Robert. *Toward an Aesthetic of Reception.* Translated by Timothy Bahti, U of Minnesota P, 1982.

Jeffords, Susan. *Hard Bodies: Hollywood Masculinity in the Reagan Era.* Rutgers UP, 1994.

Jelin, Elizabeth. *State Repression and the Labors of Memory.* Translated by Judith Rein and Marcial Godoy-Anativia, U of Minnesota P, 2003.

Jenkins, Henry, Sam Ford, and Joshua Green. *Spreadable Media: Creating Value and Meaning in a Networked Culture.* NYU P, 2013.

Johnson, Kenneth. "The Point of View of the Wandering Camera." *Cinema Journal*, vol. 32, no. 2, 1993, pp. 49–56.

Kairuz, Mariano. "Heavy Metal: La memoria del muerto, de Javier Diment." *Página 12*, 24 Mar. 2013, www.pagina12.com.ar/diario/suplementos/radar/9-8712-2013-03-26.html. Accessed 5 Nov. 2016.

Kavka, Misha. "The Gothic on Screen." *The Cambridge Companion to Gothic Fiction*, edited by Jerod E. Hogle, Cambridge UP, 2002, pp. 209–28.

Kendrick, James. *Film Violence: History, Ideology, Genre.* Wallflower, 2009.

Kendrick, Walter. *The Thrill of Fear: 250 Years of Scary Entertainment.* Grove Weidenfeld, 1991.

Kermode, Frank. *The Sense of an Ending; Studies in the Theory of Fiction.* Oxford UP, 1967

Kessler, Gabriel. *El sentimiento de la inseguridad.* Siglo XXI, 2009.

King, Geoff. "Spectacle and Narrative in the Contemporary Blockbuster." *Contemporary American Cinema*, edited by Linda Ruth Williams and Michael Hammond, 2006, pp. 334–35, 338–43, 347–49, 352.

———. "'Killingly Funny': Mixing Modalities in New Hollywood's Comedy-with-Violence." *New Hollywood Violence*, edited by Steven Jay Schneider, Manchester UP, 2004, pp. 126–64.

King, John. *Magical Reels: A History of Cinema in Latin America*. Verso, 2000.

Kirby, Lynne. *Parallel Tracks: The Railroad and Silent Cinema*. Duke UP, 1997.

Klinger, Barbara. *Beyond the Multiplex: Cinema, New Technologies, and the Home*. U of California P, 2006.

Kozloff, Sarah. *Overhearing Film Dialogue*. U of California P, 2000.

Kredell, Brendan. Introduction. *Film Festivals: History, Theory, Method, Practice*, edited Marijke de Valck, Brendan Kredell, and Skadi Loist, Routledge, 2016, pp. 15–17.

Kristeva, Julia. *Powers of Horror: An Essay on Abjection*. Translated by Leon S. Roudiez, Columbia UP, 1982.

Kuhn, Annette, and Guy Westwell. *Oxford Dictionary of Film Studies*. Oxford UP, 2012. "KV62." *IMDB*. n.d., www.imdb.com/title/tt3028024/. Accessed 5 June 2015.

Landsberg, Alison. *Prosthetic Memory: The Transformation of American Remembrance in the Age of Mass Culture*. Columbia UP, 2004.

Lanzagorta, Marco. "Horror Cinema by the Numbers." *Pop Matters*, 25 Nov. 2007, www.popmatters.com/column/horror-cinema-by-the-numbers. Accessed 25 Aug. 2016.

Lavia, Darío. "Jovenes realizadores argentinos del cine fantástico." *Cinefania*, Dec. 2004, www.cinefania.com/terroruniversal/index.php?id=121. Accessed 4 June 2015.

Lázaro-Reboll, Antonio. "'Perversa América Latina': The Reception of Latin American Exploitation Cinemas in Spanish Subcultures." *Latsploitation, Exploitation Cinemas, and Latin America*, edited by Victoria Ruétalo and Dolores Tierney, Routledge, 2009, pp. 37–54.

———. *Spanish Horror Film*. Edinburgh UP, 2012.

Leguiza, Marcelo. Personal interview. 27 Feb. 2016.

———. Personal interview. 11 June 2015.

Leen, Catherine. "City of Fear: Reimagining Buenos Aires in Contemporary Argentine Cinema." *Bulletin of Latin American Research*, vol. 27, no. 4, 2008, pp. 465–82.

Lefebvre, Henri. *The Production of Space*. Translated by Donald Nicholson-Smith, Blackwell, 1991.

Lefebvre, Martin. "On Landscape in Narrative Cinema." *Canadian Journal of Film Studies*, vol. 20, no. 1, 2011, pp. 61–78.

Lehman, Peter. "Don't Blame This on a Girl." *Screening the Male: Exploring Masculinities in Hollywood Cinema*, edited by Steven Cohan and Ina Rae Hark, Routledge, 1993, pp. 103–17.

Leitch, Thomas. "Aristotle v. the Action Film." *New Hollywood Violence*, edited by Steven Jay Schneider, Manchester UP, pp. 103–25.

Lemkin, Jonathan. "Archetypal Landscapes and Jaws." *Planks of Reason*, edited by Barry Keith Grant, Scarecrow Press, 2004, pp. 321–32.

Lerer, Diego. "Odeón, 'el netflix criollo' que ofrece gratis 700 horas de películas y series." *La Nación*, 26 Nov. 2015, http://www.lanacion.com.ar/1849074-odeon-el-netflix-criollo-que-ofrece-gratis-700-horas-de-peliculas-y-series. Accessed 16 May 2016.

———. "Rodeados de fantasmas." *Clarín*, 12 Mar. 2009, edant.clarin.com/diario/2009/12/03/espectaculos/c-02053748.htm. Accessed 12 July 2011.

———. "Un escape entre el horror y el heroísmo." *Clarín*, 27 Apr. 2006, edant.clarin.com/diario/2006/04/27/espectaculos/c-00501.htm. Accessed 12 July 2011.

Liberatto, Lisandro. "Review: Naturaleza muerta." *Altapeli*, 2 Mar. 2015. altapeli.com/bars15-review-naturaleza-muerta/. Accessed 16 Feb. 2016.

Lobato, Ramon. *Shadow Economies of Cinema: Mapping Informal Film Distribution*. Palgrave Macmillan, 2012.

———, and Julian Thomas. "An Introduction to Informal Media Economies." *Television and New Media*, vol. 13, no. 5, 2012, pp. 379–82.

Loist, Skadi. "The Film Festival Circuit: Networks, Hierarchies, and Circulation." *Film Festivals: History, Theory, Method, Practice*, edited by Marijke de Valck, Brendan Kredell, and Skadi Loist, Routledge, 2016, pp. 49–64.

Loreti, Nicanor. Personal Interview. 11 June 2009.

Lowenstein, Adam. *Shocking Representation: Historical Trauma, National Cinema, and the Modern Horror Film*. Columbia UP, 2005.

———. "Spectacle Horror and Hostel: Why Torture Porn Does Not Exist." *Critical Quarterly*, vol. 53, no. 1, 2011, pp. 42–60.

Lukinbeal, Chris. "Cinematic Landscapes." *Journal of Cultural Geography*, vol. 23, no. 1, 2005, pp. 3–22.

Lukow, Greg, and Steve Ricci. "The 'Audience' Goes 'Public': Inter-textuality, Genre, and the Responsibilities of Film Literacy." *On Film*, no. 12, 1984, pp. 28–36.

Lusnich, Ana Laura. Introduction. *Civilización y barbarie en el cine argentino y Latinoamericano*, edited by Lusnich, Editorial Biblos, 2005, pp. 9–18.

Lynch, Kevin. *The Image of the City.* MIT Press, 1960.

Magariños, Germán. Personal interview. 23 Feb. 2016.

———. Personal interview. 3 June 2015.

Magistrale, Tony. *Abject Terrors: Surveying the Modern and Postmodern Horror Film.* Peter Lang, 2005.

Marsh, Steven. *Popular Spanish Film under Franco: Comedy and the Weakening of the State.* Palgrave Macmillan, 2006.

Martin-Jones, David, and María Soledad Montañez. "Uruguay Disappears: Small Cinemas, Control Z Films and the Aesthetics and Politics of Auto-Erasure." *Cinema Journal*, vol. 53, no. 1, 2013, pp. 26–51.

Martini, Stella. *Argentina: Prensa, gráfica, delito y seguridad. Los relatos periodísticos del crimen.* C3-FES, 2007, pp. 21–54.

Massey, Doreen. Space, Place and Gender. Polity, 1994.

Massumi, Brian. "The Autonomy of Affect." The Politics of Systems and Environments, Part II special issue of Cultural Critique, no. 31, 1995, pp. 83–109.

———. "The Future Birth of the Affective Fact: The Political Ontology of Threat." Digital and Other Virtualities, edited by Antony Bryant and Griselda Pollock, pp. 79–92.

Mathijs, Ernest, and Jamie Sextion. Cult Cinema: An Introduction. Wiley-Blackwell, 2011.

Mayne, Judith. Cinema and Spectatorship. Routledge, 1993.

Mayorga, Carlos. "Ventana Sur: 'Immutable Evil,' 'Guardian,' 'Elf,' 'Under Your Feet,' Set for 2016 Blood Window." Variety, 17 Nov. 2016, variety.com/2016/film/festivals/blood-window-the-immutable-evil-the-guardian-the-elf-ventana-sur-1201920546. Accessed 18 Nov. 2016.

McKinney, Devin. "Violence: The Strong and the Weak." Film Quarterly, vol. 46, no. 4, 1993, pp. 16–22.

Melley, Timothy. Empire of Conspiracy: The Culture of Paranoia in Postwar America. Cornell UP, 2000.

Mennel, Barbara Caroline. *Cities and Cinema*. Routledge, 2008.

Message, Kylie. "Body without Organs." *The Deleuze Dictionary*, edited by Adrian Parr, Columbia UP, 2005, pp. 32–34.

Metz, Christian. *The Imaginary Signifier*. Indiana UP, 1982.

Miller, Toby, et al. *Global Hollywood 2*. BFI Publishing, 2005.

Milsztjan, Fernando. "For export de terror." *Haciendo cine*, Aug. 2007, pp. 26–30.

Mirrlees, Tanner. *Global Entertainment Media: Between Cultural Imperialism and Cultural Globalization*. Taylor and Francis, 2013.

"Mocosis." *IMDB*, n.d., www.imdb.com/title/tt3089328. Accessed 5 June 2015.

Modelski, Tania. "The Terror of Pleasure: The Contemporary Horror Film and Postmodern Theory." *Film Theory and Criticism*, edited by Leo Braudy and Marshall Cohen, Oxford UP, 2006, pp. 764–73.

Montesoro, Julia. "En nombre del cine fantástico." La Nación, 5 Dec. 2015, www.lanacion.com.ar/1851509-en-nombre-del-cine-fantastico. Accessed 4 July 2016.

Moore, Ryan. "Postmodernism and Punk Subculture: Cultures of Authenticity and Deconstruction." *Communication Review*, no. 7, 2004, pp. 305–27.

Mowitt, John. *Re-takes: Postcoloniality and Foreign Film Languages*. U of Minnesota P, 2005.

Moyano, Hernán. "Re: Cine de horror." Received by Jonathan Risner, 23 June 2014.

Mulvey, Laura. "Visual Pleasure and Narrative Cinema." *Screen*, vol. 16, no. 3, 1975, pp. 6–18.

Murray, Ray. "Re: Questions about Artsploitation." Received by Jonathan Risner, 19 Aug. 2016.

Nagib, Lucia, Chris Perriam, and Rajinder Dudrah. *Theorizing World Cinema*, I. B. Tauris, 2012.

Neale, Steve. *Genre and Hollywood*. Routledge, 2000.

Neroni, Hilary. *The Violent Woman: Femininity, Narrative, and Violence in Contemporary American Cinema*. SUNY, 2005.

Newberry, Charles. "Argentina Horror Films Going Low-Budget." *Variety*, 8 Feb. 2008, variety.com/2008/scene/markets-festivals/argentina-horror-films-going-low-budg-1117980500/. Accessed 12 Apr. 2015.

Newitz, Annalee. *Pretend We're Dead: Capitalist Monsters in American Pop Culture*. Duke UP, 2006.

Newman, Kathleen. "Notes on Transnational Film Theory." *World Cinemas, Transnational Perspectives*, edited by Nataša Ďurovičová and Kathleen Newman, Routledge, 2010, pp. 3–11.

Newman, Kim. *Nightmare Movies: Wide Screen Horror Since the 1960s*. New York: Proteus, 1984

Nichols, Bill. *Introduction to Documentary.* Indiana UP, 2001.

North, Dan. *Performing Illusions: Cinema, Special Effects and the Virtual Actor.* Wallflower, 2008.

Nouzeilles, Gabriela, and Graciela Montaldo. "Democracy and Neoliberalism." *The Argentina Reader*, edited by Gabriela Nouzeilles and Graciela Montaldo, Duke UP, 2002, pp. 473–75.

Nowell, Richard. *Blood Money: A History of the First Teen Slasher Film Cycle.* Continuum, 2011.

Nunca más: Informe de la Comisión Nacional sobre la Desaparición de Personas. EUDEBA, 1984.

Och, Dana, and Kirsten Strayer. Introduction. *Transnational Horror across Visual Media: Fragmented Bodies*, Routledge, 2013, pp. 1–13.

O'Donnell, Patrick. *Latent Destinies: Cultural Paranoia and Contemporary U.S. Narrative.* Duke UP, 2000.

Olarra Jiménez, Rafael, and Luis García Martínez. *El derrumbe argentino: de la convertibilidad al "corralito."* Planeta, 2002.

Oliveros, Mariano. "El próximo movimiento." *Haciendo Cine*, 7 Mar. 2016, www.haciendocine.com.ar/node/42607. Accessed 12 Aug. 2016.

Ostherr, Kirsten. *Cinematic Prophylaxis: Globalization and Contagion in the Discourse of World Health.* Duke UP, 2005.

Oubiña, David. Prólogo. *Cines al margen: nuevos modos de representación en el cine argentino contemporáneo*, edited by María José Moore and Paula Wolkowicz, Libraria, 2007.

———. *Estudio crítico sobre La ciénaga.* Picnic Editorial, 2009.

Page, Joanna. *Crisis and Capitalism in Contemporary Argentine Cinema.* Duke UP, 2009.

Pagnoni, Fernando. "Cine de terror argentino: Historia, temas y estética de un género en el período clásico." Horrofílmico: Aproximaciones al cine de terror en Latinoamérica y el Caribe, edited by Rosana Díaz-Zambrana and Patricia Tomé, Isla Negra, 2012, pp. 432–51.

Panessi, Hernán. "Daniel de la Vega." *Escribiendocine.* 5 Aug. 2009, www.escribiendocine.com/entrevista/0000167-daniel-de-la-vega-los-realizadores-d

e-genero-nos-vimos-obligados-a-filmar-en-otro-idioma-porque-no-encontramos-apoyo-en-nuestro-pais/. Accessed 5 May 2014.
Paradis, Kenneth. *Sex, Paranoia, and Modern Masculinity*. SUNY, 2007.
Parés, Pablo. Prólogo. *Guerreros del cine: argentino fantástico e independiente*, by Matías Raña, Fan Ediciones, pp. 13–16.
Partnoy, Alicia. *La Escuelita: relatos testimoniales*. La Bohemia, 2006.
Paul, William. *Laughing, Screaming: Modern Hollywood Horror and Comedy*. Columbia UP, 1994.
Paulus, Tom, and Rob King, eds. *Slapstick Comedy*. Routledge, 2010.
Paz, Luis. "Punk Cine." *NO. Página 12*. 2 Aug. 2012, www.pagina12.com.ar/diario/suplementos/no/12-6034-2012-08-02.html. Accessed 15 June 2015.
Peacock. "¿El fin de la cinematográfica en la Argentina?" *Micropsia*, 24 July 2013. micropsia.otroscines.com/2013/07/el-fin-de-la-critica-cinematografica-en-la-argentina/10. Accessed 8 July 2016.
Perelman, Pablo, and Paulina Seivach. *La industria cinematográfica en la Argentina: entre los límites del mercado y el fomento estatal*. Centro de Estudios para el Desarrollo Metropolitano, 2003.
Pereyra, Daniela. "Espacios para una geografía alternativa del cine." *Latidos: El pulso del cine argentino*, edited by Gabriel Patrono and Daniela Pereyra, Fan Ediciones, 2015, pp. 49–64.
Perez, Al. "Re: The Last Gateway." Email to Jonathan Risner, 25 Sept. 2009.
Pérez Llahí, Marcos Adrián. "La posibilidad de un territorio." *Cines al margen*, edited by María
José Moore and Paula Wolkowicz, Libraria, 2007, pp. 69–80.
Phillips, Kendall. *Dark Directions: Romero, Craven, Carpenter, and the Modern Horror Film*. Southern Illinois UP, 2012.
Pinedo, Isabel Cristina. *Recreational Terror: Women and the Pleasures of Horror Film Viewing*. SUNY, 1997.
Podalsky, Laura. *The Politics of Affect and Emotion in Contemporary Latin American Cinema: Argentina, Brazil, Cuba, and Mexico*. Palgrave Macmillan, 2011.
———. *Specular City: Transforming Culture, Consumption, and Space in Buenos Aires, 1955–1973*. Temple UP, 2004.
Pollachi, Paula. Personal interview, 14 June 2009.
Pollan, Dana. " 'Above All Else to Make You See': Cinema and the Ideology of Spectacle." boundary 2, vol. 11, no. 1/2, 1982–1983, pp. 129–44.

Powell, Anna. *Deleuze and Horror Film*. Edinburgh UP, 2005.

Pratt, Ray. *Projecting Paranoia: Conspiratorial Visions in American Film*. UP of Kansas, 2001.

Prawer, Siegbert Salomon. *Caligari's Children: The Film as Tale of Terror*. Oxford UP, 1980.

Prince, Stephen. "Violence and Psychophysiology in Horror Cinema." *Horror Film and Psychoanalysis: Freud's Worst Nightmare*, edited by Steven Jay Schneider, Cambridge UP, 2004, pp. 241–56.

———. Introduction. *The Horror Film*, edited by Steven Prince, Rutgers UP, 2004, pp. 1–11.

———. *Classical Film Violence: Designing and Regulating Brutality in Hollywood Cinema, 1930–1968*. Rutgers UP, 2003.

———. "Graphic Violence in the Cinema: Origins, Aesthetic Design, and Social Effects." *Screening Violence*, edited by Stephen Prince, Rutgers UP, 2000, pp. 1–44.

"Quiero hacer una película de zombies." *Infobae*, 14 May 2014, www.infobae.com/2014/05/14/1564265-ricardo-darin-quiero-hacer-una-pelicula-zombies/. Accessed 2 Apr. 2017.

Quiroga, Bernabé. "Entrevistamos a Marcelo Leguiza, la nueva promesa del cine bizarro argentino y director de MARIHUANA RADIOACTIVA INTERPLANETARIA." *Cinerd*, 26 Oct. 2010, cinerd.blogspot.com/2010/10/entrevistamos-marcelo-leguiza-la-nueva.html. Accessed 3 Mar. 2015.

Ramos Mejía, José María. *Las multitudes argentinas; estudio de psicología colectiva para servir de introducción al libro "Rozas y su tiempo."* Félix Lajouane, 1899.

Rancière, Jacques. *The Emancipated Spectator*. Verso, 2009.

Raña, Matías. *Guerreros del cine: argentino, fantástico e independiente*. Fan Ediciones, 2010.

———. Personal Interview. 18 May 2014.

Read, Jacinda. *The New Avengers: Feminism, Femininity and the Rape-Revenge Cycle*. Manchester UP, 2000.

Reati, Fernando. "Fractures and Discontinuities of Buenos Aires in Film and Fiction of the 1990s: *Mala época* and *Vivir afuera*." *Argentinean Cultural Production during the Neoliberal Years (1989–2001)*, edited by Hugo Hortiguera and Carolina Rocha, Mellen, 2007, pp. 187–204.

———. *Postales del porvenir: la literatura de anticipación en la Argentina neoliberal (1985–1999)*. Editorial Biblos, 2006.

Rébora, Alejo. Personal interview. 27 Feb. 2016.

Rébora, Alejo, and Daniela Giménez. Personal interview. 18 June 2014.

Reimer, Robert C. "Does Laughter Make the Crime Disappear?: An Analysis of Cinematic Images of Hitler and the Nazis, 1940–2007." *Senses of Cinema*, Sept. 2009, sensesofcinema.com/2009/feature-articles/does-laughter-make-the-crime-disappear-an-analysis-of-cinematic-images-of-hitler-and-the-nazis-1940-2007. Accessed 28 Sept. 2015.

Resolucion 3078/2015. Boletín Oficial de la República Argentina, 25 Nov. 2015, www.boletinoficial.gob.ar/#!DetalleNorma/136816/null. Accessed 18 July 2016.

Robbins, Helen. "'More Human Than I Am Alone': Womb Envy in Cronenberg." *Screening the Male*, edited by Steven Cohan and Ina Rae Hark, Routledge, pp. 134–47.

Rocha, Carolina. *Masculinities in Contemporary Argentine Popular Cinema*. Palgrave Macmillan, 2012.

Rodríguez, Carina. *Cine de terror en Argentina: producción, distribución y mercado, 2000–2010*. Universidad Nacional de Quilmes, 2014.

Rombes, Nicholas, ed. *New Punk Cinema*. Edinburgh UP, 2005.

Ross, Miriam. *South American Cinematic Culture: Policy, Production, Distribution and Exhibition*. Cambridge Scholars, 2010.

Rotker, Susana. *Captive: Oblivion and Memory in Argentina*. Translated by Jennifer French, U of Minnesota P, 2002.

Rubin, Martin. *Thrillers*. Cambridge UP, 1999.

Ruétalo, Victoria, and Dolores Tierney. Introduction. Latsploitation, Exploitation Cinemas, and Latin America, edited by Victoria Ruétalo and Dolores Tierney, Routledge, 2009.

Rugna, Demián. Personal Interview. 24 May 2014.

———. Personal Interview. 9 June 2009.

Russo, Juan Pablo. "Paura Flics." *Escribiendocine*, 30 Jan. 2011, www.escribiendocine.comarticulo/0002222-paura-flics-de-habitaciones-para-turistas-a-sudor-frio. Accessed 21 Jan. 2016.

Ryall, Tom. *Alfred Hitchcock and the British Cinema*. Athlone, 1996.

Sabat, Cynthia. "Elogio de la independencia: Farsa Producciones." *Había una vez una chica*. Blogger.com. 21 Dec. 2009. Accessed Oct. 2015.

"Sadomaster 2: Locura General se estrenará el próximo mes de marzo." Interview with Germán Magariños, *Terrorífilo*, 7 Jan. 2011, www.terrorifilo.com/2011/01/sadomaster-2-locura-general.html. Accessed 8 June 2015.

Salmose, Niklas. "We Spiders: Spider as the Monster of Modernity in the Big Bug and Nature-on-a-Rampage Film Genres." *Animal Horror Cinema: Genre, History and Criticism*, edited by Katarina Gregersdotter, Johan Höglund, and Nicklas Hållén, Palgrave Macmillan, 2015, pp. 146–67.

"Sangre, Sudor y Tripas: Entrevista con Germán Magariños, director de Sadomaster." 28 Feb. 2011, cinesisrosario.blogspot.com/2011_02_01_archive.html. Accessed 3 Mar. 2015.

Sapere, Pablo. Personal Interview. 23 May 2014.

———. Personal Interview. 11 June 2009.

Sarlo, Beatriz. *La ciudad vista: mercancías y cultura urbana*. Siglo Veintiuno Editores, 2009.

———. *Una modernidad periférica: Buenos Aires, 1920 y 1930*. Ediciones Nueva Visión, 1988.

———. The *Technical Imagination: Argentine Culture's Modern Dreams*. Translated by Xavier Callahan, Stanford UP, 2008.

Sarmiento, Domingo Faustino. *Facundo: Civilization and Barbarism*. Translated by Kathleen Ross, Berkeley: U of California P, 2003.

Sassen, Saskia. "The Global City: Introducing a Concept." *Brown Journal of World Affairs*, vol. 11, no. 2, 2005, pp. 27–43.

Scarry, Elaine. *The Body in Pain: The Making and Unmaking of the World*. Oxford UP, 1985.

Schaefer, Eric. "Bold! Daring! Shocking! True!": *A History of Exploitation Films, 1919–1959*. Duke UP, 1999.

Schatz, Thomas. *Hollywood Genres*. Temple UP, 1981.

Scherer, Fabiana. "El culto por lo extraño." *La Nación*. 28 Aug. 1997. www.lanacion.com.ar/75760-el-culto-por-lo-extrano. Accessed 7 May 2017.

Schneider, Steven Jay, ed. *New Hollywood Violence*. Manchester UP, 2004.

Schneider, Steven Jay, and Tony Williams. Introduction. *Horror International*, edited by Steven Jay Schneider and Tony Williams, Wayne State UP, 2005, 1–12.

Schwarzböck, Silvia. *Estudio crítico sobre Crónica de una fuga*. Picnic Editorial, 2007.

———. "La posibilidad de un arte sin Estado. El cine después de internet." *Kilómetro 111*, no. 8, 2011, pp. 9–28.
Sconce, Jeffrey. "Spectacles of Death: Identification, Reflexivity, and Contemporary Horror." *Film Theory Goes to the Movies*, edited by Jim Collins, Hilary Radner, and Ava Preacher Collins, Routledge, 1993, pp. 103–19.
———. " 'Trashing' the Academy: Taste, Excess, and an Emerging Politics of Cinematic Style." *Screen*, vol. 36, no. 4, 1995, pp. 371–93.
Scorer, James. *City in Common: Culture and Community in Buenos Aires*. SUNY, 2016.
Scott, A. O. "What It Hurts to Remember Becomes Convenient to Forget." *New York Times* 19 Aug. 2009, www.nytimes.com/2009/08/19/movies/19headless.html. Accessed 14 Mar. 2011.
Sedgwick, Eve Kosofsky. *Touching Feeling: Affect, Pedagogy, Performativity*. Duke UP, 2003.
Seigworth, Gregory J., and Melissa Gregg. "An Inventory of Shimmers." *The Affect Theory Reader*, edited by Melissa Gregg and Gregory J. Seigworth, Duke UP, 2010, pp. 1–25.
Seoane, María. " 'Somos derechos y humanos': cómo se armó la campaña." *Clarín*, 23 Mar. 2006. edant.clarin.com/diario/2006/03/23/elpais/p-01501.htm. Accessed 21 Oct. 2015.
"Se presentó La Liga de Cine de Género." *Ultracine*, 5 Dec. 2015, www.ultracine.com/index.php/se-presento-la-liga-de-cine-de-genero-argentino. Accessed 24 Aug. 2016.
Shaviro, Steven. *The Cinematic Body*. U of Minnesota P, 1993.
Shklovsky, Viktor. "Art as Technique." *Russian Formalist Criticism: Four Essays*, edited by Lee T. Lemon and Marion J. Reiss, U of Nebraska P, 1965, pp. 3–24.
Shohat, Ella, and Robert Stam. *Unthinking Eurocentrism: Multiculturalism and the Media*. Routledge, 1994.
Shonfield, Katherine. *Walls Have Feelings: Architecture, Film and the City*. Routledge, 2000.
Siseles, Hernán. "FX made in Argentina." *Haciendo cine*, 9 Nov. 2011, www.haciendocine.com.ar/node/40124. Accessed 4 Dec. 2014.
Slocum, J. David, ed. *Violence and American Cinema*. Routledge, 2001.

Smith, Murray. "Theses on the Philosophy of Hollywood History." *Contemporary Hollywood Cinema*, edited by Steve Neale and Murray Smith, Routledge, 1998, pp. 3–20.

Solanas, Fernando, and Octavio Getino. "Towards a Third Cinema: Notes and Experiences for the Development of a Cinema of Liberation in the Third World." *New Latin American Cinema*, edited by Michael Martin, vol. 1, Wayne State UP, 1997, pp. 33–58.

Sontag, Susan. *Regarding the Pain of Others*. Picador, 2004.

———. *Illness as Metaphor and AIDS and Its Metaphors*. Picador USA, 2001.

Sorlin, Pierre. *Italian National Cinema 1896–1996*. Routledge, 1996.

Staiger, Janet. *Perverse Spectators*. NYU P, 2000.

Stang, Silvia. "El 42,6% de los chicos del Gran Buenos Aires viven en la pobreza." *La Nación*, 10 Sept. 2014, www.lanacion.com.ar/1725980-el-4 26-de-los-chicos-del-gran-buenos-aires-viven-en-la-pobreza#comunidad. Accessed 15 May 2017.

Stevenson, Jack. *Land of a Thousand Balconies: Discoveries and Confessions of a B-Movie Archaeologist*. Head Press/Critical Visions, 2003.

Storey, John. *Cultural Studies and the Study of Popular Culture*. U of Georgia P, 2003.

Subero, Gustavo. *Gender and Sexuality in Latin American Horror Cinema: Embodiments of Evil*. Palgrave Macmillan, 2016.

Svampa, Maristella. *La sociedad excluyente: La Argentina bajo el signo del neoliberalismo*. Taurus, 2005.

Svampa, Maristella, and Damián Corral. "Political Mobilization in Neighborhood Assemblies: The Cases of Villa Crespo and Palermo." *Broken Promises?: The Argentine Crisis and Argentine Democracy*, edited by Edward Epstein and David Pion-Berlin, Lexington Books, 2006, pp. 117–39.

Tambling, Jeremy. *Allegory*. Routledge, 2010.

Tamburini, Claudio. *Pase libre*. Buenos Aires: Ediciones Continente, 2006.

Tasker, Yvonne. *Spectacular Bodies: Gender, Genre, and the Action Cinema*. Routledge, 2002.

Taylor, Diana. *Disappearing Acts: Spectacles of Gender and Nationalism in Argentina's "Dirty War."* Duke UP, 1997.

Tella, Guillermo. *Un crack en la ciudad: Rupturas y continuidades en la trama urbana de Buenos Aires*. Nobuko, 2007.

Thompson, Stacy. *Punk Productions: Unfinished Business*. SUNY, 2004.
Thornton, Sarah. *Club Cultures: Music, Media, and Subcultural Capital*. UP of New England, 1996.
"Trash." *IMDB*, n.d., www.imdb.com/title/tt1846800. Accessed 5 June 2015.
Trerotola, Diego. "Yo soy mi propia diva." *Página 12*, 18 Feb. 2011, www.pagina12.com.ar/diario/suplementos/soy/1-1852-2011-02-20.html. Accessed 21 Nov. 2016.
Truitt, Brian. "'You're Next' Takes Machete to Home-Invasion Conventions." *USA Today*, 8 Aug. 2013, www.usatoday.com/story/life/movies/2013/08/21/youre-next-horror-film/2674591. Accessed 23 May 2016.
Tudor, James. *Monsters and Mad Scientists: A Cultural History of the Horror Movie*. Blackwell, 1989.
"Un cine en busca de jóvenes." *Página 12*, 4 Oct. 2013, www.pagina12.com.ar/diario/sociedad/3-230518-2013-10-04.html. Accessed 14 May 2016.
Uscinski, Joseph E., and Joseph M. Parent. *American Conspiracy Theories*. Oxford UP, 2014.
Venkatesh, Vinodh. *New Maricón Cinema: Outing Latin American Film*. U of Texas P, 2016.
Von Doviak, Scott. *Hick Flicks: The Rise and Fall of Redneck Cinema*. McFarland, 2005.
White, Patricia. "Female Spectator, Lesbian Specter: The Haunting." *Sexuality and Space*, edited by Beatriz Colmina, Princeton Architectural Press, 1992, pp. 131–61.
Williams, Linda. "Film Bodies: Gender, Genre, and Excess." *Film Quarterly*, summer, 1991, pp. 2–13.
Williams, Raymond. *Marxism and Literature*. Oxford UP, 1977.
Wisker, Gina. *Horror Fiction: An Introduction*. Continuum, 2005.
Wolf, Sergio. "El Cine del Proceso: Estética de la muerte." *Cine argentino, la otra historia*, edited by Sergio Wolf, Letra buena, 1994, pp. 265–79.
———. "Las estéticas de nuevo cine argentine: el mapa es el territorio." *Nuevo cine Argentino: Temas, autores y estilos de una renovación*, edited by Horacio Bernades et al., Ediciones Tatanka, 2002, pp. 29–39.
Wong, Cindy Hing-Yuk. "Publics and Counterpublics: Rethinking Film Festivals as Public Spheres." *Film Festivals: History, Theory, Method, Practice*, edited by Marijke de Valck, Brendan Kredell, and Skadi Loist, Routledge, 2016, pp. 83–99.

Xavier, Ismail. *Allegories of Underdevelopment: Aesthetics and Politics in Modern Brazilian Cinema.* U of Minnesota P, 1997.

Yúdice, George. "Testimonio and Postmodernism." *Latin American Perspectives*, vol. 18, no. 3, 1991, pp. 15–31.

Zhang, Yingjin. *Screening China.* U of Michigan P, 2010.

Žižek, Slavoj. *Looking Awry: An Introduction to Jacques Lacan through Popular Culture.* MIT Press, 1991.

———. *The Sublime Object of Ideology.* Verso, 1989.

———. *Violence.* Profile, 2008.

INDEX

Aballay, el hombre sin miedo/Six Shooters (Spiner, 2010), 19, 188n31, 200n48
Acland, Charles, 3, 5, 10
acousmêtres, 70–71, 73, 76–77, 79
affect, 116–23, 159–60
Aguilar, Gonzalo, 20, 38, 44–45, 110
Ahí va el diablo/Here Comes the Devil (García Bogliano, 2012), 194n16
Alan Smithee's Nosferatu (Magariños, 2010), 197n32, 198n39
Alexia (Borghi, 2013), 32, 174n31
Alguien te está mirando/"Someone Is Watching You" (Cova and Maldonado, 1988), 23, 167n2
allegory, xxi–xxiii, 87–88, 125
Alonso, Lisandro, 20–21
Alta Peli (website), 18
Altaris Video, 13–14
Altman, Rick, 29, 105
Amado, Ana, 133, 145
Anarcho-Punk, 107
Andermann, Jens, xxi, xxiii, 22, 39, 45, 110–11, 167n3
Aparecidos/The Appeared (Cabezas, 2007), 146–48
apartment horror, 74–75. See also *Dead Line* (Esquenazi, 2006)
Aragón, Ricardo, 65, 78, 187n28
archetypal landscapes, 80
Argentina Druida Film, 11
Argentine horror cinema
  emergence of, xvii–xix
  film festivals and, 9–11, 16, 22–23, 27–28, 97–98, 104, 163
  Internet and, 13–15, 14, 163
  as paracinematic pleasure, 20–25
  periodization for, 8–10
  screening venues and, 14–15
  sites of production and consumption of, xv, xviii–xix, 1–8, 9–19, 25–34, 163–65
  types of films in, 12–13
  See also English-language Argentine horror films; film distribution; film financing; INCAA (Instituto Nacional de Cine y Artes Audiovisuales; National Institute of Film and Audiovisual Arts); *specific films and directors*
Argentine punk/horror cinema
  affect and, 116–23
  canon of, 94–95
  comments by viewers on, 122, 123
  fusion of horror and punk in, 104–6
  gore in, 96, 108–9, 111, 114–23, *121*
  pleasure and, 94, 102–4
  punk as cinematic genre and, 95–98, 106–10
  punk in, 98–104
  raw film aesthetics and, 110–16
argentinidad, xx, 95
Artsploitation, 27
assemblage, 83–84

237

Ataúd blanco: El juego diabólico/White Coffin (de la Vega, 2016), 163
Aterrados/"Terrified" (Rugna, 2018), 178n51
Attali, Jacques, 94, 103
Auerbach, Jonathan, 88–89
Augé, Marc, 73
auto-erasure, 61–62, 72–74, 79–81, 90–91

Bad Taste (Jackson, 1987), 195n23
Badley, Linda, 81, 178–79n3
BAFICI (Buenos Aires Festival Internacional de Cine Independiente, Buenos Aires International Independent Film Festival), 22–23
Bagg, Andrés, 72
Baño de sangre/"Blood Bath" (Pollachi), 10
Barber, Chris, 95, 190n2, 192n6
BARS. *See* Buenos Aires Rojo Sangre (BARS)
BAZOFI (film festival), 173–74n27
Benjamin, Walter, xxi, 77, 85
Bernades, Horacio, 20, 137, 141
¡Bienvenido, Mr. Marshall!/Welcome, Mr. Marshall (García Berlanga, 1953), 149, 161
Bioy Casares, Adolfo, 43
Blake, Linnie, 146, 148
Blank Generation (Kral and Poe, 1976), 93, 106, 107, 113
Blood Window, 31–32
Bloody Disgusting (website), 27
body horror cinema, 81–82. See also *The Last Gateway* (Rugna, 2007)
Bone Breaker (Esquenazi, 2005), 62
Bordwell, David, 36, 109, 195–96n23, 200n50
Borges, Jorge Luis, 43
Bosteels, Bruno, 86, 87
Breaking Nikki (Findling, 2009), 62, 129

Brinkema, Eugenie, 117–18
Brown, Todd, 30
Brussels International Fantastic Film Festival (Belgium), 28
Bucheon International Fantastic Film Festival (South Korea), 28
Buenos Aires
 as cinematic spectacle, 45–46
 in *Dead Line*, 74
 in *Death Knows Your Name*, 68–69, 69
 desuburbanization in, 54
 as hub of Argentine horror, 11–12
 in *Plaga zombie: Zona mutante*, 39–40
 retail stores in, xiii, 15–16
 screening venues in, 14–15
 Ventana Sur and, 31–32
Buenos Aires 25 años de Hardcore Punk, El documental/"Buenos Aires 25 Years of Hardcore Punk, The Documentary" (Luna y Lübbert, 2008), 191n5
Buenos Aires, 1977. See *Crónica de una fuga* (Caetano, 2006)
Buenos Aires Festival Internacional de Cine Independiente (Buenos Aires International Independent Film Festival, BAFICI), 22–23
Buenos Aires Rojo Sangre (BARS)
 BAFICI and, 22–23
 origins and role of, 9–10, 11, 12, 16, 24, 163
 punk/horror cinema and, 104
Buenos Aires Rojo Shocking, 11
Buenos Aires viceversa/Buenos Aires Vice Versa (Agresti, 1996), 38

C y K Films, 11
Caixão, Zé do, 161
captivity, 129–31, 132, 137–38
Caro, Sebastián de, 152
Carpenter, John, xxiii, 143–44, 195n23

Carri, Albertina, 20–21
Carroll, Noël, xx, 67, 116, 190n47, 200n51
La casa acecha/"The Creeping House" (de Rosa, unrealeased), 178n51
La casa de las siete tumbas/"The House of the Seven Tombs" (Stocki, 1982), xiii
La casa muda/*The Silent House* (Hernández, 2010), 181–82n2
La cautiva (Echeverría), 49
Un cazador de zombis/"Zombie Hunter" (Magariños, 2008), 97–98, 108–9, 179n6, 197n32
Charly, días de sangre/"Charly, Days of Blood" (Galettini, 1990), 171–72n14
Chion, Michel, 70–71, 76
Chronicle of a Raven. See *Jennifer's Shadow* (*Chronicle of the Raven*) (de la Vega and Parés, 2004)
CIC (Centro de Investigación Cinematográfica), 11–12, 98
Cicuta, Vic, 113
La ciénaga (Martel, 2001), 24–25
CIEVYC (Centro de Investigación y Experimentación en Video y Cine), 98
"El cine argentino: Espacios para una geografía alternativa del cine" (Pereyra), 173–74n27
cine bizarro, 104
Cine bizarro (Curubeto), 171n13
Cine Club La Cripta, 9
Cine Club Nocturna, 9
Cine fantástico y bizarro (website), 16, 47, 105–6
Cine guerrilla (blog), 96
"Cine Independiente Fantástico Argentino" ("Argentine Independent and Fantastic Cinema"), xvi
cine testimonio, 139–40, 177n49
CINE.AR PLAY, xv, 6, 15, 32

Cinefagia (website), 27
Cinefania (website), 16
Cinefania Macabra (magazine), 16
cinema clubs, 9
cinematic realism, 46
cinematic spectacles
 Buenos Aires as, 45–46
 in *Plaga zombie: Zona mutante*, 45–46
 pleasure and, 35–36, 45–46
 punk/horror cinema and, 112–13
Clarín (newspaper), 16, 87, 138, 147–48
classical horror cinema, 133, 140, 141, 145–46
comedy and humor, 148–55, 158–59
conspiracy theories, 75, 85, 86
contagion, 44
Copertari, Gabriela, xxii, 38, 41
Corman, Roger, 184n11
Cornás, Walter, 150, 153
Corral, Damián, 42
La cosa (magazine), 16, 105–6
Cova, Gustavo, xvi–xvii
Crampi, Mad, 9, 104, 105
Creed, Barbara, 82, 133
Crispin, Jimmy, 195n23
Cronenberg, David, 45, 188n32, 198n40
Crónica de una fuga (Caetano, 2006)
 Dirty War and, 137–46, *139*, 149, 154, 159, 160, 206n36
 Gothic horror cinema and, 138, 139, 141–45, *142*, 146
 as horror film, 24
 paranoia in, 86–87
Cuando tu carne grite ¡Basta!/*When Your Flesh Screams!* (Martínez, 2015), 47
cultural capital, 176–77n48
Curas zombis en azul/"Zombie Priests in Blue" (Sudak, 2013), 170n8, 179n6
Curubeto, Diego, 171n13, 184n11
cyberpunk, 112

Daemonium: soldado del inframundo/ Daemonium: Underground Soldier (Parés, 2015), 4
Darín, Ricardo, 163
Dead Line (Esquenazi, 2006)
    as apartment horror, 65, 74–78, *78*
    English-language dialogues in, 62
    paranoia in, 65, 72–78, *78*, 84–86, 88
Death Club (Merendino, 2008), 182n4
Death Knows Your Name (de la Vega, 2007)
    actors in, 187n29
    auto-erasure in, 66
    budget of, 13
    Buenos Aires in, 68–69, *69*
    comments by viewers on, 65
    distribution and, 63
    DVD distribution and, 28–29
    English-language dialogues in, 62
    haunted house trope in, 142
    paranoia in, 65–71, 84–86, 88
    reception of, 12
    special effects in, 187n31
    target audience and, 84–85
    YouTube and, 14
Deleuze, Gilles, 77, 83, 100, 164
Derrida, Jacques, 136–37
El desierto/The Desert (Behl, 2013), 17, 179n6, 199n47, 200n48
El Desquicio Producciones, 11
Detrás del Horror/"Behind the Horror" (de Llano, 2011), 95, 97–98
El día trajo la oscuridad/Darkness by Day (Desalvo, 2013), 17, 196n27
Diablo (Loreti, 2011), 19
Díaz-Zambrana, Rosana, xxi, 28, 207n44
Dick, Philip K., 195n23
dictatorship. *See* Dirty War and horror cinema
Diment, Javier, 8, 9, 19, 24, 101, 175n41. *See also specific films*
Dirty War and horror cinema
    allegory and, xxii–xxiii, 125
    comedy and parody in, 148–55, 158–59, 160–61
    Crónica de una fuga and, 137–46, *139*, *142*, 149, 159, 160, 206n36
    ethical cinematic depiction and, 133–34, 147–48
    García Bogliano and, 155–59
    gory depictions and, 146–48
    Jennifer's Shadow and, 127–29, *128*, 132, 133
    The Last Gateway and, 131–33, *132*
    themes and tropes in, 127–48
    36 Pasos and, 129–31
    viewers' expectations and, 125–27, 135–37
discipline, 129–30
2/11: Día de los Muertos/2/11: Day of the Dead (Massa, 2012), 11, 17, 28–29, 196n27
Dunaway, Faye, 127
DVD distribution, 15–16, 28–29, 150
Dying God (Lambot, 2008), 62, 187n28

Echeverría, Esteban, 43, 49
economic horror, 37–38
ENERC (Escuela Nacional de Experimentación y Realización Cinematográfica), 11–12, 98
English-language Argentine horror films
    auto-erasure in, 61–62, 90–91
    canon of, 12, 61–62
    comments by viewers on, 65
    paranoia in, 63–66, 84–91
    "star system" and, 187n28
    target audience and, 84–85, 90
    See also Death Knows Your Name (de la Vega, 2007)
EscribiendoCine (web-based periodical), 16, 96

INDEX

Escuela Nacional de Experimentación y Realización Cinematográfica (ENERC), 11–12, 98
La escuelita/The Little School (Partnoy), 140, 203–4n26
Eslabón podrido (Diment, 2015), 17
Espacios INCAA, 15, 97, 174n28, 197n32
España, Claudio, 168n13
Esperando la carroza/ Waiting for the Hearse (Doria, 1985), 195n23
Esquenazi, Sergio, 9. *See also specific films*
Evil Dead (Álvarez, 2013), 116
The Evil Dead (Raimi, 1981), 26, 180n10
Evil Dead II (Raimi, 1987), 142, 180n10
exploitation cinema, 90–91, 196n25
Extraña invasión/Stay Tuned for Terror (Vieyra, 1965), 184–85n11
extreme masculinity, 52–53

Facebook, 6, 10, 28, 39
Facundo (Sarmiento), 43
Falicov, Tamara, 31, 174n28, 176n45, 184–85n11, 194n15
family, 130–31, 133, 150–51
Fan Ediciones, 16
Fangoria (magazine), xv, 29–30, 90
Farsa Producciones (film production company), 8, 13–14, 26, 38–39, 150, 175n41
Fase 7/Phase 7 (Goldbart, 2010), 74, 200n48
Festival de Cine Inusual de Buenos Aires, 14, 97, 104, 163, 197n32
Festival de Cinepunk, 102
Festival Internacional de Cine Independiente de Mar del Plata (MARFICI), 10–11, 207n42
Festival Internacional del Cine Fantástico, 11
film distribution
  DVD distribution and, 15–16, 150
  English-language horror films and, 61–62, 63, 64–65, 84–85
  grey zone of, 1
  Internet and, 13–15, 163
  Netflix and, 163
  punk/horror cinema and, 100, 103–4
  retail stores and, xiii–xiv, 15–16
  Straight-to-Video productions and, 64–65
  transnational cultural flows and, 1–8, 25–30
  in the US, xiii–xiv
  See also YouTube
film festivals, 9–11, 16, 22–23, 27–28, 97–98, 104, 163. *See also* Buenos Aires Rojo Sangre (BARS)
film financing
  horror cinema and, 21, 26
  New Argentine Cinema and, 20
  punk/horror cinema and, 100–102, 111–12, 114–15
  See also INCAA (Instituto Nacional de Cine y Artes Audiovisuales; National Institute of Film and Audiovisual Arts)
Findling, Hernán, 9
Findling Films, 10, 11
"Flash sangriento"/"Bloody Flashback" (Manes, 1986), 171–72n14
Fonds Sud, 20
Forte, Fabián, 9, 19
Foucault, Michel, 68
found-footage horror, 140
Freeland, Cynthia, 140, 203n25, 205n32
Freud, Sigmund, 65, 71, 72, 75–76, 82–83
Fuente, Carlos de la, 97–98, 99, 103, 108, 194–95n19, 195n23. *See also specific films*

Furia Films (film production company), 11, 13–14

Garaje Olimpo (Bechis, 1999), 126, 138, 149
García Bogliano, Adrián
  Dirty War and, 155–59, 160
  English-language films and, 182n3
  punk/horror cinema and, 194n16
  role of, 9
  transnational trajectory and productions of, xvii, xix, 175n41, 176n47
  See also specific films
García Bogliano, Ramiro, 9
Getino, Octavio, 110, 148
gore
  in high-budget productions, 114–15
  in *Plaga zombie: Zona mutante*, 45
  punk/horror cinema and, 96, 108–9, 111, 114–23, *121*
  in rape-revenge films, 47
Goreinvasión (Magariños, 2004), 111, 120–21, *121*, 122, 195n20
Goretech: Bienvenidos al planeta hijo de puta/"Welcome to the Planet Son of a Bitch" (Magariños, 2012)
  Diment and, 19
  INCAA TV and, 32, 195n21
  as punk/horror film, 94–95, 105, 107, 113
  special effects and gore in, 108–9, 119, 200n48
Gorevisión (film production company)
  actors and, 187n29
  Buenos Aires and, 11
  Diment and, 19
  genres and, 108–9
  INCAA TV and, 102
  Internet and, 13–14
  low-budget productions and, 101, 111
  punk/horror cinema and, 112–13, 115
  role of, 9

  screenings and, 193n11
  SRN Distribución and, 15
  trash cinema and, 196n25
Gothic horror cinema
  Crónica de una fuga and, 138, 139, 141–45, *142*, 146
  Martel and, 24–25
  visual codes in, 141
Grité una noche/"I Screamed One Night" (García Bogliano, 2005), 26, 187n28
Guattari, Felix, 83
Gunning, Tom, 35

Habitaciones para turistas/*Rooms for Tourists* (García Bogliano, 2004), xiii, 12, 13
Haciendo cine (magazine), xvii, 16
Halbrich, Hugo, 78, 158, 187n28
Halloween (Carpenter, 1978), 71, 176–77n48, 204n29
Hammer Films, 114
haunted house trope
  in *Crónica de una fuga*, 139, 141–44, *142*
  in *Death Knows Your Name*, 142
  in *La memoria del muerto*, 56
  queer relationships and, 57
hauntology, 136
Hipersomnia/*Hypersomnia* (Grieco, 2016), 163
Historia del miedo/*History of Fear* (Naishat, 2014), 25
La historia oficial (Puenzo, 1985), 126, 148, 149, 154, 157, 160
Hollywood films
  English-language Argentine horror films and, 63
  punk/horror cinema and, 102, 109, 112–13, 114, 115–16, 122–23
horror cinema
  as disreputable, 140
  gender paradigms and, 57

INDEX

Hubert Bals Fund, 20

INCAA (Instituto Nacional de Cine y Artes Audiovisuales; National Institute of Film and Audiovisual Arts)
   Buenos Aires and, 11
   Dirty War horror films and, 148, 160
   English-language horror films and, 61
   point system (Panessi) and, 182n3
   punk/horror cinema and, 97, 101–2
   role of, xiv–xvi, 8, 12–13, 111
   support for horror cinema by, xiv–xvi, xxiii, 15, 16–17, 19, 23, 30–32
   See also Espacios INCAA
INCAA TV, xv, 15, 32, 102, 197–98n34
Los inquilinos del infierno/"The Tenants from Hell" (Leibovich and Varela, 2004), 186n24
inseguridad, 87
International Festival of Independent Cinema in Mar del Plata (MARFICI), 10–11, 207n42
Internet, xv–xvi, 13–15, 14, 163. *See also* Facebook; Twitter; YouTube
Inzomnia (Pollachi, 2007), 10
irony, 119

Jameson, Fredric, 41–42, 44, 68–69
Jennifer's Shadow (*Chronicle of the Raven*) (de la Vega and Parés, 2004)
   budget of, 12
   Dirty War and, 127–29, *128*, 132, 133
   distribution and, xiii, 176n47
   English-language dialogues in, 62
   screenings of, 14–15

Kaufman, Lloyd, xxiii
Kendrick, James, 35, 114, 119, 122, 199n47
Kermode, Frank, 108
kidnapping, 129–31, 132, 137–38

Kilómetro 111 (film journal), xv–xvi, 22
Klimovsky, León, xvii–xviii
Kryptonita (Loreti, 2015), xvi, 19
KV62: Tiempo come tiempo/"KV62: Time Eats Time" (Leguiza, 2013), 95, 96, 101, 109, 195n21

The Last Gateway (Rugna, 2007)
   actors in, 187n28
   auto-erasure in, 79–81
   comments by viewers on, 65
   Dirty War and, 131–33, *132*
   distribution and, xiii, 63
   English-language dialogues in, 62
   paranoia in, 78–86, 88
   special effects in, 188n31
   target audience and, 84–85
Latin American immigrants, 88
Lavia, Darío, xvii
Left for Dead (Pyun, 2007), 62
Leguiza, Marcelo, 98, 99, 104, 182n4, 193n11, 195n23.
   See also specific films
La Liga de Cine de Género ("The League of Genre Cinema"), xvi–xvii, 168n10
Lobato, Ramon, xiv, 3, 14, 26, 64–65, 167n5, 176n47
Loreti, Nicanor
   as actor, 150
   on Argentine cinema, 169n16
   on Dirty War, 133–34, 147
   as film critic, 29–30
   genre cinema and, 19
   role of, 9
   See also specific films
Lowenstein, Adam, xxii, 35, 51
Una luz en la ventana/"A Light in the Window" (Romero, 1942), xix

Las Madres de la Plaza de Mayo, 131
Magariños, Germán
   budget and, xxiii

Magariños, Germán (cont'd)
  distribution and, 33
  education of, 98
  gore and, 120
  INCAA TV and, 197–98n34
  influences on, 195–96n23
  low-budget productions and, 101, 103
  punk/horror cinema and, 99, 104, 108–9
  role of, 9
  screenings and, 193n11
  trash cinema and, 196n25
  See also specific films
Mala carne/Carnal (Forte, 2003), xxii, 13, 199n47
Malditos sean!/Cursed Bastards (Forte and Rugna, 2011), 32, 146, 148–49, 157–59, 160–61
Manes, Fabio, 171n13
MARFICI (Festival Internacional de Cine Independiente de Mar del Plata), 10–11, 207n42
Marihuana radioactiva planetaria/"Interplanetary Radioactive Marijuan" (Leguiza, 2010), 109
Martel, Lucrecia, 20, 24–25, 59
Massumi, Brian, 85–86, 117, 152
El matadero/The Slaughter Yard (Echeverría), 43
Mazurek, Sergio, 9
medical/hospital horror. See Death Knows Your Name (de la Vega, 2007)
La memoria del muerto/Memory of the Dead (Diment, 2011)
  as allegory of crisis, 169n15
  box-office performance of, 17
  Diment and, 19
  distribution and, 27
  horror spectacle in, 37
  mobile cinema and, 15
  neoliberalism and, 54–59

Metamorfosis FX, 12
Mocosis (Leguiza, 2014)
  budget of, 101
  English-language dialogues in, 182n4
  gore in, 121–22
  nomadism in, 110
  as punk/horror film, 94–95, 109, 121–22
Mondo macabro (movie store), xiii, 16
Mondo Psycho (Crampi, 2006)
  English-language dialogues in, 62, 182n4
  nomadism in, 110
  as punk/horror film, 94–95, 109, 197n28
  special effects and gore in, 200n48
Mórbido Film Fest (Mexico), 28, 163
mother-witch, 131, 132, 133
Mujer lobo/She Wolf (Garateguy, 2013), 15, 32, 174n31
La mujer sin cabeza/The Headless Woman (Martel, 2008), 86–87, 126
Mulvey, Laura, 76, 178–79n3, 178n1
Muñiz, Berta, 38, 150, 152, 154
Mutazion (punk collective)
  Buenos Aires and, 11
  INCAA TV and, 102
  Internet and, 13–14
  low-budget productions and, 101
  punk/horror cinema and, 96, 105, 109
  screenings and, 97, 193n11
  SRN Distribución and, 15
Mutazombie (Leguiza, 2008), 97–98

La Nación (newspaper), 16, 87, 168n10
Naturaleza muerta/Still Life (Grieco, 2014), 17, 18, 188n31, 200n48
Neale, Steve, 95, 96–97, 164
Necrofobia 3D (de la Vega, 2014), xvi, 11, 17, 32, 163
neoliberalism

in Argentina, 38, 42–43, 54, 126
  economic horror and, 37–38
  horror spectacle and, xxii–xxiii, 35–37
  La memoria del muerto and, 54–59
  No moriré sola and, 48–54
  Plaga zombie: Zona mutante and, 38–46
Netflix, 163
New Argentine Cinema
  Caetano and, 202n17
  characteristics of, xxi–xxiii
  cheaper filmmaking technologies and, 167n3
  horror cinema and, 20–25
  punk/horror cinema and, 100, 109–10
  raw film aesthetics and, 110–11
No habrás más penas ni olvido/*Funny Dirty Little War* (Olivera, 1983), 149
No moriré sola/*I'll Not Die Alone* (García Bogliano, 2008)
  DVD distribution and, 28–29
  horror spectacle in, 37
  in Japan, 176n47
  as punk/horror cinema, 194n16
  as rape-revenge film, 47–54, 52
  "star system" and, 187n28
  YouTube and, 14
No muertos/"The Undead" (Puig, 1999), 171–72n14
No sólo en cines ("Not only in cinemas") (mobile cinema), 15
Nobleza Gaucha/"Gaucho Nobility" (Cairo, Gunche, and Martínez de la Pera, 1915), 181n19
La noche de los lápices/*The Night of the Pencils* (Olivera, 1986), 149, 154
Nueve reinas/*Nine Queens* (Bielinsky, 2000), xxii, 38
Nunca asistas a este tipo de fiesta/"Never Go to This Kind of Party" (Parés, Soria, and Sáez, 2000), 148–52, 154–55, 159, 160–61

Nunca más asistas a este tipo de fiesta/"Never Again Go to This Kind of Party" (Parés, Soria, and Sáez, 2010), 148–50, 152–55, 159
Nunca más ("Never Again") report, 129, 201n6

Oliveros, Mariano, 105
Oubiña, David, 20–21, 23

Page, Joanna, xxi–xxiii, 22, 100, 175n36
Página 12 (newspaper), 16, 96, 137
paracinema, 20–25
The Parallax View (Pakula, 1974), 180n11
paranoia and paranoid horror cinema
  in *Dead Line*, 65, 72–78, 84–86, 88
  in *Death Knows Your Name*, 65–71, 84–86, 88
  English-language Argentine horror films and, 63–66, 84–91
  government agencies in, 41
  in *The Last Gateway*, 78–86, 88
  in superhero films and narcotrafficking series, 169n17
Parés, Pablo, xvii, xx, 38, 150
Partnoy, Alicia, 140, 203–4n26
Pase libre (Tamburini), 137–38, 139–40
Patagonik (film production company), 8
Paura Flics, xxiii, 9, 13–14, 134, 187n28
Peña, Fernando Martín, 171n11
Penumbra/*Penumbra* (García Bogliano, 2011), 17, 28–29, 187n28
percepticide, 134–35
piquetero movement, 42–43, 44
Pizza, birra, faso (Caetano and Stagnaro, 1998), 21, 45, 110, 202n17
Plaga zombie (Parés and Sáez, 1997), xiii, 8, 9, 12, 13, 26, 32
Plaga zombie: Zona mutante/"Plaga Zombie: Mutant Zone" (Parés and Sáez, 2001), 14, 38–46

Plaga zombie: Zona mutante: Zona tóxica/"Plaga Zombie: Mutant Zone: Toxic Zone" (Parés and Sáez, 2011), 179–80n7
Plaga zombie: American Invasion (Medeiros, 2018), 171n12
pleasure and pleasures of horror
 cinematic spectacles and, 35–36, 45–46
 concept of, xix–xxi
 paranoia and, 89–90
 punk/horror cinema and, 94, 102–4
 transnational cultural flows and, 6–8, 164–65
Pochito Producciones, 198n39
Podalsky, Laura, 45, 146, 159–60
Pollachi, Paula, 9, 10
Preso sin nombre, celda sin número/*Prisoner without a Name, Cell without a Number* (Timmerman), 203–4n26
Prince, Stephen, 51, 116, 145, 199n45, 205n33
El Proceso de Reorganización Nacional ("The National Reorganization Process"), 125. *See also* Dirty War and horror cinema
product placement, 73
prosthetic memory, 147–48
Protocolo 48: El experimento final/"Protocol 48: The Final Experiment" (de la Fuente, 2012), 95, 99, 108–9, 121–22, 129
Proyecto Epecuén/"The Epecuén Project" (Onetti and Onetti), 178n51
Puig, Alexis, 17
punk cinema, 93–94, 95–98. *See also* Argentine punk/horror cinema
punk spectacles, 112–14

queer space, 55–59
QuintaDimensión (website), 16

Rabbid EFX, 12, 187–88n32, 199–200n48

Raña, Matías, xvii, 8, 17, 46–47, 105
rape-revenge films, 46–54. *See also No moriré sola*/*I'll Not Die Alone* (García Bogliano, 2008)
Ratziel, Simón, 158
reality horror, 140
Rébora, Alejo
 low-budget productions and, 101, 103
 punk/horror cinema and, 99, 104, 112
recreational horror, 89–90
repetition, 164–65
Resurreción/*Resurrection* (Calzada, 2015), 17, 163
Rodríguez, Carina, xvii, xxi, 8, 12, 15, 18–19, 105
Rojo sangre: 10 años a puro género/"BARS: 10 years of pure genre cinema" (Aguilar, 2009), 172n16, 173n22
Romero, George, 36, 143, 180n12
Ruétalo, Victoria, xxi, 90–91
Rugna, Demián, 9, 182n3, 188n32
Run, Bunny, Run! (Crampi, 2003)
 actors in, 187n28
 English-language dialogues in, 62, 182n4
 nomadism in, 110
 as punk/horror film, 94–95, 105, 108, 197n32
 screenings of, 14
rural horror. See *The Last Gateway* (Rugna, 2007)

Sábados de Súper Acción (television program), xviii–xix
Sadomaster (Magariños, 2005)
 budget of, 13
 DVD distribution and, 28–29
 INCAA TV and, 197–98n34
 as punk/horror film, 94–95, 105, 107
 special effects and gore in, 108–9
Sadomaster 2: Locura general (Magariños, 2005)

INCAA TV and, 197–98n34
opening credits in, *93*
as parody, 197n33
as punk/horror film, 94–95, 104, 197n28
YouTube and, 14
Sáez, Hernán, 38, 150, 153
Sangre negra: Aldo Knodell debe morir/"Black Blood: Aldo Knodell Must Die" (Aguilar, 2013), 15, 32
Sapere, Pablo, xvii, 23
Sarli, Isabel, 197n34
Sarlo, Beatriz, 42, 48, 159
Sarmiento, Faustino, 43, 49–50
Sarna (film production company)
 Buenos Aires and, 11
 Internet and, 13–14
 Loreti and, 19
 low-budget productions and, 101, 103, 195n18
 punk/horror cinema and, 99, 112
 screenings and, 97
 SRN Distribución and, 15
Schiele, Kevin, 79, 187n28
Schwarzböck, Silvia, xv–xvi, 143, 144, 206n35
Sconce, Jeffrey, 19, 20, 23
Screen Anarchy (website), 27, 30
El secreto de sus ojos/*The Secret in Their Eyes* (Campanella, 2009), 80, 86–87, 149, 157
La segunda muerte/"The Second Death" (Fernández Calvete, 2011), 17, 28–29, 32, 174n31, 176n47
Sindicato de la Industria Cinematográfica Argentina (SICA; "The Union of the Cinematic Industry of Argentina"), 13
Lo siniestro (Mazurek, 2009), 17
Sitges Film Festival, xv, 28
Sonno profondo (Onetti, 2013), 15
Sonríe/*Snuff, Inc.* (Leguiza, 2012)

budget of, 101
nomadism in, 110
as punk/horror film, 94–95, 104, 109
special effects and gore in, 112, 115
YouTube and, 14
Soria, Paulo, 150, 153
Sorlin, Pierre, 2, 3–4
special effects
 gore and, 112, 114–15, 120, 121–22
 in *Plaga zombie: Zona mutante*, 45–46
 pleasures of horror and, xx
 schools and agencies for, 12
 spectacle. *See* cinematic spectacles
SRN Distribution 15, 97, 100, 102
Straight-to-Video (STV) productions, 26, 64–65, 74
structure of feeling, 85–86
Sudor frío (García Bogliano, 2010)
 actors in, 187n28
 box-office performance of, 16, 17
 Dirty War and, 146, 148–49, 155–57, 159, 160–61
 DVD distribution and, 15
 INCAA TV and, 32
 as "punk," 194n16
Sundance Film Festival, 10, 28
Los super bonarenses/"The Super Bonarenses" (Magariños, 2014), 19, 32, 101, 174n31, 195n21

Tamburini, Claudio, 137–38, 139–40. See also *Crónica de una fuga* (Caetano, 2006)
Terrorífilo (website), 16, 29, 47
testimonial literature and cinema, 139–41
They Want My Eyes (Esquenazi, 2009), 62
Timerman, Jacobo, 203–4n26
torture, 128–29, 132, 137–38, 144–46, 153–54
Trash (Rébora, 2010)
 budget of, 101
 CINE.AR PLAY and, 32

Trash (cont'd)
  nomadism in, 110
  as punk/horror film, 94–95, 107–8, 109
  special effects and gore in, 112, 115
Trash 2: las tetas de Ana L./"Trash 2: The Tits of Ana L." (Rébora, 2013)
  budget of, 101
  gore in, 121–22
  Loreti and, 19
  as punk/horror film, 94–95, 107, 109, 121–22, 197n27
trash cinema, 196n25
Tremendo amanecer/"Tremendous Dawn" (Postiglione, 2004), 199n47
36 Pasos (García Bogliano, 2006), 28–29, 129–31, 132–33, 187n28, 194n16
Troma Entertainment, 120
Twitch (website), 30
Twitter, 10, 28

Ultracine (website), 14
Ultra-Toxic (Crispin, 2005)
  English-language dialogues in, 62, 182n4
  gore in, 121–22
  as punk/horror film, 94–95, 108, 109, 111–12, 121–22
"The 'Uncanny'" (Freud), 71
Uritorco: En la cumbre solo te espera el miedo/"Uritorco: On the Summit Only Fright Waits for You" (de la Fuente, 2010), 95
Uritorco II: La casa de la montaña/"Uritorco II: The Mountain House" (de la Fuente, 2011), 95, 98, 104

Variety (magazine), xiii, xviii, 30

Vega, Daniel de la, 9, 30, 33, 63, 174–75n35, 175n41, 182n3.
  See also specific films
Vendado y frío/"Blindfolded and Cold" (Puig, 1998), 171–72n14
La venganza del sexo/The Curious Dr. Humpp (Vieyra, 1969), xvii–xviii, 184n11
Ventana Sur, 31–32
Videoflims
  DVD distribution and, 15, 150
  INCAA TV and, 197–98n34
  Internet and, 13–14
  Plaga zombie: Zona mutante and, 39
  punk/horror cinema and, 100, 104–5
Vieyra, Emilio, xvii–xviii, 184–85n11
Visitante de invierno/Winter's Visitor (Esquenazi), xv, 17, 23

War on Terror, 85–86
Witemburg, Victoria, 187n28
women, 46–47, 50. *See also* mother-witch; rape-revenge films

YouTube
  comments by viewers on, 6, 26, 38–39, 65, 123
  English-language horror films and, 65
  Farsa Producciones and, 26, 38–39, 150
  INCAA TV and, 32
  punk/horror cinema and, 100, 101
  role of, 3, 13–14, 14

Žižek, Slavoj, 84, 89, 126
zombies, 37–38. See also *Plaga zombie* series

www.ingramcontent.com/pod-product-compliance
Lightning Source LLC
Chambersburg PA
CBHW020643230426
43665CB00008B/291